# Principles of Agricultural Economics

T0303861

*Principles of Agricultural Economics*, now in its fourth edition, continues to showcase the power of economic principles to explain and predict issues and current events in the food, agricultural, and agribusiness sectors. This key text introduces economic principles in a succinct and reader-friendly format, providing students and instructors with a clear, up-to-date, and straightforward approach to learning how a market-based economy functions and how to use simple economic principles for improved decision-making.

The field of agricultural economics has expanded to include a wide range of topics and approaches, including macroeconomics, international trade, agribusiness, environmental economics, natural resources, and international development, and these are all introduced in this text. For this edition, new and enhanced material on agricultural policies, globalization, welfare analysis, and explanations of the role of government in agriculture and agribusiness is included. Readers will also benefit from an expanded range of case studies and text boxes, including real-world examples such as the Ukraine conflict, the Coronavirus pandemic, and immigration.

The work is supported by a companion website, including flash cards, study guides, PowerPoint presentations, multiple choice questions, essay questions, and an instructor's manual. This book is ideal for courses on agricultural economics, microeconomics, rural development, and environmental policy.

**Andrew Barkley** is Professor and University Distinguished Teaching Scholar in the Department of Agricultural Economics at Kansas State University, USA.

**Paul W. Barkley** is Professor Emeritus, School of Economic Sciences, Washington State University, and Adjunct Professor in the Applied Economics Department at Oregon State University, USA.

# Principles of Agricultural Economics

## Fourth Edition

## Andrew Barkley and Paul W. Barkley

Routledge
Taylor & Francis Group

LONDON AND NEW YORK

Designed cover image: rkankaro/Getty Images ©

Fourth edition published 2024
by Routledge
4 Park Square, Milton Park, Abingdon, Oxon, OX14 4RN

and by Routledge
605 Third Avenue, New York, NY 10158

*Routledge is an imprint of the Taylor & Francis Group, an informa business*

© 2024 Andrew Barkley and Paul W. Barkley

The right of Andrew Barkley and Paul W. Barkley to be
identified as authors of this work has been asserted in
accordance with sections 77 and 78 of the Copyright, Designs
and Patents Act 1988.

First edition published by Routledge 2013
Third edition published by Routledge 2020

*British Library Cataloguing-in-Publication Data*
A catalogue record for this book is available from the British Library

*Library of Congress Cataloging-in-Publication Data*
Names: Barkley, Andrew P., 1962- author. | Barkley, Paul W., author.
Title: Principles of agricultural economics/Andrew Barkley and Paul W. Barkley.
Description: Fourth edition. | Abingdon, Oxon ; New York, NY: Routledge,
    2024. | Includes bibliographical references and index.
Identifiers: LCCN 2023005730 | ISBN 9781032435787 (hardback) |
    ISBN 9781032435770 (paperback) | ISBN 9781003367994 (ebook)
Subjects: LCSH: Agriculture—Economic aspects—United States.
Classification: LCC HD1761.B32 2024 | DDC 338.1—dc23/eng/20230208
LC record available at https://lccn.loc.gov/2023005730

ISBN: 978-1-032-43578-7 (hbk)
ISBN: 978-1-032-43577-0 (pbk)
ISBN: 978-1-003-36799-4 (ebk)

DOI: 10.4324/9781003367994

Typeset in Sabon
by Apex CoVantage, LLC

Access the Instructor and Student Resources: www.routledge.com/cw/barkley

With deep and continuing gratitude to Mary Ellen Barkley and Lela Kelly Barkley.

# Contents

# Photos

# Figures

Figures

# Tables

# Boxes

# Preface

We have been pleased with the reception of the first three editions of this book. The main objective of the book is to provide students and instructors with a clear, up-to-date, and straightforward approach to learning how a market-based economy functions and how to use simple economic principles for improved decision-making. Emphasis is placed on the intuition of profit maximization and how the intuition can be used to improve both personal and professional decision-making.

Based on excellent feedback from reviewers, instructors, and current users of the book, this revision expands, updates, and improves the third edition. We have added numerous case studies that apply economic principles to real-world events in agriculture and agri-business. Enhanced material has been added on current agricultural policies, globalization, welfare analysis, and explanations of the role of government in agriculture and agribusiness. We have highlighted the consumer focus of economics as applied to food and agriculture throughout the book.

New text boxes have been added on (1) value-added agriculture, (2) inflation impact on food and agriculture, (3) monopoly power and collusion in beef/poultry/agribusiness industries, (4) effect of Coronavirus pandemic on food, agriculture, and agribusiness, (5) effect of climate change on food, agriculture, and agribusiness, (6) effect of Russia/Ukraine war on agriculture, (7) impact of risk and uncertainty on markets, (8) recent changes in government policies, (9) recent changes in international trade policies, (10) impact of the rise of China on global food and agriculture, (11) relationship between fuel markets and agricultural markets, and (12) supply chains in food and agriculture.

# Acknowledgments

Our hearty and sincere appreciation to editor Michelle Gallagher and Chloe Herbert at Taylor & Francis. Special thanks to the reviewers, instructors, and current users of the book.

# Abbreviations

| | |
|---|---|
| ADM | Archer Daniels Midland |
| AFO | animal feeding operation |
| BRIC | Brazil, Russia, India, and China |
| BSE | bovine spongiform encephalopathy |
| bu | bushel |
| CA | controlled atmosphere |
| CAB | certified Angus beef |
| CAFO | concentrated animal feeding operation |
| CAP | common agricultural policy |
| CBOT | Chicago Board of Trade |
| CD | compact disc |
| CME | Chicago Mercantile Exchange |
| COOL | country of origin labeling |
| CRP | Conservation Reserve Program |
| cwt | hundredweight |
| DDT | dichloro-diphenyl-trichloroethane |
| EC | European Community |
| EEC | European Economic Community |
| EPA | Environmental Protection Agency |
| EU | European Union |
| FDA | Food and Drug Administration |
| FDIC | Federal Deposit Insurance Corporation |
| FTA | free trade agreement |
| GATT | General Agreement on Tariffs and Trade |
| GDP | gross domestic product |
| GIS | geographical information systems |
| GM | genetically modified |
| GMO | genetically modified organism |
| GPS | global positioning system |
| H | beef growth hormones |
| ha | hectare |
| HFCS | high-fructose corn syrup |
| kg | kilogram |
| kWh | kilowatt-hours |
| lb | pound [weight] |

| LEPA | low-energy precision application |
|---|---|
| m | meter |
| MPCI | multiple peril crop insurance |
| N | nitrogen |
| NAFTA | North American Free Trade Agreement |
| NCBA | National Cattlemen's Beef Association |
| NI | national income |
| NTB | non-tariff barrier |
| NYSE | New York Stock Exchange |
| OPEC | Organization of Petroleum Exporting Countries |
| R&D | research and development |
| UK | United Kingdom |
| US | United States |
| USD | United States dollars |
| USDA | United States Department of Agriculture |
| USEPA | United States Environmental Protection Agency |
| USSR | Union of Soviet Socialist Republics (former Soviet Union) |
| USTA | United States Tennis Association |
| WHO | World Health Organization |
| WTO | World Trade Organization |

## Economic terminology

| $\pi$ | profits |
|---|---|
| $\pi_A$ | accounting profits |
| $\pi_E$ | economic profits |
| A | land |
| AFC | average fixed costs |
| APP | average physical product |
| AR | average revenue |
| ARP | average revenue product |
| ATC | average total costs |
| AVC | average variable costs |
| CS | consumer surplus |
| D | demand curve |
| DWL | deadweight loss |
| E | equilibrium |
| $E^d$ | price elasticity of demand |
| $E^d_{Y1Y2}$ | cross-price elasticity of demand |
| $E^m$ | income elasticity of demand |
| $E^s$ | elasticity of supply |
| $E^s_{Y1Y2}$ | cross-price elasticity of supply |
| ED | excess demand |
| EP | expectations of future prices |
| ES | excess supply |
| FV | future value |
| IR | immediate run |

| | |
|---|---|
| K | capital |
| L | labor |
| LR | long run |
| M | management |
| M | income |
| MC | marginal cost |
| MFC | marginal factor cost |
| MPP | marginal physical product |
| MR | marginal revenue |
| MRP | marginal revenue product |
| MRPS | marginal rate of product substitution |
| MRS | marginal rate of substitution |
| MRTS | marginal rate of technical substitution |
| MU | marginal utility |
| N | number of sellers |
| NPV | net present value |
| P | price of a good |
| P* | equilibrium price |
| $P^c$ | price ceiling |
| $P_i$ | input price |
| $P_o$ | prices of other, related goods |
| $P_{own}$ | own price of a good |
| $P_{related}$ | goods price of related goods |
| $P^s$ | price support |
| $P_X$ | input price |
| $P_Y$ | output price |
| Pop | population |
| PS | producer surplus |
| PV | present value |
| PPF | production possibilities frontier |
| q | individual-firm quantity |
| $q^d$ | individual-firm quantity demanded |
| $q^s$ | individual-firm quantity supplied |
| Q | market quantity |
| Q* | equilibrium quantity |
| $Q^d$ | market quantity demanded |
| $Q^s$ | market quantity supplied |
| SR | short run |
| t | per-unit tax |
| T | technology |
| TC | total costs |
| $TC_A$ | accounting costs |
| TFC | total factor costs |
| TFC | total fixed costs |
| TP | tastes and preferences |
| TPP | total physical product |
| TR | total revenues |
| TRP | total revenue product |

| TU | total utility |
| TVC | total variable costs |
| Y | quantity of a good; output |

## Mathematical notation

| $>$ | is preferred to |
| $<$ | is less preferred to |
| $\sim$ | is indifferent to |
| f | function |
| $\Delta$ | change |
| m | slope |
| $\Delta y/\Delta x$ | slope |
| b | y-intercept |
| $\infty$ | infinity |

# Introduction to the economics of agriculture

Photo 1.1 Introduction to the economics of agriculture

*Source:* April Cat/Shutterstock

DOI: 10.4324/9781003367994-1

## Abstract

This chapter explains why economics is important and interesting. It defines the study of economics and discusses what economics is about. We introduce and explain economic terms, including producers, consumers, macroeconomics, microeconomics, positive and normative economics, absolute prices, and relative prices. The major discussion explains why scarcity is the fundamental concept of economics. The chapter also introduces and explains economic organization, resources, trends in the agricultural economy, and a review of graphs and their construction.

### Chapter 1 Questions

1   What is economics, and what is it all about?
2   What are consumers and producers, and how do they interact?
3   What is the difference between microeconomics and macroeconomics?
4   How do economists deal with value judgments?
5   How do absolute prices differ from relative prices?
6   Why is scarcity considered the fundamental concept of economics?
7   How is an economy organized, and how does an economy function?
8   How are graphs constructed and used in economics?

## 1.0   Introduction

There were slightly more than 2 million farms in the United States (US) in 2021. Texas had the most, with more than 247,000; Alaska had the least, with 1,050. Taken together, these farms produced hundreds of crops, from apples to zucchini, from bees to turkeys, and hundreds of crops and animals in between. When sold, all products from all farms yielded a net farm income of nearly 577 billion US dollars (USD) in 2022. When the US was created in 1776, nearly 90 percent of the population lived on farms. Now, less than 2 percent of the population lives on farms. Farm output continues to grow while the farm population continues to decline. This change is due to massive technological change: improvements in the way food and fiber are produced.

Rapid technological change characterizes nearly all aspects of global agriculture. Farmers and ranchers find it advantageous to adopt new methods as quickly as possible. Mechanization and the use of agricultural chemicals have led to massive consolidation of farms and industry concentration. While this trend has resulted in fewer "family farms," it has led to lower food prices over time. These changes make the economics of food and agriculture an important and interesting subject for study.

The changes affecting agriculture have been substantial: changes in technology, changes in plant and animal breeding, changes in the diets of consumers, consumer preferences for how food is produced, changes in food exports and imports, and changes in the way agriculture relates to governments across the world.

**Economics** is a **social science**, meaning that it uses scientific methods to study the way people behave. Economists interested in **agriculture** focus on five questions:

- What should I produce?
- How much should I produce?
- How should I produce it?
- When should I produce it?
- For whom should I produce it?

Similar questions must be asked by consumers and business leaders as they allocate their time, talents, and money over opportunities to obtain the highest possible level of satisfaction. These basic questions form the foundation of the economic principles discussed in this book.

## 1.1   Economics is important and interesting!

Rapid changes in the agricultural industry make this an exciting time to study **agricultural economics**. Changes in the global economy and in the agricultural industry are occurring at a more rapid rate than at any other time in history, and these changes have huge implications for the entire domestic and global economies.

Union (EU) and Japan all subsidize their agricultural sectors.

---

**BOX 1.1**

### What do agricultural economics and agribusiness majors do?

Agricultural economics is a highly diverse, dynamic, and fascinating field! The origins of the field are the application of economic principles to farming and ranching: food production. The field has grown enormously to include a wide variety of jobs, including banks, credit unions, insurance, and law firms. A large group of students who major in agricultural economics or agribusiness work for agribusiness, both large and small. These companies provide inputs (equipment, chemical, fertilizer) and services (finance, employment, and commodity trading) to farmers and ranchers. Agribusinesses also process crops and livestock in food and fiber (meatpacking, milling, baking, and food retailing, wholesaling, food manufacturing, marketing, sales, and management).

Some work for the government in jobs such as statistician or government program administration, some conduct research on all aspects of food, agriculture, natural resources, and the environment. Many agricultural economics majors work all over the world in international trade, international development, and international business. Others work in rural development

---

and managing natural resources: air pollution, climate change, pesticides, and biofuel management. The main characteristic of agricultural economics majors is problem solving and critical thinking: the application of the economic way of thinking about benefits and costs to real world issues in food, agriculture, natural resources, and the environment. This scarce skill is highly valued, resulting in high salaries and great opportunities for students in agricultural economics and agribusiness.

Some examples show how this happens. Events that happen in other parts of the world often have a large impact on those who live in the agricultural regions of the United States. For example, armed conflict in Ukraine results in a decrease in the global supply of food. This results in higher commodity prices in the US and throughout the world, far away from the war. Extreme weather events such as droughts and hurricanes can have major effects on the food supply. These events have become more common due to climate change. Economic knowledge provides solutions to changes in supply chains in food and agriculture.

Beef exports are an important source of beef industry profits. Japan is the largest importer of US beef, followed by South Korea and China. Therefore, economic events in these nations have a large impact on the profitability of US beef producers.

Photo 1.2 Beef and rice consumption in Japan

*Source:* gresei/Shutterstock

Understanding how and why consumers purchase goods provides information useful in improving decision-making by persons employed in agriculture and agribusiness. For example, high-income nations, including the US, European Union (EU), and Japan, all subsidize their agricultural sectors.

## BOX 1.2

### The United States Department of Agriculture (USDA)

In 1862, President Abraham Lincoln established the Department of Agriculture (USDA), created to assist farmers by providing information, research, loans, and education for rural youth. Agriculture has changed a great deal since 1862, when over half of the nation's population lived on farms. However, the mission of the USDA has remained the same: "We provide leadership on food, agriculture, natural resources, and related issues based on sound public policy, the best available science, and efficient management."

Currently, the USDA promotes the marketing of farm products overseas, promotes food safety and nutrition, provides marketing assistance to farmers, protects natural resources and the environment, conducts scientific research in agriculture, promotes rural development, and helps poor individuals and families in the form of food subsidies. Today, the USDA has nearly 100,000 employees at over 4,500 locations with an annual budget over USD 195 billion (2023).

*Source:* USDA website. www.usda.gov/our_agency/about_usda. Retrieved September 28, 2022.

Economic principles help explain the reasons behind the changes in agricultural policy and the impacts of the new policies as they are legislated and implemented. The remainder of this section provides short examples to demonstrate the nature of real-life economic problems and the importance of using economics to understand them.

## 1.1.1 Meat processing

The meat processing industry earns profits by purchasing cattle and selling meat and leather. Many years of consolidation through mergers and acquisitions have resulted in four beef packers (Tyson Foods, Cargill, JBS USA, and National Beef) selling over 80 percent of all beef sold in the US. With only four major packers, there may be less competition in buying cattle from livestock producers, possibly resulting in lower cattle prices. However, there are some positive effects from having big packers. Larger packing plants and farms allow the meat production process to become more efficient, resulting in lower costs to consumers, who in turn purchase more meat. Increased meat sales increase profits for the livestock sector. The study of economics allows a deeper understanding of the causes and consequences of mergers and acquisitions in agricultural and food industries.

Coronavirus (Covid-19) had a large impact on global meat production and supply chains. When US meat processing employees became sick in 2020, some plants shut down, and others adopted safe distances between workers to slow the spread of the pandemic. These changes resulted in a decrease in meat availability and higher food prices.

## 1.1.2   Free trade among nations

**Free trade agreements** (FTAs) are formed to reduce or eliminate trade barriers between nations. Two of the most important FTAs are (1) the United States-Mexico-Canada Agreement (USMCA), formerly the North American Free Trade Agreement (NAFTA), and (2) the World Trade Organization (WTO), formerly called the General Agreement on Tariffs and Trade (GATT). These agreements have had major consequences for agricultural producers and consumers in the US and throughout the world. **Trade barriers** are laws that restrict the movement of goods across national borders. These FTAs have opened the way for increased exports of US grain (wheat, corn, milo, and soybeans) by eliminating or reducing trade barriers such as tariffs, quotas, and harsh inspection criteria. The FTAs allow the US to sell grain to Russia, Japan, Mexico, and other countries with fewer legal restrictions or taxes. This book demonstrates that the movement toward free trade generally has benefits for agricultural producers.

The trade agreements have caused some individuals and groups to question globalization and free trade. Many individuals and groups oppose trade with other nations. Some desire to be "self-sufficient," to not rely on other nations. Trade policy continues to be in the news as new trade agreements are negotiated, with large impacts on producers and consumers. Agricultural trade policy has become the major source of news, debate, and controversy since 2018, when tariffs were placed on billions of dollars of imported goods from China. China then retaliated by placing tariffs on agricultural imports.

Conflict between nations can create problems with globalization. War and international disputes can lead to supply chain disruption and loss of export markets. Recently, the highly globalized food and agricultural sector has tried to balance gains from trade with national security goals.

### BOX 1.3

## Trade barriers

Nations around the world use laws and regulations to restrict imports, exports, or both. Three common barriers include the following:

TARIFFS: Taxes paid before goods can be sold across a national border. For example, automobile consumers in the US must pay a tariff when they purchase a car made in another country.

QUOTAS: Restrictions on the quantity of goods allowed to enter the United States from another country. Quotas protect domestic producers from foreign-made products.

INSPECTION: The most subjective of the devices used to restrict imports. Inspection is used to prevent food items that are considered unsafe from entering the US economy.

*Source:* Economic Glossary. http://glossary.econguru.com/

## 1.1.3 The environment

Environmental issues play an increasingly important role in agriculture. A number of Midwestern states are well suited to growing corn (Iowa, Illinois, and Nebraska are typically the three leading states in corn production), but modern corn production often utilizes an herbicide called atrazine to eliminate weeds. Atrazine provides large agronomic and economic benefits to corn farmers in this area. Unfortunately, the chemical is also associated with human health problems, especially when it enters a domestic water supply.

The impacts of atrazine are mixed. On the one hand, the chemical provides efficient control of weeds, resulting in higher yields and higher levels of profits for corn farmers. On the other hand, atrazine contaminates the groundwater, possibly causing health problems for not only the corn farmers and their families but also for all downstream water users. Economists use a number of analytical tools to analyze trade-offs between economic benefits and environmental harm. Successful decision-making for individuals, firms, and governments involves understanding how to choose the "optimal" level of atrazine to apply to cornfields in the American Corn Belt.

## 1.1.4 Agricultural chemicals

The use of fertilizer and agricultural chemicals (such as atrazine, glyphosate [Roundup], and other herbicides, pesticides, and fungicides) has increased dramatically in the last 50 years. Environmentalists and others who are concerned about chemical residues in the food supply and in the domestic water supply have criticized the widespread use of almost all types of agricultural chemicals. As a result, the large agrochemical companies (Bayer, Dow, Novartis, Union Carbide, and others) are looking to diversify since environmental laws and regulations may impose higher costs on the producers of some agricultural chemicals in the future. Recent growth in the consumption of food produced without chemicals has led to large investments in organic food products by several large agribusiness corporations, including General Mills, Kraft/Heinz, ConAgra, and Gerber.

Each of these examples presents an issue that affects the lives of all consumers. Throughout the book, the main emphasis will be that consumers are the only source of profits in a market economy. Producers who are the best at providing consumers with what they want will earn the highest profits.

Economics can be helpful to those who want to understand the causes and consequences of these situations and events. These issues will be noted from time to time in later chapters. Economics helps provide improved understanding of our complex society, agriculture, and consumer choices. Economic principles and the framework of economic analysis lead to improved business, career, and personal decisions. The knowledge of just a few principles of economics allow for better decision-making.

The goal of this book is to help readers to "think like an economist." Throughout the book, simple economic principles will be applied to events and issues that appear in media outlets. Success in the rapidly changing global agricultural economy requires accurate information and the ability to recognize how the changes shape people's lives. Understanding economics often provides a context for dealing with current events, career decisions, and personal situations in a clear and precise manner.

It is important to note that the human condition is characterized by complex and sustained difficulties and problems. Economics improves our decision-making, but to date, it has not solved the fundamental problems of disease, shortages, and human limitations. However, many economists view recent history as a triumph of the economic way of thinking and a huge improvement in how long humans live and how well-off they are while they are alive. These upward trends are likely to continue, with solid economic decision-making guiding the way.

## 1.2   What is economics, and what is it about?

As has been mentioned, **economics** is a **social science** that centers on the study of humans as they act and interact in the marketplace. Economists study these actions and interactions. This section provides definitions and explanations of several economic concepts, then uses these ideas to provide a formal definition of economics.

### 1.2.1   Producers and consumers

Economists are particularly interested in how people produce and consume items such as food, clothing, housing, and a myriad of other things. Economists divide people into two broad groups: **producers** and **consumers**. Note, though, that many, perhaps most, people belong to both groups.

- *Producer* = an individual or firm that produces (makes; manufactures) a good or provides a service.

A **good** is a physical product such as a book or a hamburger, and a **service** is an intangible product such as a haircut, an insurance policy, or cell phone service.

- *Consumer* = an individual or household that purchases a good or a service.

These two groups of people are so important in economics that they have several names:

**Producers** = firms = business firms = sellers

**Consumers** = households = customers = buyers

Agricultural producers are individuals, families, or firms that grow and sell agricultural products. The products include field crops (including nonfood products such as cotton, tobacco, flax, and hemp) and animal products (including milk products, meats, wool, furs, and pelts).

A consumer is any person, firm, corporation, or institution who buys something. Consumers buy food items, such as pepperoni pizza and milk. They also buy clothing, houses, cars, cell phones, computers, and real estate. Consumers drive the economy since their purchases generate signals telling producers what products to place on the market.

As consumer preferences change, producers will earn profits from selling the goods that are most desired by consumers.

Most individuals are simultaneously producers and consumers. A wheat producer in North Dakota produces wheat and sells it to make a living. This same wheat producer buys food at the grocery store (whole-wheat bread), clothing (Wranglers), and perhaps a pickup truck (Ford). Even though most individuals are both producers and consumers, the lessons of economics are much more easily understood if the two roles are studied one at a time.

## 1.2.2   Macroeconomics and microeconomics

Economics divides into two major categories: **macroeconomics** and **microeconomics**.

- *Macroeconomics* = the study of economy-wide activities such as economic growth, business fluctuations, inflation, unemployment, recession, depression, and booms.
- *Microeconomics* = the study of individual decision-making units such as individuals, households, and firms.

This book is directed mainly to microeconomic behavior, or the actions and choices of individuals and individual firms. For example, it will consider issues surrounding how a feedlot owner reacts to a change in the price of cattle or the price of feed. This issue is a part of microeconomics since the feedlot is an individual decision-making unit—in this case, a business firm.

## 1.2.3   Positive and normative economics

As a social science, economics deals with topics of major consequence to public policy. There are many divergent opinions about issues such as immigration, the minimum wage, availability of health care, inflation, agricultural trade, welfare (including Social Security), animal rights, environmentalism, trade wars with other nations, and the like.

Since economics deals with all of these issues, it is important to distinguish between value judgments, which are opinion statements, and neutral statements, which are factual and descriptive. The two categories of economics that keep the opinions in one box and the facts in another are **positive economics** (facts) and **normative economics** (opinions).

- *Positive economics* = based on factual statements. Such statements contain no value judgments. Positive statements describe "what is."
- *Normative economics* = based on statements that contain opinions and/or value judgments. A normative statement contains a judgment about "what ought to be" or "what should be."

---

**QUICK QUIZ 1.1**

Examine the following statements and determine which statements represent positive economics and which statements represent normative economics.

1    The market price of wheat is USD 3.82 per bushel.
2    The market price of cotton should be higher.
3    The market price of spinach should be higher.
4    Environmentalists have an increasing voice in agricultural policy.
5    Unemployment is a major economic issue.

---

Notice in the first three examples that price changes can be both good and bad at the same time. A price increase makes the producer of that good better off, while the consumer of that good is worse off. Similarly, when the price of oil increases, oil companies earn higher levels of profits. Meanwhile, agricultural producers who must purchase oil and petroleum-based products (gasoline, diesel, fertilizer, chemicals, etc.) are worse off. Thus, economists must be careful when making normative statements and normative judgments because "facts" have different implications for different persons. Economists attempt to eliminate normative statements from their economic discussions because what is good for one individual can be bad for another.

## 1.3  Scarcity

Economics is about **scarcity**. Scarcity means that there is less than the desired quantity of something. Scarcity reflects the idea that we live in a world of finite resources and unlimited wants and desires. Humans typically want more than the available quantity of money, material goods such as cars and trucks, football championships, higher grades, and time. The notion of scarcity applies to both material goods (computers and smart phones) and intangible goods (fame, respect). The result is that humans want more than they have.

- *Scarcity* = because resources are limited, the goods and services produced from using these resources are also limited, which means consumers must make choices, or trade-offs, among different goods.

An interesting issue related to scarcity is that the major religions of the world (Judaism, Christianity, Islam, and Buddhism) suggest that it is better to give than to receive. This important ethical principle seems to be in direct contradiction with the economic principle that "people always desire more." Mother Teresa was a Roman Catholic nun who devoted her life to helping the poorest of the poor in Calcutta, India. Mother Teresa won the Nobel Peace Prize in 1979 and was beatified to sainthood in 2013. Did Mother Teresa fall victim to the idea that "more is better than less?" Yes, even philanthropists would like to have more resources to feed the hungry and help the poor. The desire to have more than is currently available is a universal trait shared by peoples of all faiths and opinions.

Economists talk extensively about "goods." If a good is scarce, it becomes an **economic good**. A good that is scarce is one for which there is an unfilled desire such as fine foods, clothes, houses, time, and vacations. **Noneconomic goods** are not scarce: they are free goods available in any quantity to any people. A consumer can have as much as she wants at no cost. Watching a beautiful sunset is a noneconomic good, because it is free. Air is free because an unlimited quantity is available for all who want to consume it. However, air is not a free good in every circumstance. Mountain climbers, scuba divers, submariners, and test pilots would consume more air if it were free. Is the air in a lecture room totally free? Indirectly, it has a price since it requires heating or cooling before it reaches the lecture hall. Clean air is not always free: people who live in urban areas would like more clean air, if it were available.

The fundamental problem of economics is **"scarcity forces us to choose." Economics** is often defined as "the allocation of scarce resources among competing ends." Scarcity constantly forces choices between what goods to buy, how to spend time, and which career goals to pursue. Economics is about making informed decisions. The study and use of economics allow individuals to make more informed personal, career, and business decisions.

## 1.4   The economic organization of society

There are many different forms of economic organization, or different ways that a society (usually a nation) can use to organize its economic activity. Three fundamental ways of organizing an economy include (1) a **market economy** (capitalism, free markets); (2) a **command economy** (dictatorship, communism); and (3) a **mixed economy** (a combination of a market economy and a command economy). These three forms of economic organization are described in this section. However, a quick diversion is needed to define and explain **resources**.

### 1.4.1   Resources

An economy must find a suitable way to allocate resources. But what qualifies as a resource that requires allocation? **Resources** are productive items used to produce

Table 1.1  Resource names and definitions

| | | |
|---|---|---|
| 1. | Land (A) | Natural and biological resources, climate. |
| 2. | Labor (L) | Human resources. |
| 3. | Capital (K) | Manufactured resources, including buildings, machines, tools, and equipment. |
| 4. | Management (M) | The entrepreneur, or individual, who combines the other resources into outputs. |

the goods and services that satisfy human wants and needs. Resources, together with the letter abbreviation used by most economists, are classified and listed in Table 1.1. These groups of resources appear in every kind of economy.

A **market economy** is an economic organization in which prices determine how resources and goods are allocated. Consumers in a market economy make purchasing decisions based on the price of goods and the money available to them. If the price of chicken increases, some consumers will eat fewer chicken products. Similarly, in a market economy, producers use prices to determine what to produce. If the price of wheat increases relative to soybeans and corn, farmers will plant more acres to wheat than they did previously. In a market system, prices drive the entire economy by conveying value, or by telling how much things are worth to producers and consumers. In a free market economy (capitalism), resources are allocated to the use that brings the highest returns. Crops are grown in California's Great Central Valley, but in the bordering foothills of the Sierra Nevada Mountains, the land is too rocky and too steep for crops. Instead, the foothill land is devoted to grazing, which provides the highest return to this rocky area. Prices allocate resources; prices affect the incentives and behavior of both producers and consumers.

In a **command economy**, resources do not automatically flow to the producer earning the highest return or to the consumer who can pay the most for the product. Resources are allocated by whoever is in charge. Examples of command economies include Cuba, where resources are allocated by a dictator, and the former Soviet Union, where high-ranking members of the Communist Party used an elaborate committee system to decide how resources would be allocated. In many socialist countries such as Sweden, resources are allocated by an elected group of decision-makers. However, a dictator who has complete control of the economic system could direct the use of resources. In either case, resources are allocated according to the discretion of a generally small group of decision-maker(s), and decisions are made by considerations other than price. Resources don't always flow to the use that brings the highest return. The people who live in a command economy may desire more fruits and vegetables. If the government's goals are different from the citizens' goals, then these fruits and vegetables will not be produced. The land, labor, and other resources may be used in the production of beef or pork, rather than fruits and vegetables. The economic returns to producing crops may be higher, but it is up to the decision-making group to decide whether to produce fruit, vegetables, or meat.

Examples of market-based economies that are characterized by both political and economic freedom include the US, Australia, Canada, Japan, and the members of the EU. Nations that do not share political and economic freedom include North Korea and Cuba. China has been moving toward a market-based economy since the 1980s, with enormous growth in economic output and incomes as a result.

Most economic systems are **mixed economies** that have elements of both market economies and command economies. The US has many markets that are free from government intervention. However, industries such as agriculture, transportation, and banking are regulated and often subsidized. Therefore, the economy of the US is a mixed economy, although the nation prides itself on being a capitalist democracy. For many years the former Soviet Union (now Russia) and China were both considered to be command economies, where elected officials planned what goods were to be produced and who would get the products. However, beginning in the 1980s, changes in both countries moved their economic systems toward free markets, particularly in agriculture. The economies of these two nations are mixed economies, with elements of both market economies and command economies.

So all real-world economies are a mixture of free market and command economies. The economic principles in this book are primarily oriented to markets since markets organize and allocate most resources in the United States.

## 1.5   A model of an economy

The model developed here describes any economy: market, command, or mixed. The individuals in the economy are divided into two categories: firms (producers) and households (consumers). In a subsistence economy, like an individual stranded on a remote island, producers and consumers are the same people: they must consume only what they produce. If there is no trade, the individuals have to produce all of their own food, clothing, and housing.

The major feature of a market economy is voluntary exchange. Producers and consumers are not forced to buy or sell anything. Even though this is true, the goods and services that consumers wish to purchase and consume must be produced. Resources are used to produce output. **Resources** are also called **inputs, factors of production**, or **factors** (economists use these terms interchangeably).

Table 1.2 shows the resources used to produce agricultural products. The model shown in Figure 1.1 is a simplified version of the real world. The real world is

### Table 1.2 Agricultural resources

| Inputs = Resources = Factors = Factors of production | Payments |
|---|---|
| 1.   Land (A) | rent |
| 2.   Labor (L) | wages, salaries |
|    = operators, family, hired | |
| 3.   Capital (K) | interest |
|    = machines, buildings, tools, and equipment | |
| 4.   Management (M) | profit |

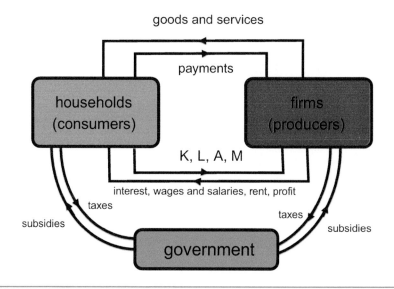

goods and services

payments

households (consumers)

firms (producers)

K, L, A, M

interest, wages and salaries, rent, profit

taxes

subsidies

taxes

subsidies

government

**Figure 1.1** Circular flow diagram of economic activity

extraordinarily complex, so we must simplify it to understand it. One of the key elements of science is simplification or modeling, also known as "reductionism." The model shown in Figure 1.1 fits with this need to use science to understand human behavior.

The arrows in Figure 1.1 show the flow of goods and services between households and firms. The two arrows across the top of the diagram show the movement of goods and services from producers (firms) to consumers (households). Households make payments to the firms to take possession of goods and services. In order to produce goods, firms must use **inputs** (also called resources, factors, and factors of production). These resources are supplied by households and include **capital** (K), **labor** (L), **land** (A), and **management** (M). Capital is produced wealth that is used in further production. In economics, the term "**capital**" refers to physical capital, such as machines, tools, buildings, and equipment. This contrasts with the typical use of the term "capital" used to describe financial capital, or money.

Firms make payments to households for the use of inputs. Interest pays for capital, wages and salaries pay for labor, rent pays for land, and profits are the payment to management.

If the lower box labeled "government" were omitted from Figure 1.1, the model would be one of a pure market economy. All real-world economies, however, include some form of government activity. Adding government to Figure 1.1 converts a market economy to a mixed economy. Both business firms and households must pay taxes to fund the government sector, and legislation allows the government to make payments to selected households and firms. These subsidies include payments to family farms, welfare checks to low-income households, schools, transportation, the postal system, and scores of other types of payments.

## 1.6   Trends in the agricultural economy

The main objective of this book is to show how economic knowledge (models, theories, and methods) can assist in the understanding of agriculture. Some background information about modern agriculture in the US is helpful. Five trends affecting the agricultural industry are especially important and are presented before returning to the study of economics. Here is a synopsis.

### 1.6.1   Fewer and larger farms

Farm numbers continue to decline. The ongoing consolidation of small farms into larger units is primarily due to technological change, including mechanization, the use of agricultural chemicals and fertilizers, and improved seeds. These changes allow for large farms to have lower costs per unit of production than small farms. Lower production costs on large-scale operations relative to small farms has resulted in huge consolidation of farms and changes in the structure of agriculture, especially during the past half century. Farms have become fewer in number but larger and more productive.

### 1.6.2   Agriculture is not just farming

Production agriculture presently employs approximately 1.4 percent of the US workforce, but the food and fiber industry, which includes processing, transport, retailing, and dozens of other things, requires approximately 14.6 percent. Although it is true that "everyone eats food," the number of persons involved in production agriculture has decreased steadily over the last century.

---

**BOX 1.4**

### The farm share of the US food dollar

Farmers and ranchers in the US receive 16 cents of every dollar consumers spend on food at home and away from home. The remaining 84 cents include food processing, packaging, transportation, food retailing, food service, energy, finance and insurance, advertising, legal and accounting costs, and other costs associated with making agricultural products meet the needs of consumers. This statistic can be controversial. Some individuals and groups suggest that farmers should receive a greater proportion of retail food prices. Some claim that the farmer's share of the food dollar reflects farmer profitability and/or well-being. Others use the statistic as evidence that processors and other food supply chain firms are "anticompetitive," or exert monopoly power. Agricultural economists have warned against these claims for many decades.

---

They suggest that these arguments are a misinterpretation of the farm share of the food dollar statistic.

The farm value of the food dollar reflects the "value-added" nature of food products that consumers desire. Raw fruits and vegetables, for example, would have a high farm share of retail prices relative to highly processed food products. However, even fruits and vegetables require transportation and grocery store costs of making the produce available at the times and locations where consumers desire them. Highly processed food products require higher levels of inputs. Making, packaging, and selling a frozen lasagna dinner incurs many costs beyond the cost of the raw (farm level) food. More processing leads to more value added. Coffee beans sold in the US would have a higher farm share of the cost than a low-fat, decaffeinated, double-shot latte.

Over time, consumer desires for more processed products have resulted in a smaller farm share of retail food prices. Profitability in agriculture stems from efficiency in the agricultural sector as it meets consumer demand in a dynamic economy, rather than the share of agricultural products in the food we eat.

*Source:* Economic Research Service (ERS), United States Department of Agriculture, (USDA/ERS) Food Dollar Series www.ers.usda.gov/data-products/food-dollar-series.aspx. Retrieved September 29, 2022.

### 1.6.3   Substitution of capital for labor

Over the past several decades, there has been an enormous movement toward mechanization, which has replaced agricultural workers with machines. This trend stems from changes in relative prices. If it is less expensive to use machines than labor, machines will be used. For example, specialized machines are used to pick cotton. These are expensive pieces of equipment, but using them is much less costly than using large crews of workers to pick the cotton by hand. The fast-food giant McDonald's hires thousands of laborers at low wages. If there is an increase in the minimum wage, McDonald's will use more machinery and hire fewer workers to operate the automatic french fry machines and drink dispensers.

### 1.6.4   Off-farm income for farm families has increased

In earlier years, farming was the sole source, or at least the major source, of income for most farm families. In today's agricultural economy, most farm families rely not only on income from agricultural sources but also on income from nonfarm jobs or investments. Typically, one individual in the family will do the farm work, while another will work in a nonfarm position. With this arrangement, a farm family's total income will not be dependent on highly variable farm income alone. On average, farm families in the US have higher levels of income and wealth than nonfarm families.

> **BOX 1.5**
>
> ## Agrotourism
>
> Agrotourism (also called agritourism) is any agricultural-based activity that hosts visitors, or tourists. Agrotourism is a growth industry and has become an important strategy to enhance incomes and the potential economic viability of small farms and rural economies. Growth in this type of niche tourism has been spurred by a large increase in consumer desire to learn more about how food is produced. Farmers and ranchers can use this growing interest in food to attract customers to their operation, educate nonfarmers about agriculture, and earn additional revenue by providing a service in high demand. Agrotourism is growing worldwide and includes picking fruits and vegetables, riding horses, tasting honey or lavender, learning about wine and cheese making, and shopping in agriculture-related gift shops.
>
> *Source:* USDA. "Know Your Farmer, Know Your Food." www.usda.gov/sites/default/files/documents/KYFCompass.pdf. Retrieved September 29, 2022.

### 1.6.5 Exports are increasingly important to the agricultural sector

The nation's ability to produce ever-larger amounts of food has increased as a result of biological breakthroughs, mechanization, and improvements in management. The production of food has grown more rapidly than the domestic consumption of food. The US has responded by exporting more and more food to consumers in other nations. This trend has made trade policy for food and agricultural products of vital importance to the profitability and sustainability of farmers across the globe, as will be discussed and analyzed in what follows. Trade barriers such as tariffs decrease agricultural exports and lower farm-sector profits.

### 1.6.6 Demand for fresh fruit and vegetables

As incomes increase, consumers will demand more high-quality goods. In the case of food, fresh fruit and vegetables are considered better tasting and more nutritious. There has been a large increase in the demand for fresh fruit and vegetables. Organic products have been characterized by large profits as consumer demand has grown.

> **BOX 1.6**
>
> ## Value-added agriculture and consumer focus
>
> In a free market economy, consumers are the only source of profits for a business firm. This is true in food and agriculture since consumers are free to purchase any type of food that they desire. Therefore, to "add value" means to provide a good or service that increases value for the customer. A successful business creates and provides value to customers.
>
> Value-added agriculture increases the value of agricultural goods by increasing consumers' willingness to pay a premium over the price for similar but undifferentiated products. These efforts could include improving a production or marketing process to differentiate the good by making it special. Cosmic Crisp apples are an example, along with organic, natural non-GMO, gluten-free, and other special categories that consumers are willing to pay for. Value-added investments can be highly profitable by penetrating into a new high-value market by creating brand identity or brand loyalty. Value-added agriculture has been subsidized since 2000 by the Value Added Producer Grant Program (VAPG), which provides grants to individual agricultural producers for the development and marking of new or enhanced value-added agricultural production.
>
> Source: "What is Value-Added Agriculture?" www.agmrc.org/business_development/valueadded_agricutlure/what-is-value-added-agriculture. Retrieved September 29, 2022.

## 1.7   Using graphs

Graphs are often used to summarize and interpret economic information. Graphs can communicate a great deal of information in a small space, which makes them useful tools to see the most important aspects of a situation or decision. A graph is a "model," and economic analysis is often an exercise in modeling. Graphs simplify the presentation of data, and social scientists must simplify the real world in order to understand it.

Most graphs allow the viewer to look at the relationship between two variables while holding everything else constant. Holding all other things constant has a special name: *ceteris paribus* (Latin for "holding all else constant"). Much of economics has to do with understanding the relationship between two variables. One of the most important concepts in economics is the demand curve. The demand curve shows the relationship between the price (P) and the quantity purchased (Q) of an economic good. A graph isolates the relationship between price and quantity while all else (time, place, prices of other goods, income, etc.) is held constant (*ceteris*

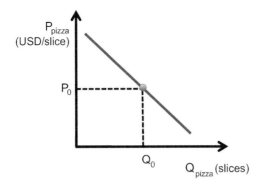

**Figure 1.2** The demand for pizza

*paribus*). The two variables, price and quantity, can be shown simultaneously on a two-dimensional surface such as the chalkboard or a computer screen.

In economics, the horizontal axis along the bottom of graph (the "x-axis") measures the value of one variable. In Figure 1.2, the quantity of a good (Q) is the measured variable on the x-axis. The numerical value of a second variable is measured from bottom to top along the vertical axis (the "y-axis") on the left-hand side of the graph.

The graph cannot be understood unless each axis has two items: **LABELS** and **UNITS**. In Figure 1.2, the label for quantity is Q (pizza) and the units are slices. The label for price is P and the units are (USD/slice). Units are typically placed in parentheses.

To understand the graph, for a given number of pizza slices ($Q_0$), the price of pizza is equal to $P_0$. As the price of pizza increases, the quantity demanded of pizza decreases.

## 1.8   Absolute and relative prices

In a market economy, prices determine the decisions made by producers and consumers. Producers and consumers do not use a single price to make decisions, but rather the price of one good relative to the price of other goods that is important.

### 1.8.1   The difference between absolute and relative prices

- *Absolute Prices* = a price in isolation, without reference to other prices. Example: the price of wheat is USD 6/bushel.
- *Relative Prices* = the prices of goods relative to each other. Example: the price of wheat increased relative to the price of corn.

The fact that the market price of wheat is equal to USD 6/bushel does not have much meaning when making a production decision about which crop to plant.

Producers need to know the price of wheat relative to the price of alternative crops such as corn, cotton, and hay. This is because it is possible for the farmer to use the land to produce an alternative crop. The farmer desires to earn the highest possible level of profit on this land, so a good economic decision is one that considers the relative prices of all crops that can reasonably be grown on the land. In general, producers will react to a relative price increase by producing more of a good since they will earn higher levels of profit by doing so. Consumers, on the other hand, will react to a price increase by buying less of a good.

Producer and consumer reactions to price changes are central to the lessons of economics. Later chapters will help explain how producers and consumers react to price changes. The following intuition will help in understanding economics.

**Producers** prefer higher prices of the goods that they produce.

**Consumers** prefer lower prices for the goods that they purchase.

Suppose that due to an increase in oil prices, all crop prices increase the same percentage. In this case, the relative prices for all crops remain the same, even though their absolute prices increase. All of the prices moved up together, so the relative prices all remained constant.

Consider the following statement: if all prices in an economy doubled, nothing would happen. At first glance, this does not seem to make sense. However, if it is known that all of the prices in the entire economy increased by the same percentage amount, in this case doubled, then relative prices remained constant, so producers and consumers would not change their decisions. Everything would cost the same relative to everything else.

Additional information suggests that if inflation were 10 percent for all goods in the economy, then the prices of everything would increase by 10 percent. This would be true for all goods, including labor services, so wages and salaries would increase by the same amount as the prices for goods. Nothing would happen, because all items in the economy would retain the same relative value. However, if oil prices were to increase due to a war in Ukraine, then consumers would use less oil and more energy from other sources. To summarize, absolute prices are accounting devices, whereas relative prices are responsible for actual decisions.

## BOX 1.7

### Inflation in agriculture

Inflation is simply a general rise in the prices of goods and services. Inflation is measured by the consumer price index (CPI), calculated each month by the Bureau of Labor Statistics (BLS), based on changes in the prices of thousands of goods and services. Inflation, or price increases, has been in the background for a long period.

From 2000 to 2020, the average annual rate of inflation was approximately 2 percent. This rate is considered by economists and business leaders to be acceptable and desirable, to help drive consumption and economic growth.

In 2020, high rates of inflation became common. The CPI reported that consumer price increased by 7 percent in 2020, returning the US and global economies to rates that prevailed in the 1970s and early 1980s.

Inflation is both good and bad for agricultural producers since both output prices (wheat, corn, beef) and input prices (labor, chemicals, fertilizer) increase. Inflation reduces the purchasing power for both producers and consumers. For example, if a beef producer gains additional revenue from beef price increases of 3 percent, her net revenues would decrease if input prices increased by 5 percent. Farm credit is also affected by inflation since the cost of borrowing increases.

Inflation can also adversely affect international trade for exported goods due to changes in exchange rates between nations. If the value of the US dollar appreciates relative to other currencies, US agricultural exports become more expensive relative to the same commodities produced and sold by other nations.

*Source:* Snell, W. "Inflation-'Good' or 'Bad' for Agricultural Producers and Consumers?"

agecon.ca.uky.edu/inflation-%E2%80%93-%E2%80%9Cgood%E2%80%9D-or-%E2%80%9Cbad%E2%80%9D-agricultural-producers-and-consumers. Retrieved January 2, 2023.

## 1.8.2   Price units

The units used to express prices are crucial to understanding how producers and consumers behave. The price of a good is not just a number of dollars, it is dollars per unit (USD/unit). The price of bread at Walmart is not just USD 1, but rather it is USD 1/loaf. The following list shows other examples.

| | |
|---|---|
| Bread | USD 2/loaf |
| Wheat | USD 7/bushel |
| Pizza | USD 15/large pizza |
| Blue jeans | USD 60/pair |
| Car | USD 23,000/car |

Prices are not expressed in dollars alone. Rather, prices are expressed in **dollars per unit.**

### 1.8.3 Constant-quality prices

The price of a good refers to constant-quality units. It means very little to say "a pair of jeans" or "a large pizza." The statement must be more specific. Fortunately, specific qualities are often used in everyday conversation. For example, "I sold two pens of cattle," or "Ten thousand cars were sold today," or "Five billion bushels of wheat were exported to Russia in February." Such specific statements tell exactly the type of good under discussion. Other examples are as follows:

"I sold two pens of heifers of average quality."
"Ten thousand Jaguars were sold last month."
"Five billion bushels of US #2 Hard Red Winter Wheat were exported in February."

Once again, a simplified real-world example describes what is happening.

## 1.9 Examples of graphs

### 1.9.1 A graph of the demand for hamburger in Miami, Florida

The demand (consumption) for hamburger is easily described using mathematics. How do consumers respond to a change in the price of hamburger in Miami, Florida? The numbers in the demand schedule in Table 1.3 show the relationship between the price of hamburger and the quantity of hamburger purchased in Miami's grocery stores.

The units are of constant quality. Specifying constant quality means that the entire quantity of hamburger in Table 1.3 is of the same quality. The units used

### Table 1.3 Hamburger demand schedule in Miami, Florida

| Price (USD/lb) | Quantity purchased (1,000 lb) |
| --- | --- |
| 2.30 | 0 |
| 2.10 | 20 |
| 1.90 | 40 |
| 1.70 | 60 |
| 1.50 | 80 |
| 1.30 | 100 |
| 1.10 | 120 |
| 0.90 | 140 |
| 0.70 | 160 |
| 0.50 | 180 |
| 0.30 | 200 |
| 0.10 | 220 |
| 0 (free!) | 230 |

for the hamburger price are dollars per pound (not just dollars) P = USD/lb. In this example the units for the quantity of hamburger is assumed to be 1,000 pounds, or Q = 1,000 lb. Figure 1.3 has both labels and units on each axis.

## QUICK QUIZ 1.2

What are the labels and units in Figure 1.3?

As fewer pounds of hamburger are placed on the market in Miami, consumers are willing to pay a higher price for it. This is due to scarcity. The lower the availability of something, the more valuable that it is, *ceteris paribus*. Figure 1.3 demonstrates the relationship between the price and quantity of hamburger, and nothing else. Everything else is held constant.

The graph simplifies the real world by omitting many otherwise important details. For example, if wages in Miami increase, will more hamburger be sold? Answering this question requires knowledge of income levels and how they are associated with changes in the consumption of hamburger. In addition, the demand for hamburger is seasonal. People buy more hamburger during the summer months for outdoor cooking. This is ignored in the graph. In this example, as in other cases, simplification helps ease understanding.

Photo 1.3 Hamburger demand in Miami, Florida

*Source:* Shutterstock

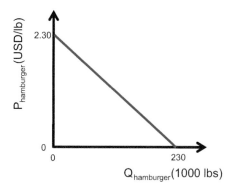

$P_{hamburger}$ (USD/lb)

2.30

0

0

230

$Q_{hamburger}$(1000 lbs)

---

**Figure 1.3 The demand for hamburger in Miami, Florida**

## 1.9.2 The slope of a line

The same information can be viewed in a slightly different way using algebra. A **function** relates two variables, say x and y. The function y = f(x) reads as "y is a function of x." The variable x is called the independent variable since the value of x does not depend on any other variable. The y variable is called the dependent variable since the value of y depends on the value that x takes. Restated, x causes y.

x = independent variable.
y = dependent variable.

The expression y = f(x) is a general function that could take any form, linear or nonlinear. A more specific functional form is the linear form, which just means that the relationship between the two variables is a straight line. The linear functional form is as follows:

1.1   y = b + mx.

This can be read, "y is a function of x, where b is the y-intercept, and m is the slope." Armed with this simple algebra, the demand for hamburger in Miami becomes an equation, where P is the price of hamburger in dollars per pound, and Q is the number of 1,000 lb units of hamburger purchased in Miami:

1.2   P = 2.30 – 0.01Q.

The demand for hamburger in Miami can be graphed using a different method. First, calculate the slope of hamburger demand in Miami. The slope is the rate at which a relationship increases or decreases. The slope is sometimes called the "rise over the run," or the "change in y divided by the change in x." In the hamburger case, the object is to find how much the price changes when the quantity of

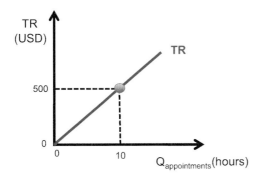

Figure 1.4 **Total revenues for a veterinary clinic in Milwaukee, Wisconsin**

hamburger purchased changes. The symbol for change is a Greek letter delta: $\Delta$. The slope is equal to the following:

1.3   $\Delta y / \Delta x = \Delta P / \Delta Q$.

In the case of hamburger in Miami in Figure 1.3, the slope equals: $-2.30 / 230 = -0.01$. Therefore, the slope of the demand line (m) equals $-0.01$, and the y-intercept (b) equals 2.30. This can be seen in the equation of the line $P = 2.30 - 0.01Q$. The graph of this economic relationship can be derived from either the demand schedule or the equation of the line.

### 1.9.3   Example: veterinary clinic in Milwaukee, Wisconsin

Suppose a veterinarian charges USD 50 for a 60-minute appointment in her clinic next to the brewery in Milwaukee. The vet's total revenue (TR) is equal to the number of appointments (Q) multiplied by the price of an appointment (P = USD 50/hour):

1.4   $TR = P * Q = 50 * Q$.

This economic relationship is a linear relationship, as shown in Figure 1.4. The slope of the line (m) equals 50, and the y-intercept equals zero.

The units for total revenue (TR) are in dollars because the price P is in dollars per hour (USD/hr), and it has been multiplied times the quantity, in hours (hr). The dollars represented by TR are the bills found in the clinic's cash register at the end of the working day.

When carefully drawn, graphs are useful tools to help organize thoughts about economic relationships. Good graphics require that every axis must include **labels** and **units**. Also, prices are always in USD/unit, not just in dollars, and the units are constant-quality units. Several of the concepts discussed in this chapter will be used throughout the course. Since the content of this book is cumulative (all new concepts build on old concepts), students who learn each concept in the beginning will have a huge advantage as the book progresses. Chapter 2 introduces the concept of production, or how we turn inputs (resources) into economically useful outputs (goods).

## 1.10   Chapter 1 Summary

1  Economics is important and interesting.
2  Economics helps us make better business, career, and personal decisions.
3  The goal of this book is to help the reader learn to "think like an economist." Thinking like an economist provides a framework for understanding economic events, career decisions, and personal situations in a clear and precise manner.
4  Economics is a social science, which is the study of human behavior.
5  A producer is an individual or firm that produces (makes; manufactures) a product.
6  A consumer is an individual or household that purchases a product.
7  Individuals are both producers and consumers.
8  Macroeconomics is the study of economy-wide activities or events.
9  Microeconomics is the study of individual decision-making units.
10 Positive economics is based on statements that are factual and contain no value judgments ("what is").
11 Normative economics is based on statements that contain opinions or value judgments ("what should be").
12 Price increases help producers and hurt consumers, whereas price decreases help consumers and hurt producers.
13 Economics is about scarcity. Scarcity means that there is less of something than is desired.
14 An economic good is any good whose quantity cannot expand without an increase in price.
15 A noneconomic good is a good that is not scarce (a free good).
16 Scarcity forces us to choose. We can't have everything that we want.
17 Economics is the allocation of scarce resources among competing ends.
18 A market economy is an economic organization in which prices determine how resources and goods are allocated (capitalism, free markets).
19 A command economy is an economic organization in which resource allocation is determined by whoever is in charge (dictatorship, communism, socialism).
20 A mixed economy has elements of both a market economy and a command economy.
21 Resources are productive items used to produce goods and services to satisfy human wants and desires. Resources include land (A), labor (L), capital (K), and management (M).
22 Firms combine resources (K, L, A, and M) to produce goods and services. Consumers make payments to firms to obtain goods and services.
23 The agricultural economy is changing rapidly. Important trends include (1) fewer and larger farms, (2) agriculture is not just farming, (3) substitution

of capital for labor, (4) rapid increases in off-farm income, (5) exports are increasingly important, and (6) an increase in the demand for fresh fruits and vegetables.

24 Graphs are useful tools to summarize and interpret information.
25 Absolute prices refer to a single price level, whereas relative prices refer to the prices of goods relative to (compared to) each other. The economic decisions of producers and consumers depend on relative prices.
26 Prices of goods are expressed in constant-quality prices.
27 Every graph must have units and labels on each axis.

## 1.11   Chapter 1 Glossary

**Absolute Price**—A price in isolation, without reference to other prices. Example: the price of wheat is USD 3/bushel (see **Relative Prices**).

**Agricultural Economics**—Economics applied to agriculture and rural areas.

**Agriculture**—The science, art, and business of cultivating the soil, producing crops, and raising livestock useful to humans. Farming.

**Capital**—Produced wealth that is used in further production. In economics, physical capital includes machinery, buildings, tools, and equipment.

*Ceteris Paribus*—Latin for "holding all else constant." An assumption used to simplify the real world.

**Command Economy**—A form of economic organization where resources are allocated by whoever is in charge, such as a dictator or an elected group of officials (see **Market Economy** and **Mixed Economy**).

**Consumer**—An individual or household that purchases a good or a service.

**Economic Good**—A good that is scarce (see **Noneconomic Good**).

**Economics**—The study of the allocation of scarce resources among competing ends.

**Factors**—Inputs provided by nature and modified by humans who use technology to produce goods and services that satisfy human wants and desires. Also called **inputs, factors of production**, or **factors**. Resources include **capital** (K), **labor** (L), **land** (A), and **management** (M).

**Factors of Production**—Inputs provided by nature and modified by humans who use technology to produce goods and services that satisfy human wants and desires. Also called **inputs, factors of production**, or **factors**. Resources include **capital** (K), **labor** (L), **land** (A), and **management** (M).

**Free Trade Agreement**—Agreements between nations to reduce or eliminate **trade barriers**.

**Good**—An **economic good**.

**Macroeconomics**—The study of economy-wide activities such as economic growth, business fluctuations, inflation, unemployment, recession, depression, and booms (see **Microeconomics**).

**Market Economy**—A form of economic organization in which resources are allocated by prices. Resources flow to the highest returns in a free market system (see **Command Economy** and **Mixed Economy**).

**Microeconomics**—The study of the behavior of individual decision-making units such as individuals, households, and firms (see **Macroeconomics**).

**Mixed Economy**—A form or economic organization that has elements of both a **market economy** and a **command economy**.

**Noneconomic Good**—A good that is not scarce; there is as much of this good to meet any demand for it. A free good (see **Economic Good**).

**Normative Economics**—Based on statements that contain opinions and/or value judgments. A normative statement contains a judgment about "what ought to be" or "what should be" (see **Positive Economics**).

**Positive Economics**—Based on factual statements. Such statements contain no value judgments. Positive economic statements describe "what is" (see **Normative Economics**).

**Producer**—An individual or firm that produces (makes; manufactures) a good or provides a service.

**Relative Price**—The prices of goods relative to each other. Example: the price of wheat increased relative to the price of corn (see **Absolute Price**).

**Resources**—Inputs provided by nature and modified by humans who use technology to produce goods and services that satisfy human wants and desires. Also called **inputs, factors of production**, or **factors**. Resources include **capital** (K), **labor** (L), **land** (A), and **management** (M).

**Scarcity**—Because resources are limited, the goods and services produced from using those resources are also limited, which means consumers must make choices, or trade-offs, among different goods.

**Service**—A type of economic good that is not physical. For example, a haircut or a phone call is a service, whereas a car or a shirt is a good.

**Social Science**—The study of society and of individual relationships in and to society, generally regarded as including sociology, psychology, anthropology, economics, political science, and history.

**Trade Barriers**—Laws and regulations to restrict the flow of goods and services across international borders, including tariffs, duties, quotas, and import and export subsidies.

## 1.12   Chapter 1 Review questions

1  Economics is

   a   an agricultural science
   b   a social science
   c   a physical science
   d   not a science, but a field of study

2  A producer is

   a   a person who purchases a product
   b   the seller of a product
   c   the buyer of a product
   d   a good sow

3  A consumer is all of the following except

   a   a buyer
   b   a household
   c   a customer
   d   a firm

4  A North Dakota wheat farmer is an example of a

   a   producer
   b   consumer
   c   both a and b
   d   neither a nor b

5 The study of growth in Mexico's level of living is an example of

a macroeconomics
b microeconomics
c political science
d consumer behavior

6 The study of how a single beef producer uses growth hormones is an example of

a macroeconomics
b microeconomics
c biological science
d consumer behavior

7 The statement "the market price of soybeans is USD 4.50 per bushel" is an example of

a positive economics
b normative economics
c a value judgment
d consumer behavior

8 The statement "the price of wheat should be higher" is an example of

a positive economics
b normative economics
c a factual statement
d consumer behavior

9 If the price of wheat rises, who is made better off?

a producers
b consumers
c both a and b
d neither a nor b

10 An increase in the price of wheat is good for

a wheat producers
b milling and baking firms
c bread consumers
d cattle producers

11 Scarcity affects

a industrial firms
b agricultural producers
c Internet users

d everyone

12 Scarcity

a reflects limited resources and unlimited desires
b affects religious persons
c forces us to choose
d all of the above

13 An example of an economic good is

a a cookie
b pollution
c garbage
d disease

14 The following is a noneconomic good

a a cookie
b a sunset
c a football
d a Lexus automobile

15 In a market economy, resources are allocated by

a prices
b whoever is in charge
c an elected group of officials
d a disaster

16 The United States is an example of:

a a command economy
b a market economy
c a mixed economy
d none of the other three answers

17 What percent of the US population is engaged in production agriculture?

a 16
b 4
c 2
d 25

18 If the price of corn increases relative to the price of other crops, *ceteris paribus*:

a farmers will plant more corn
b farmers will plant less corn

c   farmers will plant the same amount of corn

d   a corn consumer will purchase more corn

19  If the prices of all crops increase, then

a   farmers will plant more corn
b   farmers will plant less corn
c   farmers will plant the same amount of corn

d   a corn consumer will purchase more corn

20  The price of corn is written in which form?

a   USD 2
b   USD 2/bushel
c   2 bushels
d   2 bushels/USD

**Answers:** 1. b, 2. b, 3. d, 4. c, 5. a, 6. b, 7. a, 8. b, 9. a, 10. a, 11. d, 12. d, 13. a, 14. b, 15. a, 16. c, 17. c, 18. a, 19. c, 20. b

For more study questions, flash cards, and study guides, see the online materials at the companion website: www.routledge.com/cw/barkley.

# Chapter 2

## The economics of production

Photo 2.1  The economics of production

*Source:* Satin/Shutterstock

DOI: 10.4324/9781003367994-2

## Abstract

This chapter explores the physical production process. It describes the physical relationship between inputs and outputs and describes the economics of transforming inputs into products: resources into goods. The production function is defined and explained. Next, the effect of time on production is investigated by defining the immediate, short, and long runs. The role of physical production relationships is highlighted, with definitions for constant, increasing, and decreasing returns. Technological change and the law of diminishing marginal returns are defined and explained to enhance understanding of examples from food and agriculture.

### Chapter 2 Questions

1　What is production economics, and why is it useful?
2　How are physical resources combined to produce goods and services?
3　What is the physical relationship between inputs and outputs?
4　What is a production function?
5　What are the immediate run, short run, and long run in economics?
6　What are constant, increasing, decreasing, and negative returns to scale?
7　How does technological change affect production?
8　What is the law of diminishing marginal returns, and how is it used to understand economics?

## 2.1　The production function

Agricultural production is a logical place to begin the study of the economics of agriculture. During the production process, firms (also called producers) combine inputs into outputs for sale to consumers. The process can be quite complex, so the next several chapters are devoted to the production activities undertaken by firms. The discussion then shifts to the behavior of consumers, or households. All of this leads to consideration of the interactions of consumers and producers in markets.

Production is the process of making goods and services. This process requires scarce resources. As seen in the previous chapter, inputs have several different names:

2.1　Inputs = factors = factors of production = resources = A, L, K, and M

> ### QUICK QUIZ 2.1
>
> What do the letters A, L, K, and M refer to?

### 2.1.1　Wheat production in the high plains of North Dakota

Consider a wheat producer in North Dakota, a leading wheat-producing state in most years. Let Y = output = wheat, measured in bushels (bu), where f = the mathematical relationship between inputs and output:

2.2   Output = f(inputs),

2.3   Y = f(inputs), or

2.4   Y = f(K, L, A, M).

The North Dakota wheat producer uses inputs K, L, A, and M to produce wheat (Y). Chapter 1 included a short discussion of the need to simplify this complex relationship in order to understand real-world production. Graphs will lead to fuller understanding, but a two-dimensional graph is possible only if the number of inputs allowed to vary is reduced to one. Consider the relationship between inputs and outputs, and concentrate on just one input. In this case, the choice of capital is entirely arbitrary since any one of the inputs could fit into the example.

### QUICK QUIZ 2.2

How is capital defined in economics? What four types of capital are included in this definition?

As in Chapter 1, the *ceteris paribus* assumption isolates the relationship between output and the single input, capital.

### QUICK QUIZ 2.3

What does *ceteris paribus* mean?

Adopting a convention used by mathematicians helps clarify what is happening. A mathematician writes an equation to say that the variable Y is related to, or depends on, the other variables $x_1, x_2 \ldots x_n$. The equation is written as

2.5   $Y = f(x_1, x_2 \ldots x_n)$,

with numeric subscripts used to identify the variables.

### BOX 2.1

## The North American northern high plains region

Although the area has no precise definition, the North American high plains encompass the Missouri River drainage and parts of the states that lie west of the Mississippi River. The northern part of this region, including North Dakota, South Dakota, Nebraska, Kansas, Montana, Wyoming, and Colorado, is sparsely populated and is used primarily for farming and ranching. In 1910, the area supported nearly 550,000 farms. By the year 2010, the number had dropped to approximately 250,000 farms, a 55.4 percent decrease! Rainfall is scarce, so the farms of this region are devoted primarily to the production of small grains: wheat, barley, some corn, sunflower seeds, rye, and soybeans. Irrigation provides water for high-value crops in areas located above the Ogallala Aquifer. Hay grown in the region provides winter feed for large cattle herds.

*Source:* USDA/NASS. www.nass.usda.gov/. Retrieved January 3, 2023.

Following mathematical convention, the variable "$x_1$" to the left of the vertical bar is free to vary, but all variables to the right of the vertical bar, in this case, $x_2 \ldots x_n$, are held constant:

2.6　$Y = f(x_1 \mid x_2 \ldots x_n)$

In this example of wheat production in North Dakota, the only variable to the left of the vertical bar (K) varies. The variables to the right of the vertical bar (L, A, and M) are held fixed, or constant. By holding all but two variables constant, a graph can be used to describe the multidimensional relationship on a two-dimensional surface. Real physical production is a complicated biological process. Therefore, one input at a time must be isolated:

2.7　$Y = f(K \mid L, A, M).$

This equation is what mathematicians refer to as a function. Economists provide a more descriptive term by calling it a "**production function.**"

● *Production Function* = the physical relationship between inputs and outputs.

The production function is a purely physical relationship used to describe the quantity of inputs required to produce a given quantity of output. Since there are no dollar values associated with it, it is not an economic relationship.

Real-world production processes can be very complicated, making it difficult to understand the relationships among the constantly changing variables. Working with one variable at a time offers a simplified approach to this problem. For example, to determine the optimal use of the nitrogen fertilizer on wheat fields, agronomists can run controlled experiments to determine what happens to wheat yields as the amount of nitrogen is changed: either increased or decreased. They do this type of experiment on test plots, or small wheat fields that are typically adjacent to each other to keep constant the weather, growing conditions, and soil conditions across all of the plots. The idea behind the controlled experiment is to hold all inputs constant except for nitrogen and measure how the different levels of nitrogen affect the wheat yields. The wheat production function would look like this:

2.8　$Y = f(x_1, x_2 \ldots x_n).$

Where Y is wheat output, measured in bushels (bu); f is the production function, or the physical relationship between inputs and output; and the $x_i$ are inputs, which include land, labor, machinery, seed, and nitrogen. Specifying each input makes it possible to write the production function as follows:

2.9   $Y = f(N, L, K, M, A)$.

### QUICK QUIZ 2.4

What does each of the letters in this production function stand for?

To isolate the relationship between nitrogen and wheat yields, the agronomists (or other biophysical scientists) will hold constant all inputs other than the one that they are isolating, in this case nitrogen.

### QUICK QUIZ 2.5

What is the term economists use for "holding all else constant"?

2.10   $Y = f(N \mid L, K, M, A)$.

Knowledge of this relationship allows agronomists to identify the relationship between nitrogen and wheat growth. This relationship is highly important since too little nitrogen means the yields will be lower than the potential, and too much nitrogen will "burn" the crop, causing smaller yields. Figure 2.1 shows the connection between nitrogen applications and wheat yields.

Here is a major lesson: the point of maximum *physical* wheat yield (N*) is not always the optimal *economic* wheat yield. This is because nitrogen is a scarce resource and costs money to purchase. In fact, fertilizer is one of the major costs of production for farmers in most agricultural regions in the United States. If nitrogen were free, then the optimal application to a wheat field would always be N* in Figure 2.1 since this is the level of nitrogen that maximizes production. However, since it costs money to purchase and use fertilizer, the farmer will stop applying it at a point to the left of N*. Finding the optimal amount of nitrogen to apply requires application of economic principles. Economic reasoning will help determine the exact point where the benefits of using N minus the costs are maximized. For now, note that producers will not maximize *production*, because it costs too much. Instead, they will maximize *profits*. This problem will return for added explanation in Chapter 4.

A second example of a production function is a controlled experiment to find the impact of growth hormones (H) on beef production (Figure 2.2). Growth hormones are controversial since some consumers believe that the hormones are unhealthy for human consumption. Belief in this possibility is so intense that Europeans do not import American beef. Even so, cattle producers continue to use the hormones because they increase output significantly, and a vast majority of consumers in the US have not objected. A production function for beef can be written as $Y = f(H, K, L, A, M)$.

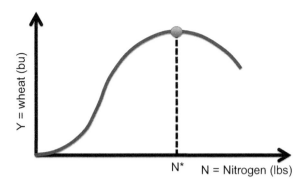

Figure 2.1 Wheat yield as a function of nitrogen application

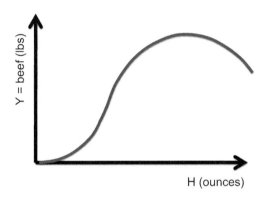

Figure 2.2 Beef output as a function of hormone use

QUICK QUIZ 2.6

What do each of these letters stand for? How are the growth hormones isolated in a scientific experiment?

BOX 2.2

## Nitrogen fertilizer use in US agriculture

Fertilizer is an organic or inorganic material, of natural or synthetic origin, that is added to soil as a nutrient to promote plant growth. Recent studies have found that a large percentage of crop yields are attributable to commercial fertilizer use, causing a large percentage of the population to rely on synthetic nitrogen fertilizer.

Mined inorganic fertilizers have been used for many centuries. Chemical, synthesized inorganic fertilizers were developed during the Industrial Revolution leading to the British Agricultural Revolution and the industrial Green Revolution of the twentieth century. Nitrogen fertilizers are made using the Haber-Bosch process (1915), which combines natural gas and nitrogen gas with a catalyst at elevated temperature and pressure to produce ammonia. Ammonia is then converted into nitrogen fertilizers such as anhydrous ammonium nitrate and urea.

The use of commercial inorganic fertilizers has increased rapidly in the last 50 years, rising almost 20-fold to the current rate of 100 million tons of nitrogen per year. In the US, use of nitrogen in agriculture has increased steadily from 2.7 million nutrient tons in 1960 to over 13.3 million nutrient tons in 2014. Corn is the biggest user of nitrogen in US agriculture, with 6.1 million nutrient tons used in 2016, followed by wheat at 1.7 million nutrient tons, and cotton at 0.3 million nutrient tons.

Applying excessive amounts of fertilizer has negative environmental effects and wastes the growers' time and money. Negative environmental effects can include eutrophication, or serious oxygen depletion, in the ocean, especially in coastal zones and lakes, causing the inability to sustain aquatic wildlife. As a result, application of nitrogen fertilizer is monitored and regulated in high-income nations. Agricultural runoff into groundwater has also been linked to "blue baby syndrome" and soil acidification. Another concern is global warming, resulting from increased levels of nitrous oxide, the third most important greenhouse gas after carbon dioxide and methane. Since the benefits of using nitrogen fertilizer are large and significant to feeding a growing world population, nations and groups will need to carefully compare these benefits of increased food production with the potential environmental costs.

*Source:* Stewart, W.M.; Dibb, D.W.; Johnston, A.E.; Smyth, T.J. (2005). "The Contribution of Commercial Fertilizer Nutrients to Food Production." *Agronomy Journal* 97: 1–6.

> ### BOX 2.3
>
> ## US beef production and consumption
>
> Humans have consumed beef since prehistoric times. Globally, it is the third most common meat after pork and poultry. Domestication of cattle began around 8000 BC to provide a source of meat, milk, and leather. Cattle were also used as draft animals until mechanization began to occur in the sixteenth and seventeenth centuries AD. Now, in the twenty-first century, the US, Brazil, and the People's Republic of China are the world's three largest consumers of beef.
>
> Beef production occurs using two major methods: grass fed on pastures and grain fed in confined pens, or feedlots. Feedlots, or concentrated animal feeding operations (CAFOs), typically feed cattle a ration of grain, protein, roughage, vitamins, and minerals. The world's largest exporters of beef are Brazil, Australia, and the US. Beef production is also important to the economies of Paraguay, Argentina, Ireland, Mexico, New Zealand, Nicaragua, Russia, and Uruguay.
>
> Beef is an excellent source of protein and minerals such as zinc, selenium, phosphorus, iron, and B vitamins. Recent health concerns from beef consumption include cancer, cardiovascular disease, and coronary heart disease; dioxins from cattle raised in the US fed on pastures fertilized with sewage sludge; *Escherichia coli* contamination; and bovine spongiform encephalopathy (BSE, or mad cow disease). Given the importance of beef in the US diet, consumers will need to continue to weigh the culinary and nutritional advantages of beef consumption with the food safety, environmental, and health concerns that arise because of modern concentrated beef production.
>
> *Source:* USDA/FAS. www.fas.usda.gov/psdonline/ Retrieved January 3, 2023.

The controlled experiment would use several pens of cattle with identical inputs (feed, water, temperature, bedding, etc.) except the level of growth hormone (H). The scientists would carefully measure and record the weight of each animal and find the physical relationship between the growth hormone and the amount of muscle on the animal.

The shape of this graph is similar to the graph of the wheat experiment. There is an "optimal" level of growth hormone for cattle production. Larger amounts of input will increase output only up to a certain point. After that, the high-dose hormone input becomes toxic and causes production to decrease.

Photo 2.2 Hormone use in beef production

*Source:* Sergey Goruppa/Shutterstock

QUICK QUIZ 2.7

Will the cattle producer use the level of growth hormones that maximizes *production*? Why or why not?

The study of production functions applies to many situations, events, and circumstances. A student studying for an exam is involved with a kind of production. In this situation output (=Y) might be test performance, or grade, and the input (=X) is the number of hours that the student studies. The output of this production process will depend on how many hours the student studies and other factors, such as intelligence and previous knowledge. However, if the student constantly drinks energy drinks and stays up all night, the test performance may actually fall. Too much studying can result in too little sleep, which in turn results in poor test performance. Thus, the relationship between the number of hours studied and the grade on a test will have the same general shape as the graphs for wheat production (Figure 2.1) and beef production (Figure 2.2). Because of differences in intelligence, preparation, alertness, and academic ability, each individual student will have a different "production function" for the examination. Each of these determinants of exam performance is held constant, *ceteris paribus* in Figure 2.3.

## 2.1.2  Profit maximization

Economists build models on the assumption that all producers desire to maximize profits. This is a simplification of the real world since there may be producers who have other goals, such as a nice lifestyle, a clean environment, world peace,

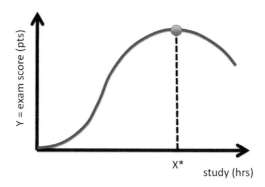

Figure 2.3 Grade as a function of study time

political power, or to pay employees more than the market wage rate. Although there are many producers who may not do everything in their power to maximize profits, this profit maximization goal is a good first approximation. Why? Because any business owner who does not pay attention to potential profits is unlikely to remain in business for long in a market economy.

Profits, denoted by the symbol $\pi$ (the Greek letter pi), have special meaning and importance in economics. Here, profits are defined as total revenue (TR) minus total costs (TC):

2.11 $\quad \pi = TR - TC.$

- **Profits** $[\pi]$ = total revenue minus total costs: $\pi = TR - TC$. The value of product sold minus the cost of producing that output.

Total revenue is simply the dollars earned from the sale of a good. Let the quantity of a good sold be given by Q units and the price of the good by P dollars per unit (USD/unit). Then, the total revenue earned by the producing firm is equal to TR = P * Q. The units for total revenue are in dollars since P is in USD/unit, and Q is in pounds, bushels, dozens, or some other appropriate measure. When P is multiplied times Q, the units cancel, and TR is in USD. Total costs represent the total costs of production of the good and are also in dollar units.

Producers of goods and services alter their production and marketing activities in a never-ending effort to maximize profits. The ability of business firms to make changes in how they produce and sell goods depends on the product that they produce. If the product is corn, major adjustments are possible at least once each year with a small number of changes occurring throughout the year. If the product is walnuts, major production decisions come only once in a generation, or even longer, but a small number of minor adjustments are possible during each growing season. If the product is lettuce grown in greenhouses, major adjustments occur almost continually. Time and timing are the critical issues. Length of time is of great importance in making profit-maximizing decisions.

## 2.2   Length of time: immediate run, short run, and long run

Radio announcers, politicians, and people on the street speak casually and knowingly about the "long run" and the "short run." In economics, however, these terms have specific meanings, but not meanings related to a specific length of time such as minutes, days, or weeks. The length of the long run, the short run, and the immediate run depend on the specific situation, as defined and explained in the next section.

### 2.2.1   Immediate, short, and long runs

The **immediate run** is a period of time during which all of the inputs available to a producer are fixed and cannot be changed. The producer cannot change the quantity of any input. A wheat producer purchases land, labor, seed, machinery, fertilizer, and chemicals. As harvest time nears, the producer is unlikely to be able to alter or use either more or less of the quantity of these inputs to affect the progress of the crop. This situation defines the immediate run.

● *Immediate Run [IR]* = a period of time in which all productive inputs are fixed.

As time passes, the producer will have more flexibility to change the quantities of inputs. In a three-month period, this producer is able to alter the number of hours of work hired, but cannot change the number of acres of land that are in production or, after a certain period, add more fertilizer. This situation is called the **short run**, defined as a period when some inputs are fixed (the quantities of inputs used cannot be altered) and some inputs are variable (the quantities of inputs can be changed).

● *Short Run [SR]* = a time span during which some factors are variable and some factors are fixed.

The quantities of some agricultural inputs are not easy to change in the short run. Land is a common example. Most producers cannot acquire more land in a short length of time. Therefore, the acres of land available to one producer remain fixed in the short run (SR). Similarly, machinery and equipment (combines, tractors, and plows) are very expensive, and many producers cannot rapidly increase or decrease the number of these inputs. During that period, when a farmer is unable to alter the quantity of inputs, the inputs are fixed, and the farmer is in the short run (SR). However, in the short run, some inputs are variable. For example, the producer could alter the level of chemicals, fertilizer, labor, or management.
   In the **long run** (LR), all inputs are variable.

● *Long Run [LR]* = a period of time in which all inputs are variable; no inputs are fixed.

Over a longer period, a producer may buy or sell machinery or land. Producers can adjust the size of their farms. An agribusiness example is the agricultural implement manufacturer, John Deere, of Moline, Illinois. In the short run, "Deere" cannot build a plant to produce more combines since this would require purchasing land, building a factory, and training a labor force. However, in the long run (several years), Deere can build a new factory and start production of an expanded line of farm machinery. The crucial aspect regarding both the short run and long run is that there is not a set length of time for the long run: the long run is however long it takes to adjust the levels of inputs. This differs from farm to farm and from business to business.

Now suppose that a farmer in the northern plains is able to increase his land holding in only two weeks (he is also a real estate broker, and his father-in-law is a banker). If all of the inputs on this farm are variable in a two-week time period, then the length of the long run is only two weeks. The length of time that defines the long run depends on the situation and the willingness of the neighbors to sell land. Most farmers face a much different situation as it can take many years to acquire new land.

A lemonade stand set up by the children living on a residential street provides a sharp contrast. In the lemonade business, the long run is very short. The children can alter the quantities of all inputs (water, glasses, lemonade mix, and stirring spoon) very quickly by running into the house. The long run may only last five minutes.

> ### QUICK QUIZ 2.8
>
> How long are the short run and the immediate run for the lemonade stand?

## 2.2.2 Fixed and variable inputs

The previous discussion provides the background necessary for the definitions of fixed and variable inputs.

- *Fixed Input* = an input whose quantity does not vary with the level of output.

A fixed input is an immediate run or a short run concept, because in the long run, all inputs are variable.

- *Variable Input* = a variable input is one that when changed, affects the level of output.

> ### QUICK QUIZ 2.9
>
> Are nitrogen and growth hormones fixed or variable inputs? Explain.

## 2.3 Physical production relationships

Understanding the production function requires discussion of transforming inputs into outputs. Suppose a corn farmer in Iowa uses capital, labor, land, and management to produce corn. The generalized production function for his farming activity is as follows:

2.12   $Y = f(L, K, A, M)$.

---

**BOX 2.4**

## Iowa corn

Corn, wheat, and rice are the world's three leading grain crops. Corn as we know it descended from the plant *teosinte* in Mexico. Today, Iowa is the leading corn-producing state, and Iowa, Illinois, Nebraska, and Minnesota account for over 50 percent of the corn grown in the US. The "Corn Belt" includes these four states, together with Indiana, Ohio, Wisconsin, South Dakota, Michigan, Missouri, Kansas, and Kentucky. The story of corn is one of success: the original corn ears were only a few inches long, but centuries of plant breeding, first by Native Americans, then by early settlers and modern scientists, have resulted in larger ears, more kernels per ear, and more ears per plant. In 1900, corn yields in Iowa averaged about 40 bushels per acre. Iowa corn yields increased to about 50 bu/acre in 1950, and 90 bu/acre in 1970. In 2018, Iowa corn growers harvested an average of 196 bushels per acre. The national average in that year was 176.4 bushels per acre.

Corn is used for many purposes, the most important being livestock feeding, where one bushel of corn converts to about 5.6 pounds of retail beef, 13 pounds of retail pork, 28 pounds of catfish, or 32 pounds of chicken. An American grocery store contains several thousand products that list corn ingredients on the label. Iowa's corn is also processed into starches, oil, sweeteners, and ethanol. Iowa leads the nation in ethanol production. Nearly one-third of the US corn crop is exported to other nations, including Japan, Mexico, Korea, Taiwan, and Egypt.

*Source:* Iowa Corn. www.iowacorn.org/ Retrieved January 3, 2023.

---

Understanding the impact of labor on corn output requires holding the levels of all other inputs constant:

2.13   $Y = f(L \mid K, A, M)$.

The production function in equation 2.13 leads to an understanding of production efficiency, the topic of the next section.

### 2.3.1 Constant, increasing, decreasing, and negative returns

The level of inputs as reported in the production function determine the level of output (the production function describes the physical relationship between inputs and output). The production process can take on different forms: **constant returns, increasing returns, decreasing returns,** and **negative returns.** The word "returns" refers to increases in output that occur as quantities of inputs increase incrementally. Think of increasing the level of inputs by one unit at a time and measuring how output responds to each change. This incremental way of approaching a problem is one cornerstone of "thinking like an economist."

In a production process characterized by **constant returns,** each additional unit of input is equally as productive as all other units of input.

- *Constant Returns* = when each additional unit of input added to the production process yields a constant level of output relative to the previous unit of input. Output increases at a constant rate.

Consider the number of cattle it takes to produce cattle hides: one animal produces one hide, no more, no less (Figure 2.4). Since each additional unit of input (in this case steers) produces exactly one additional hide, the slope of the production function for leather hides (= $\Delta Y/\Delta X$) remains constant as more inputs are used, graphically demonstrating the concept of constant returns.

- *Increasing Returns* = when each additional unit of input added to the production process yields a larger additional amount of output relative to the previous unit of input. Output increases at an increasing rate.

Managers of business firms look favorably upon this type of production process since each additional unit of input is more productive than the one just before it.

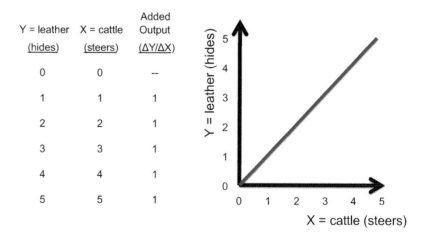

Figure 2.4 Leather production: constant returns

| Y = wheat (bu) | X = workers (persons) | Added Output (ΔY/ΔX) |
|---|---|---|
| 0 | 0 | -- |
| 10 | 1 | 10 |
| 30 | 2 | 20 |
| 60 | 3 | 30 |
| 100 | 4 | 40 |
| 150 | 5 | 50 |

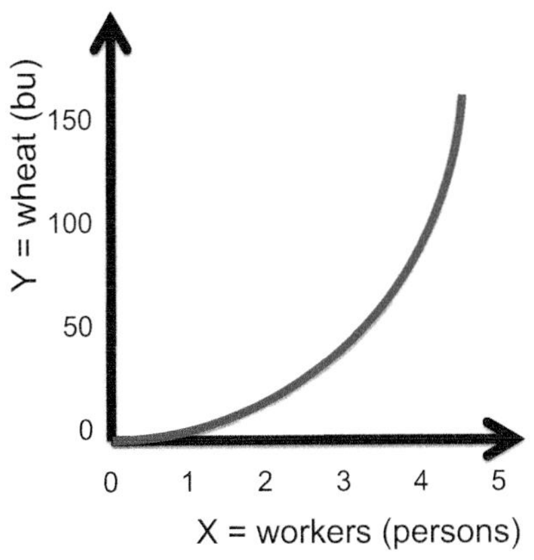

Figure 2.5 Wheat production: increasing returns

For example, if only one person tries to run both the combine and the truck during wheat harvest, the production process is inefficient. When a second worker drives the truck, the first person can spend all of her time operating the combine. As more workers join the harvest crew, holding all other inputs constant, the output increases at an increasing rate, as depicted in Figure 2.5. When **increasing returns** are present, each additional unit of input causes the level of output to increase more, relative to the previous unit of input.

### QUICK QUIZ 2.10

The production functions depicted in Figures 2.4 and 2.5 show an upward slope. Which of the graphs demonstrates increasing returns? How did you arrive at this conclusion?

**Decreasing returns** occur when the addition of one more unit of input results in a smaller increase in output than the previous unit.

- *Decreasing Returns* = when each additional unit of input added to the production process yields less additional output relative to the previous unit of input. Output increases at a decreasing rate.

Figure 2.6 illustrates a production function that exhibits decreasing returns. Suppose the example takes place in a kitchen. As more chefs appear, the productivity of the cooks increases, but at a decreasing rate. The first cook is the most productive, but adding more cooks causes the additional productivity to decline. Why? They get in each other's way and compete for use of the kitchen equipment. **Negative returns** occur when an additional unit of input actually decreases total output.

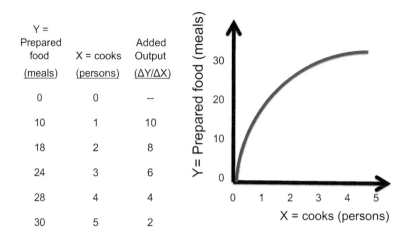

| Y =<br>Prepared<br>food<br>(meals) | X = cooks<br><br><br>(persons) | Added<br>Output<br><br>(ΔY/ΔX) |
|---|---|---|
| 0 | 0 | -- |
| 10 | 1 | 10 |
| 18 | 2 | 8 |
| 24 | 3 | 6 |
| 28 | 4 | 4 |
| 30 | 5 | 2 |

**Figure 2.6  Food production: decreasing returns**

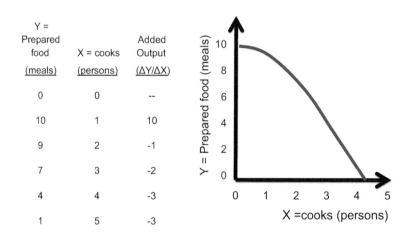

| Y =<br>Prepared<br>food<br>(meals) | X = cooks<br><br><br>(persons) | Added<br>Output<br><br>(ΔY/ΔX) |
|---|---|---|
| 0 | 0 | -- |
| 10 | 1 | 10 |
| 9 | 2 | -1 |
| 7 | 3 | -2 |
| 4 | 4 | -3 |
| 1 | 5 | -3 |

**Figure 2.7  Food production: negative returns**

In this situation, the added input is harming the production process. The cooks in the kitchen example indicates how this can happen. If the kitchen is very small, the addition of the second cook lowers the first cook's ability to prepare meals. In many situations, adding inputs results in a loss in output. Applying too much fertilizer "burns" the wheat plants and lowers the yield. Too heavy a dose of growth hormones lowers the weight gain in steers. Figure 2.7 illustrates negative returns.

- *Negative Returns* = when each additional unit of input added to the production process results in lower total output. Output decreases.

Photo 2.3 Negative returns: too many cooks in the kitchen

*Source:* Robert Adrian Hillman/Shutterstock

The negative slope in Figure 2.7 corresponds to a production function characterized by negative returns. A situation of negative returns develops anytime there is "too much of something."

## 2.3.2 A typical production function

Most production processes display stages of increasing returns, decreasing returns, and then negative returns. Why is this pattern so prevalent? Remember, the production function characterizes the physical relationship between output (Y) and a single input (X), *ceteris paribus* (holding all else constant).

The wheat farmer in North Dakota used land, labor, capital, and management to produce wheat. Suppose that this farmer has several thousand acres of wheat (farms of this size are not unusual in North Dakota) and holds all inputs constant except one: the number of combines. During harvest time, the farmer uses one combine to produce a large amount of grain. A second combine will be helpful and will allow the farmer to take advantage of having two combines working in the same field at the same time. This can actually increase production by even more than the first combine can as efficiencies are gained with the logistics of the field and the trucks needed to haul the grain to the elevator.

This may remain true for the first several combines. However, after several combines appear for use in the same field, the efficiency begins to fall. Decreasing returns set in, as combines begin to get in each other's way. When many combines are used, production can actually decrease since the farm operator must manage

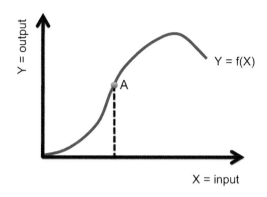

**Figure 2.8** The typical production function and diminishing returns

too many machines for a given plot of land. Figure 2.8 shows the typical production function. Notice that this function has the same shape as the earlier examples in Figures 2.1 to 2.3.

In real-world production processes, this "typical" production function usually holds. As a single input is increased, holding all other inputs constant, the productivity will typically increase with the addition of more units of input. At a certain point, adding more of the input will still yield an increase in productivity but at a decreasing rate. This is the point in the graph where the slope of the production function turns from increasing to decreasing (point A).

### 2.3.3 Total physical product

The **total physical product** (TPP) is the relationship between output (in this case corn) and one variable input (labor), holding all other inputs constant (Figure 2.9). The TPP of corn, typically measured in bushels, represents the maximum output for each level of input use. A table and graph of the TPP relationship for the corn farmer in Iowa appear in Figure 2.9.

- *Total Physical Product [TPP]* = the relationship between output and one variable input, holding all other inputs constant.

### 2.3.4 Average physical product

The **average physical product** (APP) refers to the average productivity of each unit of variable input used (Figure 2.10). Dividing the quantity of output by the quantity of input (Y/X) yields the APP that tells the number of bushels produced by each individual unit across the entire quantity of input.

- *Average Physical Product [APP]* = the average productivity of each unit of variable input used [= Y / X].

| Labor | TPP = corn |
|:---:|:---:|
| (workers) | (bu) |
| 0 | 0 |
| 1 | 10 |
| 2 | 21 |
| 3 | 33 |
| 4 | 40 |
| 5 | 45 |
| 6 | 48 |
| 7 | 42 |

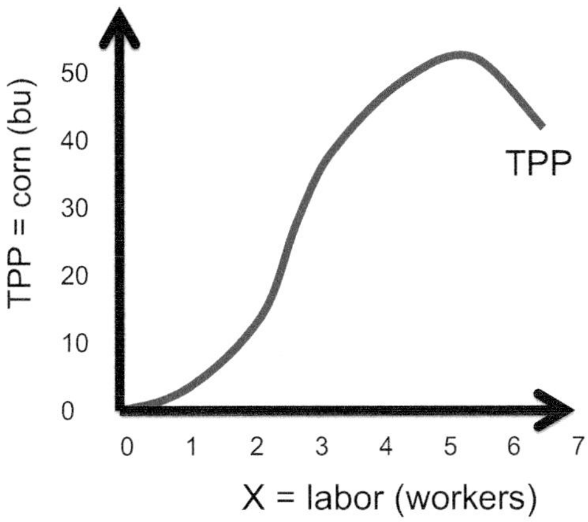

Figure 2.9 Corn production: total physical product

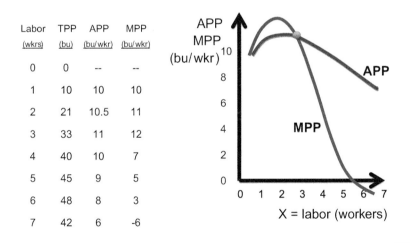

| Labor | TPP | APP | MPP |
|:---:|:---:|:---:|:---:|
| (wkrs) | (bu) | (bu/wkr) | (bu/wkr) |
| 0 | 0 | -- | -- |
| 1 | 10 | 10 | 10 |
| 2 | 21 | 10.5 | 11 |
| 3 | 33 | 11 | 12 |
| 4 | 40 | 10 | 7 |
| 5 | 45 | 9 | 5 |
| 6 | 48 | 8 | 3 |
| 7 | 42 | 6 | -6 |

Figure 2.10 Physical product of corn: average and marginal physical product

Different graphs must be used for TPP (Figure 2.9) and APP (Figure 2.10) since they are expressed in different units. Specifically, TPP is in units of output, whereas APP is expressed in units of output per unit of input.

## 2.3.5 Marginal physical product

The **marginal physical product** (MPP) is the physical product obtained from using one additional (marginal) unit of variable input (Figure 2.10). This concept tells how much more output comes from the last, or marginal, unit of input. Economists use the word "marginal" to refer to the last, or additional, or extra unit of input or output. The term appears throughout the remainder of the book. Using mathematical notation, marginal refers to a "small change," symbolized by the Greek letter delta ($\Delta$). The MPP is the change in output ($\Delta Y$) brought about by a change in input ($\Delta X$):

2.14   $MPP = \Delta Y / \Delta X$.

● *Marginal Physical Product [MPP]* = the additional amount of total physical product obtained from using an additional, or marginal, unit of variable input [$= \Delta Y / \Delta X$].

Figure 2.10 shows the APP and MPP derived from the information related to inputs (X) and outputs (Y). Output is TPP (in this case bushels of corn). To derive APP, divide TPP (in the second column) by the number of workers found

**Photo 2.4 Corn production**

*Source:* fonats/Shutterstock

in the first column. In the first row, note that if there are zero workers, no corn is produced (TPP = 0). To calculate APP for the first row, divide TPP (= 0) by the number of workers (= 0). This is not possible since a number divided by zero is undefined (or infinite). Show this by placing a dash in the first row for APP. In the second row, divide TPP = 10 by X = 1 to get APP = 10. Similarly for the remaining rows: average productivity equals Y divided by X [APP = Y / X]. The graph shows that APP increases up to a given level, then decreases. Remember that the APP refers to the average productivity of all inputs used. Notice that the TPP curve must be graphed separately from the APP and MPP curves since the units are different: TPP is in units of output, and APP and MPP are in units of output per unit of input.

Calculate MPP in a similar fashion. The MPP is the change in output given a small change in input ($\Delta Y / \Delta X$). To calculate MPP, look at a change in the input level, and calculate how much the output level changed as a result of the input change. Figure 2.10 shows that when the number of workers increases from zero to one [$\Delta X = 1 - 0 = 1$], output increases from zero bushels to ten bushels of corn [$\Delta Y = 10 - 0 = 10$]. By definition, MPP = $\Delta Y / \Delta X$ = 10 / 1 = 10, seen in the first entry in the MPP column in the table. The MPP refers to the productivity of the last unit of input, or the additional unit of input. Calculating MPP provides the answer to the question, "How much more output will be produced by adding one more unit of input?"

Look at the MPP of using a second worker. The change in input is 1 [$\Delta X = 2 - 1 = 1$], and the change in output is 11 [$\Delta Y = 21 - 10 = 11$]. The marginal productivity of labor increased with the addition of a second worker.

QUICK QUIZ 2.11

Calculate the APP and MPP from data in Table 2.1 for a beef producer. In this example, the input is bushels of corn fed to cattle and the output is meat in pounds. Graph TPP, APP, and MPP.

Table 2.1 Data for Quick Quiz 2.11

| Corn (bu) | TPP (lb) | APP (units = ?) | MPP (units = ?) |
|-----------|----------|-----------------|-----------------|
| 0 | 0 | | |
| 10 | 10 | | |
| 20 | 40 | | |
| 30 | 65 | | |
| 40 | 80 | | |
| 50 | 90 | | |
| 60 | 80 | | |

### 2.3.6 The relationship between average and marginal physical product

The APP and MPP are both derived from TPP and therefore have a direct relationship. The relationship is worth noting:

● If MPP > APP, then APP is increasing,
● If MPP < APP, then APP is decreasing.

An easy way to remember this is "average chases the marginal." Figure 2.11 shows this in the graph of the APP and MPP data for output (wheat in bushels) per input (workers).

Grades in a university-level class show the same characteristic. When each test score is earned, it is the marginal (or additional) grade. The average grade is the total number of points from all tests divided by the number of exams. Suppose that a student has taken two exams and has an average grade of 80. If this student gets a perfect score of 100 on the next (marginal) exam, the average grade increases to 87.5. The average has followed the marginal to a higher level. Similarly, a professional basketball player who has a great night will pull her average points per game up.

When the MPP is greater than the APP, the APP is increasing. In the case of a cattle feedlot, the production process is to add pounds of muscle to a steer by feeding it corn.

TPP = Total Physical Product
    = Y = beef (lb)
APP = Average Physical Product
    = Y / X = beef/corn (lb/bu)
MPP = Marginal Physical Product
    = $\Delta Y / \Delta X$ = $\Delta$beef/$\Delta$corn (lb/bu)

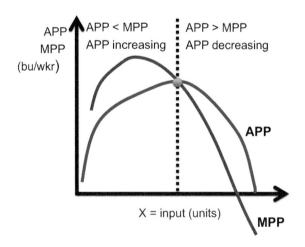

Figure 2.11 The relationship between average and marginal physical product

Draw the TPP, APP, and MPP graphs for the feedlot example in Table 2.1.

## 2.3.7 Technological change

The knowledge of productivity and the production function can help in understanding an important issue: **technological change**. An amazing number of technologies have appeared in the past decade or two: computers, software, cell phones, commercial space travel, and health care. The Internet and the information age have all occurred recently and have changed the world enormously. Technological change allows production processes to become more efficient.

● *Technological Change* = change that allows the same level of inputs to produce a greater level of output. Alternatively, technological change allows production of the same level of output with a smaller number of inputs.

Graphically, technological change is an upward shift in the production function, as in Figure 2.12. Technological change shifts the wheat production function from $Y_0$ to $Y_1$.

BOX 2.5

### The Green Revolution in India

Since the 1960s and 1970s, the term "Green Revolution" has described the development and adoption of high-yielding seed varieties in agricultural nations. The Green Revolution enhanced agricultural productivity enormously and allowed India, food-short for decades, to become self-sufficient in food grains, primarily wheat and rice. In the early 1960s, India endured a number of famines. After that, during the period from 1960 to 1990, Green Revolution techniques helped rice yields in India increase from two tons per hectare to six tons per hectare. Rice became more affordable, with rice prices dropping from over USD 550 per ton in the 1970s to less than USD 200 per ton in 2001.

Norman Borlaug, an American agronomist named the "father" of the Green Revolution, is credited with saving over a billion people from starvation through the development of high-yielding, or modern, varieties of cereal grains. These new varieties required irrigation and application of agricultural chemicals and pesticides. This resulted in industrial growth to produce these inputs, providing more jobs in the Indian economy.

The Green Revolution provided large amounts of food that allowed India and other nations to feed a rapidly growing population. However, Indian agriculture faces future challenges. The modern varieties of rice and wheat require more water, and the water table is falling in some regions. As wells are dug deeper, salinity becomes a larger problem. The use of chemicals and fertilizer has resulted in an environmental challenge, and the purchase of modern inputs requires efficient sources of credit. As India moves forward, it will continue to evolve and solve these issues, making agriculture more productive and feeding a growing world population.

*Sources:* Barta, P. "Feeding Billions, a Grain at a Time." *The Wall Street Journal*, 28 July 2007: p. A1.

Zwerdling, Daniel. "Green Revolution" Trapping India's Farmers in Debt. National Public Radio. April 14, 2009. www.npr.org/templates/story/story.php?storyId=102944731. Retrieved January 3, 2023.

Technological change in cotton production is exemplified by the success of the cotton-breeding activities carried out by scientists in cotton-producing states. Using genetic selection and biotechnology, cotton breeders have been able to develop new varieties of seeds that result in higher cotton yields. Even holding all other inputs used in cotton production (land, chemicals, fertilizer, labor, etc.) constant, the new seed varieties result in higher yields. Technological change of this kind is not limited to cotton. Output per unit of input in nearly all aspects of agriculture continues to increase as new methods of farming and raising animals for food are developed and adopted.

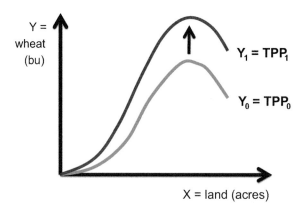

Figure 2.12 Technological change

BOX 2.6

## Cotton in Mississippi

Cotton is a major crop in Mississippi. It ranks fourth behind poultry, forestry, and soybeans in state commodities with USD 403 million of revenue produced each year. Mississippi producers plant approximately 420,000 acres of cotton annually. This number fluctuates, depending on weather and relative prices. In recent years, corn production has replaced some cotton acres in the Mississippi Delta region. The highest acreage recorded in Mississippi was in 1930, when 4.163 million acres were planted to cotton. The highest production year was 1937, when 2.692 million bales were produced on 3.421 million acres. The highest cotton yields came in 2004 with 1,034 pounds of lint produced per acre. This same year there were 2.346 million bales produced, almost as much as in 1937, with one-third of the acreage. This yield surpassed the previous yield of 934 pounds in 2003.

The production function for cotton has shifted greatly in the past few years, due to technological change. Advancements in cotton production include successful eradication of boll weevils, a major pest in cotton fields. The use of transgenic cotton varieties has increased, and a majority of Mississippi cotton producers now use transgenic varieties that eliminate some pests and save production costs. Reduced tillage techniques have enhanced cotton yields and increased profits.

*Source:* Cotton Production in Mississippi. http://extension.msstate.edu/agriculture/crops/cotton. Retrieved January 3, 2023.

## 2.4 The law of diminishing marginal returns

Knowledge of relationships between inputs and outputs allows examination of an economic "law" (meaning that the production relationship is universal). The name of this law is the **law of diminishing marginal returns**. Simply stated, this law means that as more of a single input is applied, the marginal increase in productivity will eventually decline.

- *Law of Diminishing Marginal Returns* = as additional units of one input are combined with a fixed amount of other inputs, a point is always reached at which the additional output produced from the last unit of added input will decline.

The "truth" in this law stems from one of the foundations of economics: scarcity. Adding more of a single input to a fixed quantity of other inputs means there are not enough of the other inputs to make effective use of the addition. Adding too much fertilizer to a potted houseplant does little good: the plant already has enough resources.

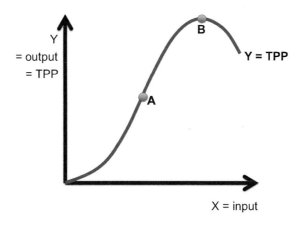

**Figure 2.13** Diminishing returns

If scarcity did not exist, adding all inputs would allow the production of more and more goods and services. In this case, every consumer would have everything that he or she desired.

Other examples of the law of diminishing marginal returns are not hard to find. The first hour of studying is the most productive. After studying for several hours, a student's energy runs low, and productivity declines. This holds true for all productive activities. Crop production in the United States follows the same rule. When the European settlers reached North America, the most productive lands were cleared and planted first, because these lands produced the largest quantity of food. As more acres of land came into production, productivity per acre fell, because of the poor quality of the remaining land. This is in accordance with the law of diminishing marginal returns. Note that productivity need not be negative for the law to hold, as is shown in Figure 2.13.

Diminishing returns begin when the rate of productivity per unit of input begins to fall (point A in Figure 2.13). Put another way, diminishing returns set in when increasing returns are exhausted. Notice: a common mistake is to think that the law of diminishing marginal returns means that the returns to adding one additional unit of input are *negative*. The law says that additional productivity must *eventually* decline.

## BOX 2.7

### Alternative agricultural production practices

Organic production systems integrate cultural, biological, and mechanical practices that promote cycling of resources, ecological balance, and biodiversity. In the US, the National Organic Program administers the production, handling, and labeling standards of organic food. In general, organic food contains no chemicals or artificial fertilizer. The yields of organic crops are often lower than conventional crops. However, the production costs are lower, and consumers pay premiums for organic products.

Sustainable development refers to intergenerational equity, meaning that the current generation should not diminish or destroy the ability of future generations to make a living or enjoy the environment. The definition of "sustainable agriculture" is complex but includes retaining natural resources, minimizing environmental damage, providing sufficient farm profits, and using low levels of inputs in farm production. One key element of sustainable agriculture is sufficiently high profits to allow farms to remain in agriculture. Sustainable food systems often emphasize reductions in soil erosion, pollution, and enhancement of soil quality.

## 2.5    The three stages of production

The concepts presented in this chapter come together to provide a large amount of information regarding the economics of production processes. Assume that producers are "rational," which simply means that they desire to maximize profits associated with their production activity. If this is so, the lessons of this chapter show that a producer will always operate within a certain range of input use. In Figure 2.14, Stage I of production is defined by a level of input use that is to the left of point A, where APP = MPP. Stage I is an "irrational" stage of production, in the sense that the producer can become more efficient if she increases the quantity of input used. The APP curve in Stage I shows this. The APP curve represents the

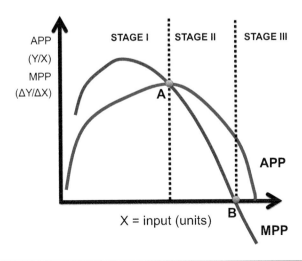

Figure 2.14  The stages of production

average productivity of the production process. Since the average productivity is increasing, the producer could become more productive by increasing the level of input use. Therefore, the rational producer will never locate in Stage I, because productivity could increase by using more inputs.

---

## BOX 2.8

### Sustainable intensification

The global population, currently at more than 7.6 billion persons, is increasing and is likely to continue to grow until about 2050, when it is expected to reach a maximum of approximately 9.8 billion people (United Nations 2017). More food will need to be produced to feed this population, and several strategies to meet this objective have been identified, including (1) bring new land into production, (2) organic agriculture, (3) biotechnology, and (4) investment in agricultural research and outreach. All of these strategies require intensification (Pretty and Bharucha 2018; Garett and Godfray, 2012).

Sustainable agricultural intensification is defined as producing more output from the same amount of land while reducing negative environmental impacts (Pretty and Bharucha 2018). There is controversy and debate about the exact meaning of "sustainable intensification," with many different individuals and groups desiring to use the term in a manner useful for them. Some believe that sustainable intensification describes the existing system of high-input, high-output agricultural production in high-income nations. Others interpret the term to refer to agroecology and organic food and fiber production.

The term "sustainable intensification" is challenging since it brings together two ideas that are often considered divergent: increased agricultural production and environmental sustainability. Scientists and farmers across the globe will continue to work together to replace old ways of doing things with enhanced methods and techniques to make sustainable intensification a reality.

*Sources:* Garett, T. and Godfray, C.J. (2012). Sustainable Intensification in Agriculture, Navigating a Course through Competing Food Systems Priorities, Food Climate Research Network and the Oxford Martin Programme on the Future of Food. Oxford, UK: University of Oxford.

Pretty, J. and Z.P. Bharucha (2018). Sustainable Intensification of Agriculture: Greening the World's Food Economy. Routledge.

Pretty, J., Toulmin, C., and Williams, S. (2011). 'Sustainable intensification in African agriculture', International Journal of Agricultural Sustainability, vol. 9, no. 1. pp. 5–24.

United Nations. World Population Projections. 2017.

Stage III is also an irrational stage of production (Figure 2.14). The third stage of production includes all input levels greater than the point at which MPP becomes negative (point B in Figure 2.14). In Stage III, the producer is using too much input since total productivity diminishes with each additional unit of input use. Total output would increase if the quantity of inputs were decreased. In other words, higher levels of productivity are possible at lower levels of input use (too many cooks in the kitchen lower the number of meals cooked). Stage II, the stage between Stage I and Stage III, is the "rational" stage of production since the producer is operating in the region of input use that is most productive. The exact point of input use that is "optimal," or profit maximizing, depends on the price of the input, or the cost of acquiring the productive resource. This profit-maximizing point is the theme of Chapter 4. In the following chapter, the costs of production are defined, explained, and explored.

## 2.6   Chapter 2 Summary

1   Production is the process of combining scarce resources into outputs.
2   A production function shows the physical relationship between inputs and outputs.
3   The point of maximum *physical* output is not always the optimal *economic* level of output.
4   A two-dimensional graph of a production function shows the relationship between one input and one output, if all else remains constant.
5   Economists assume that the goal of all producers is to maximize profits. Profits are equal to total revenue (the value of production sold) minus total costs of production.
6   The immediate run is a period of time in which all inputs are fixed. In the short run, at least one input is fixed. The long run is a period of time during which all inputs are variable.
7   The length of the long run depends on the specific situation: it is the length of time that it takes for all inputs to become variable.
8   A fixed input does not vary with the level of output. A variable input does vary with the level of output.
9   A constant returns production function shows output increasing at a constant rate for each additional unit of input used. Increasing returns occur when an additional unit of input results in more additional output than the previous unit of input. A production function characterized by decreasing returns is one where each additional unit of input increases output, but at a smaller rate than the previous unit. Negative returns occur when total output decreases as a result of adding more units of input.
10   A typical production process passes through stages characterized by increasing returns, decreasing returns, and then negative returns.
11   TPP is the relationship between output and one variable input, holding all other inputs constant. APP is the average productivity of each unit of variable input (= Y / X). MPP is the amount of additional, or marginal, physical product obtained from using an additional, or marginal, unit of variable input (= $\Delta Y / \Delta X$).
12   If MPP is greater than APP, then APP is increasing; if MPP is less than APP, then APP is decreasing. The average chases the marginal.

13 Technological change results in an upward shift in the production function. Technological change allows producing more output with the same level of inputs.

14 Stage I occurs when APP < MPP, or when APP is increasing. It is an irrational stage of production since productivity increases with the increased use of input. Stage II occurs when MPP < APP and MPP > 0. This is the rational stage of production. Stage III occurs when MPP < 0. Stage III is an irrational stage since increased input use results in lower levels of total output. The rational producer will locate input use in Stage II.

## 2.7   Chapter 2 Glossary

**Average Physical Product [APP]**—The average productivity of each unit of variable input used [=Y / X].

**Constant Returns**—When each additional unit of input added to the production process yields a constant level of output relative to the previous unit of input. Output increases at a constant rate.

**Decreasing Returns**—When each additional unit of input added to the production process yields less additional output relative to the previous unit of input. Output increases at a decreasing rate.

**Fixed Input**—An input whose quantity does not vary with the level of output.

**Immediate Run (IR)**—A period of time in which all inputs are fixed.

**Increasing Returns**—When each additional unit of input added to the production process yields a larger additional amount of output relative to the previous unit of input. Output increases at an increasing rate.

**Law of Diminishing Marginal Returns**—As additional units of one input are combined with a fixed amount of other inputs, a point is always reached at which the additional output produced from the last unit of added input will decline.

**Long Run (LR)**—A period of time during which no inputs are fixed; all inputs are variable.

**Marginal Physical Product (MPP)**—The additional amount of total physical product obtained from using an additional, or marginal, unit of variable input [=$\Delta Y$ / $\Delta X$].

**Negative Returns**—When each additional unit of input added to the production process results in lower total output relative to the previous unit of input. Output decreases.

**Production Function**—The physical relationship between inputs and outputs.

**Profits [$\pi$]**—Total revenue minus total costs: $\pi$ = TR − TC. The value of product sold minus the cost of producing that output.

**Short Run (SR)**—A period of time during which some factors are variable and some factors are fixed.

**Technological Change**—Change that allows the same level of inputs to produce a greater level of output. Alternatively, technological change allows production of the same level of output with a smaller number of inputs.

**Total Physical Product (TPP)**—The relationship between output and one variable input, holding all other inputs constant.

**Variable Input**—A variable input is one that, when changed, affects the level of output.

# 2.8   Chapter 2 Review questions

1   The production function is a(n)

   a   economic relationship
   b   physical relationship
   c   mathematical property
   d   party for producers

2   In the following production function, Y = f(L| K, A, M):

   a   *ceteris paribus* does not hold
   b   labor is held constant
   c   land is allowed to vary
   d   labor is allowed to vary

3   Economists assume that producers attempt to

   a   do the best that they can to get by
   b   maximize profits
   c   feed the world
   d   produce enough food to feed their family

4   Profits are equal to

   a   costs of production minus revenue
   b   total revenue minus total costs
   c   average revenue minus average costs
   d   marginal revenue minus marginal costs

5   The long run is defined as

   a   ten years
   b   one year
   c   depends on the situation
   d   when at least one input is fixed

6   If all inputs are variable except land for a wheat producer, then

   a   the firm is in the short run
   b   the firm is in the long run
   c   the firm is in the immediate run
   d   the firm is not in production

7   A variable input is one that

   a   changes with the weather
   b   moves up and down
   c   varies with the level of output
   d   varies with the level of other inputs

8   In decreasing returns, an additional unit of input added to a production process

   a   increases output at an increasing rate
   b   decreases output
   c   increases output, but at a decreasing rate
   d   does not change output

9   When too much of an input is used and output decreases, the production process results in

   a   constant returns
   b   increasing returns
   c   decreasing returns
   d   negative returns

10   If average productivity is 20 bu/acre and marginal productivity is 30 bu/acre, then

   a   average productivity is increasing
   b   average productivity is decreasing
   c   average productivity is constant
   d   average productivity is negative

11   The relationship between average and marginal is

   a   average causes marginal
   b   marginal causes average
   c   average chases marginal
   d   marginal chases average

Answers: 1. b, 2. d, 3. b, 4. b, 5. c, 6. a, 7. c, 8. c, 9. d, 10. a, 11. c

For more study questions, flash cards, and study guides, see the online materials at the companion website: www.routledge.com/cw/barkley.

# Chapter 3

# The costs of production

Photo 3.1 The costs of production

*Source:* cosma/Shutterstock

DOI: 10.4324/9781003367994-3

## Abstract

This chapter discusses the major motivating force behind all market-based economic behavior: profits. The economic concept of opportunity cost is highlighted, with examples of the next best alternative in professional and personal decision-making. A clear distinction between accounting profits and economic profits is described and explained. Special attention is given to cost relationships, including constant, decreasing, and increasing cost curves, and how they relate to production in real-world examples such as Walmart, feedlots, forestry, and meatpacking plants.

### Chapter 3 Questions

1 What is opportunity cost, and how does it help individuals make decisions?
2 How do accounting profits differ from economics profits?
3 What are fixed costs and variable costs, and how are they used in decision-making?
4 What are constant, decreasing, and increasing costs?
5 How do costs relate to production functions?

## 3.1   Profits

The study of production assumes that the goal of a business enterprise in a market-based economy is to maximize **profits**. This assumption applies to all firms, whether they are large multinational companies, such as Amazon or Cargill, or small family-owned businesses, such as a family farm in Delaware or a family restaurant in Salem, Oregon. The study of costs of production begins with a simple definition of profits and how the level of profits relates to the costs of production. In the simplest possible form, this relationship can be written as follows:

3.1   $\pi = TR - TC.$

**Total revenue** (TR) refers to how much money a firm earns from the sale of its output (Y). Multiplying the number of units of output (Y) by the per-unit price of the output (P) yields total revenue:

3.2   $TR = P * Y.$

The units for TR are in dollars since output (Y) times price (USD/Y) is in terms of dollars. The units of output cancel each other.

The level of **total costs** (TC) measures the payments that a firm must make to purchase the factors of production. The production of a good or service transforms inputs into outputs. These inputs are not free but require payments because they are scarce. The sum of all of the payments for inputs describes the total costs that a firm must pay to produce a given quantity of a good.

Define scarcity. What implications does scarcity have for the production process?

Commodity promotion associations often present an award to the corn or wheat producer whose fields produce the highest yield per acre in the county or state. The award winner typically wins a cash prize, publicity in the local newspaper, recognition at the county fair, and Internet coverage. These contests and awards are interesting, and even fun, but economists and agricultural economists who deal with commodity production are more interested in finding ways to help producers understand that the maximum level of profits differs from the highest level of production.

A yield contest encourages farmers to produce the maximum level of output. This requires large amounts of scarce inputs and can be a costly activity. The contest winner will have total costs (the costs of the scarce inputs) that may be much higher than the market value of the crop. A simple graph of total revenue and total costs helps illustrate this.

In Figure 3.1, the vertical distance between the TR curve and the TC curve indicates the profits ($\pi$) accruing at each level of output. Total revenue, defined as price times output, is an increasing function of output (measured on the horizontal axis of Figure 3.1). Total revenue is a linear function of output since the price of output is constant (USD/Y). The more output that the firm produces and sells, the higher the level of TR.

Total costs also rise with increasing levels of output, but due to the law of diminishing marginal returns, the costs rise at an increasing rate. This means that the production process will at some point become less productive and more costly. What does this say about county yield contests? This careful look indicates that a farmer could very well be spending too much money on the inputs just to win the award.

From an economist's point of view, the emphasis should center on profits rather than yields. An economist would advise the producer to weigh the benefits and the costs of producing a higher yield with a full understanding that the maximum yield does not automatically bring the highest level of profits. It costs too much to achieve the maximum yield. To win the award, the farmer is spending too much on inputs. The producer may be better off backing away from thoughts relating to production and awards and looking at both the benefits and the costs of each activity or each level of one activity.

From an economic point of view, the producer should determine the level of input use and compare the benefits of the input to the costs of purchasing and applying it. If the benefits of using one more unit of input are greater than the cost of the input, it is profitable to use it. The producer, however, should not purchase the input if it costs more than the benefits that stem from its use.

The comparison of benefits and costs is one of the most important "take-home lessons" from this course. In every activity, an economist will ask the question, "Do the benefits of this activity outweigh the costs?" If the rewards of the activity are larger than the costs, then the activity should be undertaken. This is true for producers deciding how much fertilizer to apply to their fields, or how much corn

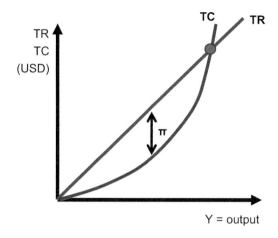

Figure 3.1 Total revenues, total costs, and profits

to produce, or for consumers trying to decide how many slices of pizza to eat, or for students deciding how many hours to study for an upcoming test.

This approach to decision-making is enormously useful, and the approach is valuable. The salaries of agricultural economics and agribusiness majors provide evidence that this is true: learning to think like an economist can provide many rewards in life, including greater financial rewards, improved personal decision-making, and more career choices. The study of the costs of production will help students gain a better understanding of how to make solid decisions.

## 3.2   Opportunity costs

The entire issue of cost takes on a new and different meaning in economics. Because of this, there is need to specify exactly what is meant by the term "costs." Total costs include two types of costs: **accounting costs** and **opportunity costs**. Accounting costs are explicit costs, or payments that a business firm must actually make in order to obtain factors of production: USD 2,000 for fertilizer, USD 25,000 for a new truck, USD 350 for seed, and the like.

● *Accounting Costs* = explicit costs of production; costs for which payments are required.

Bookkeepers and accountants consider only accounting costs. Economists include opportunity costs, which are the value of a resource in its next-best use.

● *Opportunity Costs* = the value of a resource in its next-best use. What an individual or firm must give up in order to do something.

Opportunity costs exist for every human activity. By studying economics, a student gives up the opportunity to study the "next-best alternative," which might be studying biology, listening to music, partying, or seeing a movie. When individuals decide to become farm operators, they give up the opportunity to be a professor, or a mechanic, or whatever their next-best occupational choice might be.

Suppose a college student cannot decide between studying to be a soil scientist or a veterinarian. The student cannot be both. If she becomes a soil scientist, her opportunity cost would be the income she gave up by not being a veterinarian. At another level, suppose that Jay-Z, who likely makes a fortune with his personality as an entertainer, actually would prefer to be a social worker. The opportunity cost of his being a social worker is what he would have to give up from his entertainment career: surely millions of dollars. Apparently, he prefers the millions to what might be a more satisfying life as a social worker. This concept of opportunity cost is quite powerful and is useful in explaining both economic and noneconomic behavior.

All resources (and all occupational choices) have opportunity costs associated with them. The opportunity cost of planting one acre of land to cotton is the money lost by not planting the next-best alternative crop on that acre of land. Every resource has a "next-best use," so every resource has an opportunity cost. The key idea is that in economics, total costs (TC) always include both the accounting (or explicit) costs and the opportunity costs, or what must be given up to use the resource. The following examples may help provide more confidence with this concept.

## 3.2.1 Profits (again!)

The definition of profit is $\pi$ = TR – TC. Although correct, this definition says nothing about the categories of costs included in the definition. Some simple definitions and examples help clarify the issue.

## 3.2.2 Accounting profits

**Accounting profits** are revenue minus only explicit costs. These profits are what accountants calculate and reflect only the revenue and explicit monetary costs of producing and selling a good.

- *Accounting Profits* [$\pi_A$] = total revenue minus explicit costs. $\pi_A$ = TR – $TC_A$.

Accounting profits do not consider opportunity costs. When opportunity costs are included in costs, the profit line shows economic profits—the pure profit leftover after the opportunity costs of all inputs are subtracted from total revenue.

## 3.2.3 Economic profits

- *Economic Profits* [$\pi_E$] = total revenue minus both explicit and opportunity costs. $\pi_E$ = TR – $TC_A$ – opportunity costs.

## 3.2.4 The opportunity cost of a wheat grower near Tulsa, Oklahoma

This example helps clarify the difference between accounting profit and economic profit (Table 3.1). In Case One, suppose that this producer grows and sells 25,000

| Input | Case One (USD) | Case Two (USD) |
|---|---|---|
| Chemicals | 20,000 | 20,000 |
| Machinery | 20,000 | 20,000 |
| Seed, fertilizer | 20,000 | 20,000 |
| Land (rent) | 20,000 | 20,000 |
| Hired labor | 10,000 | 15,000 |
| --------- | --------- | --------- |
| Total accounting costs | 90,000 | 95,000 |
| Opportunity costs | 10,000 | 10,000 |
| Total economic costs | 100,000 | 105,000 |
| Total revenues | 100,000 | 100,000 |
| Accounting profits | 10,000 | 5,000 |
| Economic profits | 0 | −5,000 |

Table 3.1 Oklahoma wheat producer production costs

bushels of wheat at a price of USD 4/bu. Also assume that wheat production requires ten months of managerial labor each year.

QUICK QUIZ 3.2

Define a production function.

An easy calculation can be made to find that TR = USD 100,000, as reported in Table 3.1.

QUICK QUIZ 3.3

Write out the steps taken in making this calculation.

The costs of production reported here are in round numbers to simplify the example. Actual cost data can be quite complicated. First, the explicit, or accounting costs only, are shown in the first column of numbers in Table 3.1, labeled Case One.

Continuing the story, suppose that an accountant adds up all of the accounting costs (explicit costs, which are the costs on the books) for this wheat producer. The total accounting costs (TC$_A$) are equal to USD 90,000, the sum of all of the payments made for the inputs used in wheat production in Case One.

Calculating accounting profits yields the following (Table 3.1):

3.3   $\pi_A$ = TR − TC$_A$ = USD 100,000 − USD 90,000 = USD 10,000.

Next, calculate the level of economic profits and compare the results to accounting profits. Economic profit is what is left over after all costs, including opportunity costs, are deducted ($\pi_E$ = TR – $TC_A$ – opportunity costs). Restated, economic costs include both accounting costs and opportunity costs. Use the following formula to calculate economic costs:

3.4   $TC_E$ = $TC_A$ + opportunity costs = USD 90,000 + opportunity costs.

Opportunity costs are the value of a resource in its next best use. Suppose that the Tulsa wheat producer could earn USD 1,000/month in town as a salesperson with a farm implement dealer for ten months. In this case, the opportunity cost of this individual being a wheat producer:

3.5   Opportunity cost = 10 months*USD 1,000/month = USD 10,000.

The levels of economic costs and economic profits for Case One (Table 3.1) are as follows:

3.6   $TC_E$ = USD 90,000 (accounting costs) + USD 10,000 (opportunity costs) = USD 100,000,

3.7   $\pi_E$ = TR – $TC_E$ = USD 100,000 – USD 100,000 = 0.

At first glance, it appears that this wheat producer is not doing very well since her economic profits are equal to zero. In reality, this is not a bad thing. The farmer is earning exactly what she is worth, or exactly her opportunity cost. The farmer's accounting profits are positive (= USD 10,000), which is exactly what she could be making in her next-best alternative job. So oddly enough, when economic profits equal zero, all resources earn exactly what they are worth.

## BOX 3.1

### Oklahoma wheat

Around 9,000 years ago, domestic wheat originated in the Fertile Crescent, the area that includes parts or all of the modern nations of Syria, Jordan, Turkey, Armenia, and Iraq. Wheat has been a crop in the United States since colonial times, but production expanded rapidly after 1870, when Russian immigrants brought seed for Turkey Red, a variety of wheat, with them to Kansas and the Great Plains. Wheat is the number one crop grown in Oklahoma. Most of the wheat grown there is a descendent of Turkey Red winter wheat and is used to make bread. This variety of wheat grows best in the harsh, dry climate of the southern Great Plains in Oklahoma and Texas. Wheat is well adapted to harsh environments and is a common crop in wind-swept areas too dry for rice, corn, or cotton.

Wheat is grown on more land area worldwide than any other crop and is a close third to rice and corn in total quantity produced. World leaders in wheat production include China, India, the United States, Russia, France, and Australia. Wheat supplies about 20 percent of the food calories for the world's people and is a staple in many countries. The per capita consumption of wheat in the United States exceeds that of any other single staple food.

Both whole wheat flour and all-purpose (white) flour are made from wheat kernels. A wheat kernel is divided into three major parts: bran, endosperm, and germ. All-purpose flour is made from only ground endosperm. Whole wheat flour is made by grinding the entire wheat kernel. A bushel of wheat weighs about 60 pounds and yields about 42 pounds of white flour or 60 pounds of whole wheat flour.

Unlike most other crops, hard red winter wheat is planted in the fall and harvested in the spring. In summer, wheat producers prepare the soil for planting, then plant the seed. The wheat plant will grow about six inches before the frost comes. When the weather gets cold, the wheat plant will stop growing, beginning the dormant period. On most farms in Oklahoma, cattle feed, or graze, on the young wheat plants while the plants are in their dormant period. In the spring, warm weather causes the wheat plants to grow quickly. Some varieties of wheat grow as tall as seven feet, but most are between two and four feet tall. During the early summer, the plants begin to fade from dark green to tan and finally to a golden brown. Then the wheat is ripe and nearly ready for harvest. As wheat harvest occurs, the wheat producer must avoid rain, hail, and lightning. At harvest, the farmer drives a combine across the fields to harvest the grain. When the storage bin of the combine is full, it is emptied into a truck. The truck is driven to the grain elevator in town. It takes a combine nine seconds to harvest enough wheat to make 70 loaves of bread.

*Source:* Oklahoma Ag in the Classroom. Wheat Facts. www.agclassroom. org/ok/resources_facts/agfacts_wheat.php. Retrieved January 3, 2023.

A second situation, Case Two, assumes that the farmer continues to grow and sell 25,000 bushels of wheat at the prevailing market price of USD 4/bu. Therefore, total revenue (TR) remains the same at USD 100,000. However, in this case, the federal government increases the minimum wage, so that the wages paid to the hired help increase. Now, the cost of hired workers to help with wheat harvest increases to USD 15,000, as shown in Table 3.1. To keep the example simple, assume that the increase in the minimum wage is the only change in the firm's costs

of production. If all of this is true, then TR = USD 100,000, and Case Two profits are reported in Table 3.1 and shown in equation 3.9:

3.8 $\pi_A$ = USD 100,000 – USD 95,000 = USD 5,000.
3.9 $\pi_E$ = USD 100,000 – USD 95,000 – USD 10,000 = USD –5,000.

In this case, the increase in the minimum wage results in negative economic profit. Interestingly, the farmer might stay in business. Why? Many farmers have strong ties to agriculture and will try to stay in farming even if they earn negative economic profits. This is possible because the accounting profits are positive, so the bills are paid. As before, the farmer is giving up the possibility of earning more money in her next best job. She gives up USD 5,000 to remain in agriculture. This is a very realistic scenario for many persons employed in jobs such as agricultural production or teaching, where income levels are often low but the work is compelling, satisfying, or both.

If the farmer remains in agriculture with negative economic profits, she is violating the assumption that the objective of all producers is to maximize profits. Many individuals are content to work in a job that has rewards other than money. In the current study of economics, the assumption of profit maximization is maintained to simplify the analysis. The major conclusions of economics remain the same with or without the assumption.

### ECONOMIC COSTS INCLUDE OPPORTUNITY COSTS!

Another example of economic costs relates to the full costs of attending a college or a university. The explicit, or accounting, costs of attending school include tuition, fees, room and board, textbooks, football tickets, and the like. The opportunity cost is the value of a resource in its next-best use. In this case, the student is the resource, and the opportunity cost is how much that student could earn in another field without a university-level education. Therefore, the full economic cost of attending college is not only the high cost of paying for the undergraduate education. It also includes the sacrifice of a salary and benefits that go with the job not taken in order to attend an institution of higher learning.

## 3.3   Costs and output

This section explores the relationship between the level of output produced by a firm and the costs of producing that output. Total costs will increase with increased output since this increase requires additional levels of input. The added inputs are scarce and incur costs.

### QUICK QUIZ 3.4

Should a firm always strive to produce the highest level of output?

Recall the definition of the short run. It is a period of time during which the quantity of at least one input cannot change. The number of acres of cropland in a farm provides an example. It is often difficult to change the size of a farm in a short period of time. Similarly, it may be difficult to change the size of any of the several small specialty shops or restaurants that seem to surround major university campuses. In each case, the availability of suitable land (space) seems to be the limiting factor. Each of these examples demonstrates that some inputs cannot adjust in the short run. They are "fixed."

Quantities of other inputs are variable in the short run, which means that their quantity is adjustable. For an Oklahoma wheat farm, variable inputs might include chemicals, labor, fertilizer, seed, machinery, and other items (Table 3.1). The items in this list are easy to change, even in a short period of time. Some inputs are fixed and some are variable, so costs break down into two categories: fixed costs and variable costs.

● *Total Fixed Costs [TFC]* = the total costs of inputs that do not vary with the level of output.

- *Total Variable Costs [TVC]* = the total costs of inputs that vary with the level of output.
- *Total Costs [TC]* = the sum of all payments that a firm must make to purchase the factors of production. The sum of total fixed costs and total variable costs: TC = TFC + TVC.

Fixed costs are payments to factors such as land or machines that are fixed in quantity in the short run. Variable costs are payments to factors whose quantity may change in the short run. Chemicals, labor, and fuel are included in this category.

QUICK QUIZ 3.5

How long is the long run?

In the long run, all factors are variable. This is because over a longer period of time, a producer can buy more machines and more land. Producers can adjust the size of their farm. There is no set number of years for the long run; it depends on the situation (the answer to Quick Quiz 3.5).

Since fixed factors do not vary with output, as shown in Figure 3.2, they must be paid in full, regardless of the level of output. Examples include (1) rent to the landlord that must be paid no matter what, (2) a payment to the bank for a loan taken out to purchase machines, (3) insurance on the buildings, and (4) property taxes. The key thing to remember about fixed costs is that they do not vary with output. Restating for emphasis:

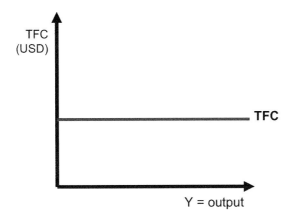

Figure 3.2 Total fixed costs (TFC)

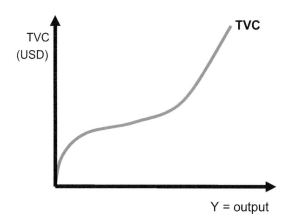

Figure 3.3 Total variable costs (TVC)

**FIXED COSTS DO NOT VARY WITH THE LEVEL OF OUTPUT.**

Variable costs are somewhat more intuitive: they vary with the level of output. In particular, they increase with the level of output because producing firms must purchase more of these resources to increase the quantity of production. This is shown in Figure 3.3.

These costs increase for a wheat farmer, for example, because more labor and more chemicals are required to increase the production of the crop. The interesting shape of the TVC curve is due to the "typical" shape of the production function discussed in Chapter 2. The slope of the TVC curve is positive, but the slope decreases in the range of output near the origin. This reflects the increasing productivity of a production process as more inputs are added initially. Further to the right, the slope of the total variable cost curve begins to increase at an increasing rate, indicating its adherence to the law of diminishing marginal returns.

**QUICK QUIZ 3.6**

State the law of diminishing marginal returns, and explain the shape of the TVC curve.

### 3.3.1 Cost curves

Total costs (TC) are the sum of total fixed costs (TFC) and total variable costs (TVC) at any given level of output. Graphically, this results in cost curves, as shown in Figure 3.4, where TFC and TVC are added vertically to get the total cost curve (TC).

In addition to total costs, the average, or per-unit, costs of producing goods are of interest. Dividing the total costs (TC) by the level of output (Y) yields average costs: AC = TC / Y. Average total costs (ATC) provide the calculation of the

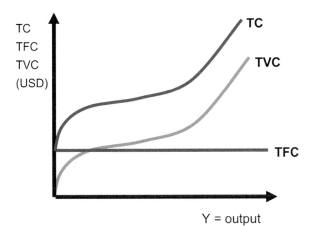

**Figure 3.4** Total cost, total fixed costs, and total variable costs

average cost of producing a single unit of output. Calculating average fixed costs (AFC) and average variable costs (AVC) uses the same steps:

- *Average Fixed Costs [AFC]* = the average cost of the fixed costs per unit of output. AFC = TFC / Y.
- *Average Variable Costs [AVC]* = the average cost of the variable costs per unit of output. AVC = TVC / Y.
- *Average Total Costs [ATC]* = the average total cost per unit of output. ATC = TC / Y.

Note that AC is identical to ATC. Marginal cost is the added cost of producing one more unit of output. The marginal, or incremental, costs help answer the question: do the benefits of producing one more unit of output outweigh the added costs? The next chapter emphasizes this issue.

- *Marginal Costs [MC]* = the increase in total costs due to the production of one more unit of output. MC = $\Delta$TC / $\Delta$Y.

The average, or per-unit, costs and marginal costs are graphed on the same graph in Figure 3.5. This is possible because they share the same units: dollar per unit of output. Similarly, the total cost curves (TC, TFC, and TVC) are on the same graph (Figure 3.4) because all of these costs are in dollars.

The per-unit cost curves shown in Figure 3.5 are closely related to the total cost curves in Figure 3.4. These curves are the "typical" cost curves for a business firm that has the "typical" production function of increasing followed by decreasing returns. In Figure 3.5, the average total costs decrease, reflecting an increase in productivity, then increase, due to decreasing returns. The marginal cost curve cuts (from below) through the minimum points on the AVC curve and ATC curves.

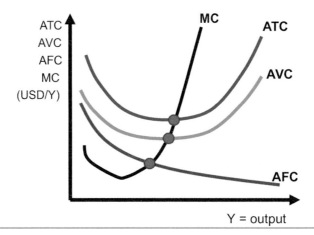

Figure 3.5 **Average and marginal costs**

## 3.4   Cost curve example: Vermont dairy farmer

A Vermont dairy farm provides a quantitative example, using cost curves similar to those introduced in the previous section. The fixed costs paid by the operator might include a rental payment to the landowner or a payment to the bank for a loan on milking machines.

> **QUICK QUIZ 3.7**
>
> What are fixed costs? Why would a loan payment be a fixed cost? List one more input for this dairy that could be a fixed cost.

Variable costs might include payments for replacement cows, feed, veterinary services, medicine, electricity, and the like.

> **QUICK QUIZ 3.8**
>
> What are variable costs? Why is electricity a variable cost? In the long run, what will the variable costs be?

The definitions of costs given earlier allow calculation of the total, average, and marginal costs for the dairy farmer. The total fixed costs are the payments for pasture rent and the loan payment to the bank. Suppose that each of these payments is equal to USD 5, so TFC = USD 10, as seen in Table 3.2.

Photo 3.3 Vermont dairy cow

*Source:* Len Green/Shutterstock

Table 3.2 Vermont dairy farm production costs

| Y = milk (1,000 lb) | TFC (USD) | TVC (USD) | TC (USD) | ATC (USD/Y) | AVC (USD/Y) | AFC (USD/Y) | MC (USD/Y) |
|---|---|---|---|---|---|---|---|
| 0 | 10 | 0 | 10 | — | — | — | — |
| 1 | 10 | 10 | 20 | 20 | 10 | 10 | 10 |
| 2 | 10 | 18 | 28 | 14 | 9 | 5 | 8 |
| 3 | 10 | 23 | 33 | 11 | 7.67 | 3.33 | 5 |
| 4 | 10 | 30 | 40 | 10 | 7.5 | 2.5 | 7 |
| 5 | 10 | 40 | 50 | 10 | 8 | 2 | 10 |
| 6 | 10 | 56 | 66 | 11 | 9.33 | 1.67 | 16 |
| 7 | 10 | 74 | 84 | 12 | 10.6 | 1.43 | 18 |

BOX 3.2

## Dairy farming in Vermont

European settlers brought dairy cows and sheep to Vermont from Plymouth Colony in the 1600s. The period 1850 to 1880 was the greatest period of growth in Vermont agriculture, and dairy products became the foundation of the state's farm sector. In a time before refrigeration, dairies frequently turned their milk into cheese or butter before it spoiled. The first vacuum-type milking machine appeared in 1865 but did not become commercially viable until the 1920s. The Vermont Dairymen's Association, formed in 1868, became a vocal and successful advocate for scientific breeding practices and the development of new technology. Vermont dairies produced high-quality butter, primarily because of the continuous improvement in the dairy herd.

Though some farmers kept Holstein and Ayrshire herds, the Jersey breed predominated in Vermont because the high level of butterfat in their milk was desired for making butter. Mechanization and rural electrification in the first half of the twentieth century allowed for larger farms. Homogenization and pasteurization increased milk safety and consumer confidence, and by the 1950s, nearly all of Vermont's milk was pasteurized. Major advancements in refrigeration and transportation made Vermont the leading supplier of fluid milk to Boston. By 1915, there were nearly 300 butter factories in Vermont.

In 1937, the federal government established a milk pricing system to maintain a stable milk supply, and in 1949, a support price system was established for dairy farmers. Through 1950–1970, this system worked well for Vermont. The problem came as productivity increased at a more rapid pace than in other industrial sectors of the economy, and production outpaced demands. The government programs could not continue to maintain a floor price without controlling the increased production. The government policy makers replaced the support price with a market-driven price.

Additional productivity increases came from conversion from milk cans to bulk storage and from consolidation. Many small dairy farms went out of business as larger farms invested in new technology and grew. Fewer milk producers remained, but those that did produced more milk.

*Source:* https://vermontdairy.com/vt-dairy-today/looking-back/. Retrieved January 3, 2023.

If the dairy were to shut down in the short run, what would the fixed costs be? If the dairy were to double the number of cows milked in the short run, what would the fixed costs be?

The cost curve definitions and a table of costs appear in Table 3.2. The first three columns on the left side of the table (Y, TFC, and TVC) provide the basic data for completing the other columns.

3.10a   TC = TFC + TVC,
3.10b   ATC = TC / Y,
3.10c   AVC = TVC / Y,
3.10d   MC = ΔTC / ΔY.

Note that the units of output for the Vermont dairy farm are 1,000 pounds of milk. Each unit of Y is equal to 1,000 pounds of milk.

The first column in Table 3.2 is output (Y) in units of 1,000 pounds. The second column is total fixed costs (TFC), which, by definition, do not vary with output. The TFC are constant at USD 10 for all units of milk produced.

Why do fixed costs not vary with the level of output? What do the fixed costs for this Vermont dairy farmer represent?

Total variable costs (TVC) appear in the third column. Variable costs change with the level of output and increase as output increases. If the firm has the "typical" production process, the total variable costs increase at a decreasing rate and then at an increasing rate. Total costs (TC) are simply the sum of the total fixed costs and total variable costs (TC = TFC + TVC). All of the total costs (TC, TFC, and TVC) are in units of dollars.

Average total costs (ATC) are total costs divided by the farm's entire output (TC / Y). These per-unit costs decrease and then increase. Average variable costs are the total variable costs (TVC) divided by the level of output (TVC / Y). The AVC curve follows the same pattern as the ATC curve. The next column is AFC, or average fixed costs. This represents the payments to fixed factors per unit of output, found by dividing total fixed costs by the amount of milk produced (AFC = TFC / Y). Average fixed costs decline as more output is produced because the dairy farmer is spreading the fixed payments (a constant numerator) over more units of output (an increasing denominator). Therefore, average fixed costs decline with larger quantities of milk produced. This provides an explanation about why many large agribusiness firms continue to increase in size: more output results in lower per-unit costs. Expansion of output can lower per-unit costs in many circumstances. This theme will appear often in the remaining chapters. Graphing these costs will provide a better understanding of their shapes and meaning.

**QUICK QUIZ 3.11**

Use the information for the Vermont dairy farmer in Table 3.2 to calculate the total, average, and marginal costs.

Total cost curves for the Vermont dairy farmer are shown in Figure 3.6.

**QUICK QUIZ 3.12**

Why are total, average, and marginal costs all shown in Table 3.2 but separate graphs are required for (1) total and (2) average and marginal costs?

**QUICK QUIZ 3.13**

Explain the shape of the cost curves in Figures 3.6 and 3.7.

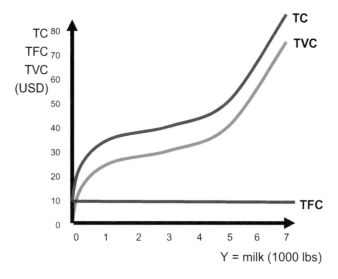

**Figure 3.6** Total costs for Vermont dairy farm

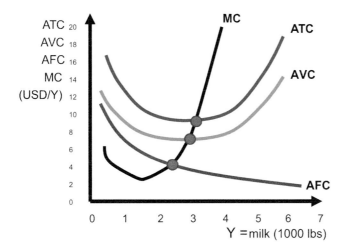

ATC 20
AVC 18
AFC 16
MC 14
(USD/Y) 12
10
8
6
4
2
0

MC
ATC
AVC
AFC

0  1  2  3  4  5  6  7
Y = milk (1000 lbs)

Figure 3.7 Per-unit costs for the Vermont dairy farm

The cost curves for the Vermont dairy farmer have the same shape as the cost curves derived earlier in Figures 3.4 and 3.5.

## 3.5 Where do cost curves come from?

The costs of production are directly related to the productivity of a firm. By most definitions, an efficient firm will have lower per-unit costs of production than a less efficient firm. This section makes the connection between the physical product curves (from Chapter 2) and the cost curves introduced in this chapter. Recall that the production function is the physical relationship between inputs (X) and output (Y), as in equation 3.11.

3.11   $Y = f(X_1, X_2, \ldots, X_n)$.

Since graphs and paper have only two dimensions, the relationship between one input and output is isolated and graphed while holding all other inputs constant, *ceteris paribus*.

3.12   $Y = f(X_1 | X_2 \ldots X_n)$.

Figure 3.8 is a graph of the typical production relationship of increasing then decreasing returns in production, together with cost curves that are increasing at a decreasing rate, then increasing at an increasing rate.

The relationship between physical product curves and cost curves is shown in the per-unit graph in Figure 3.9. The average and marginal product curves in the top half of the diagram are a mirror image of the average and marginal cost curves in the bottom half of the diagram. Mathematically, this inverse relationship demonstrates that the total variable costs of a firm are the payments made to the

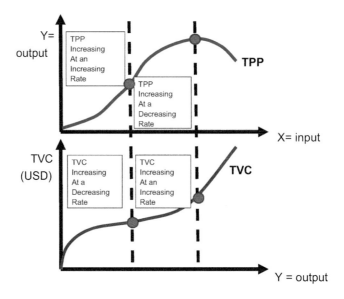

Figure 3.8 The relationship between total costs and total productivity

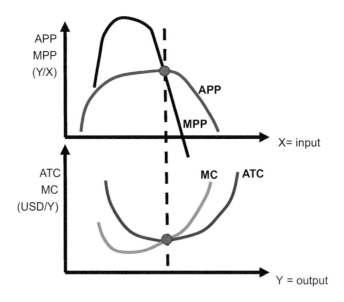

Figure 3.9 The relationship between per-unit costs and per-unit productivity

variable inputs. In this case, input $X_1$ is variable, with all other inputs held constant. Let $P_1$ be the price of input $X_1$.

3.13a  $TVC = P_1 * X_1$,
3.13b  $AVC = TVC / Y$,
3.13c  $APP = Y / X_1$.

Simple substitution allows for the following result:

3.13d  $AVC = TVC / Y = P_1 * X_1 / Y = P_1 * (X_1 / Y) = P_1 / (Y / X_1) = P_1 / APP$.

This result shows that the AVC curve is inversely related to the APP curve, as in Figure 3.9. Similarly, the marginal cost curve is inversely related to the MPP curve:

3.14  $MC = \Delta TC / \Delta Y = \Delta(P_1 * X_1) / \Delta Y = P_1 * (\Delta X_1 / \Delta Y) = P_1 / (\Delta Y / \Delta X_1) = P_1 / MPP$.

This result shows that marginal costs and marginal physical products are inversely related. Figure 3.9 summarizes the close connection between physical product curves and cost curves: an increase in productivity (increase in APP) occurs along with a decrease in costs (decrease in ATC). The relationship between average and marginal costs is the same as the relationship between average and marginal physical products.

## 3.5.1  The relationship between average and marginal costs

As noted in Chapter 2, "the average chases the marginal." This means that

3.15a  If MC > AC, then AC is increasing, and
3.15b  If MC < AC, then AC is decreasing.

Here, average costs (AC) can refer to either average total costs (ATC) or average variable costs (AVC). The earlier result occurs because the marginal cost is the additional cost associated with producing one additional unit of output. If this marginal cost is larger than the average, it "pulls" the average up. If MC, the additional costs of producing the last unit, is smaller than the average, it "pulls" the average down (Figure 3.10).

This relationship between average and marginal: "average chases marginal" is true for many examples: grades, costs, and revenue.

### QUICK QUIZ 3.14

Graph the relationship between average and marginal grades.

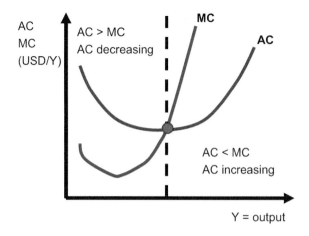

**Figure 3.10** The relationship between average costs and marginal costs

## 3.6 Constant, decreasing, and increasing cost curves

Four types of cost curves are possible: constant, decreasing, and increasing cost structures, as well as the "typical" cost curves explained earlier.

### 3.6.1 Constant cost firm

A constant cost firm is one that faces constant production costs for all units of output produced. In such a firm, the first unit of output produced costs the same as the last unit of output produced. An example is a feedlot. The operators fatten cattle until they are ready for slaughter. The fattening process is one of feeding the cattle large quantities of feed (corn, sorghum, and soybean meal) together with some vitamins and nutritional supplements. A typical feedlot pays the same amount for each bushel of feed, no matter how many steers are in the lot. Figure 3.11 shows that the firm pays the same amount for inputs.

Regardless of the number of units produced, the per-unit cost is the same at a given point in time. Since the marginal cost of producing a unit of output is fixed (constant), then MC is horizontal and AC = MC. The average chases the marginal, but in this specific case, it has "caught" it! For a constant cost firm, the average costs (AC) equal the marginal costs (MC), as shown earlier.

### 3.6.2 Decreasing cost firm

Decreasing costs occur when the per-unit costs of a firm's output decline as output increases. An example of a decreasing cost firm is the meatpacking plant in Nebraska. Packing plants, also called slaughterhouses, convert the fattened cattle into steaks, hamburger, and leather.

**Photo 3.4 Cattle feedlot**

*Source:* Tyler Olsen/Shutterstock

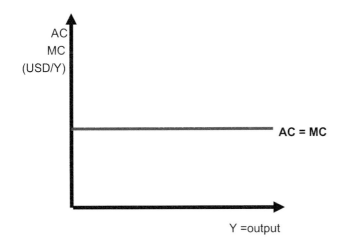

**Figure 3.11 A constant cost firm**

These are often very large facilities, with enormous electricity, water, and labor requirements. Because of this huge size, each additional pound of meat can be produced at a lower per-unit cost since the large fixed costs (the electricity, water, and labor) are spread over more units of output. Since MC < AC, AC is decreasing. The huge fixed costs mean that greater productivity comes at lower costs per unit of output, as shown in Figure 3.12.

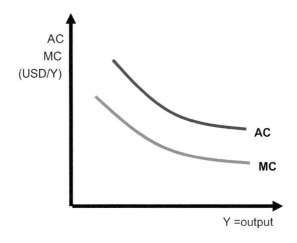

AC
MC
(USD/Y)

AC

MC

Y =output

Figure 3.12 A decreasing cost firm

Other examples of decreasing cost industries include Walmart and social networks.

BOX 3.3

## Walmart

Walmart is the most successful retailer in world history, with millions of global customers. Sam Walton, the founder, opened his first Walmart discount store in 1962, with the vision to save customers money and to help them live better. According to the Walmart website, Sam's secret was simple: give your customers what they want. From a single store in Rodgers, Arkansas, Walmart has grown to over 10,500 stores in 24 countries, employing over 2.3 million associates (employees).

One important feature of Walmart's success is logistics: how to transport goods from producers to customers throughout the globe. Walmart has one of the largest private distribution operations in the world, with over 210 regional distribution centers. Each one is over 1 million square feet in size and operates around the clock, supporting between 90 and 100 stores within a 150-mile radius. Walmart's innovations in transportation and logistics allowed the retailer to lower costs through expansion of the distribution network, resulting in low-cost products for customers. A second major factor behind Walmart's success is the development and use of technology to track its inventory, causing reduced supply chain costs.

*Source:* Wal-Mart*Corporate. http://corporate.walmart.com/our-story/our-business/. Retrieved January 3, 2023.

BOX 3.4

## Network economies

A relatively new concept in economics is "network economies," which describes networks and services that become more valuable as they are more widely used. Social network software such as Facebook and Twitter are the most obvious examples. As more individuals use these services, the more valuable they become to each individual user. Other examples of network economies include common language, common currencies such as the euro, online auctions like eBay, and air transport networks. The rapid expansion of e-commerce is another example of the use of network economies of scale by Internet merchants.

A formal definition of network economies is a good or service where the marginal cost of adding one more user to the network is nearly zero but the resulting benefits may be large. The large benefits are due to the ability of the network adopter to interact and/or trade with all of the existing members or parts of the network. Network economies have interesting economic characteristics and interesting business challenges. For example, publishing a book or a song online fundamentally changes the use of property rights to protect writers and composers. In many cases, ownership is not valued, so revenue is collected through user fees. Businesses such as book and music publishers are in the process of changing long-standing business practices to keep up with the huge advantages of the information age and network economies.

*Source:* Carl Shapiro and Hal R. Varian. "Information Rules: A Strategic Guide to the Network Economy." *Harvard Business Review Press*, 1998.

In a decreasing cost firm, the MC curve always lies below the AC curve, and the AC curve is declining. Other examples of declining cost firms include power-generating plants, cable television companies, and city water systems. These examples are all firms that require a huge network or distribution system. The high costs of installing power generators and power lines to every house in the network region result in a decreasing cost structure for an electricity plant. This also holds true for cable television companies, which must invest large amounts of money to develop the cable network throughout town. The more customers who purchase electricity and cable television, the lower the per-unit costs of production and distribution will be.

### 3.6.3   Increasing cost firm

An increasing cost firm is one whose per-unit cost of production increases with increases in output. Firms that extract fixed natural resources, such as oil, timber, or coal, typically have increasing cost structures because a fixed resource (e.g., the coal in the mine) becomes increasingly scarce as more coal is extracted. This causes the per unit cost of production to increase along with increases in output. Figure 3.13 shows the cost structure of an increasing cost firm.

For increasing cost industries, the cost of extracting the resource increases as extraction increases. This is because the lowest-cost resources are used first, with costs increasing as more resource is extracted or used. For example, the costs of digging a mine deeper or hauling lumber farther increase as more coal is extracted or more trees are cut. In this case, the MC curve is everywhere above the AC curve, and the AC curve continues to increase (average chases the marginal).

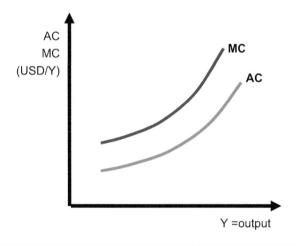

Figure 3.13  An increasing cost firm

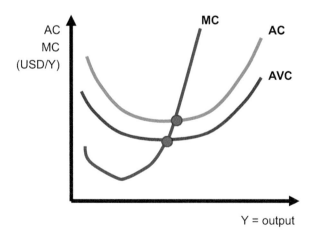

Figure 3.14  Typical cost curves

### 3.6.4   Typical cost curves revisited

The typical cost curves involve all three types of costs: decreasing AC, constant AC, and increasing AC, as illustrated in Figure 3.14.

These cost curves will help find the profit-maximizing point, the topic of the next chapter.

## 3.7   Chapter 3 Summary

1  Profits equal total revenue minus total costs. Total revenue equals the product price times the level of output. Total costs are the payments paid to acquire factors of production.
2  Accounting costs are the explicit costs of production. Opportunity costs are the value of a resource in its next-best use.
3  Accounting profits are total revenue minus explicit costs. Economic profits are total revenue minus explicit costs and opportunity costs.
4  When all resources are earning their opportunity costs, economic profits are equal to zero, and the resources are earning as much as they are worth.
5  Some farmers and ranchers remain in agriculture even if they are earning negative economic profits since they prefer a career in farming or ranching, even if it pays less than what they could earn in a different occupation.
6  Total fixed costs do not vary with the level of output.
7  Average fixed costs are fixed costs per unit of output. Average variable costs are variable costs divided by the level of output. Average total costs are total costs divided by the level of output.
8  Marginal cost is the additional cost of producing one more unit of output.
9  A typical total cost curve increases at a decreasing rate and then increases at an increasing rate as diminishing marginal returns set in.
10  If MC > AC, the average costs are increasing; if MC < AC, then average costs are decreasing.
11  A firm's cost curves reflect the firm's productivity: an increase in productivity is identical to a decrease in costs.
12  A constant cost firm faces constant production costs for all units of output produced.
13  A decreasing cost firm has per-unit costs that decrease as output increases.
14  An increasing cost firm has increasing per-unit costs as output increases.
15  A firm with "typical" cost curves is one whose average costs decrease then increase.

## 3.8   Chapter 3 Glossary

**Accounting Costs**—Explicit costs of production; costs for which payments are required.

**Accounting Profits** $[\pi_A]$—Total revenue minus explicit costs. $\pi_A = TR - TC_A$ (see Economic Profits).

**Average Costs** [AC]—Total costs per unit of output. AC = TC / Y. Note that average costs (AC) are identical to average total costs (ATC).

**Average Fixed Costs [AFC]**—The average cost of the fixed costs per unit of output. AFC = TFC / Y.

**Average Total Costs [ATC]**—The average total cost per unit of output: ATC = TC / Y. Note that average costs (AC) are identical to average total costs (ATC).

**Average Variable Costs [AVC]**—The average cost of the variable costs per unit of output: AVC = TVC / Y.

**Costs of Production**—The payments that a firm must make to purchase inputs (resources, factors).

**Economic Profits [$\pi_E$]**—Total revenue minus both explicit and opportunity costs. $\pi_E$ = TR − TC$_A$ − opportunity costs (see **Accounting Profits**).

**Fixed Costs**—Those costs that do not vary with the level of output; the costs associated with the fixed factors of production.

**Marginal Costs [MC]**—The increase in total costs due to the production of one more unit of output. MC = ΔTC / ΔY.

**Opportunity Costs**—The value of a resource in its next-best use. What an individual or firm must give up to do something.

**Profits [$\pi$]**—Total revenue minus total costs. $\pi$ = TR − TC (see Accounting Profits and Economic Profits).

**Total Costs [TC]**—The sum of all payments that a firm must make to purchase the factors of production. The sum of total fixed costs and total variable costs: TC = TFC + TVC.

**Total Fixed Costs [TFC]**—The total costs of inputs that do not vary with the level of output.

**Total Revenue [TR]**—The amount of money received when the producer sells the product. TR = P$_Y$ * Y.

**Total Variable Costs [TVC]**—The total costs of inputs that vary with the level of output.

**Variable Costs**—Those costs that vary with the level of output; the costs associated with the variable factors of production.

## 3.9   Chapter 3 Review questions

1 Corn producers interested in maximizing profits should

  a   maximize yield
  b   maximize revenue
  c   consider both costs and revenue
  d   minimize costs

2 Accounting costs include all of the following except

  a   electricity payment
  b   payment to hired workers
  c   how much money the operator could earn as a plumber
  d   fertilizer costs

3 Opportunity costs are

  a   explicit costs
  b   the value of a resource in its current use
  c   implicit costs
  d   the value of a resource in its previous use

4 Economic profits are

  a   accounting profits
  b   total revenue minus accounting costs
  c   total revenue minus accounting costs and opportunity costs

d   total revenue minus marginal costs

5   When economic profits equal zero

a   the firm should shut down
b   the firm must increase profits
c   the resources employed by the firm are underpaid
d   resources are earning exactly what they are worth

6   In a situation of negative economic profits

a   the costs of production cannot be paid
b   accounting profits are negative
c   accounting profits could be positive or negative
d   the firm will shut down

7   In the short run

a   only fixed costs exist
b   only variable costs exist
c   both fixed and variable costs are present
d   neither fixed nor variable costs are present

8   Variable costs

a   do not change with the level of output
b   increase with the level of output
c   decrease with the level of output
d   fluctuate in a manner unrelated to the level of output

9   Total variable costs divided by output equal

a   average variable costs

b   marginal costs
c   average fixed costs
d   total fixed costs

10  If MC > ATC, then

a   ATC are increasing
b   ATC are decreasing
c   ATC are constant
d   cannot be determined from the information given

11  All of the following are typical variable costs for a small business except

a   electricity
b   hired labor
c   paper
d   rental payment

12  For a firm with typical cost curves

a   the ATC increase then decrease
b   the ATC decrease then increase
c   MC is greater than ATC
d   ATC is greater than MC

13  A public utility such as an electricity provider is a(n)

a   increasing cost firm
b   decreasing cost firm
c   constant cost firm
d   cannot be determined from the information given

14  A coal mining company is a(n):

a   increasing cost firm
b   decreasing cost firm
c   constant cost firm
d   cannot be determined from the information given

**Answers:** 1. c, 2. c, 3. c, 4. c, 5. d, 6. c, 7. c, 8. b, 9. a, 10. a, 11. d, 12. b, 13. b, 14. a

For more study questions, flash cards, and study guides, see the online materials at the companion website: www.routledge.com/cw/barkley.

# Chapter 4

# Profit maximization

Photo 4.1 Profit maximization

*Source:* Thoma/Shutterstock

DOI: 10.4324/9781003367994-4

## Abstract

This chapter explores the profit-maximizing level of inputs and outputs for a firm in a competitive industry. It defines and explains perfect competition and clarifies the economic approach of comparing benefits and costs in decision-making. Graphs explain the optimal level of inputs and outputs. This chapter emphasizes the intuitive appeal of profit maximization and the rationale for using profits and losses to help determine a firm's breakeven and shutdown points. It is a comprehensive treatment of the heart of microeconomics.

### Chapter 4 Questions

1   How does a firm find the profit-maximizing level of inputs and outputs?
2   What is a perfect competitive industry, and why is it considered ideal?
3   What is the economic approach of comparing benefits and costs to make decisions, and how do you use it?
4   What causes profits and losses for a business firm?
5   What are the break-even and shut-down points, and how can they be used in business problem solving?

## 4.0   Introduction

The lessons regarding good economic decisions continue in this chapter. The materials presented here are important in economic decision-making and provide a comprehensive way of looking at the world. The "economic way of thinking" is based on comparing the benefits and costs of every human activity. It applies to purchasing a new pickup truck, attending college, or studying late. The **marginal analysis** used here is also an important tool of microeconomics that focuses attention on the advantages and disadvantages of each decision.

● *Marginal Analysis* = comparing the benefits and costs of a decision incrementally, one unit at a time.

The following paragraphs show that marginal analysis, or the economic approach to decision-making, applies to a great number of decisions, choices, and issues.

## 4.1   Perfect competition

To determine the profit-maximizing levels of inputs and outputs, we will use the concepts introduced in the preceding chapters and an additional piece of information: the price of the product $(P_Y)$. This price is the market price received by producers when they sell their output (Y). The units of the output price are in dollars per unit of output (USD/Y).

The term "output price" requires additional assumptions (simplifications) about the structure of the market in which the firm operates. The assumptions simplify the analysis in order to make some important tools of economics into something easily learned and used in the quest for the profit-maximizing levels of inputs and outputs. The major simplification is that the firm under study is in an **industry** characterized by **perfect competition**. An "industry" is a group of firms that produce and sell the same product.

● *Industry* = a group of firms that all produce and sell the same product.

**Perfect competition** means something very specific. It means that the industry has four characteristics, as specified in the formal definition.

● *Perfect Competition* = a market or industry with four characteristics: (1) a large number of buyers and sellers, (2) a homogeneous product, (3) freedom of entry and exit, and (4) perfect information.

## 4.1.1   Large number of buyers and sellers

This condition states that there are so many firms selling a product, and so many consumers who purchase it, that each individual firm is so small relative to the market that it cannot affect the price. Since numerous firms produce the same product, if one firm raises the price of the product above the price charged by the other firms, no buyers would pay the higher price, and all of the customers would go to other firms.

### UNDER PERFECT COMPETITION, INPUT AND OUTPUT PRICES ARE FIXED AND GIVEN.

In a perfectly competitive market, no individual firm can influence the price charged for the industry's product. The product price is a constant. This refers to a price at a given place and at a given point in time. This is true in an industry as diverse as agriculture. On a given day, all corn growers receive the same price for corn, and all dairy producers receive the same price for their milk.

QUICK QUIZ 4.1

Does agriculture have a "large number of buyers and sellers"?

Constant prices also hold true in the input markets that sell resources to a competitive industry. In a perfectly competitive economy, firms hire as many inputs as required without affecting the price since there are numerous buyers and sellers of inputs. Restated, each individual firm is so small relative to the market that it cannot influence factor prices. In addition, all competitive firms have access to as few or as many factors (labor, land, capital, and management) as needed. There are no additional (hidden) costs of hiring more of any input. Meeting this assumption is not always possible in the real world. If the computer industry desired to double the number of hired programmers, the wages of programmers would rise in locations such as Silicon Valley (San Jose, California) and the Seattle area where Microsoft is located. Hiring more agricultural workers in remote rural areas often requires that farmers and ranchers increase wage levels to attract enough workers, violating the assumption of perfect factor mobility. In a perfectly competitive industry, resources flow without cost to the desired jobs and locations. This is a simplifying assumption, used to make the analysis easier.

## 4.1.2   Homogeneous product

The homogeneous product assumption states that one firm's product is identical to the product sold by all other firms in the industry.

- *Homogeneous Product* = a product that is the same no matter which producer produces it. The producer of a good cannot be identified by the consumer.

The key idea is that a consumer is indifferent regarding which firm produced the good. Many agricultural products have this characteristic. Consider a truckload of wheat. A buyer could not determine who produced the crop. The same is true for a dozen eggs, or a bunch of carrots, or two pounds of cooking apples.

> ### QUICK QUIZ 4.2
>
> Are cattle an example of a homogeneous good? Is meat?

## 4.1.3   Freedom of entry and exit

Freedom to enter and exit an industry means that there are no "barriers to entry." Any firm can enter or leave the industry without encountering government obstacles or financial limitations. Most small businesses, including farming, have freedom of entry and exit. A counterexample is a public utility, such as the local producer and distributor of electric power. This industry usually requires a government permit to enter. Even with the permit, the huge financial requirements for generators, power lines, and installation costs may deter entry. Medical doctors, dentists, electricians, accountants, and many other professionals are required to obtain a license or some kind of certification in order to practice their craft. In a competitive industry, a firm can enter and exit with ease. Although entry intro agricultural production may be difficult due to high costs of land and equipment, this lack of financial ability is not considered a rigid barrier to entry. A qualified and competent individual can acquire the necessary financial resources to enter agriculture. Barriers to entry refer to legal or government restrictions.

> ### QUICK QUIZ 4.3
>
> Do farmers in the United States generally have freedom of entry and exit?

### 4.1.4 Perfect information

Information is required in any business firm. A successful firm must know the prices and availability of output and all inputs. If a single firm had "inside information" about movements in future prices, that firm would have a distinct advantage over other firms and would be able to earn higher profit levels. Gathering privileged information is in many cases illegal in the United States. However, in a perfectly competitive industry, all buyers and sellers know all prices, quantities, qualities, and technologies that they use. There are no informational advantages in an industry characterized by perfect competition.

- **Perfect Information** = a situation where all buyers and sellers in a market have complete access to technological information and all input and output prices.

> **QUICK QUIZ 4.4**
>
> How realistic is the assumption of perfect information?

The four characteristics of a perfectly competitive industry are unlikely to hold completely in the real world. However, the assumptions serve as guides to further knowledge. Entrepreneurs, scholars, business leaders, and common citizens use these and other assumptions as a starting point and then later relax them while adding complexity to the problems they must analyze. The major point to remember about perfect competition is that in the short run, prices of all inputs and outputs bought and sold by all producers and their customers are constant.

**PERFECT COMPETITION = FIXED, CONSTANT PRICES**

A competitive firm is a **price taker** since at any given moment it must take prices as fixed and given. The firm cannot change the price. Firms in market structures other than competition may be able to influence the market price of a good. If so, they are **price makers**. Competitive firms that meet the criteria listed earlier have no influence on prices and will always be price takers.

- **Price Taker** = a firm so small relative to the industry that the price of its output is fixed and given, no matter how large or how small the quantity of output it sells.
- **Price Maker** = a firm characterized by market power, or the ability to influence the price of output. A firm facing a downward-sloping demand curve.

The specific assumptions of perfect competition appear in later chapters, particularly Chapter 12. They are, however, particularly important in this chapter on profit maximization.

## 4.2 The profit-maximizing level of input

Maximizing profits is a fundamental concept in nearly all of microeconomics. It helps to review the economic approach to decision-making before facing the problem of profit maximization.

### 4.2.1 Economics: how to make better decisions

Economists look at business and personal decisions in a special way. In most every decision- making situation, an economist will compare possible benefits with probable costs. If the projected benefits are greater than the anticipated costs, the activity should be undertaken. For example, if the satisfaction gained from eating a slice of pizza is greater than the cost of the pizza, purchasing and eating the pizza is rational. This logic is sound, and it applies over a wide range of possible situations. This usefulness comes from the fact that decisions often come one at a time. The decision pondered right now is based on all the decisions that came before. This means that decision-making occurs "at the margin," or as an increment to behavior. Put another way, marginal decision-making looks at the benefits and costs of each additional unit (or each additional decision). Marginal decision-making allows determination of the profit-maximizing levels of inputs and outputs, one unit at a time. The next section uses an example from the livestock industry to make these ideas explicit.

### 4.2.2 A feedlot in Abilene, Texas: physical production

A feedlot is a business firm that purchases livestock and feeds the animals until they are ready for slaughter. The output (Y) of a feedlot is beef in pounds, and the output price $(P_Y)$ is the price of beef in dollars per pound:

4.1  Y = beef (lb),
4.2  $P_Y$ = price of beef = USD 1/lb.

> **QUICK QUIZ 4.5**
>
> Why use the economic term "holding all else constant" in this case?

> **BOX 4.1**
>
> **Feedlot**
>
> A feedlot or feed yard is a type of animal feeding operation (AFO) used for finishing beef cattle prior to slaughter. The very large beef feedlots, referred to as concentrated animal feeding operations (CAFOs), have thousands of animals in pens. Regardless of the size of the facility, the animals eat a diet composed mostly of grain.
>
> Cattle feed on pasture for the first 12 to 18 months of their life, until they weigh about 650 pounds. At that time, they transfer to a feedlot, where they continue to grow (they are fattened) for approximately three to four months, gaining up to 400 additional pounds before slaughter. The grain diet provides marbling, or fat

deposits, desired by consumers. However, a high-grain diet lowers the acidity in the animal's rumen, and antibiotics are necessary to maintain animal health.

Feedlot operators have become increasingly attentive to the environment. Odor, water quality, air quality, and land utilization are all factors that feedlot operators must consider. Most feedlots require some type of governmental permit and must have plans in place to deal with the large amount of waste that they generate. The Environmental Protection Agency (EPA) has authority under the Clean Water Act to regulate all animal feeding operations in the US. In some cases this authority is delegated to individual states. Feedlots contribute to greenhouse gases due to the methane produced by the animals. Feedlot operators also consider animal welfare through attention to practices considered sound from an ethical and economic standpoint.

*Source:* Hribar, C. Understanding Concentrated Animal Feeding Operations and Their Impact on Communities. National Association of Local Boards of Health. Retrieved January 3, 2023. www.cdc.gov/nceh/ehs/docs/understanding_cafos_nalboh.pdf.

Drouillard, J.S. "Current situation and future trends for beef production in the United States of America—A review." *Asian-Australasian Journal of Animal Sciences* 31.7 (2018): 1007.

The price of beef in this example is USD 1/lb. The assumption of perfect competition says that no matter how many pounds of beef that this feedlot sells, it will always sell for one dollar per pound. The inputs in the feedlot's production process include animals, feed, water, medicine, hormones, etc. The production function for beef fattened (fed) in this feedlot then becomes

4.3   Y = f(labor, feed, steers, water, medicine, hormones . . .).

Focusing on the profit-maximizing level of feed requires isolating the relationship between beef and feed, while holding everything else constant.

4.4   Y = f(feed | steers, labor, water, medicine, hormones . . .).

Recall that everything to the left of the vertical bar is a variable input, and everything to the right of the bar is fixed. Let X refer to the feed input, in bushels of feed. The feed price is $P_X$, in dollars per bushel of feed.

4.5   X = feed (bu),
4.6   $P_X$ = price of feed = USD 5/bu,
4.7   $P_Y$ = price of beef = USD 1/lb.

Finding the profit-maximizing level of inputs requires information related to inputs, outputs, and prices. The actual physical production process is a reminder of what the feedlot is all about: $Y = f(X)$, where Y is weight gained, or fattened beef ready for slaughter, and X is the feed input. Table 4.1 includes the physical product relationships introduced in Chapter 2.

## QUICK QUIZ 4.6

Define TPP, and define the term "production function." Define APP and MPP.

The term "APP" refers to average physical product, or the average per-unit productivity of all units of feed already used. It is the average productivity of all of the inputs. The MPP, or marginal physical product, is the productivity of the last unit of feed used. If the output generated by the last unit of input is more valuable than what the input cost, purchasing and using it in the production process is an appropriate economic decision.

## QUICK QUIZ 4.7

Could you graph the TPP, APP, and MPP curves on the same graph? Why or why not?

The graphs in Figures 4.1 and 4.2 show physical relationships between inputs and outputs, or the productive activities of the Abilene feedlot, as shown in Table 4.1. The same information can be used to derive the APP and MPP curves shown in Figure 4.2.

### Table 4.1 Abilene feedlot production process

| X = feed (bu) | Y = beef (lb) | APP = Y/X (lb/bu) | MPP = ΔY/ΔX (lb/bu) |
|---|---|---|---|
| 0 | 0 | — | — |
| 1 | 10 | 10 | 10 |
| 2 | 30 | 15 | 20 |
| 3 | 60 | 20 | 30 |
| 4 | 80 | 20 | 20 |
| 5 | 90 | 18 | 10 |
| 6 | 96 | 16 | 6 |
| 7 | 98 | 14 | 2 |
| 8 | 96 | 12 | −2 |

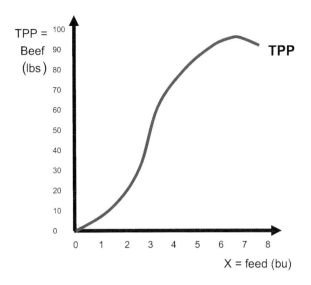

Figure 4.1 Total physical product for Abilene feedlot

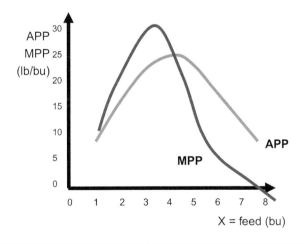

Figure 4.2 Average and marginal physical product for the Abilene feedlot

## 4.2.3   Feedlot in Abilene, Texas: value of production

The major activities of business firms break down into two categories: (1) production and (2) marketing. The previous section described production; the marketing function comes next. When the steers reach a certain weight, the feedlot operator converts physical units of output (pounds of beef) into values (dollars) by selling the cattle to the packing plant, or slaughterhouse. This analysis is a simple calculation based on the prices of the input (the price of feed, $P_X$) and the price of output (the price of beef, $P_Y$). The assumed prices are

4.8   $P_Y$ = USD 1/lb, and

4.9   $P_X$ = USD 5/bu.

A new term, **total revenue product (TRP)**, represents the total value of the firm's production. TRP converts output from physical units (pounds of beef) to dollar values.

● **Total Revenue Product [TRP]** = the dollar value of the output produced from each level of variable input. TRP = TPP*$P_Y$.

Multiplying the total physical product (pounds of beef) by the price of output (USD/pound of beef) yields the total revenue product, in units of dollars:

4.10   TRP = TPP(lb) * $P_Y$(USD/lb) = (USD).

As before, economic decision-making is about comparing the benefits with the costs of any activity. The benefit of feeding cattle in the feedlot is the revenue received from selling beef after production has occurred, or the TRP. The costs of feeding cattle are the **total factor cost (TFC)** calculated assuming that all inputs other than feed are fixed, or held constant.

● **Total Factor Cost [TFC]** = the total cost of a factor, or input. TFC = $P_X$ * X.

Using this definition, and under these assumptions, the costs are the total variable costs stemming from the use of the purchased feed.

4.11   TFC = $P_X$ * X.

The TFC are also in dollar units since they come from multiplying the quantity of the input (bushels of feed) by the unit price of the input (the price of feed, in dollars per bushel):

4.12   TFC = $P_X$(USD/bu) * X(bu) = (USD).

Table 4.2 shows the benefits and costs for the Abilene feedlot.

The left column in Table 4.2 shows the number of units of input (X). The next column, TPP, is the number of units of output produced with the level of inputs shown in the first column. The first two columns represent the production function shown in Table 4.1 and Figures 4.1 and 4.2. The Table and the two figures relate to the physical relationship between inputs and outputs. Multiplying output by price converts the physical relationship into an economic (TRP) relationship shown in the third column. In this particular example, TRP has the same numerical values as TPP, because the price of output is $P_Y$ = USD 1/lb.

Table 4.2 Profit maximization for Abilene feedlot: $P_Y$ = USD 1/lb, $P_X$ = USD 5/bu

| X = feed (bu) | Y = TPP (lb) | TRP (USD) | TFC (USD) | Profits = $\pi$ (USD) |
|---|---|---|---|---|
| 0 | 0 | 0 | 0 | 0 |
| 1 | 10 | 10 | 5 | 5 |
| 2 | 30 | 30 | 10 | 20 |
| 3 | 60 | 60 | 15 | 45 |
| 4 | 80 | 80 | 20 | 60 |
| 5 | 90 | 90 | 25 | 65 |
| 6 | 96 | 96 | 30 | 66 |
| 7 | 98 | 98 | 35 | 63 |
| 8 | 96 | 96 | 40 | 56 |

QUICK QUIZ 4.8

Calculate TRP if the price of beef was USD 2/lb. How about USD 0.50/lb?

The next column shows TFC, or the feedlot's cost of production. By assumption, all costs other than the cost of feed are assumed to be fixed, or constant. Multiplying the left column by the input price gives the total amount that the feedlot pays for feed.

The goal is to find the profit-maximizing, or optimal, level of input to purchase. To do this, calculate the profits in the last column by subtracting the total factor costs (TFC) from the total revenue product (TRP) for each level of input (X). The profits are the amount of money left over after the inputs are paid for ($\pi$ = TR – TC = TRP – TFC). A quick look at the profit column shows the highest profit occurs at USD 66, when the feedlot uses 6 bushels of feed. This straightforward calculation allows identification of the profit-maximizing level of input for a business firm. Economists working in the real world, however, would use the real cost and revenue data supplied by the firm, but the procedure is identical.

## 4.2.4 Feedlot in Abilene, Texas: marginal analysis

The main idea behind economic analysis is to find the optimal (profit-maximizing) point by looking at input use one input at a time, to find if the benefits of one additional unit of this input are greater than the costs. We do this with the help of two new concepts: the **marginal revenue product (MRP)** and the **marginal factor cost (MFC)**.

● *Marginal Revenue Product [MRP]* = the additional (marginal) value of output obtained from each additional (marginal) unit of the variable input. MRP = MPP * $P_Y$.

The units for MRP are in dollars per unit of input. MPP is the per-unit quantity of output (lb of beef per bu of feed), and the price of output is dollars per pound of beef.

4.13   MRP = MPP(lb/bu) * $P_Y$(USD/lb) = (USD/bu).

**Marginal Factor Cost** (MFC) is the additional cost of one more unit of input.

- *Marginal Factor Cost [MFC]* = the cost of an additional (marginal) unit of input; the amount added to total cost by using one more unit of input. MFC = $\Delta TC / \Delta X$.

The same information is contained in the marginal revenue and marginal cost concepts, as in the total revenue and total cost concepts. The marginal concepts are derived from the total concepts. Therefore, the marginal analysis shown here yields the same profit-maximizing solution described in the previous section. Verify this by looking at the marginal analysis for the feedlot in Table 4.3.

The first two columns of Table 4.3 repeat the input and TRP data from Table 4.2. The changes in TRP associated with each change in input use yields the MRP (MRP = $\Delta$TRP / $\Delta$X). Calculating this change for each additional unit of feed used by the feedlot yields data needed to develop the entire MRP column in Table 4.3.

A second method of calculating MRP is to calculate MPP, as in Table 4.1, and multiply MPP by the output price. This follows from the definitions of MRP and TRP:

4.14   MRP = $\Delta$TRP / $\Delta$X = $\Delta$(TPP * $P_Y$) / $\Delta$X = ($\Delta$TPP / $\Delta$X) * $P_Y$ = MPP * $P_Y$.

### QUICK QUIZ 4.9

As a check, calculate the MRP using the definition: MRP = MPP * $P_Y$.

In the case shown here, the numerical values of MRP are equal to MPP since the output price is USD 1/lb. To find the profit-maximizing level of input use, the feedlot operator will continue to increase feed use for the animals as long as the benefits outweigh the costs. The marginal costs of purchasing a unit of feed are equal to the price of feed ($P_X$ = USD 5/bu). The feedlot is assumed to operate in a perfectly competitive industry, so the price of feed is fixed and constant at five dollars per bushel for every bushel the feedlot purchases.

### QUICK QUIZ 4.10

Why does perfect competition result in constant prices for an individual firm?

An economic advisor will tell a firm (in this case, the feedlot operator) to continue with any activity (adding more feed) as long as the marginal benefits are greater than the marginal costs. Comparing the MRP and MFC columns in

**Table 4.3** Profit maximization using marginal analysis for Abilene feedlot

| X (bu) | TRP (USD) | MRP (USD/bu) | MFC (USD/bu) |
| --- | --- | --- | --- |
| 0 | 0 | — | — |
| 1 | 10 | 10 | 5 |
| 2 | 30 | 20 | 5 |
| 3 | 60 | 30 | 5 |
| 4 | 80 | 20 | 5 |
| 5 | 90 | 10 | 5 |
| 6 | 96 | 6 | 5 |
| 7 | 98 | 2 | 5 |
| 8 | 96 | −2 | 5 |

Table 4.3 shows the optimal number of bushels to feed. The comparison tells the feedlot operators to continue to buy feed as long as MRP is greater than MFC. The MRP is larger than the MFC for the first six bushels of feed. Good economic advice says that it is economically sound to continue feeding additional feed until MRP = MFC.

Once the marginal benefits (MRP) fall below the marginal costs (MFC), the feed input costs more than it returns. Productivity eventually declines with more feed.

## 4.2.5 Feedlot in Abilene, Texas: change in input price

In the real world, the market prices of inputs and outputs change continuously, so the manager stays busy continuously recalculating the optimal level of feed inputs. An illustration shows how the optimal feed decision changes when the price of the feed input changes. Suppose an early frost damages the corn and milo crops, resulting in a short supply of feed and an increase in the price of feed from USD 5/bu to USD 10/bu. The feedlot operator must now recalculate the profit-maximizing level of feed to purchase.

Table 4.4 shows that the feedlot will reduce the level of feed to five bushels: the sixth bushel would cost ten dollars but would only increase the value of output by six dollars. The firm would continue to feed more input until reaching the profit-maximizing condition (MRP = MFC) at five bushels of feed.

Not only is this a profit-maximizing result for the feedlot operator, who is increasing the feedlot's profitability, but it is also important from an economic perspective. Predictions about the agricultural economy are now possible. When the price of an input ($P_X$) increases, the quantity demanded of that input will decrease because profit-maximizing operators will reduce the level of use of this high-priced input. This is due to the "law of demand," a topic studied in Chapter 8.

Another important and interesting outcome of this model is that the number of pounds of beef that are sold to the packing plant will drop from 96 pounds to 90 pounds. Beef consumers will find less meat available in the grocery meat case,

Table 4.4 Profit maximization using marginal analysis: $P_X$ = USD 10/bu

| X (bu) | TRP (USD) | MRP (USD/bu) | MFC (USD/bu) |
|---|---|---|---|
| 0 | 0 | — | — |
| 1 | 10 | 10 | 10 |
| 2 | 30 | 20 | 10 |
| 3 | 60 | 30 | 10 |
| 4 | 80 | 20 | 10 |
| 5 | 90 | 10 | 10 |
| 6 | 96 | 6 | 10 |
| 7 | 98 | 2 | 10 |
| 8 | 96 | −2 | 10 |

which will in turn lead to an increase in the price of meat. When the costs of production of a good increase, an increase in the price of the good will result.

This explains why oil is such an important feature of the US economy. Petroleum products are direct or indirect inputs to the production of almost every good and service. Because of this, an increase in the price of petroleum products causes the price of all goods produced with oil inputs to increase. Agricultural production is particularly sensitive to the price of oil since farming requires large amounts of gasoline, diesel, oil, and other lubricants. Not only do tractors need fuel, but also fertilizer and agrochemicals are nearly all petroleum-based products. Changes in the price of oil (petroleum products) have a major effect on farmers and on all of agriculture.

### 4.2.6  Feedlot in Abilene, Texas: change in output price

The analysis of input use can also provide insight into how producers will react to changes in output prices. Suppose that the National Cattlemen's Beef Association (NCBA) is able to forge a trade pact with Russia to increase beef exports. This would increase the price of beef in the US from, say, one dollar per pound to three dollars per pound. Table 4.5 shows the results facing the feedlot when the output price increases to $P_Y$ = USD 3/lb.

The first two columns of Table 4.5 remain unchanged when the price of beef increases to USD 3/lb. The total revenue product (TRP), however, is increased by a factor of three since TRP = TPP*$P_Y$. Locating the profit-maximizing (optimal) level of input use requires calculating the profit level ($\pi$ = TRP − TFC) for each level of input use. The highest profit level is USD 259, when the feedlot uses seven bushels of feed.

The result shows that when the output price increases, a business firm will increase the use of inputs. This makes perfect sense. A business firm will earn higher levels of profits at higher output prices, because the firm will typically find it optimal to increase the amount of output it places on the market.

Table 4.5 Profit maximization for Abilene feedlot: $P_Y$ = USD 3/lb

| X = feed (bu) | Y = TPP (lb) | TRP (USD) | TFC (USD) | Profits = $\pi$ (USD) |
|---|---|---|---|---|
| 0 | 0 | 0 | 0 | 0 |
| 1 | 10 | 30 | 5 | 25 |
| 2 | 30 | 90 | 10 | 80 |
| 3 | 60 | 180 | 15 | 165 |
| 4 | 80 | 240 | 20 | 220 |
| 5 | 90 | 270 | 25 | 245 |
| 6 | 96 | 288 | 30 | 258 |
| 7 | 98 | 294 | 35 | 259 |
| 8 | 96 | 288 | 40 | 248 |

### BOX 4.2

## European price supports and the environment

Beginning after World War II, the Common Agricultural Policy (CAP) of the European Community (EC), later the EU, used high price supports for agricultural commodities to ensure enough food for European nations. The price supports worked well: Europe was transformed from a large food importer to a large food exporter in the decades 1950–1990. However, the price supports had an unintended consequence on the environment. Higher prices resulted in greater input use, including agricultural chemicals and fertilizers, which can result in damage to the environment and human health.

A comparison of France, an EU member, and the US provides an example. France and the US are both characterized by diverse and productive agricultural sectors. Both nations have modern, efficient production practices and produce similar crops and meat products. Both nations have large government subsidies for farmers. However, the EU had larger commodity subsidies, which led to greater input use. In 2020, France has approximately 18 million hectares of arable land, compared to 158 million hectares in the US. The arable land in France represents 33 percent of the total land area, and in the US, arable land represents 17 percent.

France's higher subsidy levels have led to greater production per land area. Importantly, the higher prices resulted in a French wheat yield in 2020 equal to 67 metric tons per hectare, compared to the US 33 metric tons per hectare. In 2020, France had nitrogen fertilizer usage of 110 kilograms per hectare (kg/ha), whereas the US used nitrogen fertilizer at a much lower rate: 72 kg/ha. Pesticide usage was 3.6 kg/ha in France, and 2.6 kg/ha in the US.

These data are a simple case study of the impact of higher output prices on agricultural inputs and output: higher output prices result in higher marginal revenue products, which result in greater levels of input use. More inputs result in higher crop yields and higher levels of output. Both the EU and the US have become increasingly concerned about the impact of chemicals and fertilizer on the environment. Agricultural policies in both the EU and the US are moving rapidly away from commodity subsidies and toward environmental "green" payments to farmers.

*Sources:* FAOSTAT. FAO Statistics Division 2023. Retrieved January 3, 2023.

R. Schnepf. EU Agricultural Domestic Support: Overview and Comparison with the United States. Updated June 7, 2021. Congressional Research Service R46811. https://crsreports.congress.gov/product/pdf/R/R46811. Retrieved January 3, 2023.

Higher levels of production require higher levels of input use [recall the production function: Y = f(X)]. Therefore, a major result of this analysis is that when output prices increase, profit-maximizing firms will purchase more inputs.

## QUICK QUIZ 4.11

If the price of wheat increases, wheat producers purchase more inputs. Explain why.

### 4.2.7  Graphs of optimal input use

The earlier analysis shows that a firm will respond to price changes by selecting the optimal level of input use. The firm will purchase inputs as long as the benefits (the increase in revenue brought about by using one more unit of input) are larger than the costs (the payment required to purchase the input). This result is shown using graphs when the TRP and TFC functions appear on the same graph. Figure 4.3 is an example.

The profit-maximizing level of input use for a firm occurs where the vertical distance between total revenue product (TRP) and total factor cost (TFC) is the largest. This optimal point is where the slope of the TRP function equals the slope of the TFC function. To see this, draw a line parallel (of equal slope) to the TFC line and just tangent to (barely touching) the TRP line, as shown at X* in Figure 4.3. The profit level is the highest at point X*. By moving either to the right or the left of X*, the distance between TRP and TFC decreases, reflecting lower levels of profits at any point other than X*.

There are two points where the slopes of the two functions are equal, so care is required to select the correct profit-maximizing point. At point $X_0$, the slopes of the two functions are equal to each other, but this is not a desirable point for the firm to locate. Why? Because TFC > TRP, which means that the costs of production are greater than the revenue. At this point, the firm is maximizing its losses.

The marginal analysis shown in Figure 4.4 reveals the same result that was found with the total functions in Figure 4.3. The information contained in the

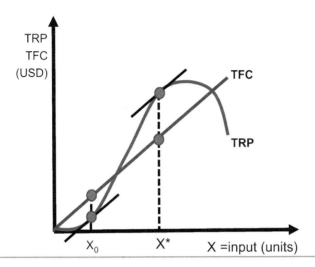

Figure 4.3 The profit-maximizing level of input: total revenue and cost

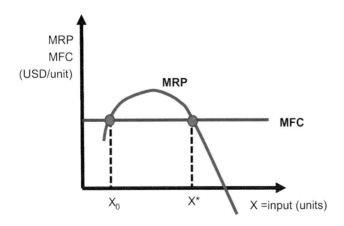

Figure 4.4 The profit-maximizing level of input: marginal revenue and cost

marginal cost and revenue functions came directly from the total functions. It is helpful to recall the definitions of MRP and MFC:

4.15   $MRP = MPP * P_Y = \Delta TRP / \Delta X$, and
4.16   $MFC = \Delta TFC / \Delta X$.

The definitions show that the MRP is the slope, or rate of change, of TRP, and the MFC is the slope of TFC. The profit-maximizing rule of input use is to continue buying inputs until MRP = MFC (Figure 4.4), or when the slopes of TRP and TFC are equal (Figure 4.3).

> ## QUICK QUIZ 4.12
>
> Why does the feedlot not use a production plan based on point $X_0$, where MRP = MFC?

## 4.2.8  Tax on the agrochemical atrazine

A study of input use can be useful in predicting how firms will respond to changes in input and output prices. One timely and important application of this analysis relates to the study of public (government) policies regarding the use of agrochemicals. Chapter 1 included a brief mention of atrazine, a common herbicide used to kill weeds in corn production. Chemical residues from atrazine appear in water supplies in areas where the chemical is used. These residues can have an adverse effect on human health.

The chemical enjoys extensive use in nearly all parts of the Corn Belt. In some cases, the level of atrazine residue is higher than the United States Environmental Protection Agency (USEPA)—recommended maximum safe level. Suppose that the government imposed a tax on atrazine as a means of reducing its use. The tax would make the chemical more expensive to farmers, who would reduce their use of the input. The reduction in use would have the desired result of lowering the residue levels in the area's drinking water.

Further, suppose that the United States Department of Agriculture (USDA) asks an economist to predict the impact of the tax on atrazine. We know that profit-maximizing producers will use the profit-maximizing level of atrazine, found where MRP = MFC. The per-unit tax (t) would increase the cost of each additional ounce of atrazine by t dollars:

4.17   $MFC = P_X + t$.

Figure 4.5 shows the impact of the tax. It increases the cost of purchasing the input from $P_X$ to $(P_X + t)$. This raises the MFC by the amount of the tax and reduces the profit-maximizing level of atrazine from $X_0^*$ to $X_1^*$.

By imposing the tax, the government has made it more costly to use an input that has economic benefits but potential environmental costs. Adjusting the tax rate can bring the level of atrazine residues to a targeted and safe level. Governments tax many goods considered to have adverse effects in a similar manner to those in atrazine: cigarettes, gasoline, lottery tickets, alcohol, etc.

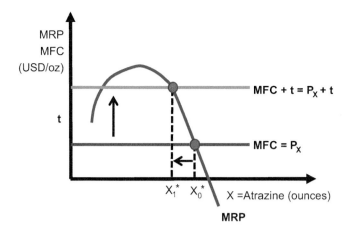

Figure 4.5 Impact of a tax on atrazine

QUICK QUIZ 4.13

Draw a graph to show the impact of a gasoline tax on agricultural production in the US. Will such a tax affect consumers of agricultural products?

## 4.3 The profit-maximizing level of output

This section discusses the optimal, profit-maximizing level of output for a business firm. The concepts and ideas presented here are applicable to a large number of business decisions, career choices, and personal issues.

### CONTINUE ANY ACTIVITY AS LONG AS BENEFITS OUTWEIGH COSTS!

Consider the output decision on a farm or for any business. Important questions include "How much wheat (or corn, potatoes, strawberries, or wool, for example) should I produce this year?" and "What is the optimal herd size for my dairy (or my hog enterprise, or my poultry flock)?" Economic analysis can be useful in providing answers to these questions. This is what it means to "think like an economist"!

### 4.3.1 Profit-maximization using total revenue and total cost curves

The questions have something in common: they all require use of the assumptions used earlier and the general assumption of the profit-maximizing firm. Now, though, attention focuses on profits, defined as total revenue (TR) minus total costs (TC):

4.18 $\pi = TR - TC$, where

- *Total Costs [TC]* = the sum of all payments that a firm must make to purchase the factors of production. The sum of total fixed costs and total variable costs. TC = TFC + TVC.
- *Total Revenue [TR]* = the amount of money received when the producer sells the product. TR = TPP * $P_Y$.

Total revenue is the amount of money earned from the production and sale of a good:

4.19  TR = TPP * $P_Y$ = Y * $P_Y$, where Y is output and $P_Y$ = price of output (USD/unit).

Total costs are the costs of production, including both fixed and variable costs. All units are in dollars.

### QUICK QUIZ 4.14

Are the costs in TC economic costs or accounting costs? Are the profits economic profits or accounting profits? Are opportunity costs included?

What are the costs facing this firm? There are both fixed and variable costs, and the total costs will increase with output.

4.20  $\pi$ = TR – TC,
4.21  $\pi$ = $P_Y$*Y – TC(Y); (TC is a function of Y).

The previous equation shows that both TR and TC are functions of the quantity produced (Y). The firm will continue to increase its level of output as long as the additional revenue from the production and sale of one more unit of the good is greater than the additional costs of production incurred when producing an additional unit of output.

A graph of total costs and total revenue often helps understanding. The total revenue curve (TR) will be a straight line since the price of output, $P_Y$, is fixed and constant. Multiplying a constant by the variable Y yields a straight line, as shown in Figure 4.6. The total cost (TC) curve has the "typical" shape, showing costs increasing at a decreasing rate and then increasing at an increasing rate.

In Figure 4.6, the vertical distance between the TR and TC functions represents profits ($\pi$ = TR – TC). The firm's objective is to maximize this distance. A line parallel to TR and tangent to the TC curve identifies this maximum distance. The point of tangency is the output level consistent with maximum profit. It occurs at output level Y*. Geometrically, this is the point where the slope of TR is equal to the slope TC (or MR = MC). Any movement to the right or left of Y* will result in a decrease in the vertical distance between TR and TC, or a reduction in profits.

As in the input case, note that there are two points in Figure 4.6 where the slope of TR is equal to the slope of TC. The firm must be sure to maximize, rather than minimize profit. The point Y* is profit maximizing since MR = MC and TR > TC.

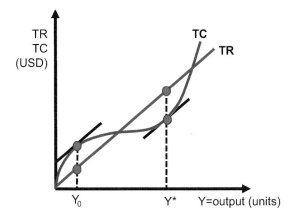

**Figure 4.6 The profit-maximizing level of output: total revenue and cost**

The first condition for profit-maximization occurs at point $Y_0$, but this point is a cost-maximization point since at $Y_0$, TR < TC.

## 4.3.2 Profit-maximization using marginal revenue and marginal cost curves

The definitions of MR and MC help summarize the profit maximization process:

- *Marginal Revenue [MR]* = the addition to total revenue from selling one more unit of output. MR = $\Delta$TR / $\Delta$Y.
- *Marginal Cost [MC]* = the addition to total cost of producing one more unit of output. MC = $\Delta$TC / $\Delta$Y.

These terms are analogous to the marginal terms in the section relating to a firm's decision relating to the use of inputs: marginal revenue product (MRP) and marginal factor cost (MFC). The marginal analysis presented here uses the same information used in the total analysis.

Marginal revenue is the slope, or rate of change, in total revenue: MR = $\Delta$TR / $\Delta$Y (Figure 4.7). TR is a constant. Therefore, MR is constant for every level of output. This is also in the formula for total revenue: TR = $P_Y$ * Y. Any change in TR comes from a change in output, Y.

4.22    $\Delta$TR = $\Delta$($P_Y$ * Y) = $P_Y$($\Delta$Y).

Substituting this into the definition of marginal revenue yields

4.23    MR = $\Delta$TR / $\Delta$Y = [$P_Y$($\Delta$Y)] / $\Delta$Y = $P_Y$,

which is why the MR line in Figure 4.7 is labeled $P_Y$.

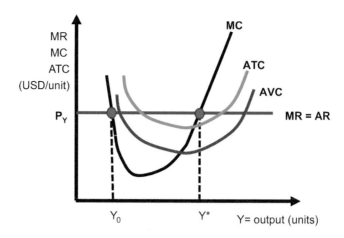

**Figure 4.7** The profit-maximizing level of output: marginal revenue and cost

Average revenue (AR) is the per-unit revenue that the firm earns from the production and sale of a good.

● *Average Revenue [AR]* = the average dollar amount received per unit of output sold. AR = TR/Y.

Average revenue is also constant at the output price since $AR = TR / Y = (P_Y * Y) / Y = P_Y$. Since MR and AR are constant, MR = AR.

> **QUICK QUIZ 4.15**
>
> What is the relationship between average and marginal? Does the relationship hold in this case?

To find the profit-maximizing level of output, the firm sets MR = MC, or $P_Y$ = MC. This condition occurs at two points in Figure 4.7: $Y_0$ and $Y^*$. These two points in Figure 4.7 are identical to the points with the same labels in Figure 4.6 since the information contained in both graphs is identical. The optimal, profit-maximizing point is $Y^*$, at that point TR > TC. Because of this, the profit-maximizing condition has two parts.

### Profit maximizing condition:

● MR = MC.
● MC must cut MR from below.

This condition is important to economics. It reiterates a theme that has appeared several times in this and earlier chapters. It comes back to the notion that an economist, or a manager in a business situation, or a person planning activities for the day. In summary form, it says that what a manager (farmer, planner, teacher, student, army general, US senator) needs to do to make good decisions, he or she must continue any activity as long as the benefits exceed the costs. The two conditions given earlier guarantee that the additional benefits are greater than the additional costs.

## 4.4 Profits and losses, break-even, and shutdown points

When is a firm earning profits or incurring losses? All of the graphs in the preceding sections show when profits are present and maximized. In addition, the search was geared toward economic profits, rather than accounting profits.

> ### QUICK QUIZ 4.16
>
> What is the difference between economic profits and accounting profits?

The cost curves depicted here include both explicit and opportunity costs. This section expands the definition of profit using both algebra and graphs to reveal the differences between maximization with and without the inclusion of opportunity costs. The explicit definition of profit is as follows:

4.24 $\pi = TR - TC$, where

4.25 $TR = TPP * P_Y = Y * P_Y = Y * MR$, and

4.26 $TC = Y * ATC$,

from the definition of average total costs, $ATC = TC / Y$.

Total revenue (TR) is simply the level of output (Y) times the output price ($P_Y$). The output price is constant in a perfectly competitive industry, so $P_Y = MR = AR$. In Figure 4.8, the firm maximizes profits by setting MR = MC, where MC cuts MR from below. Graphically, total revenue is the rectangular area defined by the horizontal distance $0Y^*$ and the vertical distance $0P_Y$. A similar rectangle identifies total costs as the per-unit costs ($ATC^*$) times the level of output ($Y^*$). This is the smaller rectangle bounded by the horizontal distance $0Y^*$ and the vertical distance $0ATC^*$.

Profits are defined as total revenue minus total costs ($\pi = TR - TC$), the rectangle identified in Figure 4.8. In the case in Figure 4.8, profits are positive ($\pi > 0$) because the price line ($P_Y = MR = AR$) is above the average total cost curve ($P_Y > ATC$). The firm will earn positive profits when this condition holds. If the price falls below the ATC curve, the firm will earn negative profits. In Figure 4.9, the price has fallen below the ATC curve ($P_Y < ATC$). The firm continues to maximize profits by setting MR = MC, where MC cuts MR from below. However, in this case, profits are negative ($\pi < 0$), and the firm is earning less than the opportunity costs of its inputs. Total revenue (TR) is the rectangle defined by the horizontal

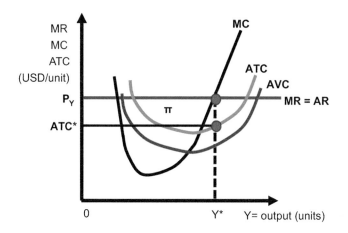

**Figure 4.8** Positive economics profits

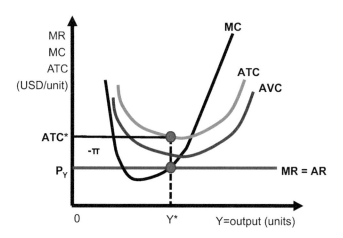

**Figure 4.9** Negative economics profits

distance (0Y*) and the vertical distance (0P$_Y$). Total costs (TC) are the larger rect-angle defined by a base of (0Y*) and a height of (0ATC*).

The rectangle identified in Figure 4.9 shows negative profits (losses). If the firm were to maximize profits, it would switch activities and use its productive inputs in their next-best use. The results show that a firm could quickly determine if profits are positive or negative by noting the following rule:

- If P$_Y$ > ATC, then profits are positive, and
- if P$_Y$ < ATC, then profits are negative.

When the output price is exactly equal to the per-unit costs, the firm is just "breaking even." Economic profits are equal to zero, but no economic losses appear.

QUICK QUIZ 4.17

QUICK QUIZ 4.17

When economic profits equal zero, is this good or bad for the firm?

### 4.4.1 The break-even point

The **break-even point** occurs when there are no economic profits or losses. At the break-even point, $P_Y$ = MC at the minimum point on the ATC, as in Figure 4.10.

- **Break-Even Point** = the point on a graph that shows that total revenue (TR) is equal to total cost (TC).

It may seem as if a firm should shut down since profits are equal to zero. However, this is the difference between accounting profits and economic profits. The cost curves consider (include) the salaries still earned by the owners of the firm. Even though profits equal zero, the returns to the owners are as high as what they could be earning in their next-best use. At the break-even point, the following condition holds:

4.27    $P_Y$ = ATC = MC = AR = MR.

Since the firm's revenue is exactly equal to the firm's costs, profits equal zero ($\pi$ = 0). If the price falls below the ATC curve, economic profits become negative. Under certain conditions, a firm may remain in business even though it is earning negative economic profits, as is explained in the next section.

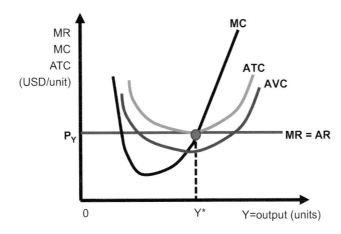

Figure 4.10 The break-even point

### 4.4.2   The shutdown point

Logic says that a firm should shut down when profits are negative, but there is a good reason why the firm will remain in production when the price falls below the ATC curve. In the short run, some of the inputs are fixed. The firm must pay the fixed costs, no matter how much is produced. If the output price falls below per-unit costs, the firm cannot cover its total costs. Since the firm is not earning enough to pay its costs of production, it might shut down. If it does shut down, it must continue to pay all of the fixed costs. For example, even if a business in a small town closes its doors, it will still have to pay the taxes, rent, and likely some utility bills. The firm might be better off remaining in business in order to pay at least part of its fixed costs. Expanded definitions of total costs help explain why:

4.28   $TC = TFC + TVC.$

Dividing all three terms by the level of output changes the equation to the following:

4.29   $ATC = AFC + AVC.$

In the short run, a firm will have both fixed and variable costs. Fixed costs do not vary with the level of output. They require payment no matter what the level

Photo 4.2 The shutdown point

*Source:* Mark Winfrey/Shutterstock

of output. In Figure 4.10, the vertical distance between the ATC and AVC curves is equal to the level of fixed costs (AFC = ATC – AVC).

In the long run, all fixed costs become variable: the ATC curve is the same as the AVC curve, and fixed costs disappear (making ATC = AVC, and AFC = 0).

QUICK QUIZ 4.18

Why do the fixed costs become variable in the long run?

If the output price lies between average total costs and average variable costs (ATC > $P_Y$ > AVC), then the firm is covering all of its variable costs and part of the fixed costs. Remaining in business is a better choice than closing down and owing all of the fixed costs. Therefore, the firm remains in business with negative profits to minimize losses. This is the optimal, profit-maximizing (cost-minimizing) solution.

If the output price falls below the average variable cost curve ($P_Y$ < AVC), then the firm will shut down. Since it cannot meet even its variable costs of production, it is losing money on each unit of output that it produces. Figure 4.11 clarifies the concept of the **shutdown point**.

● *Shutdown Point* = the level of output at which marginal revenue (MR) is equal to average variable costs (AVC).

At any price level above the shutdown point ($P_Y$ > AVC), the firm will remain in business. This is because the firm can meet all of its variable costs and at

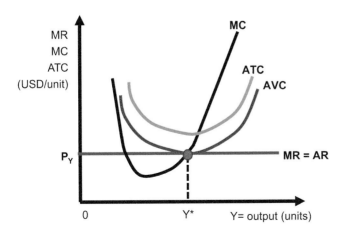

Figure 4.11 **The shutdown point**

least part of its fixed costs. At any price level below the shutdown point ($P_Y <$ AVC), the firm will shut down. This is because the firm cannot meet its variable costs of production. The firm minimizes losses by producing where MR = MC, which is where the price line intersects the MC curve and the MC curve cuts the price line from below. At this point, total costs exceed total revenue, but as long as firm is covering its variable costs, the firm will set MR = MC and continue producing.

### 4.4.3 Example: profit maximization for a catfish producer in Mississippi

Consider a commercial catfish producer as an example of a profit-maximizing firm.

4.30   TC = TFC + TVC.

**Photo 4.3** Catfish dinner

*Source:* HLPhoto/Shutterstock

Dividing these three terms by the level of output (Y) converts the total costs into average, or per-unit, costs.

4.31   ATC = AFC + AVC.

Recall that fixed costs are payments to inputs that do not vary with output. Restated, the land and building inputs remain at the same level whether the firm produces 0, or 1,000, or 1,000,000 pounds (lb) of catfish. Regardless of level of output, the fixed costs require payment. Fixed costs represent the vertical distance between the ATC and AVC curves in Figure 4.12.

In the long run, all of the fixed inputs become variable: TC = TVC and TFC = 0. Graphically, the long run curves reflect the variability of all inputs, as in Figure 4.13.

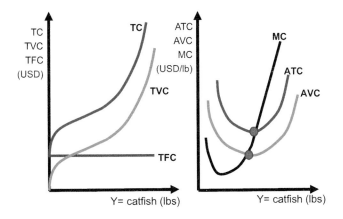

Figure 4.12  Short-run cost curves: Mississippi catfish producer

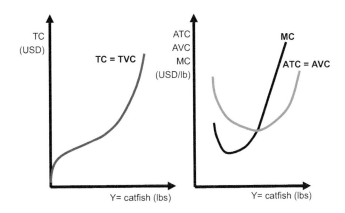

Figure 4.13  Long-run cost curves: Mississippi catfish producer

BOX 4.3

## Catfish in Mississippi

Catfish production represents over 27 percent of the value of aquaculture production in the US, making it the number-one source of aquaculture revenue. Commercial catfish production began in the 1960s, and catfish production has grown rapidly to reach annual sales of 319 million pounds in 2016. The value of the catfish crop in the US reached USD 425 million in 2003. Mississippi reported the greatest value.

The rapid growth of the catfish industry in the 1980s and 1990s led it to become one of the most important agricultural activities in states such as Mississippi, Arkansas, Alabama, and Louisiana. The combined production acreage of these four states makes up 94 percent of all catfish production acreage. Mississippi has had more acreage in catfish production than the other three states combined and has held this position since the late 1980s. The catfish industry generates an economic impact of billions of dollars and is the primary source of economic activity and employment in a number of Mississippi counties, primarily in the Mississippi Delta region.

*Source:* Commercial Catfish Production. http://Msucares.com. Mississippi State University. Retrieved January 3, 2023. http://extension.msstate.edu/agriculture/catfish.

The firm can use either the total or the marginal graphs to find its profit-maximizing level of catfish production. In the total graph (the left side of Figure 4.14), the catfish firm will find the number of pounds of catfish ($Y^*$) that will maximize the vertical distance between the TR and TC curves ($\pi = TR - TC$). The firm must make sure that the second condition of profit maximization ($TR > TC$) holds. Maximum losses occur at point $Y_0$. In the marginal graph (the right side of Figure 4.14), the firm will find the optimal, profit-maximizing point ($Y^*$) by finding the point where (1) MR = MC and (2) MC cuts MR from below. The profit-maximizing level of output is the same in both graphs.

If the catfish firm is a part of a competitive industry, the price of the output ($P_Y$) is constant for this firm. This is why the TR function is a straight line in Figure 4.14 ($TR = P_Y * Y$), and the MR function is constant ($P_Y = MR = AR$). Marginal analysis for a catfish producer involves starting at a low level of output and asking the question, "Should I produce one more unit of output?" The answer is "yes," as long as the marginal revenue (benefit) is greater than the marginal costs (loss).

The catfish producer will continue to produce more catfish until point $Y^*$ is reached. At that point, one more unit of output would raise production costs to a higher level than the price of catfish. Any point to the left or right of the profit-maximizing point ($Y^*$) will result in lower profits for the catfish firm. This chapter

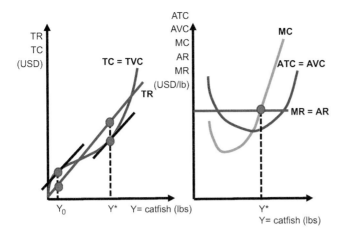

has demonstrated how to find the profit-maximizing point for both input use and output. The next chapter focuses on finding the profit-maximizing combination of inputs.

## 4.5   Chapter 4 Summary

1   Marginal analysis compares the benefits and costs of every activity, one unit at a time.
2   An industry is a group of firms that produce and sell the same product.
3   Perfect competition is defined by (1) a large number of buyers and sellers, (2) a homogeneous product, (3) freedom of entry and exit, and (4) perfect information.
4   In a perfectly competitive industry, the output price is fixed and given to a firm.
5   Total revenue product (TRP) is the dollar value of output produced from alternative levels of variable input (TRP = TPP * $P_Y$).
6   Total factor cost (TFC) is the total cost of an input (TFC = $P_X$ * X).
7   Marginal revenue product (MRP) is the additional value of output obtained from each additional unit of a variable input.
8   Marginal factor cost (MFC) is the cost of an additional unit of input.
9   Marginal analysis suggests that an individual should continue any activity as long as the marginal (incremental) benefits are greater than the marginal (incremental) costs.
10   The profit-maximizing level of input use can be found by setting MRP = MFC.
11   When the price of an input increases, the quantity demanded of that input will decrease.

12  When the output price increases, a business firm will increase the amount of input that it uses.
13  A tax placed on an input will cause a business firm to purchase less of that input.
14  The profit-maximizing level of output can be found where MR = MC.
15  When the output price is greater than average total costs, profits are positive. When the output price is below the average total costs, profits are negative. When the output price is equal to the average total costs, then the firm is breaking even and earning zero economic profits.
16  The break-even point occurs where $P_Y$ = MC at the minimum ATC point. Economic profits are equal to zero at the break-even point.
17  The shutdown point occurs where MR equals minimum AVC. At output prices above the shutdown point, the firm will remain in production. At output prices below the shutdown point, the firm will shut down.
18  Graphically, the profit-maximizing level of output can be found by locating the maximum vertical distance between the TR and TC curves. The profit-maximizing level of output can also be found by locating the point where (1) MR = MC and (2) MC cuts MR from below.

## 4.6  Chapter 4 Glossary

**Average Revenue (AR)**—The average dollar amount received per unit of output sold: AR = TR / Y.
**Break-Even Point**—The point on a graph that shows that total revenue (TR) is equal to total cost (TC).
**Homogeneous Product**—A product that is the same no matter which producer produces it. The producer of a good cannot be identified by the consumer.
**Industry**—A group of firms that all produce and sell the same product.
**Marginal Analysis**—Comparing the benefits and costs of a decision incrementally, one unit at a time.
**Marginal Cost (MC)**—The addition to total cost of producing one more unit of output: MC = $\Delta$TC / $\Delta$Y.
**Marginal Factor Cost (MFC)**—The cost of an additional (marginal) unit of input; the amount added to total cost of using one more unit of input: MFC = $\Delta$TC / $\Delta$X.
**Marginal Revenue (MR)**—The addition to total revenue from selling one more unit of output: MR = $\Delta$TR / $\Delta$Y.
**Marginal Revenue Product (MRP)**—The additional (marginal) value of output obtained from each additional unit of the variable input. MRP = MPP * $P_Y$.
**Perfect Competition**—A market or industry with four characteristics: (1) a large number of buyers and sellers, (2) a homogeneous product, (3) freedom of entry and exit, and (4) perfect information.
**Perfect Information**—A situation where all buyers and sellers in a market have complete access to technological information and all input and output prices.
**Price Maker**—A firm characterized by market power, or the ability to influence the price of output. A firm facing a downward-sloping demand curve.
**Price Taker**—A firm so small relative to the industry that the price of its output is fixed and given, no matter how large or how small the quantity of output it sells.

**Shutdown Point**—The point on a graph where marginal revenue (MR) is equal to average variable costs (AVC).

**Total Costs (TC)**—The sum of all payments that a firm must make to purchase the factors of production. The sum of total fixed costs and total variable costs: TC = TFC + TVC.

**Total Factor Cost (TFC)**—The total cost of a factor, or input: TFC = $P_X$ * X.

**Total Revenue (TR)**—The amount of money received when the producer sells the product: TR = TPP * $P_Y$.

**Total Revenue Product (TRP)**—The dollar value of the output produced from each level of variable input: TRP = TPP * $P_Y$.

## 4.7 Chapter 4 Review questions

1 A large number of buyers and sellers results in

  a  a homogeneous product
  b  a fixed and constant price
  c  freedom of entry and exit
  d  perfect information

2 All of the following have freedom of entry and exit except

  a  gas station
  b  copy store
  c  cable television
  d  clothing store

3 Which physical product curves can be graphed on the same graph?

  a  TPP and APP
  b  APP and MPP
  c  TPP and MPP
  d  TPP, APP, and MPP

4 The cost of an additional unit of input is

  a  total revenue product
  b  marginal factor cost
  c  marginal revenue product
  d  total factor cost

5 A firm will continue to purchase more input until

  a  MPP = MFC
  b  MRP = $P_Y$
  c  TRP = TFC
  d  MRP = MFC

6 When the price of corn increases, feedlots will

  a  purchase more corn
  b  purchase less corn
  c  purchase same corn amount
  d  cannot tell

7 When the price of automobiles increases, Ford Motor Company will purchase

  a  more glass, steel, and rubber
  b  less glass, steel, and rubber
  c  the same amount of glass, steel, and rubber
  d  cannot tell from the information given

8 If a tax is placed on gasoline, then a wheat producer will produce

  a  more wheat
  b  less wheat
  c  the same amount of wheat
  d  cannot tell from the information given

9 The profit-maximizing level of output can be found where:

  a  MR = MC and MC cuts MR from below
  b  MR = MC and MC cuts MR from above
  c  TR = TC
  d  The horizontal distance between TR and TC is largest

10 The shutdown point occurs where:

   a   P = min ATC
   b   P = min AVC
   c   ATC = AVC
   d   MR = MC

11 The break-even point occurs where:

   a   P = MR = MC = ATC
   b   P = min AVC
   c   AVC = ATC
   d   P = MC

**Answers:** 1. b, 2. c, 3. b, 4. b, 5. d, 6. b, 7. a, 8. b, 9. a, 10. b, 11. a

For more study questions, flash cards, and study guides, see the online materials at the companion website: www.routledge.com/cw/barkley.

# Chapter 5

## Optimal input selection

Photo 5.1 Optimal input selection

*Source:* Zeljko Radojko/Shutterstock

DOI: 10.4324/9781003367994-5

# Abstract

This chapter explains how business firms use relative prices when selecting which inputs to use. The relationship between inputs is discussed in detail, illuminating how the choice of techniques depends on relative prices. Isoquants are defined and described for three input types: perfect substitutes, perfect complements, and imperfect substitutes. Real-world examples provide insight into optimal input decisions. The marginal rate of technical substitution and the slope of the isocost line, more tools of economic analysis, help identify optimal responses to price changes. Emphasis is on how relative prices allocate resources in a market-based economy.

## Chapter 5 Questions

1 How do business firms use relative prices in decision-making about input use?
2 How do firms choose optimal production techniques, and what is the role of relative prices in the decisions?
3 What are isoquants, and how are they used to describe production techniques?
4 What are perfect substitutes, perfect complements, and imperfect substitutes in production?
5 What is the marginal rate of technical substitution (MRTS), and how is it used?
6 How are optimal input combinations selected, and how do these selections change when relative prices change?

## 5.0 Introduction

Chapter 2 introduced the physical production process, Chapter 3 covered costs of production, and Chapter 4 dealt with selecting the profit-maximizing levels of inputs and outputs. The next step asks how inputs relate to each other in the production process. In many, perhaps most, production processes, several different combinations of inputs will yield a specified level of output. For example, farm equipment can be manufactured by skilled workers (labor intensive) or by highly specialized robots (capital intensive) or by combinations of the two.

This chapter examines the selection of the optimal, profit-maximizing combination of inputs. The major message is that a firm will select inputs based on relative prices. In low-income nations where labor is inexpensive, business firms most often employ a labor-intensive production process, whereas in high-income nations, labor is often expensive, and capital-intensive production processes are used. Think of the comparison of agricultural production practices in the Great Plains portions of the United States compared to production practices in Africa. In the Great Plains, large, expensive machines till the soil, plant the crop, harvest the crop, and transport it to market. In Africa, manual labor often performs these same activities. Given the prices of labor and machinery in the two areas, farms in both areas are making rational economic decisions, even though they employ vastly different production processes.

# 5.1 The relationship between inputs

As in earlier chapters, the study of different combinations of inputs begins with the production function:

5.1   Y = f(A, L, K, M).

**QUICK QUIZ 5.1**

Define a production function and explain what the letters Y, f, A, L, K, and M stand for.

Chapter 2 analyzed the relationship between one input and one output, when all else is held constant. The quantity of one input (labor) varied, while quantities of all other inputs remained constant:

5.2   Y = f(L | A, K, M).

**QUICK QUIZ 5.2**

Explain how this production function determines whether the firm is operating in the short run or the long run.

The production function captures the physical relationship between inputs (X) and output (Y). The physical product functions (TPP, APP, and MPP) all use the same data.

**QUICK QUIZ 5.3**

Define the physical product terms TPP, APP, and MPP. Draw a graph showing each function.

Now consider the relationship between two variable inputs and the firm's output. Equation 5.3 shows a production function in which two variable inputs (L and K) are to the left of the *ceteris paribus* line, while A and M remain constant and are to the right of the line:

5.3   Y = f(L, K | A, M).

A major trend affecting US agriculture is the substitution of capital for labor (Chapter 1). Over the past several decades, the nation's agricultural sector has replaced millions of agricultural laborers with highly productive and expensive machinery. The analysis here explains why this occurred and shows how to find and measure the optimal rate of substitution of machines for labor.

A flour mill in Chicago, Illinois, provides an idea of how to determine the best combination of inputs. The term "capital" refers to physical capital and includes (1) machines, (2) buildings, (3) tools, and (4) equipment. Capital (machinery) often substitutes for labor, or workers.

A flour mill can use many possible combinations of machines and labor to grind wheat (or other grains) into flour. For example, the mill can use four workers and one machine (4 L, 1 K), or two workers and two machines (2 L, 2 K) to produce 100 five-pound bags of flour during a regular working day, as in equation 5.4:

5.4   $Y = f(L, K \mid A, M)$.

The mill manager must hire workers and a mill (a location and machinery) to produce flour from wheat. The key idea here is that there are several possible production processes for producing flour.

Figure 5.1 shows two different production practices and is different from the graphs shown in earlier chapters. The earlier graphs showed input on the horizontal axis and output on the vertical axis. In Figure 5.1, each axis represents one input in the production process. Points within the quadrant represent output and help answer a different question about production. The issue centers on selecting the profit-maximizing combination of two inputs, rather than the optimal level of one input.

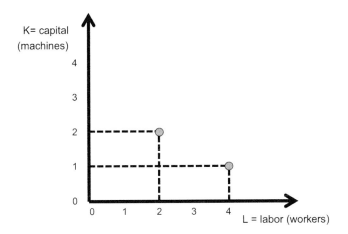

Figure 5.1 Production process for a flour mill in Chicago, Illinois

## 5.2 Isoquants

The two points shown in Figure 5.1 represent two points on an **isoquant**, which relates two variable inputs to a given level of output.

- ● *Isoquant* = a line indicating all combinations of two variable inputs that will produce a given level of output.

The prefix "iso" refers to "same, or equal," and "quant" refers to the numerical value of output. Therefore, the term isoquant means "equal quantity of output." An isoquant is a line on which every point refers to the same level of output. Figure 5.1 shows two possible production methods for the flour mill. Suppose that there are several other combinations of labor and capital that could produce the same level of output, as shown in Figure 5.2.

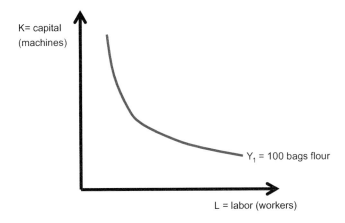

Figure 5.2 Isoquant for a flour mill in Chicago, Illinois

Every point on the isoquant, the curved line in Figure 5.2, represents the same level of output, $Y_1$ (100 5-lb bags of flour). The isoquant shows that capital and labor are substitutable: a flour mill can use any combination of K and L on the isoquant to produce the same quantity of flour. Efficient firm managers will recognize the potential for substitution among inputs and will select the profit-maximizing combination of inputs.

## 5.2.1 Examples of isoquants

Numerous combinations of inputs can produce a given quantity of most agricultural products. Corn and soybean producers in Iowa can use different combinations of land, machinery, chemicals, and labor to produce given quantities of corn and soybeans. Wheat producers make choices when selecting the appropriate amount of machinery to use.

Figure 5.3 introduces another feature of isoquants. Several isoquants, each representing a different level of output, are often drawn together as a "map." The isoquants farther from the origin represent larger outputs than the ones that are close to the origin. Moving outward from the origin and passing through isoquants shows this increase in output and the possible combinations of inputs needed to produce each level of product. Output increases with movement to the northeast in these maps since more inputs result in more outputs [$Y = f(X)$].

## 5.3 Relative prices

Different agricultural production techniques require different combinations of technology, labor, chemicals, and other inputs. Agricultural producers can select between labor-intensive methods or capital-intensive technologies, as shown in Figure 5.4.

The production technology represented by point A in Figure 5.4 shows a relatively large amount of labor and small amount of capital ($L_A$, $K_A$). Producers in many low-income nations may use this labor-intensive technology. Producers in

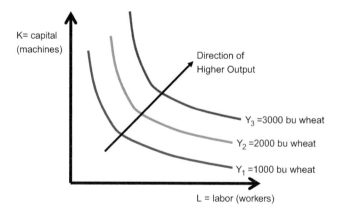

**Figure 5.3** Isoquant map for an Oklahoma wheat farm

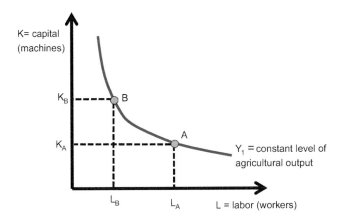

**Figure 5.4** Isoquant for an agricultural product

high-income nations typically use a capital-intensive production process in agriculture ($L_B$, $K_B$), as shown at point B. Why do producers in different nations use drastically different types of technology? The answer is **relative prices**. In regions where labor is less expensive than capital, more labor is used. In areas where labor is expensive, machines and chemicals substitute for labor because they can produce agricultural products in a less expensive manner.

Agricultural policy in the United States has paid direct subsidies to agricultural producers since 1933. Maintaining family farms has been one major goal of this policy. This policy has resulted in an agriculture that is more labor intensive than it would be without the subsidies. Why? Because the subsidies keep some small family farms in business, which prevents more labor from migrating out of agriculture and into other pursuits.

Several forces push businesses to different points on the isoquant. Lack of financial resources pushes toward more labor and less machinery. The advance of technology encourages the adoption of the newest machine and the newest variety of insecticide. Where does the adoption and substitution stop? Relative prices define the end of the struggle. Agricultural producers ask, "How much does it cost to buy labor and capital?" They select the optimal combination of inputs based on these relative prices.

American agricultural firms are therefore likely to move toward using capital-intensive production techniques such as geographical information systems (GIS), a satellite system, and computerized combines. In Africa, labor is relatively less expensive than capital. The opportunity cost of labor in many sub-Saharan African nations is quite low, near zero in some places. Job opportunities are not high for a relatively unskilled and uneducated workforce.

Therefore, the low-income nations of Africa, as well as low-income nations in other parts of the world, typically use labor-intensive techniques such as hand plowing, hoeing, weeding, and harvesting. This sounds inefficient to American and European producers, but these labor-intensive techniques can still be optimal since relative prices guide the decision (Figure 5.5).

Photo 5.3 Labor-intensive potato harvest

*Source:* usosr/Shutterstock

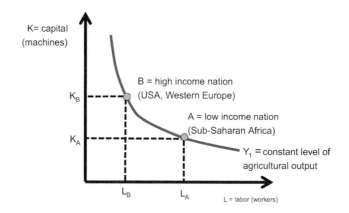

Figure 5.5 Isoquant location comparison across nations

Figure 5.5 helps explain the ongoing migration of labor out of agriculture in high-income nations. As labor has become more expensive over time due to increases in productivity and education levels, agricultural producers have replaced labor by increasing the use of machinery. This is the major result of the analysis to this point:

## THE CHOICE OF TECHNIQUES DEPENDS ON RELATIVE PRICES.

Agribusiness firms will use relative prices when choosing combinations of inputs that minimize their costs of production.

### 5.3.1 Examples: choosing the right production techniques

Car washes are different in different parts of the country. In rural areas and in small towns like Bozeman, Montana, car washes use capital-intensive production techniques. There are few workers, and fully automated machines do the work of cleaning the car. In urban areas such as New York City or Chicago, people, not machines, often wash a dirty car. This is due to relative prices. Labor is cheaper and more abundant in urban areas, so many of the car washes hire the low-skilled labor. If the price of labor increases over time, car wash owners would shift to more machines and less labor. Why? Because of the shift in relative prices.

> **QUICK QUIZ 5.4**
>
> How will McDonald's respond to changes in relative prices?

If the minimum wage increases, McDonald's must pay a higher price for labor, and the fast-food company will substitute out of labor and use more machines. Could a fast-food restaurant really do this? Yes, the decision depends on relative prices.

> **QUICK QUIZ 5.5**
>
> Explain how an automatic drink dispenser at a fast-food restaurant and agricultural tractors and combines that are driven by signals from a satellite are the result of relative prices.

Agricultural producers and agribusinesses make choices regarding the degree of mechanization based on relative costs. In the Great Plains, farming is practiced on a very large scale, with huge machines (tractors, combines, seed drills) working on thousands of acres. Contrast this with smaller farms in New England and California, which have more labor available to them.

## 5.4 Isoquant types

The production processes of firms are highly diverse: contrast the lemonade stands run by neighborhood children with the production of a good as complex as a John Deere combine. The relationships between inputs and outputs are varied and complex. This section describes several possible types of isoquants, which reflect the variety of ways that agricultural producers and agribusinesses convert inputs into output.

### 5.4.1   Perfect substitutes

**Perfect substitutes** are interchangeable inputs. High-fructose corn syrup (HFCS) is a perfect substitute for sucrose (sugar) in soda. Soda producers such as Coca-Cola and Pepsi can use either sweetener without any noticeable effect on the product.

● *Perfect Substitutes* = inputs that are completely substitutable in the production process.

The graph in Figure 5.6 shows an isoquant for perfect substitutes. The isoquant is a straight line since the two inputs substitute without impact.

Other perfect or nearly perfect substitutes include (1) cane sugar and beet sugar (no difference in the chemical composition), (2) bag seed and bulk seed, (3) 5 lb bags of flour and 10 lb bags of flour.

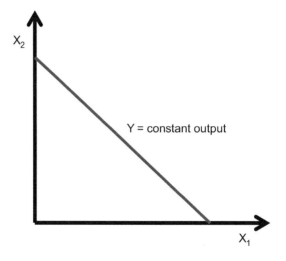

**Figure 5.6  Isoquant for perfect substitutes**

QUICK QUIZ 5.6

Are John Deere combines and CASE-IH combines perfect substitutes?

BOX 5.1

**John Deere**

Deere & Company, known by its brand name John Deere, was founded by John Deere in 1837 and is headquartered in Moline, Illinois. John Deere is the world's leading manufacturer of agricultural machinery. In 2022, it was listed eighty-fourth in the

Fortune 500 ranking. John Deere products include agricultural equipment: tractors, combine harvesters, cotton harvesters, balers, planters, and sprayers. The company also produces construction equipment, forestry equipment, diesel engines, lawn mowers, and snow blowers. In addition, John Deere provides financial services and other related activities. The company employs over 75,600 persons (2022), earns revenue of 44 billion USD (2022), and has a net income of 5.96 billion USD (2022). The company's products are recognized by the green color with yellow trim and the deer logo.

*Sources:* John Deere. www.deere.com. Accessed January 4, 2023.

Fortune 500. https://fortune.com/fortune500/2019/deere. Retrieved January 4, 2023.

## 5.4.2 Perfect complements

**Perfect complements** are resources that must be used together. Some examples come close. Think of a tractor and a plow: the plow is worthless without the tractor to pull it. The tractor is more versatile, so the complementarity is not perfect. Shoes are another example: except in very rare cases, the left shoe needs to complement the right shoe. Nuts and bolts are often perfect complements.

● *Perfect Complements* = inputs that must be used together in a fixed ratio. They operate in fixed proportions in the production process.

The isoquant for perfect complements is a right angle, showing that extra units of one input are not useful if not paired with the other input. The right angles in Figure 5.7 are isoquants. Every point on the vertical portion of each isoquant

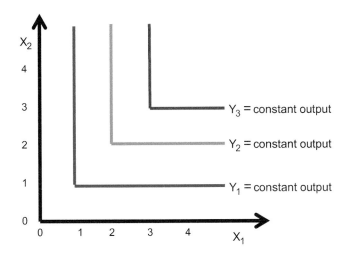

**Figure 5.7** Isoquant for perfect complements

produces the same level of output. Similarly, every point on the horizontal part of an isoquant refers to the same level of output. Adding more of one of the two inputs will have no effect on the output levels. If an extra unit of $X_1$ is added, it must be accompanied by one additional unit of $X_2$ before it becomes a useful input. Using $X_1$ and $X_2$ together increases the total product and movement to a higher isoquant.

All points on an isoquant represent the same level of output. If an agricultural producer has only one tractor, it doesn't matter how many plows she has: the tractor can only pull one plow. Similarly, if there were only one plow, any additional tractors would be wasted, as depicted in Figure 5.7.

### 5.4.3   Imperfect substitutes

**Imperfect substitutes** are the "typical" case. They are inputs that can be substituted one for another, but not perfectly. Skilled and unskilled labor are examples. These two inputs are useful in many parts of a production process, but they are not perfect substitutes.

● *Imperfect Substitutes* = inputs that are incomplete substitutes for each other in the production process.

Due to the law of diminishing marginal returns, it takes larger and larger amounts of one input to substitute for equal reductions of the other inputs. This gives the isoquant a shape that is convex (bowed toward the origin).

At point A in Figure 5.8, a firm has many workers but only one machine. Output remains constant if the firm purchases one more machine and uses three fewer workers. At point B (Figure 5.8) a firm has many machines but only one worker. At this point, the firm could replace several machines by hiring one single additional worker. Labor is scarce, so the addition of one more worker would replace several machines, and output would be unchanged. Imperfect substitutes provide

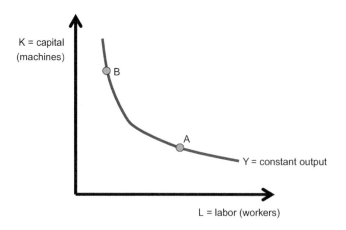

**Figure 5.8** Isoquant for imperfect substitutes

the ability to substitute between inputs. Because there are many different ways of producing goods, firm managers can select the optimal combination based on relative prices of the inputs.

## 5.4.4 Imperfect substitutes example

Soil and chemicals are imperfect substitutes when used in crop production. Many individuals believe that soil is necessary for the commercial production of food and fiber. In fact, crops can grow without soil using just water in which an appropriate mix of chemicals has been dissolved. Soil and agrochemicals are close to perfect substitutes because producers can use chemicals to replace soil.

This should not be surprising to anyone who has visited Epcot Center at Disney World in Florida, where a small number of crops grow hydroponically (in chemical-infused water). It should also not surprise anyone familiar with agriculture in the vast open spaces of the US: the Great Plains, California's Central Valley, or the Great Basin. Large parts of these areas use sand with very little soil to grow crops. With modern irrigation technology, producers can use center-pivot irrigation systems to drip nutrients into the sand (these are the big circles seen from an airplane). Figure 5.9 shows an isoquant and substitution possibilities between imperfect substitutes: soil and chemicals.

---

### BOX 5.2

## Center-pivot irrigation

Center-pivot irrigation is a method of watering crops by using a sprinkler that rotates around a pivot. Center-pivot irrigation was invented in 1949 by farmer Frank Zybach, of Dalhart, Texas. The center pivot consists of segments of galvanized steel or aluminum pipe, joined together and supported by trusses, mounted on wheeled towers with sprinklers positioned along its length. The machine moves in a circular pattern and is fed with water from the pivot point at the center of the circle. One complete rotation typically requires three days.

Center pivots are usually less than 500 meters (1,640 feet) in length (circle radius) with the most common size being the standard ¼ mile (400 m) machine. Most center-pivot systems now have drops with sprinkler heads positioned close to the crop, thus limiting evaporative losses and wind drift. Drops can also be used with drag hoses or bubblers that deposit the water directly on the ground between crops. This type of system is known as low-energy precision application (LEPA).

For center-pivot irrigation to be used, the field needs to be relatively flat. However, one major advantage of center pivots over alternative systems is the ability to function in undulating country.

This advantage has resulted in increased irrigated acreage and water use in hilly areas, including parts of the US, Australia, New Zealand, Brazil, the Sahara, and the Middle East.

*Sources:* O'Mary, M., D.R. Camp, and E.J. Sadler. "Center pivot irrigation system modification to provide variable water application depths." https://pubag.nal.usda.gov/download/14326/PDF. Retrieved January 4, 2023.

NASA/Goddard Space Flight Center. April 26, 2012. "NASA's Landsat Satellites See Texas Crop Circles—Of the Irrigation Kind." www.nasa.gov/topics/earth/features/tex-irrigation.html. Retrieved, January 4, 2023.

**Photo 5.4** Center-pivot irrigation

*Source:* B Brown/Shutterstock

Many forces cause movements along this isoquant. Soil erosion is a big issue in agriculture since cultivating the soil increases soil loss from wind and water erosion. Severe soil loss has caused producers in some areas to switch out of soil, replacing it with chemicals (hydroponic agriculture). New technologies such as "low-till" and "no-till" planting systems help reduce the threat of erosion and allow grain to be planted without having to plow the soil. These new technologies allow for the use of more soil but often require higher chemical use.

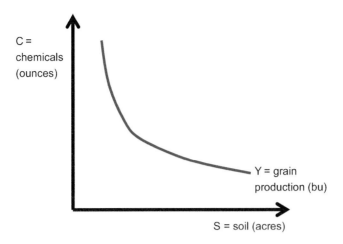

C =
chemicals
(ounces)

Y = grain
production (bu)

S = soil (acres)

Figure 5.9 Substitutability of soil and chemicals in grain
production

BOX 5.3

## No-till agriculture

No-till farming is a technique of growing crops without tilling the soil. No-till is an agricultural practice used to increase the amount of water and organic matter (nutrients) in the soil and decrease erosion. It increases the amount and variety of life in and on the soil but often requires increased chemical use for weed control.

In no-tillage farming, the seeds are directly deposited into untilled soil, which has retained the previous crop residues. Special no-till seeding equipment opens a narrow slot in the residue-covered soil. The slot is just wide enough to put the seeds into the ground and cover them with soil. The aim is to move as little soil as possible in order not to bring weed seeds to the surface and not stimulating them to germinate. No other soil tillage is done during the growth of the crop. The residues from the previous crops remain largely undisturbed at the soil surface as mulch.

Adequate weed management is the key to successful application of the system. Weed control is performed using herbicides and also through the adoption of appropriate crop rotations, including the use of adapted, aggressive species of cover crops. Some of the environment-relevant effects of no-tillage include erosion control, improvement of water quality, and increased water infiltration, which leads to reduced flood hazard and climate-related consequences through carbon sequestration in the soil—these may appear after several years of continuous, uninterrupted application. Globally, the no-till technology is used on over 100 million hectares under a wide variety of climate and soil conditions.

*Sources:* CTIC, 2023. Conservation Technology Information Center homepage www.ctic.org. Retrieved January 4, 2023.

NO-TILLAGE. www.rolf-derpsch.com/en/no-till. Retrieved January 4, 2023.

Another example of imperfect substitutes is from production agriculture in the United States. The federal government has taken millions of highly erodible acres out of agricultural production through the Conservation Reserve Program (CRP). However, when fewer acres are in production, producers substitute out of soil and into chemicals by applying higher levels of agrochemicals to the acres remaining in production.

## BOX 5.4

### Conservation Reserve Program

The Conservation Reserve Program (CRP) is a voluntary program for agricultural landowners. Through CRP, a farmer can receive annual rental payments and cost-share assistance to establish long-term, resource-conserving covers on eligible farmland. Participants enroll in CRP contracts for 10 to 15 years and receive annual rental payments based on the agricultural rental value of the land. The program provides cost-share assistance for up to 50 percent of the participant's costs in establishing approved conservation practices.

CRP protects millions of acres of American topsoil from erosion and is designed to safeguard the nation's natural resources. By reducing water runoff and sedimentation, CRP protects groundwater and helps improve the condition of lakes, rivers, ponds, and streams. Acreage enrolled in the CRP is planted to resource-conserving vegetative covers, making the program a major contributor to increased wildlife populations in many parts of the country.

*Source:* USDA. Farm Service Agency. Conservation Programs. www.fsa.usda.gov/FSA Retrieved January 4, 2023.

## 5.5   Optimal input decisions

The preceding pages and examples beg the question, "What is a systematic way to choose the optimal combination of inputs for use in a production process?" Cost-minimization is related to profit maximization since lowering costs results in increasing profits ($\pi$ = TR – TC). Relative prices drive the decision regarding what inputs to use, and changes in relative prices result in shifts out of the relatively expensive input into the relatively inexpensive input.

## 5.5.1   The marginal rate of technical substitution

The slope of an isoquant defines the **marginal rate of technical substitution** (**MRTS**). It reflects how well one input substitutes for another.

● *Marginal Rate of Technical Substitution [MRTS]* = the rate at which one input can be decreased as the use of another input increases to take its place. The slope of the isoquant: MRTS = $\Delta X_2$ / $\Delta X_1$.

A graph provides the best way to gain understanding of what the MRTS is all about.
  The slope of the isoquant in Figure 5.10 shows the MRTS between inputs $X_1$ and $X_2$. In this graph, input $X_2$ is on the y-axis, and $X_1$ is on the x-axis, so the slope of the isoquant equals $\Delta Y$ / $\Delta X$ = $\Delta X_2$ / $\Delta X_1$. In the case of imperfect substitutes, as in Figure 5.10, the slope becomes less steep in response to substituting $X_1$ for $X_2$. The value of MRTS changes with moves along the isoquant. When moving from point A to point B, the firm keeps output constant by reducing $X_2$ by one unit (from 3 to 2 on the vertical scale), and increasing $X_1$ by one input (from 1 to 2 on the horizontal scale). This results in a calculated MRTS of negative one (–1):

5.5   MRTS(AB) = $\Delta X_2$ / $\Delta X_1$ = (2 – 3) / (2 – 1) = –1.

The MRTS must always be a negative number since isoquants based on two inputs that are imperfect substitutes must always be downward sloping for rational producers.

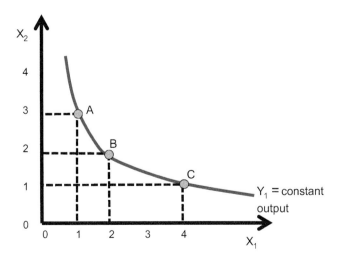

**Figure 5.10** Marginal rate of technical substitution between two inputs

The move from A to B shows that the firm can select a wide variety of input combinations that will yield the same level of output. In fact, any point on the isoquant will, by definition, result in the same level of output. The movement from A to B represents a shift out of input $X_2$ and into input $X_1$.

A move from point B to C will yield a smaller MRTS, because the slope of the isoquant becomes less steep with the move. This new MRTS (relating to the move from point B to point C) is calculated as follows:

5.6   MRTS(BC) = slope of isoquant = $\Delta X_2 / \Delta X_1$
$$= (1 - 2) / (4 - 2) = -1 / 2 = -0.5.$$

The slope of the isoquant, or MRTS, is crucial to determining which combination of inputs a firm will choose. The isoquant describes input combinations that are technically feasible. Economic information (the prices of the two inputs) allows this technical information to determine the cost-minimizing levels of input use. The next section switches from the technical information relating to input productivity to relative prices of the inputs.

## 5.5.2   The isocost line

How will a profit-maximizing producer determine how many pounds of fertilizer or what labor-intensive method or capital-intensive technique is most profitable? The producer does so by combining the technical information contained in the isoquant with cost information summarized by the **isocost line**. The prefix "iso" means the "same, or equal," and the term "cost" refers to the value placed on inputs. Therefore, the term isocost means "equal costs." An isocost line is a line on which every combination of inputs has the same value or costs.

● **Isocost Line** = a line indicating all combinations of two variable inputs that can be purchased for a given, or same, level of expenditure.

Consider an agricultural implement dealer facing a USD 10/hour price of labor, a USD 100/ machine price of capital, and total expenditures equal to USD 1,000. This is enough information to use in developing an algebraic equation for an isocost line:

5.7   $TC = P_1X_1 + P_2X_2.$

Given "economic data" from the example, this becomes

5.8   $TC = (USD\ 10/hour) * X_1 + (USD\ 100/machine) * X_2 = 10L + 100K,$

where $X_1$ is labor (L) and $X_2$ is capital (K). The terms in this equation rearrange to yield the equation of a line: $y = b + mx$, where b is the y-intercept and m is the slope. This is done to isolate the value of the variable measured on the vertical axis (K in this example) on the left-hand side of the equation. Total expenditures (TC) is equal to USD 1,000, so

5.9   $TC = 10L + 100K$, and
5.10   $1,000 = 10L + 100K.$

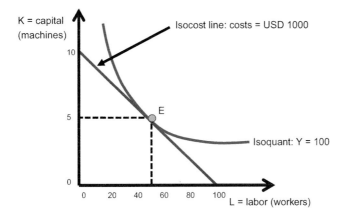

K = capital (machines)

Isocost line: costs = USD 1000

E

Isoquant: Y = 100

L = labor (workers)

Figure 5.11 **Equilibrium for input combination between capital and labor**

To isolate K on the left side of the equation, subtract 10L from both sides:

5.11    $1,000 - 10L = 100K$.

Reverse sides to move K to the left-hand side:

5.12    $100K = 1,000 - 10L$.

Finally, divide both sides by 100 to get:

5.13    $K = 10 - 0.1L$.

This is the equation for the isocost line. This line is graphically shown in Figure 5.11: the y-intercept is equal to 10 and the slope is equal to 0.1 (= 10 / 100). Use of this simple algebra can be used for any two-variable isocost line. In summary:

5.14    $TC = P_1X_1 + P_2X_2$,
5.15    $P_2X_2 = TC - P_1X_1$,
5.16    $X_2 = TC / P_2 + (-P_1 / P_2) * X_1$.

The slope of the isocost line equals $(-P_1 / P_2)$, and the y-intercept equals $(TC / P_2)$. This equation contains the information on relative prices and helps locate the optimal, cost-minimizing combination of inputs for a business firm.

### 5.5.3 Equilibrium: the tangency of the isoquant and the isocost line

As an example, the analysis is used to help an agricultural implement dealer find the optimal combination of machines and workers for the firm to employ. This

requires combining the isoquant and the isocost line in the same graph, as in Figure 5.11. To find the optimal combination of inputs, the firm will locate at the point of tangency of the isoquant and the isocost line (the only point where the two lines are barely touching). In Figure 5.11, this occurs at the point (50, 5), where the firm purchases 50 hours of labor and five machines.

Note that this point is exactly "in the middle" of the isocost line. This is due solely to the location of this particular isoquant and is not always the point where the firm will locate. The actual point depends on the technology (represented by the isoquant) and the relative prices (represented by the isocost line).

The firm's objective is to minimize costs. It can meet this objective by finding an **equilibrium** point at the tangency, where the slope of the isoquant is equal to the slope of the isocost line. Equilibrium is a point where the firm is doing as well as it possibly can, given the situation, and does not desire to change.

● *Equilibrium* = a point or situation from which there is no tendency to change.

Once the manager locates the equilibrium point, he or she has no forces pushing for change: the firm is "at rest." The equilibrium condition can be shown algebraically to be where the slope of the isoquant (= MRTS = $\Delta X_2 / \Delta X_1$) is equal to the slope of the isocost line (= $-P_1 / P_2$).

5.17   $\Delta X_2/\Delta X_1 = -P_1/P_2$.

We can rearrange this equation (by cross-multiplication) to find the equilibrium condition for optimal input use:

5.18   $P_2\Delta X_2 = -P_1\Delta X_1$.

This equation shows that in equilibrium, the changes in expenditures on each input are equal. The relationship states that a firm manager will continue to substitute inputs until the amount spent for the added units of one input is just equal to the money saved by the reduction in the amount spent on the other input. To make this idea clear, consider the case when the equality in the equilibrium condition provided earlier does not hold:

If $P_2\Delta X_2 > -P_1\Delta X_1$, then more $X_1$ should be used because the cost of adding one more unit of $X_2$ is greater than the cost saved by decreasing the use of $X_1$.

If $P_2\Delta X_2 < -P_1\Delta X_1$, then more $X_2$ should be used because the cost of adding one more unit of $X_1$ is greater than the cost saved by decreasing the use of $X_2$.

This equilibrium condition indicates that the optimal, cost-minimizing, combination of inputs occurs when the physical rate of substitution (MRTS) is equal to the economic rate of substitution (the price ratio). The equilibrium condition provides the least-cost solution for the firm.

At point A in Figure 5.12, the firm is not in equilibrium since the slope of the isoquant (MRTS) is greater (steeper) than the price ratio:

5.19  $P_2\Delta X_2 > -P_1\Delta X_1$.

This inequality signals to the manager to substitute out of the expensive input ($X_2$) and into the less expensive input ($X_1$). This substitution will continue until point E is reached, where $\Delta X_2 / \Delta X_1 = -P_1 / P_2$. At point E, the firm is in equilibrium.

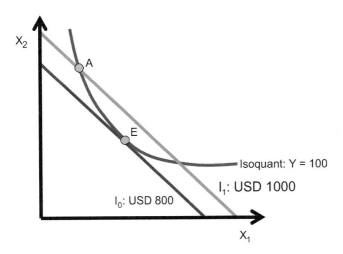

Figure 5.12 Disequilibrium example for input combination

Figure 5.12 shows that through the process of input substitution (moving from point A to point E), the firm reached a lower isocost line ($I_0$), with a cost savings of USD 200 (USD 1,000–USD 800). The next step enquires about a corn producer's selection of inputs.

### 5.5.4   Example: corn producer near Newton, Iowa

The goal of a corn producer near Newton, Iowa, is to minimize costs. The producer's objective is to produce 100 bushels of corn at the lowest possible cost. The production of corn requires N inputs ($X_1$, $X_2$, $X_3$ . . . $X_N$), and the two most expensive inputs are land ($X_1$) and fertilizer ($X_2$). Focusing on these two major inputs requires holding quantities of all other inputs constant. The corn producer's production function is:

5.20   $Y = f(X_1, X_2 \mid X_3 . . . X_N)$, where
5.21   $X_1$ = land (acres), and
5.22   $X_2$ = fertilizer (lb).

The objective is to find the optimal (lowest cost) combination of land and fertilizer to use to produce corn in Iowa. Figure 5.13 shows an isoquant that reflects all combinations of inputs (land and fertilizer) that produce the same level of output (corn).
    The slope of the isoquant is the marginal rate of technical substitution = MRTS = $\Delta X_2 / \Delta X_1$. Since land and fertilizer are substitutes, there are many

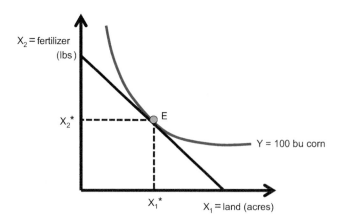

**Figure 5.13** Equilibrium for input combination between fertilizer and land

combinations of the two inputs that will meet the objective and produce 100 bushels.

The producer will want to locate the cost-minimizing combination of inputs for the production of 100 bushels of corn. She can do this with the use of the isocost line. To minimize the costs of producing 100 bushels, the corn producer locates the tangency point of the isoquant and isocost lines: the point where the slope of the isoquant equals the slope of the isocost line (MRTS = price ratio):

5.23 $\Delta X_2 / \Delta X_1 = -P_1/P_2$.

The equilibrium point in this hypothetical example is where the changes in expenditures from substituting land and fertilizer along the isoquant are equalized: the money released from the sale of land is equal to the cost of the fertilizer needed to make up for the lost land.

5.24 $-P_2\Delta X_2 = P_1\Delta X_1$

If the change in expenditure for one input were greater than the change in the other input, the producer could lower costs by moving toward the equilibrium point.

Interestingly, the equilibrium condition for selecting the optimal combination of inputs follows the same logic as the profit-maximizing condition of input use. Recall that the profit-maximizing rule for input use is to set the marginal revenue product (MRP = MPP * $P_Y$) equal to the marginal factor cost (MFC = $P_X$):

5.25 MRP = MFC,
5.26 MPP * $P_Y$ = $P_X$,
5.27 $(\Delta Y / \Delta X)$ * $P_Y$ = $P_X$,
5.28 $\Delta Y$ * $P_Y$ = $\Delta X$ * $P_X$.

Equation 5.28 shows that the profit-maximizing condition results in an equilibrium where the incremental increase in revenue ($\Delta Y$ * $P_Y$) is equal to the incremental increase in input costs ($\Delta X$ * $P_X$). The next section shows how producers (input users) react to changes in the price of inputs.

## 5.6 Optimal responses to price changes

Relative prices drive the economic decisions of producers in their quest to maximize profits and/or minimize costs. Since prices are constantly changing, the question becomes how producers respond to changes in prices. Economic intuition says that when it is possible, shift out of expensive inputs and into less-expensive inputs. A contemporary choice of this kind comes up with respect to finding the correct combination of agrochemicals and land to use in the production process.

The discussion of isoquants and isocost lines focused on setting the MRTS equal to the slope of the isocost line, or the price ratio ($P_1 / P_2$). The equilibrium condition highlights the importance of relative prices in the economy: if the price of one input changes, the price ratio also changes, resulting in a new equilibrium combination of inputs.

### 5.6.1   Price change for the farm implement manufacturer

Consider the farm implement manufacturer (John Deere) to see how input price changes affect input selection. This firm used labor (L = workers), and capital (K = machines) to produce implements. The price of labor is USD 10/hour, the price of machines is USD 100/hour, and total expenditures are USD 1,000, as shown in Figure 5.14.

Suppose the wage rate increases from USD 10/hour to USD 20/hour, shifting the isocost line from $I_0$ to $I_1$. Focus attention on the shift in isocost lines by recalling the algebraic equation (y = b + mx) of the isocost lines:

5.29   $X_2 = TC/P_2 + (-P_1 / P_2)X_1.$

The y-intercept of the isocost line (TC / $P_2$) remains unchanged because the total expenditures (TC) and the price of machines ($P_2$) have remained unaltered. The slope ($-P_1 / P_2$), however, becomes steeper due to the increase in the price of labor ($P_1$). The slope of $I_0$ is equal to the price ratio prior to the price change: $-P_1 / P_2$ = $-10 / 100 = -0.1$. After the wage increase, the price ratio increases to $-P_1 / P_2$ = $-20 / 100 = -0.2$. This change is shown in Figure 5.14. The addition of isoquants to Figure 5.15 provides information on the firm's need to change its input mix in response to the change in relative prices.

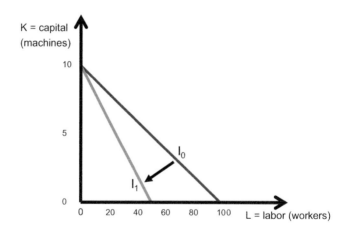

Figure 5.14 Isocost shift due to a wage increase for farm implement manufacturer

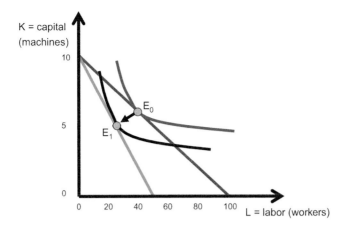

Figure 5.15 Equilibrium change due to a wage increase for implement manufacturer

If the total expenditures of the firm remain constant at USD 1,000, the firm ends up on a lower isoquant, showing that production drops due to the increase in input price. This reflects the discussion in the previous chapter: if the price of an input increases, production costs increase, and the firm lowers its level of output. The price change also alters relative prices (the slope of the isocost line) and results in a substitution out of labor and into capital.

The corn producer's goal was to produce 100 bushels of corn at the lowest possible cost. If the price of land increases, the slope of the isocost will change, but this firm manager will desire to remain on the same isoquant in order to remain at the production goal of 100 bushels. The price change will cause a shift in the cost-minimizing combination of inputs, shown in Figure 5.16.

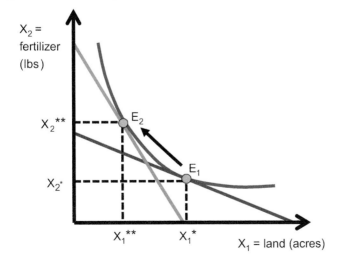

Figure 5.16 Equilibrium change due to a land price increase

The increase in the price of land causes the slope of the isocost line to become steeper. To remain on the same isoquant, the producer will shift out of the more expensive input (land) and into the less expensive input (fertilizer) in order to reach a new equilibrium at ($E_2$). At the new equilibrium, fewer acres of land and more fertilizer are employed.

## 5.6.2 Example: the impact of gambling on input selection in Minnesota

The general principles outlined in the previous sections are useful in exploring any changes in relative prices, including unusual situations like the impact of gambling casinos on the optimal selection of inputs to use in agriculture. Minnesota is the point of reference, but the issue could appear in any number of places. Over the past few years, several large gambling casinos have located in the Midwest, including Minnesota. These casinos, often built on agricultural land, reduce the number of acres available for agricultural production in this area. The casinos employ

Photo 5.6 Impact of gambling on land price near casino

*Source:* Lipik/Shutterstock

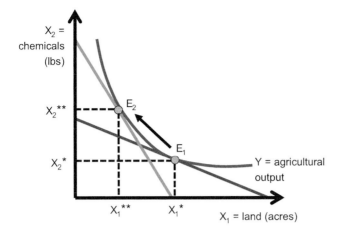

several hundred persons. Many have moved to the area and purchased houses. The increase in visitors has also increased the demand for hotel rooms, restaurants, gasoline stations, and convenience stores. As a result, the business climate in these areas has improved dramatically. The casinos have also caused an increase in the price of land due to their own needs for buildings and parking space and the increase in the population of the area. Graphical analysis helps understand how gambling has affected the use of land and agrochemicals in Minnesota agriculture.

If the price of land ($P_1$) increases, the price ratio increases, and the isocost line becomes steeper. To produce the same amount of agricultural output or to remain on the same isoquant, the producers in the area must use more chemicals to replace the land that has been lost.

## 5.6.3 Relative prices rule!

Relative prices determine the optimal level of output (Chapter 3), the optimal level of inputs to use (Chapter 4), and the cost-minimizing combination of inputs to use (Chapter 5). Chapter 6 will show how relative prices also determine the most profitable combination of outputs to produce. Relative prices run the entire market-based economy since the decisions of business firms are all determined by the relative prices of scarce resources. Relative prices reflect consumer preferences, so the best decisions in food and agriculture will be consumer centered.

## 5.7 Chapter 5 Summary

1  A firm will select inputs based on relative prices.
2  There are many different combinations of inputs that can produce the same level of output.

3  An isoquant is a line that represents all combinations of two variable inputs that will produce a given level of output.
4  Different nations use drastically different production practices based on relative prices.
5  When labor is cheap relative to capital, a labor-intensive production practice will be used.
6  Agribusiness firms will choose combinations of inputs that minimize their costs of production.
7  Perfect substitutes are inputs that can be interchanged completely. The isoquant for perfect substitutes is a straight line.
8  Perfect complements are inputs that must be used together in a fixed ratio. The isoquant for perfect complements has an "L" shape.
9  Imperfect substitutes are inputs that substitute for each other incompletely. The isoquant for imperfect substitutes is convex to the origin.
10  The marginal rate of substitution (MRTS) is the rate one input can be decreased as the use of another input increases. The MRTS is the slope of the isoquant.
11  The isocost line indicates all combinations of two variable inputs that can be purchased at the same level of expenditure.
12  To find the optimal combination of inputs, the firm will locate at the point where the isoquant is tangent to the isocost line. At this point, the marginal rate of technical substitution equals the relative price ratio.
13  An equilibrium is a point from which there is no tendency to change.
14  Changes in relative prices result in shifts in the isocost line and changes in the equilibrium combination of inputs. Firms will substitute out of relatively expensive inputs and into relatively less expensive inputs.
15  Relative prices rule: relative prices determine the optimal level of output, the optimal level of inputs, and the cost-minimizing combination of inputs to use.

## 5.8   Chapter 5 Glossary

**Equilibrium**—A point or situation from which there is no tendency to change.
**Imperfect Substitutes**—Inputs that are incomplete substitutes for each other in the production process.
**Isocost Line**—A line indicating all combinations of two variable inputs that can be purchased for a given, or same, level of expenditure.
**Isoquant**—A line indicating all combinations of two variable inputs that will produce a given level of output.
**Marginal Rate of Technical Substitution (MRTS)**—The rate at which one input can be decreased as the use of another input increases to take its place. The slope of the isoquant. MRTS = $\Delta X_2 / \Delta X_1$.
**Perfect Complements**—Inputs that must be used together in a fixed ratio. They operate in fixed proportions in the production process.
**Perfect Substitutes**—Inputs that are completely substitutable in the production process.
**Relative Prices**—The prices of goods relative to prices of other goods (see **Absolute Price**).

## 5.9 Chapter 5 Review questions

1 To draw an isoquant, the graph must show

   a  one input on each axis
   b  one input and one output
   c  one output on each axis
   d  cost of production on the vertical axis

2 Each point on the isoquant shows the same level of:

   a  output
   b  profit
   c  inputs
   d  expenditures

3 Relative prices are captured in the

   a  equilibrium point
   b  isoquant
   c  isocost line
   d  vertical axis

4 The optimal combination of inputs depends on

   a  land grant university recommendations
   b  tradition
   c  resource availability
   d  relative prices

5 In the wide open spaces of the American West, farms are likely to be

   a  larger than in the Eastern US
   b  smaller than in the Eastern US
   c  the same size as in the Eastern US

   d  cannot determine from the information given

6 Sugar and high-fructose corn syrup (HFCS) are

   a  perfect substitutes
   b  perfect complements
   c  imperfect complements
   d  imperfect substitutes

7 A pen and a pencil are

   a  substitutes
   b  complements
   c  unrelated
   d  irreplaceable

8 Capital and labor are

   a  perfect complements
   b  perfect substitutes
   c  imperfect substitutes
   d  unrelated

9 If the price of the input on the x-axis decreases, then the slope of the isocost line will:

   a  become steeper
   b  become less steep
   c  shift out parallel
   d  shift in parallel

10 Labor-intensive agricultural production practices are most likely to occur in:

   a  Florida
   b  Kansas
   c  Texas
   d  sub-Saharan Africa

**Answers:** 1. a, 2. a, 3. c, 4. d, 5. a, 6. a, 7. a, 8. c, 9. b, 10. d

For more study questions, flash cards, and study guides, see the online materials at the companion website: www.routledge.com/cw/barkley.

# Optimal output selection

Photo 6.1  Optimal output selection

*Source:* Jim Parkin/Shutterstock

DOI: 10.4324/9781003367994-6

## Abstract

This chapter covers the intuition behind profit maximization and how this intuition can be used to improve both personal and professional decision-making. Emphasis is on economic decision-making, or comparing costs against benefits in all choices. The concepts discussed here include how an agribusiness firm selects outputs under continuously changing prices. The production possibilities frontier is defined and explained, as is the marginal rate of product substitution, and the isorevenue lines are used to find the optimal combination of outputs. The chapter concludes with a brief review of profit-maximization rules for input use, outputs, and input combination.

### Chapter 6 Questions

1   What is economic decision-making?
2   How can comparing benefits and costs be used to improve business, career, and personal choices?
3   How do agribusiness firms select outputs?
4   How do output decisions change when relative prices change?
5   What is the production possibilities frontier (PPF), and how does it clarify economic choices?
6   What is the marginal rate of product substitution (MRPS), and how is it used to select optimal output combinations?
7   What is an isorevenue line, and how is it used?
8   How can profit maximization be summarized for input use, outputs, and input combinations?

## 6.0   Introduction

Agriculture and the agricultural economy are changing rapidly as new technologies such as no-till crop production, global positioning systems (GPS), sophisticated machinery, and bio-technology have been introduced and adopted by agricultural producers. With this constant change, producers must spend great amounts of time searching for the commodities that are best for their available resources. Agricultural producers and agribusinesses must be prepared to deal with rapid and large changes in relative prices. In the Midwestern Corn Belt states, large increases in corn and soybean production followed the biofuel-driven increases in the prices of these two crops during the period 2008–2013. Commodity prices later fell dramatically, causing large declines in profitability in the global grain industry.

Agribusinesses are also changing. As mergers and consolidations take place, large agribusiness corporations shift into new product lines and sometimes abandon old ones. On farms and in factories, the decisions about which products to produce are made using a combination of technical and economic information. This chapter is devoted to understanding how firms, farm and nonfarm, make decisions about which outputs to produce and sell.

# 6.1 The production possibilities frontier (PPF)

Most firms can produce more than one output. Farm managers worldwide often must choose between several competing crops: wheat, corn, milo, soybeans, and hay. Animals, primarily beef, hogs, and chickens, are also alternative sources of income on some farms. Packing plants have numerous outputs that could be produced, depending on the relative profitability of each product. They could grind all of their meat into hamburger or slice it into steaks. Most business firms that are able to produce any of several outputs require some guidance when making final decisions regarding which products bring the most economic benefit to the firm.

Relative prices continue as important variables in economic decisions. Other important variables include diversification and risk minimization. Firms and businesses will often make production choices based on reducing their exposure to risk or relying too heavily on a single product. These need to be mentioned even though the main focus continues to be relative prices.

A **production possibilities frontier (PPF)** describes a firm's possible combinations of outputs.

● *Production Possibilities Frontier [PPF]* = a curve depicting all possible combinations of two outputs that can be produced using a constant level of inputs.

A farmer-stockman in the northern Great Plains provides an example of how managers make decisions regarding the optimal combination of outputs. Suppose farmer-stockmen can allocate their resources to the production of two outputs: wheat ($Y_1$) or cattle ($Y_2$). The production function, or the technical relationship between inputs (X) and outputs (Y), is adaptable to include multiple outputs:

6.1   $Y_1, Y_2 = f(|X_1, X_2, X_3 \ldots X_N)$.

Here, all inputs are held fixed and are used to produce two outputs: $Y_1$ (wheat) and $Y_2$ (cattle). The firm under consideration has fixed resources (K, L, A, and M). Variables listed to the right of the vertical line in equation 6.1 indicate that these variables are available in fixed quantities, "holding all else constant," or *ceteris paribus*.

> QUICK QUIZ 6.1
>
> What are the four inputs K, L, A, and M? Name the four items that comprise capital.

The firm depicted in Figure 6.1 allocates these resources between the two outputs: raising cattle ($Y_2$) or growing wheat ($Y_1$). If the decision-maker allocates all of the resources to cattle, then the firm produces all cattle and no wheat. If all of the resources go to wheat, the firm produces all wheat and no cattle. The firm can also select an intermediate point where some resources are devoted to each

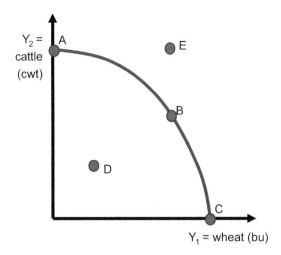

of the two possible products. Figure 6.1 shows all of the possible combinations of outputs produced with a fixed level of inputs. The units for cattle are measured in hundredweight (cwt is the abbreviation of hundredweight, or 100 pounds), and the units for wheat are bushels (bu).

Point A represents complete specialization in beef, and point C shows output when all productive resources are committed to wheat. Point B represents a situation that divides resource use between cattle and wheat production. Point D is attainable by the firm, but such a combination of products is irrational because it does not make use of all available resources. Points inside (below) the PPF are physically possible to achieve but can be improved upon by selecting combinations of wheat and cattle located on the PPF. Point E is not physically attainable, given the fixed level of resource use, as it lies outside of the PPF.

### 6.1.1   The shape of the PPF

The law of diminishing marginal returns causes the PPF to be concave to the origin (bowed out). The reason is that the first unit of input used for either beef or wheat is the most productive. Adding more units of inputs causes the productivity level to decrease.

Specialization of a firm's resources into what it does best allows the firm to use its best grazing acres to produce cattle and the best farmland to produce wheat. The PPF is concave to the origin because specialization allows the inputs to move to their most productive use. If the resources were not specialized, the PPF would be a straight line since output could not be increased by specialization. Finding the profit-maximizing combination of output requires use of information contained in the PPF and information on the economic value of the two outputs (relative prices).

If the level of inputs changes or technological change occurs, the PPF will shift. For example, if the farmer-stockman increased the number of acres in the farm, then the PPF would shift out and to the right, as shown in Figure 6.2. Technological change may also result in an outward shift of the PPF since it is a change in the relationship between inputs and outputs. Technological change results in more output produced with the same level of inputs.

Technological change in both cattle production and wheat production results in an outward shift in the PPF (Figure 6.2).

A shift in the PPF will also occur if technological change affects only one output. If a new variety of wheat comes from university wheat breeding programs, the PPF will shift out for wheat but remain in place for cattle, as shown in Figure 6.3.

With this type of technological change, the y-intercept remains the same, because if all of the firm's resources are devoted to the production of cattle, the total quantity produced will remain the same. If the resources are all devoted to wheat, however, more bushels of output will result from the same level of inputs. The technical change favors wheat, and the PPF shifts to the right. The firm will be able to produce more of

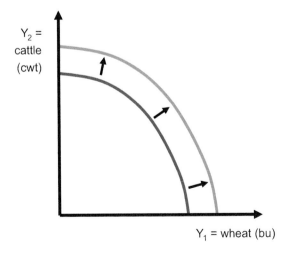

Figure 6.2 **The impact of technological change on the production possibilities frontier**

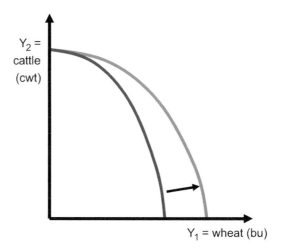

**Figure 6.3** Technology change on one output of the production possibilities frontier

both outputs since resources previously devoted to wheat will now become available for beef production. But how does the firm select the optimal, or profit-maximizing, combination of outputs? The rate of change in the PPF provides the key.

## 6.2   The marginal rate of product substitution (MRPS)

The slope of the PPF at any point reveals the rate of substitution between the two outputs at that point. This rate is the **marginal rate of product substitution (MRPS)**. It represents the decrease in one output $(Y_1)$ that must occur if the other output $(Y_2)$ is to increase.

### QUICK QUIZ 6.4

Why must one output decrease if the other increases?

- *Marginal Rate of Product Substitution [MRPS]* = the rate at which one output must decrease as production of another output is increased. The slope of the production possibilities frontier (PPF) defines the MRPS: MRPS = $\Delta Y_2 / \Delta Y_1$.

The slope of production possibilities frontier at any point is the change (reduction) in cattle production required by the desired change (increase) in wheat production at that point. The slope of a function is the "rise over the run," or $\Delta Y_2 / \Delta Y_1$. The MRPS represents the physical trade-off that the farmer-stockman must make when determining the optimal allocation of inputs between the two products.

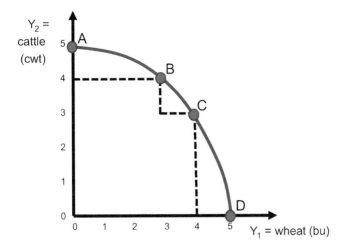

Figure 6.4 Production possibilities frontier for a
farmer-stockman

Figure 6.4 extends the study of the concave-shaped PPF by calculating the MRPS at different points along the PPF for cattle and wheat. The rate of substitution between outputs (MRPS) changes with movement along the PPF. When the PPF is concave to the origin, the MRPS is increasing in magnitude from left to right. Start at point A, the point of complete specialization in cattle. At this point, the resources available for cattle production yield 5 hundredweight (cwt) of cattle but no wheat. If the firm takes enough resources from cattle production to reduce cattle output by one unit (from 5 to 4 cwt), cattle resources switch to wheat production. Figure 6.4 shows that resources taken from cattle production will yield three bushels if used for wheat. The MRPS, or the slope of the PPF, measures this movement out of cattle and into wheat:

6.2  $\text{MRPS(AB)} = \Delta Y_2 / \Delta Y_1 = (4 - 5) / (3 - 0) = -1/3.$

The first inputs used in wheat production are the most productive. As the firm adds more inputs, productivity per unit of added resource declines. As cattle production is reduced one more unit from four bushels to three bushels, wheat production increases, but not as much as it did between points A and B. Using the MRPS as a measure, the move from A to B shows the following:

6.3  $\text{MRPS(BC)} = \Delta Y_2 / \Delta Y_1 = (3 - 4) / (4 - 3) = -1.$

The absolute value of the MRPS has increased from one-third to one, reflecting decreasing returns. As the firm continues to switch resources from cattle to wheat, the productivity continues to decline:

6.4  $\text{MRPS(CD)} = \Delta Y_2 / \Delta Y_1 = (0 - 3) / (5 - 4) = -3.$

The MRPS increases when the production functions are subject to decreasing returns. In all economic situations, inputs will be subject to decreasing returns, resulting in a PPF that is concave to the origin. Remember, though, that the PPF derives from the production functions of the two outputs. The shape of the PPF and its slope (MRPS) depend on the production function, or the physical relationship between inputs and outputs [Y = f(X)]. With the physical production possibilities in place and understood, attention turns to the economic relationships that determine the profit-maximizing combination of outputs.

## 6.3   The isorevenue line

To complete the firm's search for the profit-maximizing combination of outputs requires combining the physical production information shown by the PPF with the economic information relating to the relative prices of $Y_1$ and $Y_2$. Market price information allows a firm to select the optimal combination of output. Relative prices provide the firm with information about the value of producing a good or a combination of goods. In the farmer-stockman example, the firm is interested in allocating inputs between cattle and wheat: how many cattle to raise and how much wheat to grow. The firm can determine this by looking at the revenue earned from the production and sale of beef and grain. An isorevenue line provides the revenue information in the same way that the isocost line helped with cost information in Chapter 5.

● **Isorevenue Line** = a line showing all combinations of two outputs that will generate a constant level of total revenue.

An isorevenue line for the farmer-stockman can be graphed using assumptions about the price of wheat [($P_1$) is USD 5/bu] and the price of cattle [($P_2$) is USD 100/cwt]. Recall the definition of total revenue (TR):

6.5   $TR = P_1Y_1 + P_2Y_2$,
6.6   $TR = 5 * Y_1 + 100 * Y_2$.

To illustrate a specific isorevenue line, let TR = USD 500. Figure 6.5 shows an isorevenue line. As in the case of the isocost line, there are an infinite number of isorevenue lines: one for each dollar value of total revenue. The isorevenue line is shown using mathematics to find the profit-maximizing level of output. The algebraic equation (y = b + mx) for the isorevenue line derives from the definition of total revenue:

6.7   $TR = P_1Y_1 + P_2Y_2$,
6.8   $P_2Y_2 = TR - P_1Y_1$,
6.9   $Y_2 = TR / P_2 + (-P_1 / P_2) * Y_1$.

Equation 6.9 shows that the y-intercept is equal to TR / $P_2$. The y-intercept of an isorevenue line is the situation where all of the revenue comes from the good on the y-axis (cattle in Figure 6.5). In this situation, no wheat is sold, so $Y_1$ = 0, and

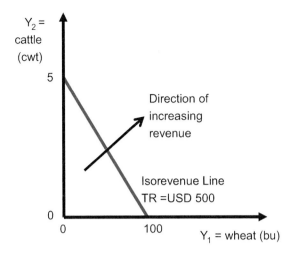

**Figure 6.5 Isorevenue line for a farmer-stockman**

$TR = P_2 Y_2$. Given this, it can be shown that the quantity of cattle sold is $Y_2 = TR / P_2$. The slope of the isorevenue line represents relative prices and is equal to the price ratio $(-P_1 / P_2)$. The slope of the isorevenue line contains all of the economic information that the firm needs to choose the profit-maximizing level of input.

> **QUICK QUIZ 6.5**
>
> The derivation of the equation of the isorevenue line is similar to the derivation for the isocost line. Derive the algebraic equation for the isocost line.

To complete the firm's search for the profit-maximizing combination of goods requires combining the physical production information in the PPF with the economic information in the relative prices.

## 6.4   The optimal output combination

To maximize profits, the firm will want to reach the highest isorevenue line possible, consistent with the technical information from the PPF and the relative price information summarized in the isorevenue line. Since higher levels of revenue appear on lines to the northeast, the profit-maximizing firm will locate on the isorevenue line that is tangent to the PPF, represented by point E in Figure 6.6.

This point of tangency shows where the slope of the PPF (the MRPS) is equal to the slope of the isorevenue line (the price ratio). Point E is an equilibrium point for the firm—the firm can do no better than point E given current prices and the current stage of technology.

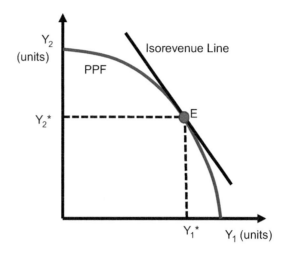

Figure 6.6 Optimal output combination

Why is point E an equilibrium point for the firm?

The profit-maximizing rule for optimal output selection is to set the MRPS equal to the slope of the isorevenue line, or the output price ratio:

6.10 MRPS = slope of isorevenue line,
6.11 $\Delta Y_2 / \Delta Y_1 = -P_1 / P_2$,
6.12 $\Delta Y_2 * P_2 = -\Delta Y_1 * P_1$.

This is a familiar result. The firm's manager should shift resources toward the output with the highest revenue. Intuition alone is sufficient to indicate that the firm loses its hold on equilibrium as soon as it moves away from this point. The strategy to maximize profits is to employ resources in the output that generates the highest returns.

If $\Delta Y_2 * P_2 > -\Delta Y_1 * P_1$, then the firm should move out of $Y_1$ and into $Y_2$, and

if $\Delta Y_2 * P_2 < -\Delta Y_1 * P_1$, then the firm should move out of $Y_2$ and into $Y_1$.

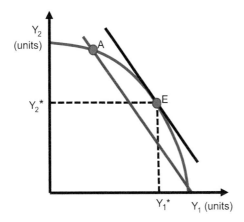

**Figure 6.7** Locating the profit-maximizing point

The graph in Figure 6.7 demonstrates this situation. Point A is a feasible point of production since it lies on the PPF. However, the point is not a profit-maximizing point for the firm since higher revenue is available at point E. To see this, note that at point A, the slope of the isorevenue line is steeper than the slope of the PPF (the MRPS). The following relationship holds at point A:

6.13    $MRPS(A) <$ the price ratio,

6.14    $\Delta Y_2 / \Delta Y_1 < -P_1 / P_2$,

6.15    $\Delta Y_2 * P_2 < -\Delta Y_1 * P_1$.

The profitable strategy for this firm is to reduce the inputs devoted to $Y_2$ and shift them to the production of $Y_1$. At point A, the revenue associated with good $Y_1$ is higher than the revenue earned from the production and sale of $Y_2$.

The firm will shift resources out of $Y_2$ and into $Y_1$ until it reaches the equilibrium point E. At E, the firm cannot earn higher revenue from the production of the two goods: E is an optimal, profit-maximizing point. If the price of one output changes, the price ratio will shift, and the isorevenue lines will have a different slope. The firm will then shift resources between outputs until it reaches the new equilibrium.

## 6.5    Price changes and the optimal output combination

Relative prices allocate resources in a market economy.

During the period 2008–2013, the price of corn increased relative to the price of other grains. This caused a major shift of agricultural land use in the United States. Land moved out of wheat, soybeans, milo, and cotton production and into the production of corn. The PPF in Figure 6.8 shows how grain producers shifted resources from wheat to corn in response to the change in relative prices.

At point A, grain farmers produce $Y_1^*$ bushels of wheat and $Y_2^*$ bushels of corn. The initial prices of wheat ($P_1$) and corn ($P_2$) define the slope of the isorevenue line ($-P_1 / P_2$). When the relative price of corn increases, the denominator of the price ratio increases, resulting in a decrease in the slope of the isorevenue line. Point A becomes less profitable after the price change.

Grain producers relocate to point B in Figure 6.8 by shifting resources out of wheat and into corn. During the period 2008–2013, biofuels caused this to happen. Corn and soybean acres were at an all-time high, and there was a reduction in acres planted to wheat. Economic theory did an excellent job of explaining this shift in the outputs in many grain-producing areas.

**Photo 6.2 Corn and ethanol**

*Source:* Jim Barber/Shutterstock

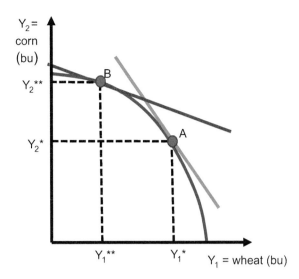

Figure 6.8 Locating the profit-maximizing point between wheat and corn

## Biofuels

A biofuel is a type of fuel whose energy is derived from biological carbon fixation. Biofuels have become increasingly popular in recent years because of higher oil prices, the desire for energy independence, concern over greenhouse gas emissions from fossil fuels, and support from government subsidies.

Bioethanol is an alcohol made by fermentation, mostly from carbohydrates produced in sugar or starch crops such as corn or sugarcane. Cellulosic biomass, derived from nonfood sources such as trees and grasses, is also being developed as a source for ethanol production. In its pure form, ethanol can be used as a fuel for vehicles, but it is usually used as a gasoline additive to increase octane and reduce the volume of harmful vehicle emissions. Bioethanol is widely used in the US and in Brazil.

Biodiesel is made from vegetable oils and animal fats. Biodiesel in its pure form can be used as a fuel for vehicles, but it is usually used as a diesel additive to reduce levels of particulates, carbon monoxide, and hydrocarbons emitted into the atmosphere by diesel-powered vehicles. Biodiesel is produced from oils or fats and is the most common biofuel in Europe.

The US production of ethanol and biodiesel has grown significantly in recent years as consumers have shifted away from fossil fuels to alternative energy and fuel sources. The future of the biofuel industry is difficult to predict since the industry depends on (1) oil prices; (2) government policies, including subsidies to biofuel producers, fuel regulations, and environmental regulations; and (3) corn prices. Since both oil and corn are globally produced and traded, forecasting future biofuel prices and returns is difficult.

Biofuels have become an important strategy for enhancing farm income through the large demand for fuels. Recent research has favorably evaluated higher rates of blending ethanol with gasoline (Farrell et al. 2018).

*Sources:* Demirbas, A. (2009). "Political, economic and environmental impacts of biofuels: A review." *Applied Energy* 86: S108–S117. Retrieved January 4, 2023.

Farrell, John, John Holladay, and Robert Wagner. (2018). "Fuel blendstocks with the potential to optimize future gasoline engine performance: Identification of five chemical families for detailed evaluation." Technical Report. U.S. Department of Energy, Washington, DC. DOE/GO-102018–4970. Retrieved January 4, 2023.

Irwin, Scott. (2015). "2014 really was an amazing year for ethanol production profits." FarmDocDaily. University of Illinois at Urbana-Champaign. March 5, 2015. Retrieved January 4, 2023.

BOX 6.2

## Biofuels: The impact of fuel prices on agriculture

Historians estimate that agriculture has been practiced for over 9,000 years. For thousands of years, food and fiber was produced using manual labor, later replaced by animal power: horses, mules, and oxen. At about 1900, agriculture was revolutionized by the introduction of gasoline powered equipment. As farmers adopted mechanization, agriculture became dependent on petroleum products: gasoline, diesel, and oil. Modern agriculture was initiated with the introduction of agricultural chemicals and synthetic fertilizers after World War II. Most pesticides, herbicides, and fungicides are derived from petroleum products, and nitrogen fertilizer is produced from natural gas. These purchased inputs were widely adopted, leading to enormously increased food production, and hunger and malnutrition decreased drastically. Since 1950, modern agricultural production practices depend heavily on fuel to produce and distribute food and fiber. When oil prices increase, production costs increase. During 2022, the conflict in Ukraine resulted in large increases in fuel prices: USDA estimated that the cost of fuel, labor, and electricity increased 34 percent during the invasion.

Biofuels were developed as a substitute for petroleum products due to high oil prices during the 1980s. Biofuels can be produced with any biomass, but in the United States, corn, sorghum, and soybeans are the major inputs. As the demand for biofuels increased during the 1980s and 1990s, the prices of these crops increased relative to other crops. Farmers shifted acreage out of other crops and into biofuel crops, and profitability increased. The growth of biofuels during 2008–2013 created high returns to agricultural production, but was dependent on high oil prices. When oil prices decreased in the 2010s, biofuel prices followed, reducing agricultural output prices and profitability.

These trends have resulted in two major impacts of fuel prices on agriculture: increasing both revenues through biofuel demand and costs through fuel prices. It is difficult to generalize the net overall effect of oil price changes on agriculture. Gains and losses vary depending on which outputs are produced and the level of fuel, chemical, and fertilizer use for each farm or ranch.

*Sources:* American Farm Bureau. "High Fuel Prices Squeeze Farms and Ranches." June 28, 2023. www.fb.org/newsroom/high-fuel-prices-squeeze-farms-and-ranches. Retrieved January 4, 2023.

## 6.6 Review of profit-maximization rules

The first six chapters of this book have outlined profit-maximizing and cost-minimizing rules for the optimal use of inputs and the optimal combinations of outputs. There is a striking symmetry between the profit-maximizing and cost-minimizing rules developed for use by a business firm. This brief section reviews the profit-maximizing rules for:

1   The optimal level of input use (Chapter 4),
2   The optimal level of output (Chapter 4),
3   The optimal input combination (Chapter 5),
4   The optimal output combination (Chapter 6).

### 6.6.1  Rule for optimal input use

To maximize profits by selecting the proper level of input use, set the marginal benefits (the marginal revenue product = MRP) equal to the marginal costs (the marginal factor cost = MFC). Recall the definitions: MRP = MPP * $P_Y$, and MPP = $\Delta Y / \Delta X$.

6.16  MRP = MFC,
6.17  MPP * $P_Y = P_X$,
6.18  $(\Delta Y / \Delta X) * P_Y = P_X$,
6.19  $\Delta Y * P_Y = \Delta X * P_X$.

The profit-maximizing rule states that the firm manager should continue to use an input until the additional benefits of using the input to produce and sell a good ($\Delta Y * P_Y$) are equal to the additional costs of employing the unit of input ($\Delta X * P_X$).

### 6.6.2  Rule for optimal output production

To maximize profits by selecting the level of output, set the marginal benefits (the marginal revenue = MR) equal to the marginal costs (= MC). Next, recall the definitions: MC = $\Delta TC / \Delta Y$, and MR = $P_Y$, assuming a competitive industry. For a firm with a single input, total costs are the input price times the quantity of input utilized (TC = $P_X * X$).

6.20  MR = MC,
6.21  $P_Y = \Delta TC / \Delta Y$,
6.22  $P_Y = \Delta(P_X * X) / \Delta Y$,
6.23  $\Delta Y * P_Y = \Delta X * P_X$.

The profit-maximizing rule states that the firm manager should increase output until the additional benefits of production ($\Delta Y * P_Y$) are equal to the additional costs of producing one more unit of output ($\Delta X * P_X$). Compare this result with that for the optimal level of input rule.

### 6.6.3  Rule for optimal input combination

To minimize costs by selecting the optimal combination of inputs, the firm manager will set the slope of the isoquant (MRTS) equal to the slope of the isocost line (the price ratio). Recall the definition: MRTS = $\Delta X_2 / \Delta X_1$.

6.24  MRTS = slope of isocost line,
6.25  MRTS= $-P_1 / P_2$,
6.26  $\Delta X_2 / \Delta X_1 = -P_1 / P_2$,
6.27  $-\Delta X_2 * P_2 = \Delta X_1 * P_1$.

The cost-minimizing rule states that the firm manager should purchase inputs until the additional expenditures on each input are equal.

### 6.6.4   Rule for optimal output combination

To maximize profits by selecting the optimal combination of outputs, the firm manager will set the slope of the production possibilities frontier (MRPS) equal to the slope of the isorevenue line (the price ratio). Next, recall the definition: $MRPS = \Delta X_2 / \Delta X_1$.

6.28    $MRPS$ = slope of isorevenue line,
6.29    $MRPS = -P_1 / P_2$,
6.30    $\Delta Y_2 / \Delta Y_1 = -P_1 / P_2$,
6.31    $-\Delta Y_2 * P_2 = \Delta Y_1 * P_1$.

The profit-maximizing rule states that the firm manager should produce output until the additional revenue from each output are equal.

### 6.6.5   Thinking like an economist

Relative prices drive all economic decision-making: firms determine what to produce, how to produce, and what quantity to produce based on relative prices. The main idea behind thinking like an economist is to weigh the benefits and costs of every activity. If the benefits outweigh the costs, then the activity should be undertaken. This holds true for all aspects of production, as shown in Chapters 2 through 6. The next chapter shifts the focus from producers to consumers. Consumers make economic choices in much the same way that producers do: a consumer will buy a good if the benefits outweigh the costs.

## 6.7   Chapter 6 Summary

1   The production possibilities frontier (PPF) is a curve that represents all combinations of two outputs produced with a constant level of inputs.
2   The PPF is concave to the origin due to the law of diminishing returns.
3   Technological change results in an outward shift in the PPF.
4   The marginal rate of product substitution (MRPS) is the rate of decrease required in one output in order for the output of another product to be increased. It is also the slope of the PPF.
5   An isorevenue line depicts all combinations of the two outputs that generate a constant level of total revenue.
6   To find the revenue-maximizing combination of outputs, a firm will reach the highest isorevenue line possible by locating at the tangency between the PPF and the isorevenue line.
7   Relative price changes result in shifts in the isorevenue line and a reallocation of resources.

## 6.8   Chapter 6 Glossary

**Isorevenue Line**—A line depicting all combinations of two outputs that will generate a constant level of total revenue.

**Marginal Rate of Product Substitution [MRPS]**—The rate at which one output must decrease as production of another output is increased. The slope of the production possibilities frontier (PPF) defines the MRPS: MRPS = $\Delta Y_2 / \Delta Y_1$.

**Production Possibilities Frontier [PPF]**—A curve depicting all possible combinations of two outputs that can be produced using a constant level of inputs.

## 6.9 Chapter 6 Review questions

1   The production possibilities frontier shows

   a   all combinations of two inputs that can produce a constant level of output
   b   all combinations of two outputs that can be produced with a constant level of inputs
   c   all levels of one output that can be produced with varying levels of inputs
   d   an isoquant

2   A point located inside the PPF is

   a   efficient and attainable
   b   efficient but not attainable
   c   not efficient but attainable
   d   neither efficient nor attainable

3   A point located outside of the PPF is

   a   efficient and attainable
   b   efficient but not attainable
   c   not efficient but attainable
   d   neither efficient nor attainable

4   The marginal rate of product substitution refers to

   a   the physical trade-off between inputs
   b   the physical trade-off between outputs
   c   the economic trade-off between inputs
   d   the economic trade-off between outputs

5   The MRPS is

   a   constant along the PPF
   b   increasing in absolute value along the PPF
   c   decreasing in absolute value along the PPF
   d   increasing or decreasing, depending on if there is increasing or decreasing returns

6   The slope of the PPF is due to

   a   the isoquant
   b   relative prices
   c   the production functions of the two outputs
   d   the cost of inputs

7   The isorevenue line is derived from

   a   the isoquant
   b   relative prices
   c   the production functions of the two outputs
   d   the cost of inputs

8   The profit-maximizing combination of outputs can be found at the tangency of

   a   the PPF and the isorevenue line
   b   the PPF and the isocost line
   c   the isocost and isoquant lines
   d   the isoquant and isorevenue lines

**Answers:** 1. b, 2. c, 3. b, 4. b, 5. b, 6. c, 7. b, 8. a

For more study questions, flash cards, and study guides, see the online materials at the companion website: www.routledge.com/cw/barkley.

# Chapter 7

## Consumer choices

**Photo 7.1** Consumer choices

*Source:* studio online/Shutterstock

DOI: 10.4324/9781003367994-7

## Abstract

In a market economy, consumers are the driving force behind all production decisions since successful business firms "give consumers what they want." This chapter enhances the understanding of how consumers decide what to purchase. Economists consider consumers to be rational, or purposeful and consistent. This assumption allows economists to predict and explain consumer choices. In particular, economists are able to make strong predictions about how consumers respond to changes in income and relative prices. The law of diminishing marginal utility explains why consumers prefer variety. Real-world examples include meat consumption in the US and China and the diamond-water paradox.

### Chapter 7 Questions

1   Why are consumers the source of all profits in a free market economy?
2   Why do successful firms give consumers what they want?
3   How do consumers decide what to buy?
4   Why are consumers considered rational and consistent?
5   How do consumers respond to changes in income and relative prices?
6   What is the law of diminishing marginal utility, and how does it affect consumers?
7   Why do consumers prefer a variety of goods?
8   What is the diamond-water paradox, and why is it useful?

## 7.0   Introduction

The circular flow diagram in Chapter 1 summarized an economy composed of two groups: producers and consumers. Chapters 2 through 6 explained the profit-maximizing behavior of producers. This chapter answers the question: what role do consumers play in a market economy? Consumers spend their incomes on the goods and services produced by firms. In a market economy, consumers are the driving forces behind all production decisions since producers will give consumers what they want by responding to relative prices. This chapter explains the behavior of consumers, and the following chapters explain the interactions between producers and consumers in domestic and international markets. The lessons begin with a study of rational behavior: the consumers' counterpart of profit maximization.

## 7.1   Rational behavior

Economic logic assumes that all human behavior is purposeful and consistent. The term "**rational behavior**" in economics is different from the dictionary definition of the term. The dictionary definition states that an individual's rational behavior is "fully competent, or sane." In economics, rational means that individuals do the best they can, given the constraints they face.

●   *Rational Behavior* = individuals do the best that they can, given the constraints they face. Rational behavior is purposeful and consistent.

Suppose that students seeking a good grade were to skip class in order to play a video game. Is this rational? It would be hard to claim this as "rational," using the dictionary definition of the word since it is counter to the students' objective to perform well. However, according to the economic definition, this behavior would be rational if the benefits of the activity outweighed the costs. Any behavior is considered rational as long as its benefits outweigh its costs.

Another way to think about rational behavior is to imagine that individuals do the best they can, given the constraints that they face. Consumers maximize their own happiness given a budget. For example, a college professor gets a paycheck twice a month and uses the income to purchase food, clothes, housing, water, electricity, toothpaste, etc., as long as each purchase adds to her satisfaction. In this way, consumers maximize their satisfaction given a budget constraint. Notice the similarities with how economists describe producer behavior: producers maximize profits given input and output prices, as well as technology. Casting the consumers' problems in the same terms, all individuals (consumers) do the best they can by maximizing satisfaction, given the constraints that they face: income and prices.

The study of consumer behavior begins with consumers who have preferences for some goods over others. Examples are everywhere. Which is preferred:

- Pizza or cheeseburgers?
- Wranglers or Levi's?
- McDonald's or Burger King?
- Hamburgers or sushi?
- White bread or wheat bread?
- House in the country or high-rise apartment?
- Mercedes or Kia?
- Fur stole or wool coat?
- Small liberal arts college or large state university?

## BOX 7.1

### Behavioral economics

Economics as a social science assumes that all economic decision-making is "rational." Behavioral economics integrates irrational, emotional, and psychological aspects into models of decision-making and market outcomes. This approach allows for human behavior to be subject to emotion, error, poor judgment, inconsistency, and lack of knowledge. Behavioral models of individual and institutional behavior typically include insights from psychology into economic models.

This tradition has a long history, including Adam Smith's 1759 work, *The Theory of Moral Sentiments*, which included psychological explanations of individual behavior and the nature of morality and ethics. Behavioral economics highlights the use of heuristics, or simple rules of thumb, in decision-making, rather than strict logic. The field also emphasizes how decision-makers "frame" their choices based on past experience and emotion. The behavioral approach also emphasizes inefficiencies and anomalies that arise from nonrational behavior.

Behavioral economics has been controversial since some behavioral economists focus on the divergence between the rational assumption of standard economics and the nonrational assumptions of the behavioral approach. However, social scientists are in search of the truth, and the insights from the behavioral approach can advance understanding of individual decision-making and market outcomes. Simplifying assumptions in science are not meant to be factual but rather a method of organizing thoughts about the complex real world. The objective of science is to explain and predict. If a new model or new approach can make better, more useful explanations and predictions, then it will be adopted and integrated into a field such as economics.

*Source:* Simon, H.A. (1987) "Behavioral Economics." The New Palgrave Dictionary of Economics Palgrave McMillan, London (2023). Retrieved January 4, 2023.

Consumer choices about what goods to buy depend on preferences and the relative prices of goods and services. The benefits of consuming a good come from the satisfaction that comes from consuming it. The costs of consuming a good are the total monetary and non-monetary costs of obtaining the good: the price plus such things as the time costs associated with the purchase of the good (having to drive to Walmart, locate the good, and then stand in line to pay for it, etc.). A consumer will purchase a good if the benefits, or the gains in satisfaction, are greater than the costs of obtaining it.

This way of thinking provides simple information for firms that desire to maximize profits. Therefore, manufacturers and merchants rely on consumers so they must always do the following:

- Pay attention to what consumers want since consumer preferences determine what they buy.
- Pay attention to prices since consumer decisions stem from relative prices.

Successful and profitable firms are the ones that do the best job of providing consumers with what they want. The next section relates to the formation of consumer preferences.

## 7.2 Utility

The specialized language of economics makes broad use of the word "utility." It means much more than just usefulness. It takes on a meaning relating to satisfaction, or happiness, or fulfilment. If an object has utility in an economic sense, then it is bringing some kind of reward to its owner or the person who is using it. Food has utility because it keeps people alive. A football game has utility because it entertains the spectators. Social friends have utility because they are there to help or to be helped. In language that is more straightforward:

- *Utility* = satisfaction derived from consuming a good.

Utility is a concept applicable to all goods and services, whether or not they move through markets. Consumers increase their utility by purchasing new CDs, clothes, appendectomies, houses, vacations, or trucks. Utility can also come from nonmarket goods or experiences: babies, singing in a choir, love, gossiping with the neighbor, or watching the sunset. What is it that gives babies, singing, and gossiping the capacity to confer "utility"? The next section is devoted to answering that question.

### 7.2.1 Cardinal and ordinal utility

About 200 years ago, Jeremy Bentham (1748–1833) and a number of other economists struggled to find a way to measure utility. They tried to assign an actual numerical value to the amount of satisfaction that each good or service produced and conferred on its user. These economists developed a hypothetical unit, called a "util," to measure consumers' levels of happiness, or satisfaction.

- *Utils* = hypothetical units of satisfaction derived from consumption of goods or services.

Assigning quantitative measures to levels of satisfaction yields a measure called **cardinal utility**.

- *Cardinal utility* = assigns specific, but hypothetical, numerical values to the level of satisfaction gained from the consumption of a good. The unit of measurement is the hypothetical util.

Recall that cardinal numbers are the simple numbers used for counting: 1, 2, 3 . . . 10, 14, 19, etc. These early economists and other social scientists tried to develop the util as a measure of satisfaction assignable to each good. Their list might include the following:

- Apple = 20 utils,
- Orange = 10 utils,
- Hamburger = 50 utils,
- Beethoven symphony download = 100 utils,
- New clothes = 200 utils,
- New automobile = 40,000 utils.

BOX 7.2

## Obesity

The prevalence of obesity in the US has more than doubled from 13.4 percent of the population in 1960–1962 to 41.9 percent in 2017–2020. The fundamental cause of obesity is not hard to find: an energy imbalance caused by consuming too many calories and not getting enough physical activity to use them. Obesity is a serious public health issue since obesity is related to increased health care costs not only for the individual but for society as well. These costs are large and growing (Finkelstein et al. 2009). The determinants of body weight include genetic makeup, metabolism, behavior, environment, culture, and socioeconomic status. Behavior and environment play a large role. Total calories consumed per person in the US increased from 2,157 in 1979 to 2,700 in 2008 (USDA/ERS 2007). American diets have more meat and grains and less fruits and vegetables than dietary recommendations. Energy-dense calories form sugar and fat are also consumed in quantities greater than the recommended levels. Overweight and obese people spend more time watching television and less time exercising and sports than others in 2007 (US BLS). Fast-food consumption and food purchased away from home also increased over time.

Consumers have inelastic demand for most foods, and nonprice attributes are more important than prices in food choices. Could taxes or subsidies help shift consumers out of sugar and fat and into fruits and vegetables? Recent research suggests that a 10 percent reduction in the prices of fruits and vegetables would increase consumption by 2 to 5 percent in low-income households (Dong and Lin 2009). A 20 percent tax on caloric-sweetened soft drinks, juice drinks, and sports drinks would reduce consumption by 24 percent (Smith, Lin, and Lee 2010). Research also suggests that about 4 percent of all US individuals and families do not have access to healthy food. These individuals and families live in what have begun to be called "food deserts" (USDA/ERS AP-036, 2009). Others have too much access to unhealthy food, called "food swamps," meaning numerous fast-food restaurants but with no healthy alternatives. Obesity is especially concentrated in low-income households.

The causes and consequences of obesity are complicated and difficult to comprehend fully. This is particularly vexing since the underlying cause of obesity is simple: eating more calories than are expended in physical activities. Many commentators and analysts claim that American farm subsidies have contributed significantly to obesity by making fattening foods relatively cheap and abundant. Careful research by Okrent and Alston (2012) demonstrated that the impact of agricultural subsidies on obesity is modest, with negligible effects on the prices paid by consumers for food, and thus negligible influence on dietary patterns and obesity.

*Sources:* Dong, D., & Lin, B. H. (2009). Fruit and vegetable consumption by low-income Americans (Vol. 70). Washington, DC: USDA.

Finkelstein, E. A., Trogdon, J. G., Cohen, J. W., & Dietz, W. (2009). Annual medical spending attributable to obesity: payer-and service-specific estimates. *Health Affairs*, 28(5), w822–w831.

Smith, T. A., Lin, B. H., & Lee, J. Y. (2010). Taxing caloric sweetened beverages: potential effects on beverage consumption, calorie intake, and obesity. *USDA-ERS Economic Research Report No. ERR-100.*, U.S. Department of Agriculture, Economic Research Service, July 2010.

Okrent, A. M., & Alston, J. M. (2012). The effects of farm commodity and retail food policies on obesity and economic welfare in the United States. *American Journal of Agricultural Economics*, 94(3), 611–646.

US. BLS. (2009) National Longitudinal Surveys.

USDA/ERS (2007) National Health and Nutrition Examination Survey (NHANES).

*USDA/ERS (2009) Access to Affordable and Nutritious Food:* Measuring and Understanding Food Deserts and Their Consequences AP-036. Washington DC: USDA, June.

These scientists and scholars soon found that assigning utils was impossible. People cannot assign a meaningful value to the level of satisfaction because the measures of satisfaction differ among individuals and are not observable. Since science requires accurate and measurable observations, the early scholars concluded that they could not use cardinal utility measures to quantify an individual's feelings or level of satisfaction. Once economists and others realized that measuring utility was impossible, they turned attention to **ordinal utility**, or ranking goods in order of preference (A is preferred to B, B is preferred to C, C is preferred to D, etc.). Ordinal utility replaced the earlier concept of cardinal utility.

● *Ordinal Utility* = a way of considering consumer satisfaction in which goods are ranked in order of preference: first, second, third, etc.

Ordinal preferences do not depend on specific numbers or values. Instead, the rankings of goods and services with respect to the satisfaction they provide relative to other goods allow economists to observe consumers and develop principles of human behavior to help understand consumer choices. Cardinal utility continues to provide examples of how consumer behavior works, as shown in the next section.

## 7.2.2   Positive and normative economics

Recall from Chapter 1 that economists do not make value judgments about the utility (satisfaction) that consumers derive from goods. Whatever it is that consumers desire, economists take as factual without bringing their own preferences or opinions to bear on the situation. Economists make no normative statements about what consumers desire to buy.

> ### QUICK QUIZ 7.1
>
> Define, explain, and compare positive and normative economics.

> ### QUICK QUIZ 7.1A
>
> You are an economist assigned to study the price of soybeans. Will you use positive methods or normative methods?

> ### QUICK QUIZ 7.1B
>
> You are an economist assigned to study consumer preferences for soybeans. Will you use positive methods or normative methods?

## 7.2.3   Utility, total utility, and marginal utility

Economists use the term **utility** to refer to the amount of satisfaction that a consumer receives from the consumption of a good. In this use, the utility of a good stems from answers to questions such as, "How much satisfaction (utility) did you get from consuming those strawberries?" **Marginal utility (MU)** is the additional amount of satisfaction gained from consuming one more unit of a good, and **total utility (TU)** is the cumulative satisfaction received from the entire collection of the good or service, in this case, strawberries.

- *Marginal Utility [MU]* = the change in the level of utility when consumption of a good is increased by one unit: $MU = \Delta TU / \Delta Y$.
- *Total Utility [TU]* = the total level of satisfaction derived from consuming a given bundle of goods and services.

Applying these concepts to a hypothetical example of consumer behavior enhances understanding. The example here is drinking bottles of cold water after a long, hot

**Table 7.1** Total and marginal utility derived from drinking cold water on a hot day

| Y = quantity consumed (bottles) | TU = total utility (utils) | MU = marginal utility (utils/bottle) |
|---|---|---|
| 0 | 0 | — |
| 1 | 10 | 10 |
| 2 | 16 | 6 |
| 3 | 19 | 3 |
| 4 | 20 | 1 |
| 5 | 20 | 0 |
| 6 | 18 | −2 |

day of work. In this case, one major prediction regarding consumer behavior is that "first is best." The first unit of a good consumed yields the most satisfaction. The second unit is less satisfying. Additional satisfaction, or utility, comes from each unit consumed, but typically, the amount of satisfaction from each successive bottle of water diminishes.

To demonstrate this idea, consider the relationship between the quantity of a good consumed (Y) and the satisfaction derived from consuming it. Think of picking peaches in California's Sacramento Valley. Suppose that you have worked all day and are hot, tired, and thirsty (picking tree fruits is hard and dirty work most often done in the heat of the summer). The orchard owner brings the picking crew a large cooler filled with bottles of cold drinking water. Table 7.1 summarizes the satisfaction that you receive from drinking the water at the end of the hot day of hard work. Cardinal utility forms the basis for developing a numerical example of how consumers make decisions.

### QUICK QUIZ 7.2

Define and explain the concepts of cardinal and ordinal utility.

### BOX 7.3

## California agriculture

California agriculture is truly amazing. The state has a larger and more diverse farm sector than any of the other states. In 2017, California farms had cash receipts equal to USD 45.1 billion. The state accounted for 12 percent of the nation's agricultural sales. Over 400 different commodities are grown in California, including olives, honey, pecans, pistachios, avocados, Christmas trees, wool, wheat, figs, artichokes, corn, and cotton. The state produces nearly half of US-grown fruits, nuts, and vegetables. Nine of the nation's top ten producing counties are in California. The top five California commodities are (1) milk and cream, (2) grapes, (3) almonds, (4) nursery products, and (5) cattle and calves.

Johnston and McCalla, economists at the University of California at Davis, identified seven major forces driving California agriculture: (1) producers in California serve high-value and emerging markets, mostly distant and foreign; (2) California agriculture is highly dependent on land and water resources; (3) California agriculture is characterized by the absence of water in the right place, providing the incentive to irrigate; (4) California agriculture has always depended on a large supply of agricultural field labor from Asia and the Americas; (5) California agriculture has grown rapidly and almost continuously, although it has been periodically buffeted by natural catastrophes such as floods and droughts, and economic shocks such as the Great Depression, and various recessions; (6) California agriculture requires high levels of management skills—both technical and economic. It has always been dominated by large-scale operations that have grown in complexity and sophistication; and (7) agriculture in California has always been on the technological frontier in developing, modifying, or "borrowing" new technologies, such as large-scale mechanical technology, irrigation equipment, horticulture/plant varieties, pest control, food processing, and wine making.

*Sources:* USDA/NASS Statistics by State, California Ag Statistics, 2019.

US Census Bureau. Census of Agriculture. 2017.

Johnston, Warren E., and Alex F. McCalla. "Whither California Agriculture: Up, Down or Out? Some Thoughts about the Future." Giannini Foundation Special Report 04–1. 2004.

The first bottle of water brings great satisfaction: 10 utils. The second bottle brings additional satisfaction since the total utility increased to 16 utils. However, the additional satisfaction gained from the second bottle is lower: the marginal utility is six additional utils gained from the consumption of the second bottle. This makes perfect sense: the first bottle is the most satisfying. In keeping with earlier notation, the variable Y denotes the total output of a firm and the output is now being consumed.

Looking at the rate of change in total utility (MU = $\Delta$TU / $\Delta$Y) allows calculation of the marginal utility. The move from no bottles to one bottle changes TU from zero to 10 utils ($\Delta$TU = (10 – 0) = 10), and the change in quantity consumed

is equal to one util ($\Delta Y = (1 - 0) = 1$). Thus, the marginal utility at this level of consumption is equal to ten utils/bottle: $MU = \Delta TU / \Delta Y = 10 / 1 = 10$.

As more bottles are consumed, total utility increases, but at a decreasing rate. This is due to the consumer's increasing level of satisfaction. The fifth bottle does not provide any additional satisfaction, so the consumer is fully satisfied and indifferent between drinking the bottle or not.

### QUICK QUIZ 7.3

Have you ever had enough water so that when you are asked if you would like another bottle, you say, "I could take it or leave it"? Use economic terminology to describe this situation.

Something interesting occurs with consumption of the sixth drink. It moves the consumer past the point of indifference to one of dissatisfaction. Table 7.1 shows this where the marginal, or additional, satisfaction becomes negative. The sixth bottle makes the consumer feel worse than if he or she did not drink it at all. Remember that a rational consumer would never undertake any activity in which the costs outweigh the benefits, so the rational consumer in the example would not accept the sixth bottle of water.

### QUICK QUIZ 7.4

Would anyone ever be irrational enough to drink more than the utility-maximizing level of bottles of water, or any other beverage?

Graphs of the TU and MU functions look similar to, and have some of the same characteristics as, some of the graphs used in earlier chapters. Since the MU represents the rate of change in TU, it also represents the slope of the TU function (recall that the slope of any function is "rise over run," or m = $\Delta y$ / $\Delta x$).

### QUICK QUIZ 7.5

Explain why TU and MU are drawn on separate graphs.

Figure 7.1 shows that as consumption of water increases, the level of utility (satisfaction) increases, but at a diminishing rate. In the example, the consumer becomes satiated at five bottles; any additional consumption of water will result in a decrease in total utility. The marginal utility graph in Figure 7.2 shows the additional utility gained from the consumption of one more bottle of water. Marginal utility decreases with additional consumption of the good. This decreasing rate of marginal utility is the topic of the next section.

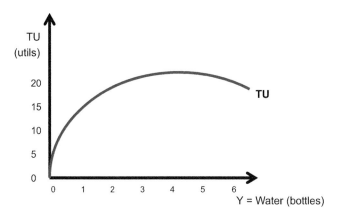

Figure 7.1 Total utility from consuming water on a hot day

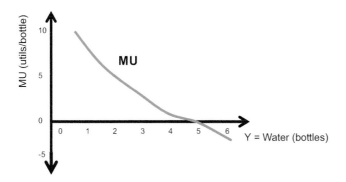

Figure 7.2 Marginal utility from consuming water on a hot day

## 7.3   The law of diminishing marginal utility

The previous section showed that as the consumption of water increases, marginal utility decreases. Each additional unit consumed gives the consumer less additional utility than the one before. This does not mean that total utility declines: four is preferred to three; more is better than less. However, more is better than less at a declining rate. At some point, the consumer can consume too much of a good: water becomes a noneconomic good at the point where its marginal utility becomes negative. This pattern of consumer utility is pervasive—so pervasive, in fact, that economists have referred to it as a "law."

- *Law of Diminishing Marginal Utility* = marginal utility declines as more of a good or service is consumed during a given time period.

There is no actual proof of this; it is just intuition that appears to be so widespread that it is called a "law." This law is powerful enough to explain a great deal about the way consumers behave. The law of diminishing marginal utility implies that consumers will not spend all of their income on one good because the marginal utility of continuing to buy more of the same good declines. Instead, consumers use their money to buy a variety of goods.

## 7.4   Indifference curves

Understanding consumer behavior requires considering the properties of consumer preferences. As in earlier cases, understanding consumer behavior requires several assumptions. The assumptions simplify the real world to provide greater understanding of consumer choices. The major assumptions associated with the study of consumer behavior include the following:

- Assumption #1. Preferences for goods and services are complete.

When given any two goods, a consumer can determine if he or she prefers A to B, prefers B to A, or is indifferent between A and B. Let the symbol ">" mean "is preferred to," the symbol "<" mean "is less preferred to," and the symbol "~" mean "is indifferent to." Completeness of preferences requires that for any two goods, A and B, the consumer can tell if

7.1a  A > B (A is preferred to B),
7.1b  B > A (B is preferred to A), or
7.1c  A ~ B (the consumer is indifferent between A and B).

Complete preferences allow economists to study all goods since the consumer is able to rank how any good compares to all other goods in the generation of utility.

● Assumption #2. Consumers are consistent.

Using the same notation as earlier, consistency of preferences means that

7.2  if A > B and B > C, then A > C.

"Transitive preferences," or simply "transitivity," means that consumers do not change their preferences haphazardly. Economists assume that consumer behavior is purposeful and consistent, so purchases must be consistent. This can be a difficult assumption in the real world since the transitivity among a few goods, or the entire universe of goods, applies only in one place, time, and context.

Consumer behavior is complicated and known to be quite changeable. A quick look at selecting which political candidate to support helps make this point. One voter may choose the Democrat candidate until the Republican candidate makes a series of promises that are attractive to the voter. Two problems arise. First, if one candidate makes new promises, is the voter still comparing the same two goods? Second, the transitivity requirement must hold for only a brief moment. The result of these problems places boundaries around the notion of indifference. Nonetheless, it is an important attribute needed for the study of consumer preferences to move ahead.

● Assumption #3. Nonsatiation: More is preferred to less.

Consumers can never have enough! This assumption states that a consumer will always want more of a good. It states that a consumer will never consume "too much" of a good and reach the point where marginal utility becomes negative.

These three assumptions are basic to models about consumer preferences. The objective of developing such models is to explain and then to predict consumer behavior. Relative prices drive a market economy. This simple notion received much attention in earlier chapters. It should not be surprising when consumer behavior must respond to the same rigorous questions: "What happens when prices change?"

## 7.4.1  Consumer responses to relative price changes

Suppose that freezing weather in Florida kills a significant fraction of the nation's citrus fruit crop. The frost results in reduced supplies of citrus fruit and the prices of oranges, grapefruit, lemons, and limes increase accordingly. How will consumers respond to the increase in the price of citrus fruit?

Photo 7.3 Florida oranges

*Source:* Devi/Shutterstock

BOX 7.4

## Florida oranges

Florida is a major agricultural state and ranks first in the United States in the value of production of oranges, grapefruit, tangerines, sugarcane for sugar and seed, squash, watermelons, sweet corn, fresh-market snap beans, fresh-market tomatoes, and fresh-market cucumbers.

   The Florida citrus industry encompasses a range of economic activities, including fruit production in 27 counties of central and south Florida, fresh fruit grading, packing and shipping to domestic and international markets, fruit processing for juice extraction, and juice packaging for retail distribution. The Florida citrus-bearing grove area has declined from over 750,000 acres in the year 2000 to around 419,452 acres in 2020, a reduction of 44 percent, while production volume utilized has declined by 71 percent, primarily due to losses from citrus greening disease (also known as Huanglongbing or HLB), which entered the state in 2005.

Globally, orange production is greatest in Brazil, the US, and Mexico, while China produces mandarins, and India grows lemons and limes. In what is now Haiti, in 1493, Christopher Columbus oversaw the first plantings and early growth of citrus trees in the New World. Oranges with their high level of vitamin C helped prevent scurvy in sailors during long sea voyages.

*Sources:* USDA/NASS Statistics by State, Florida Ag Statistics, 2023.

US Census Bureau. Census of Agriculture. 2017. Retrieved January 4, 2023.

Economic Contributions of the Florida Citrus Industry in 2016–2017. https://fred.ifas.ufl.edu/PDF/economic-impact-analysis/FRE-EconomicCont ributionsFLCitrusReport2019-20FINAL.pdf. Retrieved January 4, 2023.

Economists assume that consumers maximize their own utility, subject to a budget constraint. This is a serious assumption since consumers of all ages and stations in life are constantly buffeted by forces explicitly designed to change the choices they make as consumers or citizens. Advertising aims explicitly at changing consumer preferences. Political rhetoric works the same way, and ever-present peer pressure causes consumers to make frequent changes in the pattern of their purchases.

The question here narrows in the hope that lessons from economics can help sort out what happens when the relative prices of consumer goods (food, clothing, books, vacuum cleaners, entertainment, etc.) change. When this occurs, consumers shift their purchases into less expensive goods and away from more expensive goods. **Indifference curves** help show this movement between goods.

## 7.4.2  Indifference curves

The word "indifferent" means that an individual, a consumer in this case, does not have a preference between two outcomes; it doesn't matter one way or the other. An indifference curve is a graphed function that shows all combinations of two goods that provide exactly the same degree of satisfaction to a consumer. Since each point provides the same satisfaction, the consumer is indifferent between any two points on the curve. If a friend asks, "What would you like to do tonight?" and you respond, "I don't care," then you are indifferent. Similarly, when you cannot decide between a new yellow shirt and a new blue shirt, you are indifferent.

An indifference curve shows a consumer's willingness to trade one good for another. If a consumer has a case of Pepsi, how many bottles is she willing to trade to get one hamburger? Similarly, if a Texas cattle producer raises cattle and has a freezer full of meat, how many pounds of beef would she trade for two pounds of fruit and vegetables? The indifference curve shows exactly how a consumer is willing to trade one good for another. The formal definition of an **indifference curve** is as follows:

- *Indifference Curve* = a line showing all possible combinations of two goods that provide the same level of utility (satisfaction).

### 7.4.3 Indifference curve example: pizza and Coke

Pizza and Coke make a highly regarded snack, or even a simple dinner, but the proportions between the two may change depending on the purpose: snack or dinner. A given consumer may be indifferent between several combinations of the popular foods. The indifference curve $I_0$ in Figure 7.3 shows a group of points, each representing the same degree of satisfaction. A consumer is indifferent between any pair of points on the curve. The indifference curve represents consumer preferences for only two goods: slices of pizza and bottles of Coke. The shape of the indifference curve comes from the fact that the supply of each of the goods is limited. Put another way, the curve takes its shape from the scarcity associated with the two goods.

QUICK QUIZ 7.6

Define the concept of scarcity, and explain why it is the foundation of economics.

Now consider Coke at point B on the indifference curve shown in Figure 7.3. At this point, the consumer has a more-than-adequate amount of pizza and very little Coke. Therefore, he is willing to give up several slices of pizza in exchange

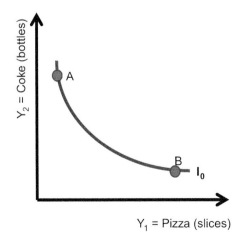

**Figure 7.3** An indifference curve for pizza and Coke

for one Coke. The opposite is true at point A. Where Coke is plentiful and pizza is scarce, the consumer is willing to give up several Cokes to obtain one slice of pizza.

These trade-offs make the indifference curve convex to the origin, reflecting the law of diminishing utility. The first unit of consumption of a good is the most highly valued. There are four properties of all indifference curves, as explained next.

### 7.4.4  Four properties of indifference curves

7.3a  Downward sloping
7.3b  Everywhere dense
7.3c  Cannot intersect
7.3d  Convex to origin

Explanations for these four properties follow.

1  **Downward Sloping.** By assumption, more is preferred to less. Figure 7.4 shows that this must be true. If an indifference curve were upward sloping, then a point such as B, with more of both goods than point A, would, by definition, produce the same level of utility ($I_0$) as point A, which has lower amounts of both goods.

An indifference curve that slopes upward (Figure 7.4) violates the definition of "indifference." Point B shows more of both goods than point A, but since it lies on the same indifference curve as point A, it seemingly produces the same level of utility. This cannot be true. This reasoning applies to all combinations of two goods, and it follows that all real-world indifference curves are downward sloping. Put another way, the property of nonsatiation (more is preferred to less) ensures that indifference curves must be downward sloping. A consumer must

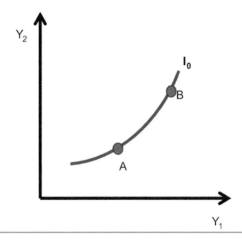

Figure 7.4 Proof that an indifference curve cannot be upward sloping

give up some of one good in order to get the other good. The slope of the indifference curve represents the consumer's willingness to trade, or sacrifice, one good for another.

2   **Everywhere Dense.** This property means that there is an indifference curve through every single point in the positive quadrant. Every combination of the two goods produces some level of satisfaction. The term "everywhere dense" means that there are an infinite number of isoquants in the plane.

---

**QUICK QUIZ 7.7**

Why do we only draw some of the indifference curves in the graphs?

---

3   **Cannot Intersect.** Indifference curves cannot intersect since that would mean that two different levels of utility were equal to each other at the point of intersection. To untangle this problem, assume that two indifference curves intersect, as in Figure 7.5.

First, notice that points A and B are on the same indifference curve ($I_1$). Each point provides the same level of utility. Next, notice that points B and C are on the same indifference curve ($I_2$), so they each represent the same level of utility. If A and B have equal levels of utility, and B and C have equal levels of utility, then it follows that A and C must have equal levels of utility (A ~ B and B ~ C, so A ~ C). However, Figure 7.5 shows that combination A produces a higher level of utility than combination C since A has more of each good than C (A > C).

Therefore, indifference curves cannot intersect. A contradiction follows if they do. The equations A ~ C and A > C cannot both be true at the same time.

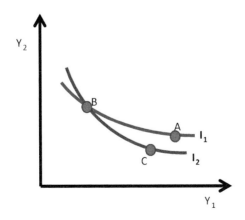

**Figure 7.5 Proof of why indifference curves cannot intersect**

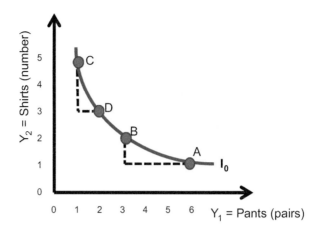

---

**Figure 7.6 The law of diminishing marginal utility**

Therefore, indifference curves must not touch since each curve represents a different level of utility.

4   **Convex to Origin.** This property states that the indifference curves must bend inward toward the origin (be convex to the origin). This is due to the law of diminishing marginal utility: the first unit of a good is the most satisfying! The graph in Figure 7.6 shows this.

The law of diminishing marginal utility is used to show that if a consumer has many pairs of pants (point A: six pairs of pants, one shirt), she is willing to trade three pairs of pants for one additional shirt (point B: three pairs of pants, two shirts). On the other hand, if the consumer had five shirts and only one pair of pants (point C), she would be willing to give up two shirts for the second pair of pants (point D: two pairs of pants and three shirts). A consumer's willingness to trade one good for another depends on how much of each good that he or she has. The first unit provides the higher level of satisfaction, and consumption of subsequent units provide less additional utility, as shown in Figure 7.6.

## 7.4.5   Indifference curves for substitutes and complements

Consider the case of two goods that are **perfect substitutes,** meaning that the consumer is indifferent between the consumption of either good. Suppose a consumer is purchasing shirts that are identical in every aspect other than color. If the consumer is indifferent between blue shirts and green shirts, then these two goods are perfect substitutes in consumption, as shown in Figure 7.7.

● *Perfect Substitutes (consumption)* = goods that are completely substitutable so that the consumer is indifferent between the two goods.

The indifference curve for perfect substitutes is a straight line with a constant slope. In Figure 7.7, the consumer is indifferent between any combination of blue

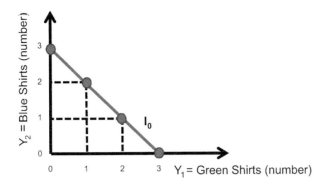

Figure 7.7 **Perfect substitutes in consumption**

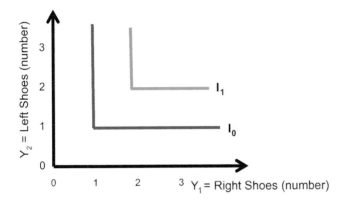

Figure 7.8 **Perfect complements in consumption**

and green shirts that adds up to three shirts. This indifference curve is a special case since it is not convex to the origin. The consumer is willing to trade one good for the other at a constant rate, so the goods are, in a way, the same good, "shirts." The opposite case of perfect substitutes is **perfect complements**.

● *Perfect Complements (consumption)* = goods that must be purchased together in a fixed ratio.

Here, consuming one of the two goods requires consuming some of the other good at the same time. For example, except in rare cases, consuming a left shoe commits a person to consume a right shoe (Figure 7.8). The level of utility along indifference curve $I_0$ does not increase when the consumer buys additional right shoes to go with one left shoe. Left and right shoes must be consumed together in order to produce satisfaction for the consumer. Similarly, as left shoes accumulate without the right shoes that match them, the utility level stays constant. Utility increases only with the purchase of one of each good: a right shoe and a left shoe. This is also a special case of an indifference curve since the curve is not convex to the origin. Almost all goods are "imperfect substitutes," meaning that they can be substituted with each other, but not perfectly. Convex indifference curves characterize these goods.

## 7.5 The marginal rate of substitution

The slope of the indifference curve reflects the rate of change between goods and is called the **marginal rate of substitution (MRS)**.

- *Marginal Rate of Substitution [MRS]* = the rate of exchange of one good for another that leaves utility unchanged. The MRS defines the slope of an indifference curve. MRS = $\Delta Y_2 / \Delta Y_1$.

The term "marginal" refers to a small change. The term "substitution" refers to the trade-off between the goods. Thus, the MRS is the number of units of good $Y_2$ that must be given up per unit of good $Y_1$, if the consumer is to remain indifferent or retain the same level of satisfaction.

### 7.5.1 The diamond-water paradox

The literature of economics includes many examples of unusual relationships existing between goods. Among these is a 200-year-old paradox called the diamond-water paradox. The issue is very simple: why is water, an absolute necessity to life, so inexpensive (often free), while diamonds, stones used as romantic baubles and ornamentation but with no necessary use at all, are outrageously expensive?

> ### QUICK QUIZ 7.8
>
> Use simple economic reasoning to explain the diamond-water paradox.

The economic answer to the paradox centers on scarcity. Diamonds are valuable because they are scarce, whereas water is inexpensive because it is relatively plentiful. Would people ever give up diamonds for water? It sounds unlikely, but the transaction would take place if you had only diamonds and no water. Would anyone give up water for diamonds? Certainly, if they had enough water to meet their needs. The graph in Figure 7.9 shows this.

The slope of the indifference curve in Figure 7.9 is easily interpreted to be the MRS between the two goods. The MRS between points A and B shows the willingness of a consumer to trade diamonds for water.

7.4    MRS (AB) = $\Delta Y_2 / \Delta Y_1$ = (3 − 5) / (2 − 1) = −2.

Photo 7.4 Diamond-water paradox

*Source:* Sebastian Duda/Shutterstock

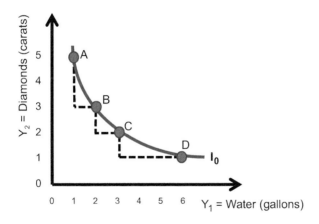

Figure 7.9 The diamond-water paradox

At point A, diamonds are relatively plentiful, so the consumer is willing to give up two diamonds for one more gallon of water. But what happens to the MRS when the consumer trades for one more unit of water?

7.5   $MRS(BC) = \Delta Y_2 / \Delta Y_1 = (2 - 3) / (3 - 2) = -1.$

The absolute value of the rate of substitution has declined, as shown in Figure 7.9, where the slope of the indifference curve has decreased. This reflects the fact that as water becomes more plentiful (less scarce); the consumer is willing to give up fewer diamonds to acquire more water. The calculation of the MRS for the next gallon of water is

7.6    $MRS(CD) = \Delta Y_2 / \Delta Y_1 = (1 - 2) / (6 - 3) = -1/3.$

The MRS continues to fall in absolute value with the consumption of more units of water. Previous sections of this chapter established the connection between the law of diminishing marginal utility and the convexity of the indifference curve.

A college student's allocation of time displays the same characteristics as the trade-offs between goods. Suppose that there are two ways for a college student to spend time: (1) studying and (2) relaxing. The possibilities are depicted in Figure 7.10. If a student has been working all of the time, he may be willing to give up several hours of work to get the first hour of play. As a student increases the amount of play, extra hours of play become less valuable, as shown in Figure 7.10.

The indifference curve in Figure 7.10 shows that it is likely that most students will eventually settle at a position somewhere near the middle of the graph. The notion of "balance" suggests that a student will want to consume some of each good. An indifference curve reflects consumer preferences. However, consumers must spend within their limits, or, in language that is more technical, they must comply with a budget constraint, the theme of the following section. After studying the budget constraint, it will be combined with indifference curves to find a utility-maximizing (most satisfying) equilibrium point that combines what consumers want with what they can afford.

QUICK QUIZ 7.9

What is an equilibrium?

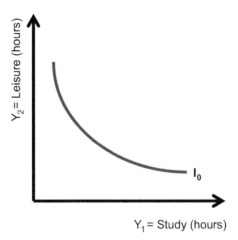

Figure 7.10 Time allocation for a college student

## 7.6  The budget constraint

Indifference curves are everywhere, as shown in this graph, with the satisfaction provided by one good shown on each axis. This collection of indifference curves (as in Figure 7.11) is called an indifference curves map.

The indifference curves shown in Figure 7.11 each include a group of points that represent combinations of the two goods. In addition, each point (combination) on a single curve yields the same amount of satisfaction. Given the assumption that more is preferable to less, the level of utility increases as one moves to the northeast from the graph's origin to curve $I_0$, to curve $I_1$, and to curve $I_2$. The consumer's budget limits him to considering only those combinations on the highest attainable indifference curve. The consumer is constrained by a budget. Utility, or consumer preference, is represented by the indifference curves, and the budget constraint represents the amount that the consumer has to spend on the goods.

● *Budget Constraint* = a limit on consumption determined by the size of the consumer's budget and the prices of goods.

A line added to Figure 7.11 shows the consumer's budget constraint. Assume that a consumer spends all of his income on only the two goods (food and clothes) in Figure 7.12. Define the variables of a budget constraint as

7.7a  $M$ = income (USD),
7.7b  $Y_1$ = food (calories),
7.7c  $P_1$ = price of food (USD/calorie),
7.7d  $Y_2$ = clothes (outfits),
7.7e  $P_2$ = price of clothes (USD/outfit).

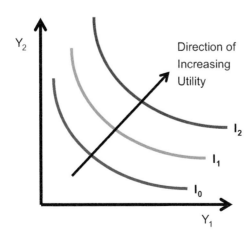

Figure 7.11  An indifference curve map

The budget line stems from the assumption that the consumer spends his entire income on food and clothes. The equation for the line states that income must be greater or equal to the combined expenditures on food ($Y_1$) and clothing ($Y_2$).

7.8   $M \geq P_1Y_1 + P_2Y_2$.

If all income is spent on food and clothing, then the inequality in Equation 7.10 becomes an equality:

7.9   $M = P_1Y_1 + P_2Y_2$.

This equality (the budget constraint) shows that the amount of money available (M) is exactly equal to the amount spent on food and clothing. Some specific numbers illustrate a budget constraint.

7.10   $M$ = USD 100/month; $P_1$ = USD 1/calorie; $P_2$ = USD 20/outfit.

This information defines a line on the graph in Figure 7.12, showing combinations of food and clothing affordable with the given budget.

The y-intercept shows the affordable quantity of clothing if all of M goes for clothing. The x-intercept shows the maximum amount of food that M can purchase. The x-intercept is found by calculating how many calories of food could be purchased at an income level of USD 100/month and a price of food equal to USD 1/calorie ($M/P_1$ = USD 100/(USD 1/calorie) = 100 calories).

The y-intercept is found by calculating how many outfits of clothing could be purchased if all of the income were spent on clothing ($M / P_2$ = USD 100 / (USD 20/outfit) = 5 outfits). Finding these two intercepts and connecting them with a straight line provides a "picture" of the budget constraint. The slope of this **budget line** is the "rise over the run," or $\Delta y / \Delta x = \Delta Y_2 / \Delta Y_1 = -5 / 100 = -0.05$.

● ***Budget Line*** = a line indicating all possible combinations of two goods that can be purchased using the consumer's entire budget.

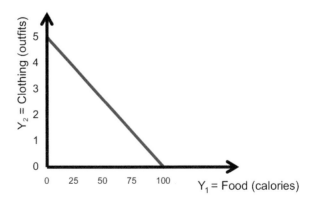

**Figure 7.12 The budget constraint**

The equation of a line is given by y = b + mx, where b is the y-intercept and m is the slope. The equation of a budget constraint leads to derivation of the equation for the budget line. This derivation should look familiar: it is similar to the derivation of the isocost and isorevenue lines used to study the behavior of producers (Chapters 5 and 6).

7.11a   $M = P_1Y_1 + P_2Y_2$,
7.11b   $P_2Y_2 = M - P_1Y_1$,
7.11c   $Y_2 = (M / P_2) + (-P_1 / P_2) Y_1$.

The y-intercept equation (7.13b) is equal to M / P$_2$, which is equal to USD 100 / (USD 20/ outfit) = 5 outfits (this confirms the earlier calculation). The calculation of the slope of the budget line, is confirmed by m = $\Delta y / \Delta x = -P_1 / P_2$ = relative prices. The slope of the budget constraint represents the relative prices of the two goods.

The **opportunity set** is the triangle formed by the budget line, as in Figure 7.13.

● *Opportunity Set* = the collection of all combinations of goods within the budget constraint of the consumer.

The triangle formed by the axes and the budget line is called the opportunity set, because any combination of goods in the set is within the given budget and affordable. Points such as A that are outside of the opportunity set are not feasible: the consumer does not have enough money to afford them.

A consumer will desire to maximize utility, subject to the budget constraint as shown in Figure 7.13. The consumer will desire to locate as far to the northeast as possible while staying within the opportunity set. The next section shows how a consumer will select the utility-maximizing point by combining the preference information from the indifference curves with budget information in the budget line.

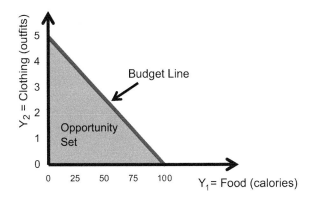

Figure 7.13 The opportunity set

## 7.7 Consumer equilibrium

The term "equilibrium" describes a situation where there is no tendency to change. When an economy is in equilibrium, producers and consumers are doing the best that they can, given the constraints that they face. In equilibrium, producers are maximizing profits, subject to technology and prices, and consumers are maximizing utility, subject to a budget constraint and prices. Equilibrium is an "optimal" point.

A "map" of indifference curves summarizes consumer preferences. The curves represent the trade-offs between food ($Y_1$) and clothes ($Y_2$). The slope of an indifference curve is the MRS, which represents a consumer's relative preferences for the two goods, $Y_1$ and $Y_2$. It answers the question, "How many units of $Y_1$ am I willing to give up to receive an additional unit of good $Y_2$?" This depends on the consumer's preferences for each good. The MRS reflects the marginal utility for each good and defines how much additional satisfaction a consumer can receive from each unit of the good.

7.12   $MRS = \Delta Y_2 / \Delta Y_1 = MU_1 / MU_2$

A consumer will want to reach the highest possible level of satisfaction. This optimal, or highest, level of utility will be the highest indifference curve that is still within the opportunity set, or the indifference curve that is tangent to the budget line.

Point E in Figure 7.14 represents the consumer's optimum, or equilibrium point. In this example, the equilibrium combination includes 50 calories of food and 2.5 outfits. This equilibrium point is arbitrarily set at the "halfway" mark on the budget constraint between the vertical (food) and horizontal (clothing) axes. However, there are numerous possible equilibria, each depending on the location of the consumer's indifference curve. Regardless of how many indifference curves come under consideration, the optimal, or equilibrium point, from which there is no tendency to change always appears at the point where the indifference curve is tangent to the budget line.

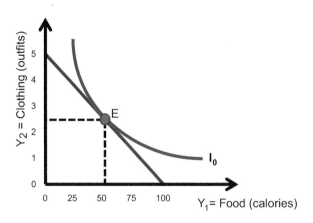

**Figure 7.14** Consumer equilibrium

The slope of the budget line represents relative prices, as it is equal to the price ratio ($-P_1 / P_2$). The budget line represents what the consumer can buy. The slope of the indifference curve defines the consumer's preferences. This graphical analysis is a story about a shopping trip taken in order to match two things:

1 What the shopper can afford (the budget constraint)
2 What the shopper prefers to consume (the indifference curve)

The mathematical equation for the equilibrium reflects this story:

7.13a Slope of the indifference curve = slope of the budget line,
7.13b MRS = price ratio,
7.13c $\Delta Y_2 / \Delta Y_1 = -P_1 / P_2$,
7.13d $MU_1 / MU_2 = -P_1 / P_2$,
7.13e $-MU_1 / P_1 = MU_2 / P_2$.

This equilibrium condition states that a consumer should equalize the additional utility gained from the consumption of a good (MU) divided by the price of the good, for all goods. If a consumer can gain more satisfaction from one unit of cost from one good than from another good, then the consumer should shift consumption away from lower-utility goods and into the higher-utility goods. This allows the consumer to reach the highest indifference curve possible while remaining within the budget constraint.

## 7.8   The demand for meat in Phoenix, Arizona

Learning about consumer behavior helps observers understand real-world issues in the agricultural economy. Currently, there is an important issue in the red meat industry: the per capita consumption of beef in the US has declined rather steadily to reach a 55-year low in 2015 of 54.1 pounds of beef per capita. There has been an increase since then, and per capita beef consumption was 57.2 pounds per capita in 2018. Economists argue about whether this decrease stems from price changes (beef is expensive relative to meats such as pork and chicken) or health issues (some consumers perceive red meat to be unhealthy).

### 7.8.1   Consumer equilibrium for the Phoenix consumer

A simple model of consumer behavior helps analyze this issue. Assume that the budget for weekly expenditures on meat is 20 dollars (M = USD 20), the price of beef is 4 dollars per pound ($P_1$ = USD 4/lb), and the price of chicken is 2 dollars per pound ($P_2$ = USD 2/lb). Figure 7.15 shows the budget line for the Phoenix consumer.

QUICK QUIZ 7.10

Locate the opportunity set in Figure 7.15.

Photo 7.5 Demand for meat in Phoenix, Arizona

*Source:* gresei/Shutterstock

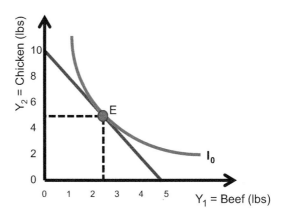

Figure 7.15 Phoenix consumer equilibrium

The opportunity set for meat is the area 0-10-5 that shows all possible combinations of beef and chicken that could be purchased with the consumer's budgeted meat expenditures (M = USD 20). The opportunity set makes up the triangle in Figure 7.15. If the entire budget was spent on beef, the consumer could purchase five pounds of meat (x-intercept, $M/P_1$ = USD 20 / USD 4/lb = 5 lb).

If, alternatively, the consumer spent all of her income on chicken, 10 pounds of chicken could be purchased (y-intercept, $M/P_2$ = USD 20 / USD 2/lb = 10 lb). The opportunity set reflects what is possible for the consumer to purchase.

The indifference curves represent the consumer's preferences. The slope of the indifference curve is the marginal rate of substitution (MRS = $MU_1$ / $MU_2$). The slope of the budget line reflects relative prices and is equal to $-P_1$ / $P_2$. The equilibrium for purchases of meat occurs where the MRS is equal to the relative price ratio, as shown in Figure 7.15. At the equilibrium point (E), the Phoenix meat eater consumes 2.5 pounds of beef and 5 pounds of chicken.

## 7.8.2   An increase in income for the Phoenix consumer

If the local Phoenix economy expands, wages and salaries paid to the workers in the area will rise. This, in turn, allows these consumers to spend more money on meat. Suppose that total meat expenditures rise from $M_0$ = USD 20/week to $M_1$ = USD 40/week.

This increase in income is good for consumers, it is good for the beef industry, and it is good for beef producers in the US and other beef-producing nations. Figure 7.16 shows the impact of the increase in income on the consumer's meat purchases.

The original consumer equilibrium for the meat eater in Phoenix ($E_0$) is 2.5 pounds of beef and 5 pounds of chicken. After the income increase, the equilibrium shifts to 5 pounds of beef and 10 pounds of chicken ($E_1$).

> ### QUICK QUIZ 7.11
>
> What defines the location of the equilibrium point on the budget line?

Changes in income have a large impact on consumption. An increase in income will have an impact on the beef industry. When income levels increase, consumers typically spend more money on "luxury" goods such as beef.

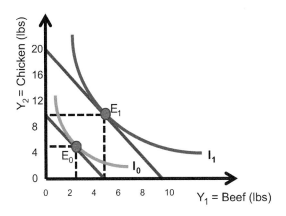

Figure 7.16  **Effect of an increase in income on Phoenix consumer equilibrium**

Consumer choices

QUICK QUIZ 7.12

Can you think of any goods that would have a decrease in consumption when income levels increase?

### 7.8.3  The impact of general inflation on the Phoenix consumer

A simultaneous and continued increase in all prices in an economy is referred to as a general inflation. Chapter 1 includes a short discussion indicating that inflation would not affect the economy at all since the price of labor (wages and salaries) would increase at the same rate as the prices of all other goods and services. If all prices in the economy double, for example, including wages and salaries, then the consumption and production of goods and services would remain unchanged. In the real world, inflation does not increase all prices in a uniform and simultaneous fashion.

The simple model of consumer behavior sheds light on this issue by investigating the logic behind it. The following price and income data reflect a general inflation where all prices double. The subscripts refer to the good (1 = beef; 2 = chicken), and the superscripts refer to time periods zero and one.

| *Before:* | *After:* |
|---|---|
| $M^0$ = USD 20/week | $M^1$ = USD 40/week |
| $P_1^0$ = USD 4/lb | $P_1^1$ = USD 8/lb |
| $P_2^0$ = USD 2/lb | $P_2^1$ = USD 4/lb |

The budget line ($M = P_1 Y_1 + P_2 Y_2$) will be identical before and after the inflation.

| *Before:* | *After:* |
|---|---|
| $20 = 4Y_1 + 2Y_2$ | $40 = 8Y_1 + 4Y_2$ |
| $2Y_2 = 20 - 4Y_1$ | $4Y_2 = 40 - 8Y_1$ |
| $Y_2 = 10 - 2Y_1$ | $Y_2 = 10 - 2Y_1$ |

Since the budget line remains unchanged, the equilibrium does not change. The general inflation has no effect on the economy. Relative prices have not changed, so nothing happens.

### 7.8.4  The impact of a change in beef prices on the Phoenix consumer

The situation is different for changes in relative prices. Suppose that the cost of production for beef deceases due to technological changes in packing plants. Prior to the change, $P_1^0$ = USD 4/lb and after the change, $P_1^1$ = USD 2/lb. The price and income data are as follows, where the subscript refers to the good (1 = beef; 2 = chicken), and the superscript refers to time periods zero and one.

| $M^0$ = USD 20/week | $P_1^0$ = USD 4/lb | $P_2^0$ = USD 2/lb |
|---|---|---|
| $M^1$ = USD 20/week | $P_1^1$ = USD 2/lb | $P_2^1$ = USD 2/lb |

206

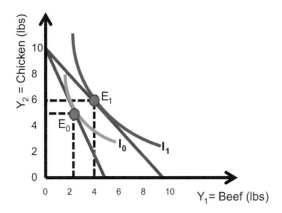

**Figure 7.17** **Decrease in beef price effect on Phoenix consumer equilibrium**

The budget constraint changes since the relative prices of beef and chicken change. The slope of the budget line is the relative price ratio.

*Before:*                     *After:*

$20 = 4Y_1 + 2Y_2$      $20 = 2Y_1 + 2Y_2$
$Y_2 = 10 - 2Y_1$        $Y_2 = 10 - Y_1$

In Figure 7.17, the consumer equilibrium before the price change is ($E_0$), 2.5 pounds of beef and 5 pounds of chicken. After the price change, the budget line shifts to reflect an increase in purchasing power since the price of beef is lower. The y-intercept remains at 10 since both income (M) and the price of chicken ($P_2$) have remained unchanged. The x-intercept shifts from 5 pounds ($M^0 / P_1{}^0$ = USD 20 / USD 4/lb = 5 lb) to 10 pounds ($M^1 / P_1{}^1$ = USD 20 / USD 2/lb = 10 lb).

The consumer equilibrium after the technological change ($E_1$) moves to four pounds of beef and six pounds of chicken, as shown by the tangency of the indifference curve and the budget line (MRS = the price ratio). The consumer can expand the consumption of both goods, even though the price of chicken remains constant. This occurs because of the increase in the consumer's purchasing power associated with the price decrease. The price of beef has a strong effect on consumer purchases of both beef and chicken.

The technological change increased the amount of beef sold in Phoenix. Any circumstance that causes a relative price decrease will result in more of the good being sold. Cattle producers are better off since consumers purchase more beef (note that the price of cattle does not decrease, just the price of meat in the grocery store). Similarly, any factor that increases the relative price of beef in the grocery store will have an adverse effect on the cattle producers.

## 7.8.5 The impact of a change in chicken prices on the Phoenix consumer

Does a change in the price of chicken affect the beef market? Definitely, yes. Just as the beef price decline caused an increase in the consumption of both beef and chicken, a change in the price of chicken will affect both the beef and the chicken markets since they are substitutes. Suppose that there is a decrease in the relative price of chicken from USD 2/lb to USD 1/lb:

$M^0$ = USD 20/week      $P_1^0$ = USD 4/lb      $P_2^0$ =U SD 2/lb
$M^1$ = USD 20/week      $P_1^1$ = USD 4/lb      $P_2^1$ = USD 1/lb

The budget line shifts due to the price change.

*Before:*                              *After:*

$20 = 4Y_1 + 2Y_2$            $20 = 4Y_1 + Y_2$
$Y_2 = 10 - 2Y_1$               $Y_2 = 20 - 4Y_1$

Figure 7.18 shows that the x-intercept does not change, but the budget line pivots upward and outward. The original equilibrium ($E_0$: 2.5 lb beef; 5 lb chicken) and the equilibrium after the price change ($E_1$: 2 lb beef; 12 lb chicken). With the price decrease of chicken, the consumer substitutes out of the more expensive product (beef) and into the less expensive product (chicken). Beef and chicken are substitutes: consumers will shift their purchases toward the less expensive product.

Relative prices rule. Any change in the relative price of beef will affect the quantity of beef purchased, whether the real change as opposed to the relative change is a change in the price of beef or a change in the price of chicken.

## QUICK QUIZ 7.13

Are beef and chicken substitutes or complements in consumption? Why? Are beef and chicken perfect substitutes or imperfect substitutes in consumption? Why?

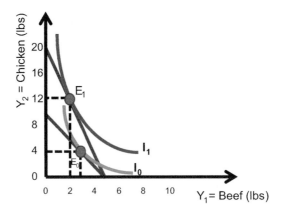

**Figure 7.18** Decrease in chicken price effect on Phoenix consumer equilibrium

### 7.8.6 Conclusions for the beef industry based on consumer theory

Given the previous example, what conclusion stems from the demand for beef in Phoenix, Arizona? Let the quantity of beef purchased by consumers be the demand for beef, $Q^d_{beef}$. The demand for beef is a function of income and the prices of beef and chicken: $Q^d_{beef} = f(M, P_1, P_2)$. A summary of this analysis appears next.

1   $P_1\downarrow$: The price of beef decreases:
    $P_1\downarrow$: $Q^d_{beef}$ increases
2   $P_2\downarrow$: The price of chicken decreases:
    $P_2\downarrow$: $Q^d_{beef}$ decreases
3   $M\uparrow$: Income increases:
4   $M\uparrow$: $Q^d_{beef}$ increases

---

**BOX 7.5**

## Food labeling

Labels on food are mandated by the government to provide consumers with information about their purchases. In the US, the Food and Drug Administration (FDA) administers nutritional labels in the attempt to encourage consumers to purchase healthier foods. The performance of free markets and free trade depend critically on how knowledgeable consumers are about the products they do or do not purchase.

For many food products, consumers are unable to determine the product quality by visual inspection. An example is organic lettuce: it is impossible to know if the lettuce is truly organic, or if a producer or distributor merely added the label to increase the price of a product characteristic that is currently in high demand. Product characteristics of this type involve organic, natural, country or area of origin, nutrition and health, GMO-free, and humane treatment of animals. There may be an important role for government to regulate food products that claim these characteristics. However, private markets could also resolve this issue since each firm has an incentive to provide accurate information, or it is likely to lose customers in the long run.

There has been a great deal of debate about the merits and consequences of labeling food. Beef retailers in the US were required to label to reveal in which country the beef product originated. The labeling was somewhat facetiously called "Country of Origin Labeling," or COOL. This labeling appears to be simple but is actually quite complicated and costly to keep track of which nations the beef cattle were in during the course of their lifetime and after slaughter. The economic concept behind this law is difficult to know with accuracy. A second highly debated and highly controversial labeling law is "GMO-free." Economists, food industry experts, and government regulators have devoted a great deal of time and attention to the expected and unanticipated effects of this type of law. Currently (2023), there is no agreement about the benefits and costs of labelling foods as being "GMO-free."

*Source:* McCluskey, J. (2000). "A game theoretic approach to organic foods: an analysis of asymmetric information and policy." *Agricultural and Resource Economics Review*, vol. 29, no. 1, pp. 1–9.

Armed with the knowledge of the consumer's demand for beef, an economist can provide advice to the beef industry:

- Lower production costs in every way possible. Lower $P_1$ to sell more beef.
- Pay attention to consumer preferences: especially to the prices of competing products such as chicken ($P_2$).
- Look to consumer groups with growing incomes (M) for new markets: low-income nations.

These three statements apply to any good, with the basic message for producers to pay careful attention to their consumers. This chapter has identified the optimal, utility-maximizing point for the consumer. The model of consumer behavior yielded the major determinants of consumer demand: relative prices and income. The next two chapters explain how markets work. Supply (Chapter 8) and demand (Chapter 9) curves show the behavior of sellers and buyers. Chapter 10 is a study of markets, where buyers and sellers interact.

## 7.9   Chapter 7 Summary

1 In economics, we assume that individuals are rational. Rational behavior indicates that individuals do the best that they can, given the constraints that they face. Rational behavior is purposeful and consistent.
2 Utility is the satisfaction derived from consuming a good.
3 Cardinal utility assigns specific values to the level of satisfaction gained from the consumption of a good.
4 Ordinal utility ranks consumer satisfaction from the consumption of a good.
5 Total utility is the level of satisfaction derived from consuming a given bundle of goods and services. Marginal utility is the change in the level of utility as consumption of a good is increased by one unit.
6 The law of diminishing marginal utility states that MU declines as more of a good is consumed.

7 Three assumptions about consumer behavior are (1) preferences are complete, (2) consumers are consistent, and (3) more is preferred to less (nonsatiation).

8 An indifference curve is a line showing all of the combinations of two goods that provide the same level of utility.

9 Indifference curves have four properties: (1) downward sloping, (2) everywhere dense, (3) can't intersect, and (4) convex to the origin.

10 Perfect substitutes are goods that a consumer is indifferent between. Perfect complements are goods that must be purchased together in a fixed ratio. Most goods are imperfect substitutes, meaning that they can be substituted with each other, but not perfectly.

11 The marginal rate of substitution (MRS) is the rate of exchange of one good for another that leaves utility unaffected and defines the slope of the indifference curve. The slope of the indifference curve is equal to the marginal valuation of the two goods.

12 The budget constraint is the limit imposed on consumption by the size of the budget and the prices of the two goods.

13 A consumer maximizes utility by locating at the tangency of the indifference curve and the budget line.

14 The opportunity set includes all combinations of goods within the budget constraint of the consumer.

# 7.10 Chapter 7 Glossary

**Budget Constraint**—A limit on consumption determined by the size of the budget and the prices of goods.

**Budget Line**—A line indicating all possible combinations of two goods that can be purchased using the consumer's entire budget.

**Cardinal Utility**—Assigns specific, but hypothetical, numerical values to the level of satisfaction gained from the consumption of a good. The unit of measurement is the hypothetical util (see Ordinal Utility).

**Indifference Curve**—A line showing all possible combinations of two goods that provide the same level of utility (satisfaction).

**Law of Diminishing Marginal Utility**—Marginal utility declines as more of a good or service is consumed during a given time period.

**Marginal Rate of Substitution [MRS]**—The rate of exchange of one good for another that leaves utility unchanged. The slope of an indifference curve: MRS $= \Delta Y_2 / \Delta Y_1$.

**Marginal Utility [MU]**—The change in the level of utility when consumption of a good is increased by one unit: MU $= \Delta TU / \Delta Y$.

**Opportunity Set**—The collection of all combinations of goods within the budget constraint of the consumer.

**Ordinal Utility**—A way of considering consumer satisfaction in which goods are ranked in order of preference: first, second, third, etc. (see Cardinal Utility).

**Perfect Complements (consumption)**—Goods that must be purchased together in a fixed ratio.

**Perfect Substitutes (consumption)**—Goods that are completely substitutable, or the consumer is indifferent between the two goods.

**Rational Behavior**—Individuals do the best that they can, given the constraints they face. Rational behavior is purposeful and consistent.

**Total Utility [TU]**—The total level of satisfaction derived from consuming a given bundle of goods and services.

**Utility**—Satisfaction derived from consuming a good.

**Utils**—Hypothetical units of satisfaction derived from consumption of goods or services.

## 7.11   Chapter 7 Review questions

1   An individual who stays up so late that he feels sick the next day is

   a   rational
   b   irrational
   c   not an economic individual
   d   cannot tell from the information given

2   Placing a numerical value on the consumption of a piece of apple pie is an example of

   a   normative economics
   b   cardinal utility
   c   ordinal utility
   d   positive economics

3   Modern economics uses which type of consumer theory?

   a   cardinal utility
   b   ordinal utility
   c   total utility
   d   public utility

4   Marginal utility refers to

   a   the extra level of electricity from a public utility
   b   the level of satisfaction from consuming a good
   c   utility derived from consuming a good
   d   a change in utility when consumption is increased by one unit

5   When a consumer is indifferent between consuming an additional unit of a good:

   a   TU is negative
   b   MU is equal to zero
   c   TU is equal to zero
   d   MY is negative

6   All of the following are assumptions about consumer behavior except

   a   complete preferences
   b   consistent consumers
   c   nonsatiation
   d   relativity

7   Indifference curves are convex to the origin due to

   a   the law of diminishing marginal utility
   b   the law of diminishing returns
   c   relative prices
   d   the law of demand

8   A tractor and a plow are

   a   substitutes
   b   complements
   c   perfect substitutes
   d   not enough information to answer

9   Peanut butter and jelly are

   a   substitutes
   b   complements
   c   perfect substitutes
   d   not enough information to answer

10   The indifference curve represents

   a   consumer income
   b   consumer preferences
   c   what consumers can afford
   d   what consumers actually purchase

11  An increase in the price of chicken will affect

 a  the amount of chicken purchased
 b  the amount of beef purchased
 c  the relative price of beef and chicken
 d  all of the above

12  A general inflation will lead to

 a  a decrease in the consumption of beef

 b  an increase in the consumption of beef
 c  no change in the consumption of beef
 d  unemployment

13  If income decreases, then the consumption of beef will

 a  increase
 b  decrease
 c  not change
 d  not enough information to answer

**Answers:** 1. b, 2. b, 3. b, 4. d, 5. b, 6. d, 7. a, 8. b, 9. b, 10. b, 11. d, 12. c, 13. b

For more study questions, flash cards, and study guides, see the online materials at the companion website: www.routledge.com/cw/barkley.

# Supply

Photo 8.1 Supply

*Source:* Joel Shawn/Shutterstock

DOI: 10.4324/9781003367994-8

## Abstract

This chapter explains the first of the two most famous building blocks of economics: supply and demand. These tools are crucial to understanding markets and how they function to allocate goods and resources. The chapter describes the derivation of a supply curve. The concept of supply shows how quantities placed on a market respond to increases or decreases in the price of the good. Determinants of market supply are presented. Next, the concept of elasticity, or responsiveness, of producers to changes in prices is introduced. Movements along the supply curve and shifts in supply are discussed and explained.

### Chapter 8 Questions

1. How do supply and demand interact?
2. How is the aggregate supply curve derived?
3. How does the supply curve change when relative prices change?
4. What are the determinants of the supply curve?
5. What is the price elasticity of supply, and why is it important for understanding food and agricultural markets?
6. What is the difference between a movement along and a shift in a supply curve?

## 8.0 Introduction

Chapters 1 through 7 describe and explain the behavior of individual economic units. These economic actors use marginal analysis to locate the optimal point in their economic decisions. Producers select the profit-maximizing combinations of inputs and outputs, and consumers purchase combinations of goods to maximize their own utility or satisfaction. Consumers determine what to purchase in order to maximize satisfaction, given their income and relative market prices. This chapter shows the explicit connection between individuals and markets by deriving market, or aggregate, supply curves. The chapter also explains the determinants of market supply and introduces the concept of elasticity, or responsiveness, of producers to changes in prices and other economic conditions. Chapter 9 discusses consumer demand, and Chapter 10 shows how supply and demand interact to determine the prices and quantities of goods.

## 8.1 Supply

A supply function shows the relationship between the quantity of a good available for sale in a market and its price. Points on a supply function represent the quantity of a specific good that will be placed on the market at each price.

- *Supply* = the relationship between the price of a good and the amount of that good available at a given location and at a given time.

In more formal terms, supply refers to a direct functional relationship between the price and quantity of a good:

8.1   $Q^s = f(P)$,

where $Q^s$ is the quantity supplied of a good, and P is the price of the good. When the price of a good increases, the quantity supplied of a good also increases.

## 8.1.1   The individual firm's supply curve

In the next several chapters, the notation $Q^s$ denotes the market, or aggregate (total), level of quantity supplied, and $q^s$ denotes a single firm's supply, which is the firm's contribution to $Q^s$. This allows for a distinction between graphs for single firms and graphs for an entire market supply. As shown next, market supply is the aggregated supply of all individual firms that produce and sell the same product.

Understanding supply and demand at the aggregate, or market, level, requires understanding the component parts of an individual firm's supply curve. Specifically, deriving the supply curve for an entire market begins with a study of the costs incurred by an individual firm, as shown in Figure 8.1.

An individual profit-maximizing producer will continue to produce a good until MR = MC. The situation shown in Figure 8.1 relates to a firm in a competitive industry. A competitive firm is a price taker, and therefore the firm has no control over the price of the product it sells. The price is fixed, constant, and equal to the MR line associated with each price: $P_0$, $P_1$, and $P_2$.

> ### QUICK QUIZ 8.1
>
> Why does the assumption of competition result in a fixed price? Why is the price equal to the MR?

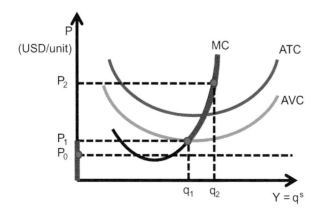

Figure 8.1  Individual-firm short-run supply curve

For example, at a given point in time, price $P_2$ is fixed and given. The firm cannot change it. At the market price of $P_2$ in Figure 8.1, this single firm will maximize profits by setting MR = MC, or P = MC at $q_2$ units of output. If the firm produced one more unit of output ($q_2 + 1$), the additional (marginal) costs would increase to a level above the marginal revenue line, and profits would decrease. At one less unit of output ($q_2 - 1$), profits would fall since marginal revenue would be higher than the marginal costs.

The individual firm will always expand output until MC equals price. Therefore, the MC curve defines the relationship between the market price of a good and the quantity supplied by the individual firm. Since supply refers to a direct, functional relationship between the price and the quantity supplied of a good, the marginal cost curve represents the supply curve of the individual firm. This is true for all prices, as long as the price is above the shutdown point.

> ## QUICK QUIZ 8.2
>
> Define the shutdown point for a firm in the short run and the long run (see Chapter 3).

In the short run, the firm will continue to produce as long as price is greater or equal to the average variable cost ($P \geq AVC$). At prices below AVC, the firm will shut down because costs are higher than revenue. The price $P_1$ in Figure 8.1 defines the shutdown price. For all prices above $P_1$, the individual firm's supply curve is equal to the MC curve, and for all prices below $P_1$, the supply curve is equal to zero (the heavy line on the vertical axis below $P_1$ in Figure 8.1).

● *Supply Curve for an Individual Firm* = the firm's marginal cost curve above the minimum point on the average variable cost curve.

Notice that there are two segments to the individual firm's supply curve: (1) above the shutdown point, supply is equal to the marginal cost curve, and (2) below the shutdown point, the supply curve is equal to zero. In the long run, the shutdown point is the ATC curve since ATC = AVC in the long run, as in Figure 8.2.

> ## QUICK QUIZ 8.3
>
> Why does ATC = AVC in the long run? Draw an individual firm's long-run supply curve (see Chapter 3).

## 8.1.2   The market supply curve

Aggregating all the supply curves of the individual firms in the market yields the market supply curve (sometimes called the industry, or aggregate, supply curve). Figure 8.3 provides the derivation of such a supply curve.

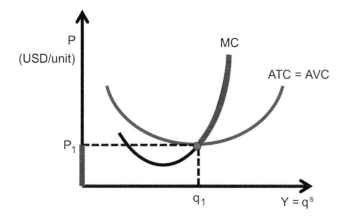

Figure 8.2  Individual-firm long-run supply curve

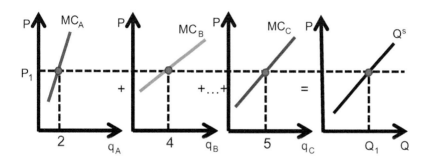

Figure 8.3  Derivation of a market supply curve

The term "horizontal summation" refers to the aggregation of the quantity supplied by each firm into the market supply curve. Figure 8.3 shows the aggregation procedure for three firms, taken as representative of all firms in an entire market. The ellipsis ( . . . ) represents the numerous other firms that are in the same market but are not included in the diagram due to lack of space.

Adding together the MC curve of each of the firms in the industry yields the market supply curve $Q^s$ shown in the far-right graph. Each of the three graphs to the left refers to an individual firm, represented by the symbol "q." The "Q" represents the market supply curve to indicate that the units scale (measurement on the horizontal axis) for the total market is much larger than the units scale for the individual firms.

At an initial price of $P_1$ dollars per unit, firm A sets MR = MC and produces two units of output. Firm B follows the same behavioral rule and produces four units of output. Similar logic causes firm C to produce five units of output. Adding together

Table 8.1 The hypothetical market supply
of bread in New York City

| Price (P)<br>(USD/loaf) | Quantity supplied (Q$^s$)<br>(1,000 loaves) |
| --- | --- |
| 1 | 10 |
| 2 | 20 |
| 3 | 30 |
| 4 | 40 |
| 5 | 50 |

all of the individual firm supply curves (including those that are represented by the ellipsis) yields the point on the market supply curve for price $P_1$:

8.2  $Q_1 = q_A + q_B + \ldots + q_C.$

Following this horizontal summation procedure for different price levels produces a market supply curve ($Q^s$). Keep in mind that only three of the numerous firms in the industry appear in the example. The definition of the **market supply curve**:

● *Market Supply Curve* = the relationship between the price and quantity supplied of a good, *ceteris paribus*, derived by the horizontal summation of all individual supply curves for all individual producers in the market.

Summarizing data on how each individual firm in a market adjusts production levels in response to changes in price produces a hypothetical market supply schedule, as shown in Table 8.1. Real-world supply schedules would look very much the same, with real data substituted for prices and quantities.

The definition of the supply schedule is straightforward:

● *Supply Schedule* = a schedule showing the relationship between the price of a good and the quantity of a good supplied.

The information from the supply schedule leads to a graph of a market supply curve that summarizes the relationship between the price and quantity supplied of a good.

## 8.1.3  The law of supply

The key information provided in a supply schedule is that when the price of a good increases, the quantity supplied increases due to the profit-maximizing behavior of individual firms. This positive, or direct, relationship between price and quantity supplied is so pervasive in market economies that economists are comfortable calling it a "law":

● *Law of Supply* = the quantity of goods supplied to a market varies directly with the price of the good, *ceteris paribus*.

Photo 8.2 Bread supply

*Source:* senk/Shutterstock

The information contained in the supply schedule is the basis for a market supply curve, as shown in Figure 8.4.

There is an unusual but universal feature of this market supply graph. Economists study supply (the behavior of producers) and demand (the behavior of consumers). When they graph a supply curve, they are graphing the relationship

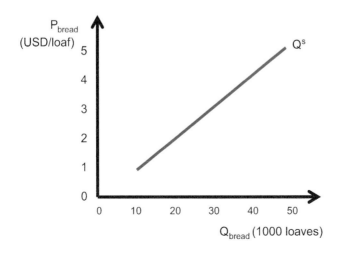

Figure 8.4 Market supply curve for bread in New York City

between the price and quantity supplied of a good. Price is the independent variable since it causes (determines) the quantity of a good sold. Price causes quantity supplied.

8.3a   $P \rightarrow Q^s$ (P causes $Q^s$),
8.3b   P = independent variable,
8.3c   $Q^s$ = dependent variable,
8.3d   $Q^s$ = f (P).

The study of competitive industries in Chapter 4 showed that individual producers
in such industries take prices as given and respond by deciding how much of their
product to place on the market. The individual firms are too small relative to the
entire market to have any effect on the price of a good. Therefore, price causes
quantity supplied.
     Mathematicians locate the independent variable on the horizontal (x) axis and
the dependent variable on the vertical (y) axis. For example, Figure 8.5 shows the
physical relationship between precipitation and the yield of wheat.

8.4a   $x \rightarrow y$ (x causes y),
8.4b   y = f(x),
8.4c   x = fixed = independent variable,
8.4d   y = dependent variable.

Economists draw supply and demand curves "backward" because Alfred Marshall, the first economist to draw supply and demand curves, drew them that way.
Marshall lived in England and in 1890 was among the first economists to study the
relationship between price and quantity using graphical analysis. Economists have
not changed. Analysts and students have continued to use these graphs and labels
since Marshall's time, even though it breaks with the mathematicians' tradition of
placing the independent variable on the horizontal axis and the dependent variable
on the vertical axis.

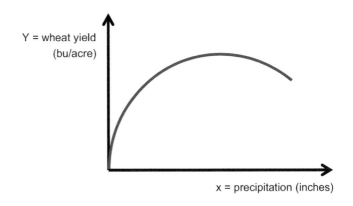

Figure 8.5 Wheat yield as a function of precipitation

In Figure 8.4, price is the independent variable, but it is on the vertical axis. Quantity supplied is the dependent variable, on the horizontal axis. Be aware when working with graphs of supply and demand that the graphs are "backward," since price is the independent variable.

In summary, a market supply curve shows the positive relationship between the price and quantity supplied of a good. The law of supply states that when the price of a good increases, the quantity supplied will also increase, holding all else constant.

To maximize profits, individual firms will produce greater levels of output when prices are higher. A graph of market supply (Figure 8.4) isolates the relationship between price and quantity supplied by holding everything in the economy constant (*ceteris paribus*). Only the price and quantity supplied of a good can vary. The market supply curve provides information about how a market economy functions. The next section expands and explains that information.

## 8.2   The elasticity of supply

The profit-maximizing behavior of business firms leads to a positive (upward-sloping) relationship between the price and quantity supplied of a good. The rate of change in one variable in response to a change in the other variable is of critical importance. It comes down to the question: "How much will quantity supplied increase (decrease) for a given increase (decrease) in the price?" The term "**elasticity**" describes this relationship, and understanding the relationship is important to understanding how a market economy functions.

### 8.2.1   Elasticity defined

**Elasticity** is a measure of the responsiveness of one variable to a small change in another variable:

- *Elasticity* = the percentage change in one economic variable in response to a percentage change in another economic variable.

The elasticity of supply measures how quantity supplied changes when the price of a good increases by 1 percent:

- *Elasticity of Supply* = the percentage change in the quantity supplied in response to a percentage increase in price.

Mathematically, the elasticity of supply ($E^s$) is given by

8.5   $E^s = (\text{\% change in } Q^s)/(\text{\% change in } P) = \%\Delta Q^s / \%\Delta P.$

### 8.2.2   Elasticity classifications

The formula $E^s = \%\Delta Q^s / \%\Delta P$ shows that the price elasticity of supply is the responsiveness (measured by the percentage change) in quantity supplied, given a 1 percent change in the good's own price.

The price elasticity of supply measures the movements along a supply curve. A hypothetical example of the supply curve for bread in New York City appears in Figure 8.4. The degrees of responsiveness of producers to price changes fall into three categories: (1) **inelastic supply**, (2) **elastic supply**, and (3) **unitary elastic supply**.

An **inelastic** supply curve is one that shows relatively small changes in quantity supplied in response to changes in price: a 1 percent change in price results in a less than 1 percent change in quantity supplied. Mathematically, this is equivalent to $\%\Delta Q^s < \%\Delta P$, or $E^s < 1$.

- *Inelastic Supply* = a change in price brings about a relatively smaller change in quantity supplied.

An **elastic** supply curve is one that shows a relatively large change in quantity supplied in response to changes in price: a 1 percent change in price results in a larger than 1 percent change in quantity supplied. Mathematically, this is equivalent to $\%\Delta Q^s > \%\Delta P$, or $E^s > 1$.

- *Elastic Supply* = a change in price brings about a relatively larger change in quantity supplied.

The third category of elasticity is **unitary elastic,** which takes its name from an elasticity of supply equal to one. This means that the change in quantity supplied is equal to the change in the price of a good ($\%\Delta Q^s = \%\Delta P$, or $E^s = 1$).

- *Unitary Elastic Supply* = the percentage change in price brings about an equal percentage change in quantity supplied.

The percentage change of a variable is the change in the variable ($\Delta x$), divided by the level of the variable ($\Delta x / x$). If a student's test scores improve from 80 points to 90 points, the percentage change in tests scores would be this: $(t_1-t_0) / t_0 = (90 - 80) / 80 = 10 / 80 = 0.125$. Similarly, the percentage change in quantity supplied is equal to $\Delta Q^s / Q^s$, and the percentage change in price is equal to $\Delta P / P$.

8.6   $E^s = (\Delta Q^s / Q^s) / (\Delta P / P) = (\Delta Q^s / \Delta P) * (P / Q^s)$.

The degree of price responsiveness of a firm depends on the flexibility of the firm's production processes as it responds to a change in price. In the immediate run, the firm has very little flexibility, so supply is very inelastic. Over a longer time period, the firm has more opportunities to make production choices and changes, so supply becomes more elastic.

Suppose that the price of bread in New York City suddenly increases from USD 1/loaf to USD 2/loaf. What is the elasticity of supply? Start with the mathematical expression for the supply elasticity:

8.7   $E^s = (\Delta Q^s / Q^s) / (\Delta P / P) = (\Delta Q^s / \Delta P) * (P / Q^s)$.

Data in Table 8.1 show that if bread costs USD 1/loaf, 10,000 loaves are supplied to the market. When the price rises to USD 2/loaf, 20,000 loaves are produced. So

$\Delta Q^s = 20{,}000 - 10{,}000 = 10{,}000$, and $\Delta P = $ USD 2/loaf – USD 1/loaf = USD 1/loaf. These numbers substitute directly into the elasticity formula, but what numbers for "$Q^s$" and "$P$" are the correct ones to use? The initial values of price and quantity (USD 1/loaf and 10,000) yield a different number for the supply elasticity than the ending values (USD 2/loaf and 20,000 loaves). Therefore, it is common practice to use the average values of prices and quantities to calculate the elasticity of supply over relatively small changes in price. This practice leads to the calculation of what is called the "arc elasticity."

- *Arc Elasticity* = a formula that measures responsiveness along a specific section (arc) of a supply or demand curve and measures the "average" price elasticity between two points on the curve.

To calculate the arc elasticity, use the average value of price and quantity in the formula for price elasticity. Let $Q^s_{average}$ and $P_{average}$ be the average values of price and quantity:

8.8a  $Q^s_{average} = (Q^s_1 + Q^s_0) / 2$,
8.8b  $P_{average} = (P_1 + P_0) / 2$.

Substituting these terms into the elasticity equation results in

8.9  $E^s = (\Delta Q^s / \Delta P) * (P_{average}/Q^s_{average}) = (\Delta Q^s / \Delta P)*[(P_1 + P_0) / (Q^s_1 + Q^s_0)]$.

The twos in the denominators drop out since there is a two in both the numerator and the denominator. This formula yields the elasticity of supply of bread for a price increase from USD 1/loaf to USD 2/loaf, where "lf" is the abbreviation for "loaf":

8.10
$E^s = (\Delta Q^s / \Delta P) * [(P_1 + P_0) / (Q^s_1 + Q^s_0)]$.
$= [(20{,}000 \text{ lf} - 10{,}000 \text{ lf}) / (\text{USD } 2/\text{lf} - \text{USD } 1/\text{lf})]*$
$[(\text{USD } 2/\text{lf} + \text{USD } 1/\text{lf}) / (20{,}000 \text{ lf} + 10{,}000 \text{ lf})]$
$= [10{,}000 \text{ lf} / \text{USD } 1/\text{lf}] * [\text{USD } 3/\text{lf} / 30{,}000 \text{ lf}]$
$= (10{,}000 / 30{,}000) * (3 / 1) = 1$.

In this case, the supply elasticity of bread in New York City is unitary elastic.

## QUICK QUIZ 8.4

Define and explain the terms elastic, inelastic, and unitary elastic.

Interestingly, there are no units for elasticity. All of the loaves and dollars cancel each other out since they appear in both the numerator and the denominator:

## ELASTICITIES HAVE NO UNITS!

This feature of elasticities is highly desirable since it allows analysts to compare responsiveness to economic change across all goods and services in a uniform fashion. Comparing the change in the quantity available of two different goods such as apples and hamburgers to a change in price of a good is impossible since different goods have different units. Calculating elasticities enables an observer to compare the responsiveness of any goods since the units are identical: they are unitless.

### 8.2.3 Own-price and cross-price supply elasticities

It is possible to calculate elasticities of supply for changes in price and for changes in any other economic variable. The most commonly used elasticity is the **own-price elasticity of supply**.

- *Own-Price Elasticity of Supply* = measures the responsiveness of the quantity supplied of a good to changes in the price of that good.

Another common elasticity is the **cross-price elasticity of supply**, which measures the responsiveness of quantity supplied of one good to a change in the price of a related good. A related good is any good that has an impact on the production of the good under consideration. Slaughtering cattle yields two major products: beef and hides (leather). If the price of hides increases, this will affect not only the quantity of hides supplied but also the quantity of beef supplied.

- *Cross-Price Elasticity of Supply* = a measure of the responsiveness of the quantity supplied of a good to changes in the price of a related good.

### 8.2.4 The relationship between elasticity and slope

To get a better idea about how to calculate supply elasticities, assume that there are only two firms in the soft drink industry: Coke and Pepsi. Table 8.2 shows hypothetical price and quantity supplied information for the two beverages.

The arc elasticity of supply for Coke is as follows:

$$E^s_{coke} = (\Delta Q^s \, \Delta P) * [(P_1 + P_0) / (Q^s_1 + Q^s_0)],$$

8.11    $E^s_{coke} = [(50 - 25) / (0.75 - 0.50)] * [(0.75 + 0.50) / (50 + 25)],$

$$E^s_{coke} = [25 / 0.25] * [1.25 / 75] = 100 * 0.0167 = 1.67.$$

Table 8.2 Price and quantity supplied data for Coke and Pepsi

| Soda price (USD/can) | Coke $Q^s$ (mil cans) | Pepsi $Q^s$ (mil cans) | Soda market (mil cans) |
| --- | --- | --- | --- |
| 0.50 | 25 | 20 | 45 |
| 0.75 | 50 | 25 | 75 |

The supply of Coke is elastic, meaning that a 1 percent increase in the price of Coke results in a 1.67 percent increase in the quantity of Coke supplied. This means that Coke has a relatively flexible production function and can respond to changes in price. The data in Table 8.2 also allows the calculation of the arc elasticity of supply for Pepsi:

8.12 $\quad \begin{aligned} E^s_{pepsi} &= (\Delta Q^s / \Delta P) * [(P_1 + P_0) / (Q^s_1 + Q^s_0)], \\ E^s_{pepsi} &= [(25 - 20) / (0.75 - 0.50)] * [(0.75 + 0.50) / (25 + 20)], \\ E^s_{pepsi} &= [5 / 0.25] * [1.25 / 45] = 20 * 0.0278 = 0.55. \end{aligned}$

The elasticity of supply of Pepsi is relatively **inelastic**. A 1 percent increase in the price of Pepsi results in only a 0.55 percent increase in the quantity of Pepsi supplied. Compared to Coke, Pepsi's production process is less flexible, and therefore, the company is less able to respond to changes in the price of Coke.

Calculation of the soda market (Coke and Pepsi taken together) elasticity of supply follows the same steps as the calculation of the individual firm's supply elasticities. The market elasticity of supply lies between the two individual firm elasticities since the market is composed of only the two firms.

8.13 $\quad \begin{aligned} E^s_{market} &= (\Delta Q^s / \Delta P) * [(P_1 + P_0) / (Q^s_1 + Q^s_0)], \\ &= [(75 - 45) / (0.75 - 0.50)] * [(0.75 + 0.50) / (75 + 45)], \\ E^s_{market} &= [30 / 0.25] * [1.25 / 120] = 120 * 0.0104 = 1.25. \end{aligned}$

As expected, the soda market supply elasticity is between the individual firm elasticities: $0.55 < 1.25 < 1.67$.

## QUICK QUIZ 8.5

Is the market supply for soda elastic or inelastic? Explain.

## QUICK QUIZ 8.6

What is arc elasticity? Hint: see Section 8.2.2.

Figure 8.6 shows two supply curves with different elasticities. The elasticity of supply reflects how responsive a firm is to a change in price. The slope of the supply function reflects this.

In Figure 8.6, the firm with the more elastic supply ($q^s_B$) has a flatter slope than the firm with the more inelastic supply ($q^s_A$). Firm A is less responsive to the price increase from $P_0$ to $P_1$ and increases output from $q^0_A$ to $q^1_A$. Firm B is more responsive to the change in price and increases output from $q^0$ to $q^1_B$. The own-price elasticity of a firm, or the responsiveness of a firm to a change in price, depends on the ability of the firm to adjust inputs and outputs in response to a change in price.

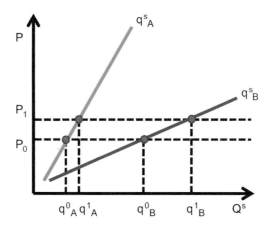

**Figure 8.6** Elasticities of supply for two firms

Although the price elasticity of supply relates to the slope of the supply curve, it is not equal to the slope:

8.14   Slope = $\Delta y / \Delta x = \Delta P / \Delta Q$ Elasticity = $(\Delta Q / \Delta P) * (P / Q)$.

When two supply curves share the same graph, an observer can easily determine which curve is more elastic by looking at the relative slope of the two curves. However, this is not an accurate test for curves on different graphs because the slope depends on the scale of the graph. A steeply sloped curve may be elastic: it depends on the scale used for the graph.

## 8.3   Change in supply; change in quantity supplied

This section introduces terminology useful when working with supply curves. The terms "supply" and "quantity supplied" refer to two different things. This is a common source of confusion to newcomers to the world of supply and demand. With a little practice, however, the terms become less intimidating and very useful in determining the impact of economic variables on the quantity of a good placed on the market. A change in the price of a good causes a *movement along a supply curve* referred to as a **change in quantity supplied**:

● *Change in Quantity Supplied* = a change in the quantity of a good placed on the market due to a change in the price of the good. A movement along the supply curve.

The changes in the market supply of hamburgers in Elko, Nevada, shown in Figure 8.7 make this clear.

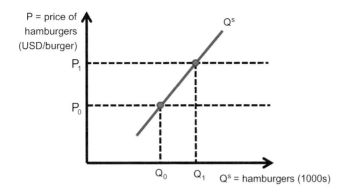

Figure 8.7 Market supply of hamburgers in Elko, Nevada

Photo 8.3 Hamburger supply

*Source:* robertlamphoto/Shutterstock

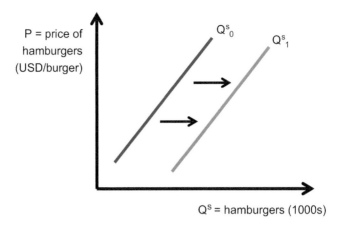

P = price of
hamburgers
(USD/burger)

$Q^s_0$

$Q^s_1$

$Q^S$ = hamburgers (1000s)

**Figure 8.8** An increase in the supply of hamburgers in Elko, Nevada

The supply curve shows the increase in the number of hamburgers supplied to the market in Elko after an increase in price. In Figure 8.7, the price of hamburgers increases from $P_0$ to $P_1$. This causes a movement from $Q_0$ to $Q_1$ along the given supply curve. The movement reflects a change in the *quantity supplied*. This change in price and quantity does not reflect changes in any of the variables (production techniques, extent of market, labor prices, manufacturing technology, and the like) used in the "manufacture" of a hamburger. It reflects the response to an increase in price—that is all. Because the change takes into consideration only the starting and ending prices and the starting and ending quantities, the existing supply curve records all known information related to the change. The curve showing the supplier's capabilities stays in place. This does not represent a "change in supply."

The graph of the market supply curve for hamburgers holds everything constant other than the price and quantity supplied. Therefore, if anything other than the price of hamburgers changes, it causes a shift in the entire supply curve, or a **change in supply**:

● *Change in Supply* = a change in the supply of a good due to a change in an economic variable other than the price of the good. A shift in the supply curve.

Figure 8.8 shows a change in supply.

A rightward shift in the supply curve represents an increase in supply since more hamburgers will reach the market at each price. Similarly, a shift in the supply curve to the left would show a decrease in supply (fewer hamburgers at each price). The increase in supply in Figure 8.8 could result from an increase in the technology available to the firm or a decrease in production costs. Shifts in the entire supply function represent a change in nonprice determinants of supply. The following section explains these supply determinants.

## 8.4 Determinants of supply

The supply of a good results from the interaction of many economic variables. The list of supply determinants generally considered to be most important includes such things as (1) input prices, (2) production technology, (3) prices of related goods, and (4) the number of sellers. Therefore, a formula for a supply curve for a good includes own price (P), input prices ($P_i$), technology (T), prices of other, related goods ($P_o$), the number of sellers (N), and a category "Other," representing all other determinants of supply:

8.15  $Q^s = f(P \mid P_i, T, P_o, N, \text{Other})$.

A graph of a supply curve condenses all of the determinants into the relationship between the quantity supplied of a good ($Q^s$) and the own price of the good (P), while all other variables are held constant (the *ceteris paribus* assumption).

### QUICK QUIZ 8.7

Why are all variables other than the price held constant?

The nonprice determinants of supply are often called "supply shifters" because a change in any one of them results in a shift in the entire supply curve (a change in supply). However, if only the price of a good changes, the result is a movement along the existing supply curve, or a change in quantity supplied.

### 8.4.1 Input prices

The prices that firms pay to purchase inputs have a direct effect on the cost of production (Chapter 3). These prices multiplied by the quantities of inputs purchased represent the costs paid by the producing firm. Since the individual firm's supply curve is the marginal cost curve on any level of output above the shutdown point, any increase in the price of an input will increase the cost of production and hence shift the supply curve upward and to the left.

### QUICK QUIZ 8.8

Define the shutdown point and distinguish it from the break-even point.

Figures 8.9 and 8.10 show how an increase in input prices shifts the supply curve. The comparison allows thinking of the decrease in supply in two ways. First, Figure 8.9 shows that if the price of ground beef increases, the supply of hamburgers shifts upward and to the left since the marginal cost of a hamburger increases. This results in a decrease in supply.

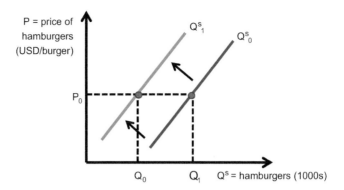

**Figure 8.9  A decrease in the supply of hamburgers in Elko, Nevada, at constant price**

### QUICK QUIZ 8.9

Explain why this is not a decrease in quantity supplied.

At a given price of hamburgers ($P_0$), the firm will decrease its output of hamburgers from $Q_1$ to $Q_0$ in response to the increase in the price of ground beef. An increase in the price of an input causes an increase in the cost of production that results in a decrease in supply, or a shift of the supply curve to the left.

Figure 8.10 shows the same shift in the supply curve of hamburgers due to the increase in the price of ground beef, but the interpretation differs. In this case, the firm raises the price of hamburgers from $P_0$ to $P_1$ to cover the cost of production at the given level of output, $Q_0$.

## 8.4.2  Technology

Technological change allows the production of more output with the same level of inputs or the same level of output produced with fewer inputs (Chapter 2). Either way, improved technology will lower the cost of production for every level of output. The entire supply curve shifts to the right.

### QUICK QUIZ 8.10

Does a shift in the supply curve indicate a change in supply or change in quantity supplied?

Figure 8.11 shows technological change that allows the firm to produce a greater quantity at the same cost.

A rightward shift in supply is an increase in supply. More output produced at the same price, or the same level of output produced at a lower price.

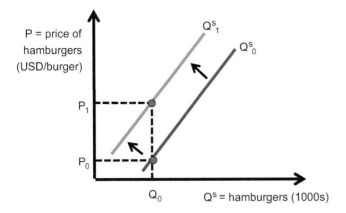

Figure 8.10  A decrease in the supply of hamburgers in Elko, Nevada, at constant quantity

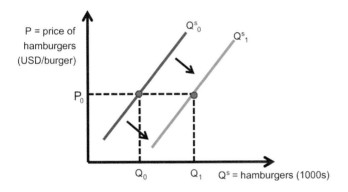

Figure 8.11  The impact of technological change on the supply of hamburgers

## BOX 8.1

### Genetically modified organisms (GMOs)

Farmers, ranchers, scientists, and hobbyists have altered the characteristics of plants and animals ever since the beginning of agriculture. Desirable characteristics, such as higher-yielding plants and more docile animals, have been carefully developed by breeding plants and animals with desired characteristics. The process was accelerated with knowledge of genetics, beginning in the 1860s. Genetic information allowed farmers to develop plants and animals through selective breeding or selecting desirable traits with genes, or DNA.

In the 1950s, scientists discovered methods of changing an organism's DNA. The basic idea of producing GMOs involves altering a living plant or animal's genetic makeup through mutation, deletion, or adding genetic material. When genetic material from a different donor species is combined with that of a recipient species, the resulting DNA, or recombinant DNA, is called a "transgenic organism." First produced in 1972, this "transgene" technique provided a way of modifying the DNA in food, giving rise to the genetically modified organism, or GMO. In 1992, the first commercially produced GMO food, a tomato, was approved for sale in the US. Since then, genetically modified (GM) crops have become widely adopted for desirable traits such as resistance to pests, herbicides, or environmental conditions such as drought.

This area of research grew rapidly as genetically modified, economically suitable food products were developed. Monsanto (now Bayer) was the industry leader, with "Roundup Ready" seeds for corn, cotton, and soybeans. These seeds were resistant to the herbicide Roundup, allowing for crops to be treated with Roundup, without damage to the crop. The economic advantages of GMO crops are large, and quick adoption followed in many nations.

GMOs are controversial for many reasons, including the ethics of producing GM crops. Many consumers believe that there could be unanticipated consequences to either human health or to the environment from GMO production and consumption. Even now, 50 years after the Roundup ready tomato was marketed, farmers in the EU member nations are prohibited from growing or importing GMOs. Recently, some evidence has suggested that glyphosate, the major ingredient of Roundup, could be a carcinogen. Glyphosate use has increased dramatically since the introduction of herbicide-resistant crop use. This, together with glyphosate-resistant weeds, has increased concern about the continued success of GMOs.

Although there is no evidence that GMOs cause harm, a recent report found that 49 percent of US adults believed that eating GMO foods are "worse" for one's health, 44 percent say they are "neither better nor worse," and 5 percent believe they are better (Pew 2018).

Sources: Lynas, Mark. (2018). *Seeds of Science: Why We Got It So Wrong on GMOs*. London, UK: Bloomsbury Sigma.

Pew Research Center, "Public Perspectives on Food Risks," http://pewresearch.org, Nov. 19, 2018. Retrieved January 11, 2023.

BOX 8.2

## Animal welfare

Many consumer groups and others show increasing concern about animal suffering during the production of poultry, meat, and livestock, as well as the food products that include their use. The topic of how best to treat animals in the food production system is challenging, difficult, and controversial. Decisions about animal welfare involve how processing practices affect production costs, as well as how animals are treated and general ethical considerations. Some consider animal welfare, or the happiness and pain experienced by animal, while others recognize animal rights, which are common principles that constrain how people treat animals. Divided public opinion characterizes these issues. Given the diverse opinions on such things as poultry cage space, debeaking birds, free-range animals, and forced molting (restarting the production cycle by depriving hens of food), the most common policy approach is voluntary labeling of food products.

In 2008, California passed a law requiring regulation of confinement practices for farm animals, including egg-laying hens. The law took effect in 2015. Egg producers and other animal agricultural industries have been actively involved in this new regulation since it sets a precedent for future oversight of all animal production systems. The egg industry has moved forward in response to federal legislation that would regulate animal welfare issues in egg production, all other agricultural industries have taken notice.

Temple Grandin, a well-known beef industry leader and spokesperson, has provided "core standards" based on the belief that (1) animals have basic needs and (2) a failure to fulfill these needs places animals under unnecessary stress. These standards include the following: (1) animals must have the opportunity to care for, interact with, and nurture their young; (2) hogs must be able to build nests during farrowing; (3) animals must have sufficient space to move, exercise, and socialize with herd mates; (4) animals must have a dry area where they can lie down at the same time without soiling their bellies; and (5) animals require clean air, including tolerable (noninjurious) ammonia levels.

Livestock producers, researchers, and industry leaders often agree that farming practices that result in healthy, unstressed animals promote higher levels of production and profitability. In some cases, consumers are willing to pay for food that has been produced by animals produced within animal welfare standards.

Producers are concerned that the increased willingness to pay for such products is not enough to cover increased production costs.

Increased concern for animal rights continues to change consumption choices. Recent growth in plant-based meat, opposition to fur-based clothing, and new laws about how animals must be cared for are growing rapidly (Park and Valentino 2019).

*Sources:* Grandin, T. (2010). *Improving Animal Welfare: A Practical Approach.* Wallingford, UK: CABI.

National Research Council. (2010). Toward Sustainable Agricultural Systems in the 21st Century. Committee on Twenty-First Century Systems Agriculture, Board on Agriculture and Natural Resources, Division on Earth and Life Studies.

Yon Soo Park, Yon Soo, and Benjamin Valentino. "Who supports animal rights? Here's what we found." *The Washington Post.* July 26, 2019. www.washingtonpost.com/politics/2019/07/26/who-supports-animal-rights-heres-what-we-found/. Retrieved January 11, 2023.

### 8.4.3 Prices of related goods

In the real world, many firms produce more than one good. Multiproduct firms will choose which good or goods to produce based on relative prices.

**Graph the firm's optimal output selection.**

Changes in relative prices affect goods that are related in the production process. A meat processing plant produces both beef and leather. If the price of leather increases, it will affect (1) the quantity supplied of leather and (2) the supply of beef. Test your knowledge of the difference between a change in supply and a change in quantity supplied by explaining why an increase in the price of beef affects (1) the quantity supplied of beef and (2) the supply of leather.

Beef and leather are complements in production defined as follows:

● *Complements in Production* = goods that are produced together (e.g., beef and leather).

The **cross-price elasticity of supply** ($E^s_{Y1Y2}$) for complements in production is positive: if the price of one of the complements increases, it results in an increase in the supply of the complementary good:

8.16   $E^s_{Y1Y2} = (\Delta Q^s_{Y1} / \Delta P_{Y2}) * [(P_{Y2}^0 + P_{Y2}^1)/(Q^s_{Y1}^0 + Q^s_{Y1}^1)] > 0.$

**Substitutes in production** are the opposite of complements in production. Two goods competing for the same resources are substitutes in the production process:

● *Substitutes in Production* = goods that compete for the same resources in production (e.g., wheat and barley compete for farmland).

The cross-price elasticity of demand for substitutes in production is negative:

8.17   $E^s_{Y1Y2} = (\Delta Q^s_{Y1} / \Delta P_{Y2}) * [(P_{Y2}^0 + P_{Y2}^1)/(Q^s_{Y1}^0 + Q^s_{Y1}^1)] < 0.$

An increase in the price of a substitute (for example, barley) causes a decrease in the supply of its substitute good (for example, wheat). The price change causes farm managers to shift resources into the good with the now relatively higher price and out of the good with the now relatively lower price. Restated, the increase in the price of a substitute good results in a decrease in the supply of its substitute good.

## 8.4.4   Number of sellers

The impact of the number of sellers is direct: more sellers result in a larger supply of a good when they bring new resources into the production of a good. If this is the case, the supply curve will shift to the right, reflecting an increase in supply. If firms exit the industry and take productive resources with them, the supply curve shifts to the left, resulting in a decrease in supply.

There are many other determinants of supply, or "supply shifters." In agriculture, the weather is an important determinant of supply. When weather conditions are favorable, agricultural output increases, resulting in a shift in supply. Government programs can also shift the supply curves of agricultural goods. Government subsidies result in a shift in supply to the right, and increased taxes shift supply curves to the left.

---

### BOX 8.3

## Food supply chains

The food supply chain refers to the process of moving food from farm to table. The process includes food production, processing, distribution, consumption, and waste disposal. The US food supply chain is complex yet effective at ensuring that all individuals and families have food available. Food production and processing are found across the entire world, allowing for the continuation of food security through supply shocks such as weather events, pandemics, and conflicts between nations.

Food moves through the supply chain in a domino-like fashion. If there is a complication or bottleneck at one point in the supply chain, the entire chain can be disrupted, and consumers may not be able to purchase food in the short run. The US food supply chain covers long distance, and consumers have become more disconnected from agricultural production over time. Consumers in the US eat kiwis from New Zealand, bananas from Ecuador, and coffee from Brazil. The intricate market relationships between buyers and sellers at each point in the food supply chain provide flexibility and resilience to changes in supply and demand. When production is affected by weather events in one area, food distributors can shift purchases to another region, and consumers retain the ability to buy a wide variety of high-quality food.

During the Coronavirus (Covid-19) pandemic, meat processing plants had high levels of illness among employees. The industry quickly adapted by distancing workers from each other and maintaining production. Similarly, when Russia invaded Ukraine in February 2022, Ukrainian wheat production and exports were adversely affected. Grain merchandisers reacted by modifying the wheat supply chain, resulting in a relatively stable supply of wheat. This type of flexibility demonstrates how markets and relative price movements signal shortages and surpluses, which result in a steady supply of food to consumers through food supply chains.

## BOX 8.4

### The impact of risk and uncertainty on markets

Risk is defined as a situation where the outcomes of a decisions are known, and the probability of each possible outcome is known. Uncertainty is broader, defined as a situation where the potential outcomes are unknown to the decision-maker. Risk and uncertainty play a prominent role in markets. Agricultural markets are subject to risk and uncertainty that comes from many sources: weather, production vectors such as insects and plant disease, and price risk form market changes. Most recently, food and agricultural market have been subject to supply chain blockages and labor supply shortages.

An example of risk in agriculture is planting a crop of wheat. Historical data provide the probability of different yields per acre to be known. Although the final yield outcome is risky, the outcomes fit a probability distribution. Uncertainty occurs when producers don't know the probability distribution. Uncertainty occurs when producers don't know the probability of possible outcomes: weather, price, and production events are unknown. In a free market economy, profits can occur only when there is uncertainty: not only do producers need to manage uncertainty, they need to seek it out.

Risk can be managed through insurance markets, such as crop insurance, that aggregate a large number of individuals with uncertainty: volume can reduce uncertainty. Investment firms also do this when they invest in a broad portfolio of assets. Risk and uncertainty are a large part of a free market economy. To be successful, producers and consumers must manage risk and seek out uncertainty: not all decisions and ideas will succeed. A successful strategy is often to try many ideas with the hope that one will work.

*Source:* Frank Knight (1921). Risk, Uncertainty, and Profit. Boston, MA: Hart Schaffner, and Marx: Houghton Mifflin Company.

Producer behavior was summarized, together with the details of the supply curve and their determinants. In the next chapter, consumer behavior will be highlighted, then Chapter 10 will bring supply and demand together in markets.

## 8.5 Chapter 8 Summary

1 Supply is the amount of a good available in a given location, at a given time, and at a given price.
2 The marginal cost curve above the minimum average variable cost curve is the supply curve of the individual firm.
3 The horizontal summation of all individual supply curves yields the market supply curve.
4 A supply schedule is a Table showing the relationship between the price of a good and the quantity of a good supplied.
5 The law of supply states that the quantity of goods offered to a market varies directly with the price of a good, *ceteris paribus.*
6 An elasticity is the percentage change in one economic variable with respect to a percentage change in another economic variable.
7 The elasticity of supply is the percentage change in the quantity supplied with respect to a percentage change in price [$E^s = \%\Delta Q^s / \%\Delta P$]. An inelastic supply curve is relatively unresponsive to changes in price ($E^s < 1$); an elastic supply curve is relatively responsive to changes in price ($E^s > 1$); a unitary elastic supply curve describes a good for which a percentage change in price results in an equal percentage change in quantity supplied ($E^s = 1$).
8 The elasticity of supply becomes more elastic as time passes.
9 Elasticities are unitless and can be compared across different goods.
10 The own-price elasticity of supply measures the responsiveness of quantity supplied of a good to changes in the price of that good.

11 The cross-price elasticity of supply measures the responsiveness of quantity supplied of a good to changes in the price of a related good.

12 The change in quantity supplied occurs when the change in quantity of a good sold is a result of a change in the price of a good. Graphically, this is a movement along a supply curve.

13 A change in supply occurs when the change in quantity of a good sold is a result of a change in an economic variable other than the price of a good. Graphically, this is shown with a shift in the supply curve.

14 Determinants of supply include (1) input prices, (2) technology, (3) prices of related goods, and (4) the number of sellers.

15 Complements in production are goods that are produced together. Substitutes in production are goods that compete with the same resources in production.

## 8.6   Chapter 8 Glossary

Arc Elasticity—A formula that measures responsiveness along a specific section (arc) of a supply or demand curve and measures the "average" price elasticity between two points on the curve.

Change in Quantity Supplied—A change in the quantity of a good placed on the market due to a change in the price of the good. A movement along the supply curve.

Change in Supply—A change in the supply of a good due to a change in an economic variable other than the price of the good. A shift in the supply curve.

Complements in Production—Two or more goods produced together in the same production process (e.g., beef and leather).

Cross-Price Elasticity of Supply—A measure of the responsiveness of the quantity supplied of a good to changes in the price of a related good.

Elastic Supply—A change in price brings about a relatively larger change in quantity supplied.

Elasticity—The percentage change in one economic variable in response to a percentage change in another economic variable.

Elasticity of Supply—The percentage change in the quantity supplied in response to a percentage increase in price.

Inelastic Supply—A change in price brings about a relatively smaller change in quantity supplied.

Law of Supply—The quantity of goods supplied to a market varies directly with the price of the good, *ceteris paribus*.

Market Supply Curve—The relationship between the price and quantity supplied of a good, *ceteris paribus*, derived by the horizontal summation of all individual supply curves for all individual producers in the market.

Own-Price Elasticity of Supply—Measures the responsiveness of the quantity supplied of a good to changes in the price of that good.

Substitutes in Production—Goods that compete for the same resources in production (e.g., wheat and barley compete for farmland).

Supply—The relationship between the price of a good and the amount of that good available at a given location and at a given time.

Supply Curve for an Individual Firm—The firm's marginal cost curve above the minimum point on the average variable cost curve.

Supply Schedule—A schedule showing the relationship between the price of a good and the quantity of a good supplied.

Unitary Elastic Supply—The percentage change in price brings about an equal percentage change in quantity supplied.

## 8.7   Chapter 8 Review questions

1   The individual firm supply curve is the

   a   horizontal summation of the market supply curve
   b   MC curve above the maximum ATC
   c   MC curve above the minimum ATC
   d   MC curve above the minimum AVC

2   The market supply curve is

   a   the MC curve above the minimum ATC
   b   the horizontal summation of all individual firm supply curves
   c   the vertical summation of all individual firm supply curves
   d   not enough information provided to answer

3   The law of supply states that

   a   producers will always maximize profits
   b   the price of a good and quantity supplied have a positive relationship
   c   supply equals demand
   d   the law of diminishing returns affects supply

4   An elasticity measures

   a   how prices affect inflation
   b   the law of supply
   c   how economic influences the stock markets
   d   how responsive one variable is to another variable

5   The elasticity of fruit is _____ relative to the elasticity of apples.

   a   more elastic
   b   less elastic
   c   the same level of elasticity
   d   not enough information provided to answer

6   If the price of a good increases 1 percent and quantity supplied increases 2 percent, then the supply of the good is

   a   elastic
   b   inelastic
   c   unitary elastic
   d   cannot tell from the information given

7   If a change in the price of apples results in a change in the quantity supplied of oranges, then the goods are:

   a   own-price elastic
   b   cross-price elastic
   c   related
   d   unrelated

8   If the price of fish increases, then there is a change in:

   a   the supply of fish
   b   the quantity supplied of fish
   c   the amount of fish sold
   d   cannot tell from the information given

9   Each of the following is a determinant of supply except

   a   number of sellers
   b   technology
   c   tastes and preferences
   d   input prices

10  If the price of corn increases, then there is a(n)

a   increase in the supply of corn
b   decrease in the supply of corn
c   increase in the quantity supplied of corn
d   decrease in the quantity supplied of corn

**Answers:** 1. d, 2. b, 3. b, 4. d, 5. d, 6. a, 7. c, 8. b, 9. c, 10. c

For more study questions, flash cards, and study guides, see the online materials at the companion website: www.routledge.com/cw/barkley.

# Chapter 9

## Demand

Photo 9.1 Demand

*Source:* Pressmaster/Shutterstock

DOI: 10.4324/9781003367994-9

## Abstract

This chapter highlights how consumers respond to changes in prices, income, and other economic variables. The demand curve is derived that shows the quantity of a good that consumers will purchase at different prices. The pervasiveness and importance of the law of demand is outlined, and the elasticity of demand is defined and explained. Demand determinants are discussed in detail, including prices, prices of related goods, income, tastes and preferences, expectations of future prices, and population. Business strategies for agribusinesses are emphasized. Demand, together with supply studied in the previous chapter, together form the foundation of economics: markets.

### Chapter 9 Questions

1  How do consumers react to changes in prices, income, and other economic variables?
2  How is the aggregate demand curve derived?
3  What is the law of demand, and how does it help economists understand consumer behavior?
4  How is the elasticity of demand defined, and why is it a useful and important concept?
5  What are the determinants of demand?
6  How can the knowledge of consumer demand lead to better business decisions?
7  How is demand related to markets?

## 9.0  Introduction

Chapters 1 through 7 describe and explain the behavior of individual economic units (producers). These economic actors use specific methods to locate the optimal point in their economic decisions. Producers select the profit-maximizing combinations of inputs and outputs, and consumers purchase combinations of goods to maximize their own utility or satisfaction. Consumers use similar logic when they decide what to purchase. The decision is based on maximizing satisfaction given income, relative prices, tastes, and a number of other factors. This chapter shows the explicit connection between individuals and markets by deriving market, or aggregate, demand curves. The chapter also explains the determinants of market demand and reintroduces the concept of elasticity, or responsiveness of consumers to changes in prices and other economic conditions. Chapter 10 shows how supply and demand curves interact to determine the prices and quantities of goods. The study of consumer behavior is important to producers since consumer choices are the main determinant of profitability.

## 9.1  Demand

While supply curves stem from the marginal cost curves of individual producers, demand curves derive from decisions made by consumers when they decide which goods and services to buy. Demand reflects the purchases that consumers make as they strive to maximize utility, given prices and income. "Demand" is a technical term that describes consumer purchases, or

- *Demand* = consumer willingness and ability to pay for a good.

A good's price is the most important determinant of demand, and a **demand curve** is a graphic representation commonly used to show the relationship between the price of a good and the quantity demanded of that good.

- *Demand Curve* = a function connecting all combinations of prices and quantities consumed of a good, *ceteris paribus*.

This section shows the derivation of an individual consumer's demand curve and then finds the market demand curve by adding together all the individual curves.

## 9.1.1   The individual consumer's demand curve for macaroni and cheese in Pittsburgh, Pennsylvania

The goal here is to derive an individual consumer's demand curve. Begin by assuming that a college student in Pittsburgh has USD 40/week to spend on food. The student purchases two types of food: macaroni and cheese ($Y_1$), which each initially cost USD 2/box ($P_{Y1}$ = USD 2/box), and pizza ($Y_2$), which costs USD 5/pizza ($P_{Y2}$ = USD 5/pizza). Suppose that the grocery store lowers the price of macaroni and cheese from the initial price of USD 2/box to USD 1/box, and later, to USD 0.50/box. These data can be used to derive the relationship between the price of macaroni and cheese and the quantity demanded ($Q^d$). The data help answer the question, "How do changes in price affect the quantity demanded of a good?"

The student's budget for food is USD 40/week, so income (M) equals USD 40/week. In this case, "income" refers to the amount of money allocated to food purchases in a given time period. The following facts allow an observer to graph the consumer's equilibrium as shown in Figure 9.1. The consumer's equilibrium points at each price level are identified in the graph.

9.1a   $Y_1$ = mac-n-cheese      $P_{Y1}$ = USD 2/box
9.1b   $Y_2$ = pizza          $P_{Y2}$ = USD 5/pizza

The graph shows the budget line for the student:

9.2a   $M = P_{Y1}Y_1 + P_{Y2}Y_2$,
9.2b   $Y_2 = (M / P_{Y2}) + (-P_{Y1} / P_{Y2}) * Y_1$,
9.2c   $Y_2 = (40 / 5) + (-2 / 5) * Y_1 = 8 - 0.4 * Y_1$.

The y-intercept ($M / P_{Y2}$) is equal to eight, and the slope is –0.4, as shown in Figure 9.1. Consumer equilibrium is located where the marginal rate of substitution (MRS), or the slope of the indifference curve, is equal to the price ratio, or the slope of the budget line. In Figure 9.1, this initial equilibrium is at the point (10, 4), or ten boxes of macaroni and cheese and four pizzas.

As the price of macaroni and cheese falls, the consumer's opportunity set increases. Figure 9.1 shows that the consumer can purchase more of both goods when the price of macaroni and cheese falls since the consumer's purchasing power increases. By lowering the price of a good and observing how the quantity purchased of a good changes, the grocer can derive the relationship between price and quantity demanded, or a demand curve.

## QUICK QUIZ 9.1

What is the opportunity set in Figure 9.1?

Table 9.1 shows the data needed to derive a **demand schedule** for the Pittsburgh student.

- *Demand Schedule* = information on prices and quantities purchased of a good, *ceteris paribus*.

A demand curve displays the relationship between the price and quantity of a good purchased, or:

9.3   $Q^d$mac cheese = $f(P_{Y1}, P_{Y2}, M)$.

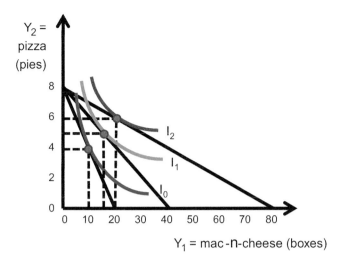

$Y_2 =$ pizza (pies)

$Y_1 =$ mac-n-cheese (boxes)

Figure 9.1 Derivation of a demand curve for macaroni and cheese

Table 9.1 Price and quantity data for student consumption choices

| Price of mac-n-cheese ($P_1 =$ USD/box) | Quantity of mac-n-cheese ($Y_1 =$ boxes) | Quantity of pizza ($Y_2 =$ pies) |
| --- | --- | --- |
| 2 | 10 | 4 |
| 1 | 15 | 5 |
| 0.5 | 20 | 6 |

The consumer's equilibrium points identified in Figure 9.1 and Table 9.1 lead to the derivation of the demand curve for the student, if everything other than the price of macaroni and cheese is held constant. Figure 9.2 shows the resulting demand curve.

The demand curve in Figure 9.2 includes the same information that appears in the consumer equilibrium graph in Figure 9.1. The variable on the y-axis is now the price of macaroni and cheese ($P_{Y1}$) rather than the quantity of pizza ($Y_2$), as in Figure 9.1. The demand curve depicted in Figure 9.2 displays the relationship between the price of macaroni and cheese, and the quantity purchased of the good, *ceteris paribus*. The mathematical expression for this is

9.4   $Q^d$mac cheese $= f(P_{Y1} \mid P_{Y2}, M)$.

A similar process allows derivation of demand curves for all pairs of goods and services.

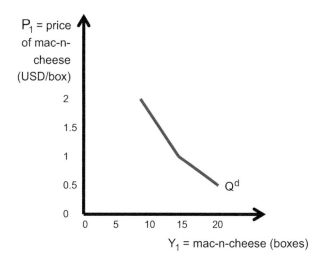

**Figure 9.2** Demand curve for macaroni and cheese

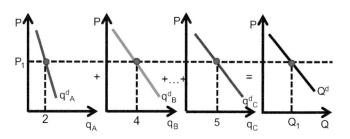

**Figure 9.3** Derivation of a market demand curve

## 9.1.2  The market demand curve

Deriving a market demand curve requires summing all of the individual demand curves in the market. As in the case with supply curves, this summation (or aggregation) requires specific steps to complete. The individual consumer demands (q) are summed horizontally to obtain the market demand curve ($Q^d$), as shown in Figure 9.3.

The market demand curve for any product is the horizontal summation of all of the individual demand curves for that product, in this case, consumers A, B, and C. Note that there are many consumers whose demand curves do not appear in Figure 9.3: the ellipsis ( . . . ) represents all of the remaining consumers in the market. To add demand curves horizontally, take a given price such as $P_1$, and sum the quantities demanded by each consumer at that price.

Following Figure 9.3 and assuming that the product is loaves of bread, consumer A buys two loaves, B purchases four loaves, and C buys five loaves, each consumer paying the same price: $P_1$. Adding all of these quantities together yields the total quantity of bread purchased ($Q^d = 2 + 4 + \ldots + 5$). Next, select a different price and repeat the horizontal summation process. The **market demand curve** is the outcome of this procedure. It appears on the right-hand side of Figure 9.3.

- *Market Demand Curve* = the relationship between the price and quantity demanded of a good, *ceteris paribus*, derived by the horizontal summation of all individual consumer demand curves for all individuals in the market.

### 9.1.3 The law of demand

An increase in the price of a good results in a lower quantity of the good purchased. This regularity of consumer behavior, so consistent across products and services, is called the **law of demand**.

- *Law of Demand* = the quantity of a good demanded varies inversely with the price of the good, *ceteris paribus*.

Stated very simply, the law of demand says that "the demand curves slope down." This is true for all individual consumers, as well as all market demand curves. There can be exceptions to this law, but these occur only in rare and unusual circumstances.

Figure 9.4 shows a demand curve for steak dinners in Philadelphia. A move from right to left along the curve indicates that as the good becomes increasingly scarce, it increases in value. This is consistent with the law of diminishing marginal utility discussed in Chapter 7: the first steak dinner is the best (provides the most utility). However, as consumers eat more steak dinners, the satisfaction derived from each successive steak dinner diminishes.

Supply (a concept dealing with producer behavior) and demand (derived from consumer behavior) are of critical interest and importance in economics. Graphing a supply curve or a demand curve demonstrates the relationship between price and

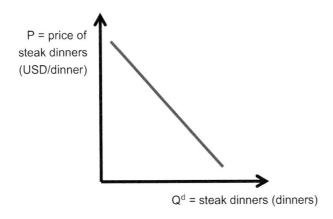

Figure 9.4 The demand for steak dinners in Philadelphia

Photo 9.3 Steak dinner

*Source:* Kasai Bialasiewicz/Shutterstock

quantity. As has been noted, these graphs are conventionally drawn with price (the independent variable) on the vertical axis and quantity demanded (the dependent variable) on the horizontal axis. Price causes quantity demanded.

QUICK QUIZ 9.2

Why do economists draw supply and demand curves "backward"?

9.5a   $P \rightarrow Q^d$       P = independent variable,
9.5b   $Q^d = f(P)$       $Q^d$ = dependent variable.

Consumers of commonly purchased goods take prices as given and decide how much to buy. Assuming a competitive economy, each individual consumer is so small relative to the market that he or she cannot affect the price of a good. Therefore, price causes quantity demanded.

Why does the assumption of competition result in constant prices faced by an individual buyer?

To summarize, the demand curve captures the relationship between the price of a good (P) and the quantity demanded ($Q^d$), *ceteris paribus*. The law of demand states that if the price of a good increases, then the quantity demanded will decrease, *ceteris paribus*. The next section deals with elasticity of demand, a concept used to indicate how responsive consumers are to changes in prices and other economic variables.

## 9.2   The elasticity of demand

"Elasticity," introduced earlier in Chapter 8, measures the changes in one variable that come in response to changes in another variable. The price elasticity of demand tells how responsive the quantity demanded is to a change in price. The price elasticity of demand answers the question, "How much does quantity demanded change when price changes?" Figure 9.5 makes this clear.

When the price of steak dinners falls from $P_0$ to $P_1$, the law of demand states that consumers in Philadelphia (and all other places!) will purchase more steak dinners. The price elasticity of demand tells how many more steak dinners consumers purchase after a drop in price. The price elasticity of demand relates to the slope of the demand curve. The major determinant of the elasticity of demand is the availability of substitutes.

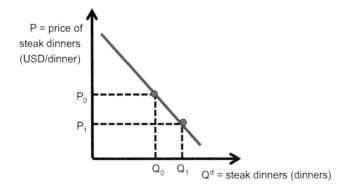

**Figure 9.5 A price change for the demand for steak dinners in Philadelphia**

## THE AVAILABILITY OF SUBSTITUTES DETERMINES THE ELASTICITY OF DEMAND.

If there are very few substitutes for a good, then consumers will find it difficult to "substitute out" of goods that are more expensive and into less expensive goods. However, if substitutes are available, then the consumer's reaction to a price change will be responsive, or elastic, to the change. Think of cigarettes. The many brands available make it easy to respond by switching to another brand when the price of a common brand increases.

---

### BOX 9.1

## Tobacco in North Carolina

Tobacco production and processing are among the most historically important industries in North Carolina. However, increased globalization and reduced numbers of barriers to free trade in agricultural products have resulted in challenges for tobacco producers in North Carolina and the southeast US.

Settlers brought tobacco from Virginia to North Carolina as early as 1663. Tobacco became one of the most important crops in North Carolina, and it remains an important part of the state's agricultural economy. The crop represents about 15 percent of the total value of all crops grown in North Carolina. Processing tobacco is an important industry in the state, which ranks first among tobacco-producing states.

Phillip-Morris produces approximately one-half of all US-produced cigarettes—much of it in North Carolina. RJ Reynolds is currently North Carolina's second-largest tobacco company. The livelihood of US tobacco farms is threatened by foreign tobacco production and decreased demand for tobacco products. In October 2004, Congress eliminated tobacco quotas, reducing profitability for smaller tobacco producers, as the value of imported tobacco increased from USD 690 million in 2004 to USD 752 million in 2011, shifting the tobacco supply curve to the right and causing price to fall.

*Sources:* US Census Bureau: Foreign Trade Division, USA Trade Online. US Import and Export Merchandise trade statistics. usatrade.census.gov. Retrieved January 11, 2023.

---

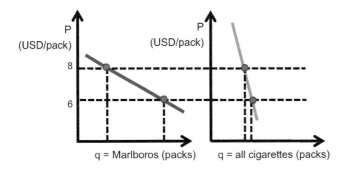

**Figure 9.6** Price elasticity of demand for Marlboros and all cigarettes

Suppose that a hypothetical student, who is a smoker, is studying for a final exam and finds herself in need of nicotine. The student goes to the nearby convenience store to purchase cigarettes. All brands have always sold for USD 6/pack. Now suppose that the price of Marlboro cigarettes increases to USD 8/pack, whereas all other brands continue to sell for USD 6/pack. The student is likely to be responsive to this change in price because of the many substitute brands available: if the price of Marlboros is relatively higher, then the student could shift her purchase to Lucky Strikes or Camels, for example.

On the other hand, if the price of all brands of cigarettes increases to USD 8/pack, then the student is likely to purchase a pack of her favorite Marlboros, even though the price has increased. Why? Because the demand for goods like cigarettes is very inelastic (when a smoker needs a smoke, she needs a smoke). The left panel of Figure 9.6 shows that if the price of one specific brand of cigarettes increases, then consumers shift out of the relatively expensive brand and into relatively less expensive brands. The right-hand panel shows the demand for all cigarettes. There, a price increase does not result in a large substitution out of her favorite brand since there are no good substitutes (cigarettes are cigarettes, and the student needs a smoke!). In the first case, the price difference was large enough to cause the student to make a change. She responded to the change so her demand for the cigarettes was elastic. In the second case, all brands had a high price, so substitution was not possible. The purchaser was unresponsive, so demand for the product was inelastic. In general, the elasticity of demand depends on the availability of substitutes and how willing consumers are to switch their purchases to another good.

**QUICK QUIZ 9.4**

Which is more elastic (responsive) to changes in price: the demand for oranges or for all fruit?

**Photo 9.4** Cigarettes

*Source:* Minerva Studio/Shutterstock

The elasticity of demand for narrowly defined goods is greater than for more broadly defined goods since there are more substitutes available. For example, if the price of blue shirts (narrowly defined) increases, buyers will switch into green shirts, but if the price of all shirts (broadly defined) increases, consumers have few opportunities to purchase a less expensive shirt. Therefore, the elasticity of demand for blue shirts is greater than the elasticity of demand for all shirts. Next, we turn to calculation of demand elasticities.

## 9.2.1 The own-price elasticity of demand

The definition of own-price elasticity of demand is as follows:

- *Own-Price Elasticity of Demand* = the percentage change in the quantity demanded in response to a percentage change in price.

The formula for calculating the price elasticity of demand at a single point on a demand curve is

9.6   $E^d = (\Delta Q^d / Q^d) / (\Delta P / P) = (\Delta Q^d / \Delta P) * (P / Q^d).$

Economists calculate elasticities rather than slopes of demand functions because the slopes of curves are not directly comparable. Recall that it is not possible to graph variables measured in different units in the same quadrant. In Figure 9.7, it appears that purchases of apples are more responsive to price changes than purchases of oranges. Actual calculations of the elasticities are necessary to show if this is the case. The reason is that the units of the graphs are different for apples and oranges.

---

### BOX 9.2

## Washington apples

Currently, the state of Washington has over 175,000 acres of irrigated apple orchards located on the eastern slope of the Cascade Mountains. The area produces 10 to 12 billion apples each year in orchards planted by the settlers as early as the 1820s. The rich soil from volcanic ash, plentiful sunshine, and arid climate provide excellent growing conditions for tree fruits such as apples and pears. The arid climate results in fewer insect and disease problems, making commercial apple production attractive. Today, the typical apple orchard is 100 acres, but some are as large as 5,000 acres. An estimated 40,000 pickers work in the fields during the annual apple harvest. US consumers eat an average of 19 pounds of fresh apples each year, compared to about 46 pounds consumed each year by Europeans. More than half of the fresh crop of eating apples grown in the US is from the orchards in Washington State.

Production practices have evolved continuously, as new technologies and new varieties have been developed and adopted. Recently, high-density plantings use dwarf trees to bring apples into production faster and allow growers to respond more rapidly to changes in consumer tastes and preferences. Smaller trees also reduce the need for labor and equipment during the harvest season. Controlled atmosphere (CA) storage occurs in large, airtight warehouses with reduced oxygen levels and temperatures held constant at 32 to 36 degrees Fahrenheit. This allows for a constant supply of fresh apples throughout the year.

Although there are more than 7,500 varieties of apples worldwide, the top nine varieties of apples grown in Washington State include Red Delicious, Golden Delicious, Gala, Fuji, Granny Smith, Braeburn, Honeycrisp, Cripps Pink, and Cameo. The Red Delicious variety represents about 34 percent of apples grown in the state. Organic apples are about 9 percent of the apple acreage in Washington, with growing demand.

*Source:* Washington State Apple Commission. Waapples.org/did-you-know. Retrieved January 11, 2023.

Photo 9.5 Washington apples

*Source:* Kissofdeath/Shutterstock

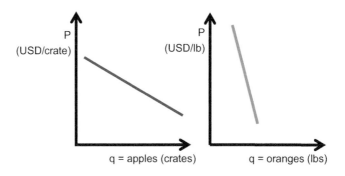

Figure 9.7 Demand for apples and oranges

Elasticities are unitless and therefore attractive to social scientists that make comparisons among elasticities across all goods. The definition of price elasticity makes this clear (equation 9.7):

9.7   $E^d = (\Delta Q^d / \Delta P) * (P / Q^d)$.

Since the price (P) and quantity demanded ($Q^d$) appear in the numerator and the denominator, the units of each cancel, leaving no units for an elasticity calculation.

Hence, economists use elasticities rather than slopes to measure the responsiveness of consumer purchases to changes in prices and other economic variables. These unitless elasticities allow an unbiased comparison of the market values of apples and oranges.

To summarize the discussion, elasticities measure how responsive consumers are to changes in price. An elastic demand curve shows that consumers are more responsive to price changes, while an inelastic demand curve reveals that consumers not so likely to change their buying habits in response to price changes. The elasticities are comparable across all goods. The major determinant of the elasticity of demand is the availability of substitutes. If substitutes are available, then, when the price of a good increases, consumers switch to the lower-priced product.

The price elasticity of demand explains many market-related situations. For example, gasoline stations in college towns often charge higher prices for gasoline the day before the beginning of spring break. On this day when several thousand students are preparing to leave town, the demand for gasoline is relatively inelastic: many of the students will fill their car's tank. Station owners know this and increase the price of fuel to take advantage of the fact that the students will pay higher prices in order to fulfill their vacation plans.

Veterinarians often charge higher prices for rich people with poodles than for poor people with mixed-breed mutts. Why? Because wealthier people are more likely to be willing and able to pay higher prices for vet services than poor people are. The elasticity of demand for medical services is lower (more inelastic) for rich persons than for poor.

Airline tickets usually cost more if purchased on the same day as the flight. Why? Because travelers who have not made flight arrangements prior to the day of the flight have an inelastic demand for airline travel. They are flying in response to an emergency or an urgent situation and are willing to pay higher prices for the flight. The elasticity of demand for airline tickets becomes more inelastic as the day of the flight approaches. Airlines take advantage of this by increasing prices as flight time approaches.

For practice using the elasticity concept, consider the calculation of an arc elasticity of the demand for wheat. The definition of the price elasticity of demand is

9.8    $E^d = \%\Delta Q^d / \%\Delta P = (\Delta Q^d / \Delta P) * (P / Q^d)$.

Calculating the price elasticity of demand requires knowledge of the changes in price and quantity. In words, this is equivalent to the percentage change in quantity demanded that has come in response to a percentage change in price. Suppose that the price of wheat increases from USD 3/bu to USD 5/bu, resulting in a decrease in the quantity of wheat demanded from $Q_1 = 20$ billion bushels to $Q_2 = 16$ billion bushels.

9.9a   $P_1$ = USD 3/bu        $Q_1$ = 20 billion bushels,
9.9b   $P_2$ = USD 5/bu        $Q_2$ = 16 billion bushels,
9.10a  $\Delta P = P_2 - P_1 = 5 - 3 = 2$,
9.10b  $\Delta Q = Q_2 - Q_1 = 16 - 20 = -4$.

The next step in the calculation requires selection of a price and a quantity to plug into the formula. Which P is correct: $P_1$ or $P_2$? Since using either of these prices would result in a different calculation, use the average price. The **arc elasticity** formula shows how this happens:

9.11    $E^d = \%\Delta Q^d / \%\Delta P = [(Q_2 - Q_1) / (P_2 - P_1)] * [(P_1 + P_2) / (Q_1 + Q_2)]$.

This formula uses the average (or mean) prices and quantities for the price and quantity levels. Since the average price is equal to $[(P_1 + P_2) / 2]$, and the average quantity is equal to $[(Q_1 + Q_2) / 2]$, the twos cancel out, resulting in equation 9.11 given earlier.

The law of demand states that if the price increases, consumers will purchase less wheat. Therefore, the sign of the price elasticity of demand will always be negative. The magnitude of the elasticity depends on the availability of substitutes for wheat. Consumers could switch from wheat bread and flour tortillas to corn bread and corn tortillas, for example. The elasticity formula quantifies the responsiveness of consumers to a change in the price of wheat and puts the result that pertains to a change in consumer behavior into a single easily understood number:

9.12    $E^d = (Q_2 - Q_1) / (P_2 - P_1) * (P_1 + P_2) / (Q_1 + Q_2) = (16 - 20) / (5 - 3) * (3 + 5) / (20 + 16) = -0.44$

The law of demand states that the sign of the price elasticity of demand must always be negative. The absolute value of the elasticity converts the elasticity to a positive number, as in equation 9.13:

9.13    $| E^d | = 0.44$.

This elasticity provides a summary of how much quantity demanded changes given a change in price. The price elasticity relates to the demand curve shown in Figure 9.8. The absolute value less than one (= 0.44) indicates that the demand for wheat is relatively inelastic. There are few good substitutes for wheat.

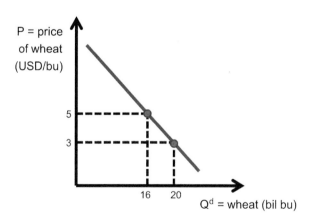

Figure 9.8 The demand for wheat

## 9.2.2 Responsiveness classifications

The relative magnitude of the price elasticity of demand for different goods provides useful information. For example, the quantity demanded of food remains relatively constant since food is a physiological necessity. If the price of food increases, most consumers continue to eat approximately the same amount. In more formal terms, the demand for food is inelastic because the quantity demanded does not vary with changes in price. Examples of common goods with inelastic demands include necessities of all types (food, housing, medicine, tobacco, gasoline, toothpaste, newspapers, and the like).

- *Inelastic Demand* = a percentage change in price brings about a smaller percentage change in quantity demanded.

Recall the definition of elasticity:

9.14   $E^d = \%\Delta Q^d / \%\Delta P$.

In the case of a good with an inelastic demand, the percentage change in price is greater than the percentage change in quantity demanded ($\%\Delta Q^d < \%\Delta P$). Therefore, when demand for a good is inelastic, the absolute value of the price elasticity of demand is less than one, $|E^d| < 1$, as shown in Figure 9.9.

The demand for food depicted in Figure 9.9 is inelastic. The quantity demanded is relatively unresponsive to a change in price. In such a case, the magnitude of the elasticity of demand is relatively small. If the price of the good increases by 1 percent, then the quantity demanded will decrease by less than 1 percent.

Consider how consumers respond to changes in the price of expensive meals in upscale restaurants. If the restaurant increases the price of one specific item on the menu, customers will switch away from the relatively high-cost meal and select

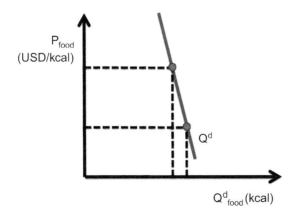

Figure 9.9 Demand for an inelastic good: food

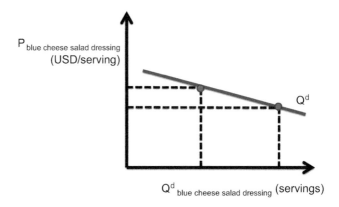

**Figure 9.10** Demand for an elastic good: blue cheese salad
dressing

lower-cost menu items. Since substitutes are available, consumers are responsive
to changes in price. Menu items are goods with **elastic demands**.

- *Elastic Demand* = a percentage change in price brings about a larger percentage change in quantity demanded.

A 1 percent increase in the price of a good with an elastic demand results in a
greater than 1 percent decrease in the quantity demanded. In the case of elastic
demand, $| E^d | > 1$, since $\%\Delta Q^d > \%\Delta P$. In a graph of an elastic demand, such as
for blue cheese salad dressing (Figure 9.10), the percentage change in quantity
demanded is larger than the percentage change in price.

Substitutes exist for the blue cheese salad dressing, so the demand for this item
is elastic. Recall that the demand for food as a whole is inelastic since there are no
good substitutes. Even so, food items for which demand is elastic might include
Florida oranges, Idaho potatoes, McDonald's Big Macs, avocados, and fresh
peaches.

### QUICK QUIZ 9.5

Explain why each of the goods listed has an elastic demand.

The third and last category of price elasticity of demand is **unitary elastic
demand**.

- *Unitary Elastic Demand* = the percentage change in price brings about an
equal percentage change in quantity demanded.

Table 9.2 Demand elasticity classifications

| | |
|---|---|
| Unitary | $|E^d| = 1$ |
| Inelastic | $|E^d| < 1$ |
| Elastic | $|E^d| > 1$ |

Mathematically, the formula for unitary elasticity is as follows:

9.15 $E^d = \Delta Q^d / \Delta P \ast (P_1 + P_2) / (Q_1 + Q_2) = 1$.

In this case, the quantity demanded of the good falls by the same percentage as the price of the good rises. Table 9.2 summarizes the three categories of the price elasticity of demand.

The magnitude of the price elasticity depends on the availability of substitutes. Alternative purchases typically become more available over time, resulting in the demand for a particular product becoming more elastic. Consumers become more responsive to changes in prices as time passes. Suppose that the price of electricity increases. An individual consumer cannot typically change sources of electricity in the short run. Therefore, the demand for electricity in the short run is inelastic: households purchase the same level of kilowatt-hours (kwh) and are likely to stay at approximately the same level even when prices increase.

Over time, and within some limits, consumers substitute out of electricity by purchasing natural gas furnaces, water heaters, and kitchen appliances. Some households may even invest in solar power, wind power, and other alternative sources of power. Since consumers have more choices as time passes, the demand for electricity becomes more elastic over time.

## 9.2.3 The elasticity of demand and total revenue

A business firm's pricing strategy is based on the price elasticity of demand for its product. Consider a firm that is attempting to maximize total revenue (TR = P * Q, where P is the per-unit price and Q is the quantity sold). Figure 9.11 shows the demand curves for a product with an inelastic demand and a product with an elastic demand. The inelastic demand case suggests that a firm can increase total revenue by decreasing output and increasing price: added revenue from the price increase will outweigh the decrease in output sold. Alternatively, with the help of some familiar equations:

9.16a $\quad TR = PQ$,
9.16b $\quad \Delta TR = \Delta(PQ) = \Delta P \Delta Q$.

When demand is inelastic, as it is in the left graph of Figure 9.11, the positive price increase ($\Delta P$) is larger than the decrease in quantity sold ($\Delta Q$), so reductions in quantity sold result in an increase in total revenue. Given an inelastic demand, a

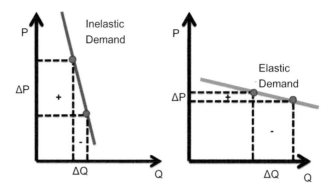

Figure 9.11 Demand for inelastic and elastic goods

firm will reduce output to increase price and revenue. Making the product scarce causes total revenue to increase.

The strategy of reducing output backfires for a firm facing an elastic demand: the reduction in quantity would be greater than the price increase, resulting in a decrease in total revenue. This is because the decrease in quantity ($\Delta Q$) is larger than the increase in price ($\Delta P$). This is shown in the right graph of Figure 9.11.

QUICK QUIZ 9.6

Describe the impacts on total revenue of an agricultural policy that reduces the number of acres of land planted to wheat in the US.

The relationship between the price elasticity of demand and total revenue explains why business firms are so interested in the elasticity of demand for the goods sold by the firm. An effective pricing strategy requires knowledge of how customers will respond to a change in price: it requires knowledge regarding the elasticity of demand for the products it sells.

## 9.2.4   Own-price and cross-price demand elasticities

Elasticities of demand are associated with (1) the good's own price and (2) the price of a related good. Recall that the own-price elasticity of demand measures the responsiveness of the quantity demanded of a good to changes in the price of that good. A related good is one that has an impact on the consumption of another good. The **cross-price elasticity of demand** measures how the demand for one good changes when the price of a related good changes.

- *Cross-Price Elasticity of Demand* = a measure of the responsiveness of the quantity demanded of a good to changes in the price of a related good.

The cross-price elasticity is written as $E^d_{Y1Y2} = \%\Delta Q^d_{Y2} / \%\Delta P_{Y1}$. This formula states that the cross-price elasticity of demand is the percentage change in quantity demanded of good $Y_2$ given a percentage change in price of good $Y_1$. If two goods $Y_1$ and $Y_2$ are unrelated, then the change in the price of $Y_1$ has no effect on the consumption of good $Y_2$, and the cross-price elasticity is equal to zero ($E^d_{Y1Y2} = 0$). There are two types of related goods in consumption: **substitutes** and **complements**.

- ***Substitutes in Consumption*** = goods that are consumed on an "either/or" basis, such as wheat bread and white bread.

Corn and milo (sometimes called "grain sorghum") are substitutes in consumption for feeding cattle. A feedlot operator can purchase either of these two feed grains since they are nearly equivalent nutritionally. If the price of corn increases, then the demand for milo increases as feedlots substitute out of corn and into milo. Thus, the cross-price elasticity of demand is positive for substitutes.

9.17   $E^d_{Y1Y2} = \%\Delta Q^d_{Y2} / \%\Delta P_{Y1} > 0$

Electric appliances (stoves, furnaces, and hot water heaters) and natural gas appliances are frequently substitutes. Most homes in the northern United States have either gas or electric appliances (sometimes both), depending on the relative prices of natural gas and electricity. Within some limits gasoline and bicycles are substitutes. As the price of gasoline rises, short-distance commuters switch to bicycles.

Complements in consumption are goods consumed together, for example, bread and butter, or biscuits and gravy, or dress shirts and neckties.

- ***Complements in Consumption*** = goods that are consumed together, such as peanut butter and jelly.

If the price of bread increases, consumers will purchase less bread and as a consequence, they need less butter. The demand for butter decreases when the price of bread increases. This means that the cross-price elasticity of butter with respect to bread is negative:

9.18   $E^d_{Y1Y2} = \%\Delta Q^d_{Y2} / \%\Delta P_{Y1} < 0.$

Unrelated goods might include ice cream, houses, and laptops. The number of homes purchased is likely unrelated to the price of ice cream or the price of laptops. Consequently, the price of houses has no impact on the demand for ice cream or the demand for laptop computers. In these cases, the **cross-price elasticity of demand** is equal to zero.

9.19   $E^d_{Y1Y2} = \%\Delta Q^d_{Y2} / \%\Delta P_{Y1} = 0.$

## 9.2.5   The relationship between elasticity and slope

As with supply curves, the elasticity of demand relates to the slope of the demand curve but is not equal to it. Use caution when comparing the slopes of two demand

curves drawn in different graphs. The slope may reflect different scales on the horizontal and vertical axes and thus be misleading. Elasticities across goods are comparable only when the actual elasticities are calculated.

## 9.3 Change in demand; change in quantity demanded

Earlier in this chapter, data from a consumer equilibrium graph showed that successively lowering the price of macaroni and cheese increased the quantity purchased. This showed that the demand curve is a function of the relationship between price and quantity demanded, *ceteris paribus* (holding all else constant). The demand curve reflects a consumer's willingness and ability to purchase a good at each of several prices for the good.

The demand curve for high-quality Certified Angus Beef (CAB) demonstrates the difference between a change in demand and a change in quantity demanded. Graphically, a change in the price of beef is represented by a movement along an existing demand curve. This movement along the curve represents a change in the quantity demanded. This shows that if the price of beef decreases while all else is held constant, consumers will eat more beef.

QUICK QUIZ 9.7

Why does the quantity of beef demanded decrease when the price of beef increases?

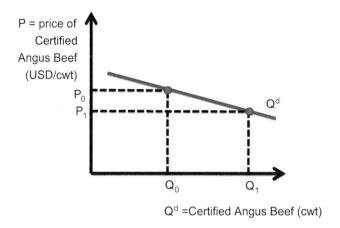

**Figure 9.12  Increase in the quantity demanded of Certified Angus Beef**

- ***Change in Quantity Demanded*** = when a change in the quantity of a good purchased is a result of a change in the price of the good. A movement along a demand curve.

The movement along a demand curve is due to a change in the price of the good or a change in quantity demanded, as depicted in Figure 9.12.
   If anything other than the good's own price changes, then there is a shift in demand, known as a **change in demand**.

- ***Change in Demand*** = when a change in the quantity of a good purchased is the result of a change in an economic variable other than the price of the good. A shift in the demand curve.

An increase in income causes the entire demand curve to shift out (to the right) since an increase in purchasing power will result in consumers buying more beef at each price. This is a change in demand due to consumers being able to afford to eat more beef, as shown in Figure 9.13.

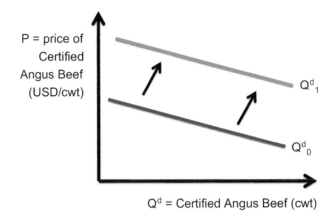

P = price of
Certified
Angus Beef
(USD/cwt)

$Q^d_1$

$Q^d_0$

$Q^d$ = Certified Angus Beef (cwt)

Figure 9.13 An increase in the demand for Certified Angus Beef

### 9.3.1 Examples of demand changes

1   The price of corn and the demand for soda
    What does the price of corn have to do with the price of soda? Corn is a major
        input in the production of soda since high-fructose corn syrup (HFCS)
        is the sweetener used for most sodas. Therefore, as the price of corn
        increases, the price of soda increases. Does this cause a shift or a move-
        ment in demand? It causes a change in the price of soda, so the result is a
        movement along the demand curve for soda, seen in Figure 9.14.

2   The impact of cold weather on cattle
    Very cold weather can slow the growth of or even kill cattle. An extreme
        weather event of this kind reduces the number of cattle available for
        slaughter. This, in turn, results in an increase in the price of beef. The
        result is a movement along the demand curve, as shown in Figure 9.15.

3   The price of milo's impact on the demand for corn
    Milo and corn are nearly perfect substitutes as cattle feed, and either grain is
        suitable for use in a feedlot.
    An increase in the relative price of milo results in a movement along the
        demand curve for milo and a shift in the demand for corn, or an increase
        in the demand for corn (Figure 9.16).

4   College
    The tuition at public colleges (universities) in the United States is a topic of great
        concern. Suppose that tuition is considered to be the "price" of a college degree.
        An increase in tuition will result in a movement along the demand curve or a
        change in quantity demanded, as shown in Figure 9.17. Some students will
        shift out of college and into employment when the price of college increases.

5   The effect of a decrease in income on the demand for veterinary services
    If an economic variable other than the price changes, it results in a change
        in demand, or a shift in the demand curve, as seen in Figure 9.18. If the
        income level in a community declines, for example, then the purchasing
        power of individuals and households falls and less money is available to

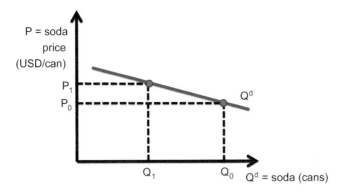

Figure 9.14  A decrease in the quantity demanded of soda

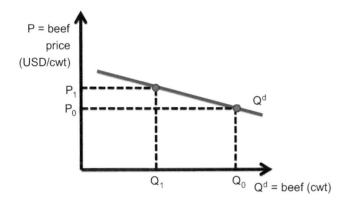

Figure 9.15  A decrease in the quantity demanded of beef

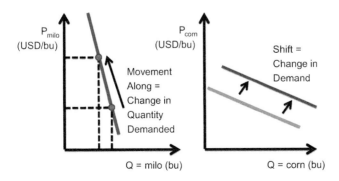

Figure 9.16  Change in demand and change in quantity demanded

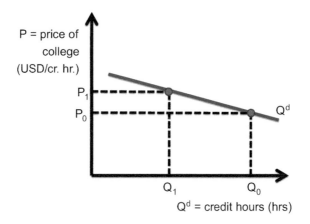

Figure 9.17 An increase in tuition, the price of college

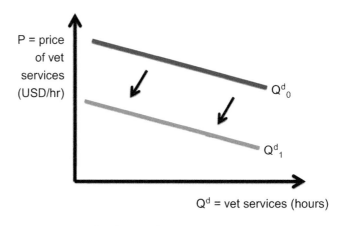

Figure 9.18 A decrease in the demand for veterinary services

spend on veterinary services. Individuals and families will forego veterinary services such as preventative medicine and annual check-ups. These
services may seem "optional" for pets when spendable income is low.

## 9.4 Determinants of demand

The own price of a good ($P_{own}$) is the most important determinant of demand.
Other determinants of demand include the price of related goods ($P_{related\ goods}$),
income (M), tastes and preferences (TP), expectations of future prices (EP), and
population (Pop), as written in this demand function:

9.20   $Q^d = f(P_{own}, P_{related\ goods}, M, TP, EP, Pop)$.

There are other determinants, but this list includes the most important ones. Each needs additional discussion. The first demand determinant is the good's own price. The law of demand says that if the price of a good increases, then the quantity demanded decreases, *ceteris paribus*.

---

**QUICK QUIZ 9.8**

When the price of a good changes, is it followed by a change in demand or a change in quantity demanded?

---

## 9.4.1 Prices of related goods

A second determinant of demand appeared in Section 9.2.4. There it was shown that substitutes in consumption are goods that can be purchased on an "either/or" basis. Corn and milo are both feed grains and are substitutes in the production of beef. Depending on the relative prices of the two grains, feedlot managers will purchase either one. If the price of corn increases, consumers (feedlots) substitute out of corn and into milo. If the price of corn increases, the quantity demanded of corn decreases, and the demand for milo increases.

Complements in consumption are goods that are used together, such as bread and butter. If the price of butter increases, the quantity demanded of butter decreases, and the demand for bread will decline as well.

## 9.4.2 Income

Changes in income levels have a significant impact on the demand for goods and services. Think of the vast differences between the types of goods that a homeless person consumes compared to the consumption habits of a very wealthy person. Increases in the incomes have a huge impact on the type and magnitude of goods and services that consumers demand and purchase.

---

**BOX 9.3**

### US wheat exports

On average, about 7.5 million bushels of wheat enter international markets each year. Approximately 10 percent of this total comes from the US. Much of the wheat exported from the US goes to low-income nations. In a low-income nation in sub-Saharan Africa or Asia, incomes are at or near subsistence levels, and any increase in income increases expenditures on food. When income levels rise in Korea, China, or Pakistan, the US exports more wheat to these countries, increasing the incomes of wheat producers in the US.

*Source:* USDA/ERS. Retrieved January 11, 2023.

---

The relationship between income and consumption is highly important to agriculture. As incomes increase, purchases shift from goods such as ramen noodles and macaroni and cheese to steak and roses. The demand for agricultural goods produced in the US strongly depends on the level of income in other countries.

Over a century ago, a German statistician named Ernst Engel (1821–1896) studied the relationship between consumers' incomes and their expenditures. His studies resulted in a functional relationship between income and consumption called the **Engel curve** and written as follows:

9.21    $Q^d = f(M \mid P_{own}, P_{related\ goods}, TP, EP, Pop)$.

- **Engel Curve** = the relationship between income and quantity demanded, *ceteris paribus*.

Engel's studies of the consumption patterns of individuals led him to a relationship now called **Engel's law**.

- *Engel's Law* = as income increases, the proportion of income spent on food declines, *ceteris paribus*.

Notice that Engel's law says that the proportion of income spent on food, not the total dollars spent on food. This means that as people become wealthier, they spend more dollars on food, but the proportion of income spent on food increases at a declining rate. Engel's law has major implications for agriculture. It implies that as income increases, production agriculture decreases in importance relative to the rest of the economy. This has happened over the course of US history. In the pre-revolutionary years, nearly every European who settled in what is now the United States was a farmer. Now, early into the twenty-first century, less than 2 percent of the US population is engaged in farming. Engel was right. As levels of living in the United States increased, agriculture lost importance as a part of the overall economy.

Engel's law can be observed in the Engel curve for food, as shown in Figure 9.19. The curve shows the relationship between income (M) and the quantity of food purchased ($Q^d$). Near the origin, where income is equal to zero, a one dollar increase in income likely results in a one dollar increase in expenditures for food.

At low levels of income, most of the budget goes for food. As income levels increase, purchases of food continue to increase (the slope of the Engel curve is positive), but at a decreasing rate reflecting the increasing purchase of nonfood items. At a certain point, food purchases reach a maximum and begin to fall, indicating that wealthy individuals may not spend as high a proportion of their incomes on food as individuals with lower levels of income. Statistical evidence shows that this is true.

## QUICK QUIZ 9.9

Does the Engel curve show that middle-income families purchase less food than low-income families? Explain why or why not.

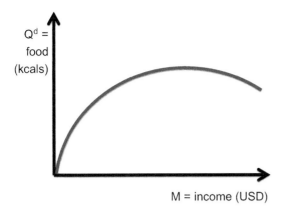

**Figure 9.19** An Engel curve for food

An example introduced in Section 9.1.1 provides a closer look at Engel's law by showing the derivation of two Engel curves. The Pittsburgh college student in the example purchases only two goods: macaroni and cheese (mac-n-cheese, $Y_1$) and pizza ($Y_2$). The student has a weekly income of USD 40. The price of macaroni and cheese is two dollars per box for ($P_{Y1}$ = USD 2/box), and the price of pizza is five dollars per pizza pie ($P_{Y2}$ = USD 5/pie). To summarize:

9.22a  M = USD 40/week,
9.22b  $Y_1$ = mac-n-cheese, $P_{Y1}$ = USD 2/box,
9.22c  $Y_2$= pizza, $P_{Y2}$ = USD 5/pie.

The objective here is to show how the consumer's equilibrium purchases change with a change in income. This requires increasing the income available for food expenditures from USD 40/week to USD 60/week, and then to USD 80/week, as in Figure 9.20.

The small circles in Figure 9.20 indicate the consumer's equilibrium points at each income level. The student buys more pizza as income is increased. The graph also shows increases in the consumption of macaroni and cheese when income increases from USD 40/week to USD 60/week. However, when income increases to USD 80/week, the purchases of macaroni and cheese decline.

### QUICK QUIZ 9.10

What determines the shape and location of the budget lines drawn for each level of income?

The Engel curve depicts the relationship between income and quantity demanded. The data in Table 9.3 form the bases of Engel curves for both macaroni and cheese and pizza, as depicted in Figure 9.21.

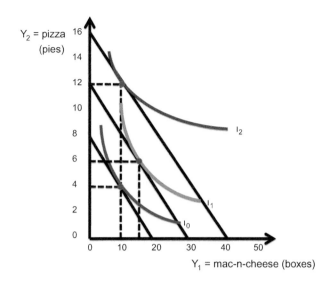

Figure 9.20 Derivation of Engel curves for macaroni and cheese and pizza

The mathematical expression in equation 9.23 shows the relationship between income (M) and quantity demanded ($Q^d$), holding all else constant:

9.23 $Q^d = f(M \mid P_{own}, P_{related\ goods}, TP, EP, Pop)$.

The graph on the right side of Figure 9.21 shows how pizza consumption increases as income increases. The relationship between income and pizza purchases is positive, meaning that increased income leads to increased purchases of pizza. Economists call the type of good whose consumption increases as income increases a **normal good**.

- *Normal Good* = a good whose consumption increases in response to an increase in income.

Normal goods might include such goods as food, clothing, and automobiles. Other goods exhibit decreased consumption levels as income increases: **inferior goods**.

Table 9.3 Consumer purchases and income

| M income (USD/week) | Y₁ Qᵈ mac-n-cheese (boxes) | Y₂ Qᵈ pizza (pies) |
|---|---|---|
| 40 | 10 | 4 |
| 60 | 15 | 6 |
| 80 | 10 | 12 |

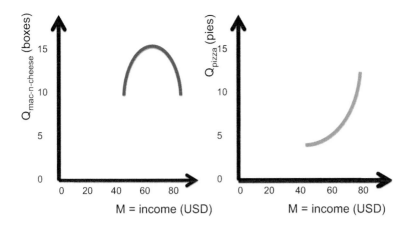

Inferior goods could include used clothing or macaroni and cheese. As incomes rise, consumers substitute out of inferior goods and into normal goods.

- *Inferior Good* = a good whose consumption declines in response to an increase in income.

The left side of Figure 9.21 shows that the consumption of macaroni and cheese increases as income increases from USD 40/week to USD 60/week (macaroni and cheese is a normal good in this range) but declines as income rises from USD 60 to USD 80 per week (macaroni and cheese is an inferior good in this range). As people earn more money, they first increase their consumption of inexpensive foods (e.g., macaroni and cheese, ramen noodles, spaghetti). When incomes reach a certain level, consumers begin to shift out of inexpensive foods and into more expensive foods, such as steak and seafood.

A **luxury good** is a good purchased at an increasing rate when income increases. Pizza consumption as shown in Figure 9.21 is an example. A luxury good is a specific type of normal good since the relationship between income and quantity consumed is positive.

- *Luxury Good* = a good whose consumption increases at an increasing rate in response to an increase in income.

A **necessity good** is also a normal good, but one where consumption increases at a decreasing rate as income increases:

- *Necessity Good* = a good whose consumption increases at a decreasing rate in response to an increase in income.

The relationship between income and consumption is crucial to farmers and to other producers of goods or services. Taking food as perhaps the best example, as the level of living increases in low-income nations such as Haiti and Korea, consumers substitute out of less expensive calorie sources, such as grains, and into more expensive sources, such as beef and chicken. This increase in meat consumption has a large, positive effect on the incomes of food producers in the United States.

Some meat consumed in Asia originates in the United States. It takes approximately seven pounds of grain to produce one pound of beef. Therefore, increases in Asia's consumption of US meat increases the demand for feed grains, which are major crops produced in the Great Plains region of the US. Any increase in the development of low-income nations that leads to an increase in income will enhance the demand for meat consumption, which in turn will result in an increase in the well-being of producers in the United States.

Economists summarize the relationship between income and consumption with the **income elasticity of demand**.

● *Income Elasticity of Demand* = the percentage change in the demand for a good in response to a percentage change in income.

The mathematical formula for the income elasticity of demand is:

9.24   $E^m = \%\Delta Q^d / \%\Delta M = (\Delta Q / Q) / (\Delta M / M)$.

This formula is a "point elasticity" that can be used to find the income elasticity of demand at any point on an Engel curve. The arc elasticity formula is as follows:

9.25   $E^m = \%\Delta Q^d / \%\Delta M = \Delta Q / \Delta M) * (M_1 + M_2 / Q_1 + Q_2)$.

The income elasticity of demand allows the classification of goods into three categories, based on the responsiveness of consumers to changes in their incomes (Table 9.4).

The study of the relationship between income and consumption leads to one important conclusion. Agricultural producers and agribusinesses can improve their economic situation by following the saying, "Give the consumers what they want!" As average incomes increase in the United States, consumers will shift out of inferior goods and into luxury goods. In agriculture, luxury goods include organic fruits and vegetables, free-range chicken, and hormone-free beef.

### Table 9.4 Good responsiveness to income

| | | |
|---|---|---|
| Normal goods | $E^m > 0$ | $\%\Delta Q^d > 0$ |
| Luxury goods | $E^m > 1$ | $\%\Delta Q^d > \%\Delta M$ (normal good) |
| Necessity goods | $0 < E^m < 1$ | $\%\Delta Q^d < \%\Delta M$ (normal good) |
| Inferior goods | $E^m < 0$ | $\%\Delta Q^d < 0$ |

# Natural and organic beef

As incomes rise, consumers have increasingly demanded meat products perceived to be healthier and less harmful to the environment. Natural and organic beef products are more popular and are likely to become even more popular over time. Currently, natural beef comprises a small but growing percentage of the total beef market, at approximately 2.7 percent of all beef consumed in the US. Producers of natural beef may use a USDA label if (1) the product is minimally processed, (2) the product contains no artificial ingredients, and (3) the product contains no preservatives. The company or organization owning the brand name of this beef is responsible for the administration and regulation of these requirements. Natural beef contains no antibiotics or growth hormones.

Organic beef is a much more stringent label, requiring no antibiotics or growth hormones and no feed that includes nonorganic sources such as fertilized pastures or agricultural chemicals such as herbicides. Certification is administered and monitored by the USDA and requires a great deal of time, effort, and documentation. Natural and organic beef products are more expensive than conventional beef products. Understandably, organic beef is typically much more expensive than natural beef due to the high cost of acquiring organic feed grain. Approximately 1 percent of all beef consumption is organic beef.

Beef cattle producers must carefully weigh the benefits of natural and organic beef (price premiums) with the additional costs of modifying their production practices.

*Source:* "Production Claims at Retail." March 5, 2021. www.beefitswhatsfordinner.com/retail/sales-data-shopper-insights/production-claims-at-retail Retrieved January 11, 2023.

An economist recommends that agricultural producers and agribusinesses not waste time or effort opposing this type of good. Instead, they should just "Give the consumers what they want!" and revenue will increase. There is a large and increasing demand for expensive agricultural goods in high-value markets. This relates to the changing tastes and preferences of consumers who live in high-income nations.

## 9.4.3 Tastes and preferences

The tastes and preferences of consumers are a major determinant of the demand for goods and services in the US, and although this is true, it is also true that tastes and preferences change with time—sometimes quite quickly. Tobacco use, for example, has dropped dramatically for the entire population in the US, although smoking among young persons is higher now than it was 30 years ago. Similarly, food safety has become a much more important determinant of consumer demand for agricultural products, due to outbreaks of salmonella in poultry and *Escherichia coli* in beef. Organic fruits and vegetables are a small but rapidly growing sector in food marketing. Consumer tastes and preferences are always changing, based on trends, relative prices, fads, and other, sometimes difficult-to-isolate factors.

> ## BOX 9.5
>
> ## Antibiotic use in food production
>
> Antibiotics (also called antimicrobial drugs) are used extensively in meat production, both in the US and throughout the world. Antibiotics are added to animal water or feed to promote weight gain. Although antibiotics are used to cure animal disease, most antibiotic use is subtherapeutic or prophylactic. Drugs are used to proactively maintain animal health and increase weight.
>
> The use of antibiotics in animal agriculture has been and continues to be controversial, due to concerns of overuse in livestock production, which could lead to antimicrobial drug-resistant bacteria (USFDA 2012). The US Government Accounting Office (USGAO 1999) reported increased consumer concern for antibiotic effectiveness due to (1) overprescription by medical doctors, (2) improper use by patients, (3) routine use in meat production, and (4) resistant strains of bacteria. Many nations have banned the use of antibiotics for growth promotion. The FDA implemented a five-year plan for antimicrobial stewardship in 2017, to be implemented between 2019 and 2023. The plan increases veterinary oversight for use of most medicated feeds, which has reduced sales of medically important antibiotics by 28 percent (Maday 2019). Antibiotic use is anticipated to continue to decrease over the course of the five-year plan.
>
> *Sources:* US Food and Drug Administration (FDA). "The Judicious Use of Medically Important Antimicrobial Drugs in Food-Producing Animals." CVM GFI #209. April 2012.
>
> US General Accounting Office (GAO). "Food Safety: The Agricultural Use of Antibiotics and Its Implications for Human Health." RCED-99–74: April 28, 1999.
>
> Maday, J. "FDA Plans Next Moves on Antimicrobials." Bovine Veterinarian. August 13, 2019. www.bovinevetonline.com/article/fda-plans-next-moves-antimicrobials. Retrieved January 11, 2023.

### 9.4.4  Expectations of future prices

The expectations of future prices also have an impact on the demand for a good. If the expectation for the price of gold were to increase, would a consumer or an investor buy or sell gold? If a person could buy gold today at USD 1,000/ounce and sell it later for USD 1,700/ounce, that person could make a huge return on the investment. Expected future prices of agricultural products have a similar effect on today's demand. If the price of a good or commodity is expected to decrease, then the demand for the good will soon decrease, as consumers wait to purchase until the price decreases. Traders working at the Chicago Board of Trade, the Chicago Mercantile Exchange, and the New York Stock Exchange (NYSE) earn their living by buying and selling goods and commodities. They anticipate, or "guess," whether the prices will rise of fall and make purchases and sales accordingly. This "futures trading" is a major subject of study among agricultural economists. This topic is further explored in Chapter 16.

### 9.4.5  Population

Although the list could be expanded, population is the final determinant of demand mentioned here. Population growth has a direct and important impact on consumption. More people will buy more goods, particularly necessities such as food. The result is similar to an increase in income in low-income nations. If the population of Ethiopia increases, then Ethiopia's demand for wheat will increase: if the population of Ethiopia increases, the country's demand for food will rise.

The last few pages have dealt with the determinants of demand. Chapter 10 uses much of this information to explain how markets operate. The supply and demand curves from Chapter 8 and this chapter merge into one graph to aid the study of the interaction between producers and consumers.

## 9.5  Chapter 9 Summary

1. Demand is the consumer willingness and ability to pay for a good.
2. The demand curve is a function connecting all combinations of prices and quantities consumed for a good, *ceteris paribus*.
3. The demand schedule presents information on price and quantities purchased.
4. The market demand curve is the horizontal summation of all individual demand curves.
5. The law of demand states that the quantity of a good demanded varies inversely with the price of a good, *ceteris paribus*.
6. The price elasticity of demand relates how responsive quantity demanded is to changes in price [$E^d = \%\Delta Q^d / \%\Delta P$]. An inelastic demand curve is one where a percentage change in price results in a relatively smaller percentage change in quantity demanded ($|E^d| < 1$). An elastic demand is one where a percentage change in price results in a larger percentage change in quantity demanded ($|E^d| > 1$). A unitary elastic demand curve is one where the percentage change in price results in an equal percentage change in quantity demanded ($|E^d| = 1$).
7. The own-price elasticity of demand measures the responsiveness of the quantity demanded of a good to changes in the price of the same good.

8   The cross-price elasticity of demand measures the responsiveness of the quantity demanded of a good to changes in the price of a related good.

9   Substitutes in consumption are goods that are consumed on an "either/or" basis. Complements in consumption are goods consumed together.

10   A change in quantity demanded results from a change in the price of a good. A change in quantity demanded is a movement along a demand curve.

11   A change in demand results from a change in an economic variable other than the price of a good. A change in demand is a shift in the demand curve.

12   Demand is determined by (1) the price of the good, (2) prices of related goods, (3) income, (4) tastes and preferences, (5) expectations of future prices, and (6) population.

13   An Engel curve shows the relationship between consumer income and the quantity of good consumed, *ceteris paribus*. Engel's law states that as income increases, the proportion of income spent on food declines.

14   The income elasticity of demand is the percentage change in the demand for a good in response to a percentage change in consumer income [$E^m = \%\Delta Q^d / \%\Delta M$].

15   A normal good is one whose consumption increases in response to an increase in income ($E^m > 0$). The consumption of an inferior good declines in response to an increase in income ($E^m < 0$). A luxury good's consumption increases at an increasing rate in response to an increase in income ($E^m > 1$), while a necessity good's consumption increases at a decreasing rate in response to an increase in income ($0 < E^m < 1$).

## 9.6   Chapter 9 Glossary

**Change in Demand**—When a change in the quantity of a good purchased is the result of a change in an economic variable other than the price of the good. A shift in the demand curve.

**Change in Quantity Demanded**—When a change in the quantity of a good purchased is the result of a change in the price of the good. A movement along the demand curve.

**Complements in Consumption**—Goods that are consumed together, such as peanut butter and jelly.

**Cross-Price Elasticity of Demand**—A measure of the responsiveness of the quantity demanded of a good to changes in the price of a related good.

**Demand**—Consumer willingness and ability to pay for a good.

**Demand Curve**—A function connecting all combinations of prices and quantities consumed of a good, *ceteris paribus*.

**Demand Schedule**—Information on prices and quantities purchased of a good, *ceteris paribus*.

**Elastic Demand**—A percentage change in price that brings about a larger percentage change in quantity demanded.

**Elasticity**—The percentage change in one economic variable resulting from a percentage change in another economic variable.

**Elasticity of Demand**—The percentage change in the quantity demanded in response to a percentage change in price.

**Engel Curve**—The relationship between income and quantity demanded, *ceteris paribus*.

**Engel's Law**—As income increases, the proportion of income spent on food declines, *ceteris paribus*.

**Income Elasticity of Demand**—The percentage change in the demand for a good in response to a percentage change in income.

**Inelastic Demand**—A percentage change in price brings about a smaller percentage change in quantity demanded.

**Inferior Good**—A good whose consumption declines in response to an increase in income.

**Law of Demand**—The quantity of a good demanded varies inversely with the price of the good, *ceteris paribus*.

**Luxury Good**—A good whose consumption increases at an increasing rate in response to an increase in income.

**Market Demand Curve**—The relationship between the price and quantity demanded of a good, *ceteris paribus*, derived by the horizontal summation of all individual consumer demand curves for all individuals in the market.

**Necessity Good**—A good whose consumption increases at a decreasing rate in response to an increase in income.

**Normal Good**—A good whose consumption increases in response to an increase in income.

**Own-Price Elasticity of Demand**—The percentage change in the quantity demanded in response to a percentage change in price.

**Substitutes in Consumption**—Goods that are consumed on an "either/or" basis, such as wheat bread and white bread.

**Unitary Elastic Demand**—The percentage change in price brings about an equal percentage change in quantity demanded.

## 9.7   Chapter 9 Review questions

1  An individual demand curve for pizza can be derived with the following:

   a  prices of pizza, one other good, and income
   b  price of pizza and two other goods
   c  income
   d  price of pizza

2  If the price of milo increases:

   a  consumers will buy more milo
   b  consumers will buy less milo
   c  consumers will buy the same amount of milo
   d  cannot tell with the information given

3  Which has the least elastic demand curve?

   a  apples
   b  fruit
   c  food
   d  oranges

4  If a firm faces an inelastic demand curve, then it will desire to

   a  maintain output at the current level
   b  increase output to increase revenue
   c  decrease output to increase revenue
   d  purchase more inputs

5 If the price of pork increases, then the following will result:

   a  a change in pork demand and a shift in pork demand

   b  a change in pork demand and a movement along the pork demand curve

   c  a change in quantity of pork demanded and a shift in pork demand

   d  a change in quantity of pork demanded and a movement along the pork demand curve

6 If potential buyers expect the price of gold to increase, then the

   a  demand for gold will increase today

   b  demand for gold will decrease today

   c  quantity demanded of gold will increase today

   d  quantity demanded of gold will decrease today

7 The income elasticity of demand for food is:

   a  $0 < E^m < 1$

   b  $E^m > 0$

   c  $E^m < 1$

   d  $E^m = 0$

8 If the price of corn decreases, then the

   a  quantity demanded of corn will decrease

   b  quantity demanded of corn will increase

   c  demand of corn will decrease

   d  demand of corn will increase

9 If the price of corn decreases, then the

   a  quantity demanded of milo will decrease

   b  quantity demanded of milo will increase

   c  demand of milo will decrease

   d  demand of milo will increase

10 Peanut butter and jelly are

   a  complements in consumption

   b  complements in production

   c  substitutes in consumption

   d  substitutes in production

**Answers:** 1. a, 2. b, 3. c, 4. c, 5. d, 6. a, 7. a, 8. b, 9. c, 10. a

For more study questions, flash cards, and study guides, see the online materials at the companion website: www.routledge.com/cw/barkley.

# Markets

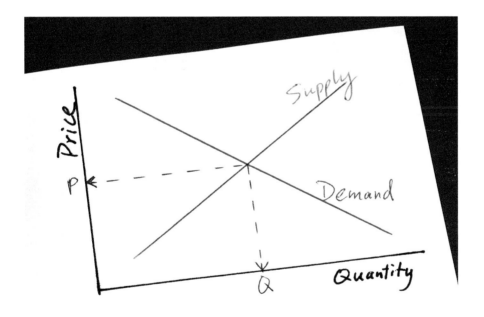

Photo 10.1 Markets

*Source:* JohnKwan/Shutterstock

DOI: 10.4324/9781003367994-10

## Abstract

Markets bring buyers and sellers together to exchange goods and services. Markets provide efficient, self-correcting institutions that provide goods that producers want to sell and consumers want to buy. In this chapter, market equilibrium and mathematical models of supply and demand are introduced and explained. An analytical tool called comparative statics leads to the analysis and understanding of changes in supply and demand. The models explained here provide timely, important, and interesting explanations of real-world events. Quantitative models of markets are described and explained.

### Chapter 10 Questions

1   What are markets, and how do they work?
2   Why are markets considered to be self-correcting?
3   How is market equilibrium defined and how is it used to understand markets?
4   How are mathematical markets used to understand producers' and consumers' behavior?
5   What are comparative statics, and how are they used to explain and predict market outcomes?
6   How are quantitative market models used to understand markets?

## 10.0   Introduction

Prices of goods and services are critical features of a free market economy. Producers who understand how and why the prices of goods and resources change over time can use this information to increase profitability. Consumers make better choices if they understand market forces that determine price changes. This chapter describes and explains how buyers and sellers interact in markets: the foundation of a market-based economic system.

## 10.1   What is a market?

A **market** is an institution or a process that allows buyers and sellers to interact. A market is not necessarily a **marketplace**, which is a physical location where buyers and sellers go to exchange goods. A marketplace can be a farmer's market or the commodity trading pits of the Chicago Board of Trade.

● *Marketplace* = a physical location where buyers and sellers meet to trade goods.

A market can be located in a physical space, such as a shopping mall in Salt Lake City, Utah, but it need not be. Buying and selling goods on the Internet from a firm such as Amazon or eBay makes the Internet into a market, even though the buyers and sellers are not in the same physical location and may never exchange

a word. A market appears wherever there is interaction between buyers and sellers of a good:

- *Market* = the interaction between buyers and sellers.

This interaction between buyers and sellers determines the price of a good and
the quantity of the good that changes hands. One key feature of markets is that
they are voluntary. Individual buyers and sellers determine quantities and prices.
The next section describes how the voluntary actions of numerous producers and
consumers lead to a market equilibrium.

Keep in mind that this chapter's lessons relating to supply, demand, and prices
are presented under the assumption that all other economic conditions are held
constant during the negotiations over potential prices and quantities of the good
being traded. This assumption, called the *ceteris paribus* assumption, was presented in Chapter 1 and has been mentioned frequently in each successive chapter.
The assumption is necessary to allow focusing attention on a single item of interest, which in economics is almost always the price or quantity of a good. Using this
assumption simplifies the complicated real world, making it easier to understand.

## 10.2   Market equilibrium

Markets work by bringing together producers who desire to sell their product at
the highest possible price, and consumers who desire to purchase goods at the lowest possible price. Although the goals of buyers and sellers are opposite from one
another, voluntary trades allow for the objectives of both groups to be met. This section describes how the behavior of numerous individual buyers and sellers converge
on a price or quantity from which there is no tendency to change, or **equilibrium**.

- *Equilibrium* = a point from which there is no tendency to change.

The market supply and market demand curves derived in Chapters 8 and 9 appear
together on a single graph in Figure 10.1. The market supply curve ($Q^s$) is the horizontal sum of all of the individual firms' supply curves. It represents the quantity
of a good that all producers taken together are willing and able to offer for sale at
each price. The voluntary nature of the supply curve is evidence that firms freely
offer a quantity of a good to the market in order to maximize their profits.

The market demand curve ($Q^d$) depicts the horizontal sum of all individual
consumer demand curves. Individual demand curves show the quantity of a good
that a consumer is willing and able to purchase at each price. The market demand
curve reflects the voluntary behavior of many consumers seeking to maximize their
individual levels of satisfaction.

The **market equilibrium** occurs at the intersection of the supply curve and the
demand curve at point E in Figure 10.1. At this point, the quantity supplied ($Q^s$)
by firms at a given price is equal to the quantity demanded ($Q^d$) by consumers at
the same price.

- *Market Equilibrium* = the point at which the quantity supplied by producers at
  a given price is equal to the quantity demanded by consumers at that same price.

At point E (and only at point E), the following market equilibrium condition holds:

10.1 $Q^* = Q^s = Q^d$.

Only one price equates the quantity of a good supplied by producers with the quantity purchased by consumers. This price is the **equilibrium price**, shown by point P* in Figure 10.1.

● ***Equilibrium Price*** = the price at which the quantity supplied equals the quantity demanded.

The equilibrium price is also the **market price** since it is the price determined in the market and agreed to by buyers and sellers.

● *Market Price* = the price where quantity demanded is equal to quantity supplied.

The **equilibrium quantity** is $Q^*$, where the quantity supplied is identical to the quantity demanded.

● ***Equilibrium Quantity*** = the point where quantity supplied is equal to quantity demanded.

The intersection of supply and demand determines the market equilibrium. Why not another price or quantity? Every price other than P* is not an equilibrium price, and every quantity other than $Q^*$ is not an equilibrium quantity. Any point other than point E in Figure 10.1 is a **disequilibrium** point unsatisfactory to either buyers or sellers or both. In disequilibrium, freely operating market forces come into play to cause the market to move toward the equilibrium point, E.

● ***Disequilibrium*** = a market situation in which the market price does not equalize supply and demand.

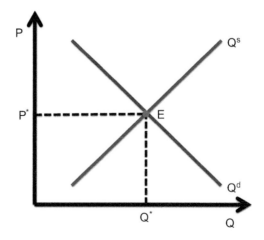

Figure 10.1 **Market equilibrium**

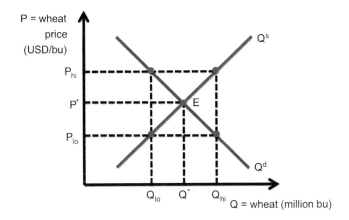

Figure 10.2 Figure 10.2 **Market forces in a wheat market**

The voluntary behavior of buyers and sellers will result in a movement toward equilibrium (point E), where the quantity supplied equals the quantity demanded. Consider the hypothetical market for wheat depicted in Figure 10.2.

The supply curve in the wheat market ($Q^s$) shows the quantity of wheat that wheat producers will offer for sale at each of a range of prices. Intuitively, the supply curve represents the cost of wheat production. Low-cost producers are located to the left, where the supply curve is low, and high-cost producers are located to the right, at higher prices.

### QUICK QUIZ 10.1

How is the supply curve for wheat derived for an individual firm? For the industry?

The demand curve for wheat ($Q^d$) shows the quantity of wheat that buyers will purchase at each of a range of prices. In the wheat market, the major consumers are millers who purchase wheat then grind it into the flour used for baking bread or tortillas. The demand curve for this wheat represents the consumers' willingness and ability to pay for it. Scarcity causes the demand curve to slope downward from left to right. As more wheat becomes available, millers offer lower prices to meet their needs for wheat.

### QUICK QUIZ 10.2

How is the demand curve for wheat derived?

Why is everything other than price (and quantity) held constant in the graph of supply and demand? How does this simplification affect the study of the market for wheat?

The price of wheat always gravitates toward the equilibrium point, E. Suppose that the price of wheat is $P_{hi}$. At this relatively high price of wheat, the law of demand indicates that consumers (flour millers) will purchase only a small quantity of the grain. Specifically, at price $P_{hi}$, they will purchase $Q_{lo}$ million bushels of wheat. Wheat suppliers, however, expand wheat production when the price of wheat is high. They will provide $Q_{hi}$ million bushels to the market when the price reaches $P_{hi}$. At price $P_{hi}$, the quantity supplied ($Q_{hi}$) exceeds the quantity demanded ($Q_{lo}$). This situation yields a **surplus**, which is the horizontal distance between $Q_{hi}$ and $Q_{lo}$ in Figure 10.2.

● *Surplus* = a market situation in which producers are willing to supply more of a good than consumers are willing to purchase at a given price ($Q^s > Q^d$).

A surplus occurs at any price higher than the equilibrium price ($P^*$). In a surplus situation, there is more wheat available for sale than flour millers are willing to purchase. Consider the manager of a grain elevator (the grain storage facility) somewhere in the northern Great Plains. A larger-than-usual harvest has resulted in a full elevator and a huge pile of wheat "stored" on the ground. No millers are buying any wheat at the current high price ($P_{hi}$). Pressure develops for the elevator manager to sell the wheat as quickly as possible since rain or moisture will cause the wheat grains to sprout, which lowers the value of the wheat. What does the manager do? She lowers the price of wheat to sell it.

As the price of wheat drops from $P_{hi}$, suppliers (wheat producers and elevators) reduce the quantity of wheat offered to the market and consumers increase the quantity demanded of wheat, as shown along the demand curve. Suppliers lower the price of a good until they are able to sell their product and eliminate the surplus. The price continues to drop until the quantity of wheat supplied ($Q^s$) comes in line with the quantity of wheat demanded ($Q^d$). This occurs only at the equilibrium price ($P^*$) and the equilibrium quantity ($Q^* = Q^s = Q^d$).

This story holds true not only for wheat crops but also for any good or service. If the price of a good is greater than the equilibrium price, producers (sellers) will continue to lower the price until the market price is the equilibrium price. Any price higher than $P^*$ is a disequilibrium price since there is a tendency to move toward the equilibrium point (E). Once at equilibrium, there is no tendency to change since quantity supplied is equal to quantity demanded, and there is no surplus. Buyers and sellers agree on quantity and price.

If the price of wheat falls to $P_{lo}$, wheat suppliers will cut back production to $Q_{lo}$ and wheat consumers (millers) will increase quantity demanded to $Q_{hi}$. This situation results in a **shortage** since the quantity demanded ($Q_{hi}$) is greater than the quantity supplied ($Q_{lo}$). The shortage is the horizontal distance between $Q_{lo}$ and $Q_{hi}$ in Figure 10.2.

- **Shortage** = a market situation in which consumers are willing and able to purchase more of a good than producers are willing to supply at a given price ($Q^s < Q^d$).

Shortages occur at all prices below the equilibrium price ($P^*$). Suppose a flour miller has contracted with several bread bakers for a large quantity of flour. At the price $P_{lo}$, the miller is unable to acquire any wheat due to the shortage. What should he do? Offer a higher price to increase the amount of wheat available. The increase is shown along the supply curve. As the price increases, the quantity demanded decreases along the demand curve. The price will continue to be "bid up" by wheat consumers until it reaches the equilibrium point E and the shortage disappears. This occurs in the market for wheat and in the market for any good or service where a shortage occurs. Any price below $P^*$ is a disequilibrium price. The independent actions of buyers and sellers cause the price to gravitate toward its equilibrium point.

At any price other than the equilibrium price, market forces (the behavior of buyers and sellers) will bring the price back into equilibrium at the market equilibrium price and quantity. Walmart behaves in a similar way. It places items on sale by lowering prices when a store has a surplus (price too high) in its inventory. Walmart does not reorder this item. If the shelves are empty, Walmart shoppers request more of the good because they cannot purchase the quantity desired. There is a shortage (price too low), and Walmart increases the price and reorders more of the good until the equilibrium is reached. In this simple way, Walmart has become the most successful retailer in the world by using simple economic principles.

This simple supply-and-demand model can help predict price movements in the economy. Individuals who become expert at such predictions often become grain merchandisers, commodity traders, or stockbrokers. The individuals in these professions often use simple and intuitive supply-and-demand models to "buy low and sell high," further discussed in Chapter 16. In all other businesses and professions, the tools related to supply and demand are useful in determining how market forces will affect the price and quantity of inputs and outputs.

## 10.3 Comparative statics

The study of markets provides managers of business firms with a powerful method of understanding and analyzing how prices of the firm's inputs and outputs change over time. This knowledge can lead to improved decision-making and higher levels of profit for the firm. The interaction of supply and demand results in an equilibrium market price and quantity. The study of the impacts of changes in supply and demand relationships is called **comparative statics**, a method of comparing one equilibrium point with another.

● *Comparative Statics* = a comparison of market equilibrium points before and after a change in an economic variable.

The study begins with the impacts of changes in demand, then moves to changes in supply, and, finally, to simultaneous changes in both supply and demand. Careful consideration of these comparative static examples provides useful insight into analyzing any economic policy, change, or situation.

### 10.3.1 Changes in demand

The large and enduring increases in China's per capita income are likely to continue to have a positive impact on the demand for beef and grain produced in the United States. Consumers with increasing income levels tend to substitute out of inexpensive calorie sources, such as grains, and into more expensive sources, such as beef and seafood. Figure 10.3 shows this increase in demand for beef.

The outward shift in the demand curve (from $Q^d_0$ to $Q^d_1$) is a change in demand (not a change in quantity demanded) since the source of the change is a nonprice variable (the increase in per capita income in China). The equilibrium point in Figure 10.3 changes from $E_0$ to $E_1$ because of the change in demand. As the demand curve shifts upward and to the right, it sweeps across the supply curve from one equilibrium point to another. The change increases the price of beef from $P^*_0$ to $P^*_1$, causing a change in quantity supplied, or a movement along the supply curve, as shown in Figure 10.3.

**A SHIFT IN DEMAND RESULTS IN**

1 A CHANGE IN DEMAND, and
2 A CHANGE IN QUANTITY SUPPLIED.

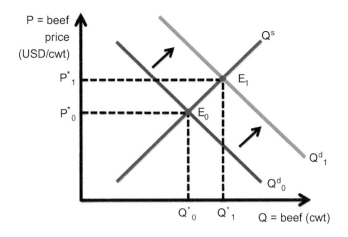

Figure 10.3 An increase in the demand for beef

An increase in demand, as shown in Figure 10.3, results in an increase in the equilibrium price and quantity of beef. Any economic variable that increases demand for a good will result in a higher price and a larger quantity of the good moving through the market. This could be due to an increase in income or population, an expectation that the good's price will increase even more in the future, or a change in consumer tastes and preferences, to name a few possible sources of increases in demand.

## BOX 10.1

### The substitution of beef, pork, and chicken in the US

To what extent do consumers actually "substitute," or switch, from one meat product to another? This question was researched using data from US consumers in 1995 by Brester and Schroeder. Price elasticities for the own prices and cross prices were estimated for beef, pork, and poultry. The results show that meats are most responsive to changes in their own price, with elasticities ranging from −0.33 (poultry) to −0.69 (pork). This means that if the price of meat increases by 1 percent, the quantity demanded of the meat will decrease by the percentage shown in the table. Cross-price elasticities measure the responsiveness of consumers to a change in the price of a related good. The substitution between meats is relatively small in percentage terms; however, the dollar value of the substitution is large since even small elasticities can have large aggregate effects in high-volume commodity markets.

**Price Elasticities of Meat Demand**

|  | $P_{beef}$ | $P_{pork}$ | $P_{poultry}$ |
|---|---|---|---|
| $Q_{beef}$ | −0.56 | 0.10 | 0.05 |
| $Q_{pork}$ | 0.23 | −0.69 | 0.04 |
| $Q_{poultry}$ | 0.21 | 0.07 | −0.33 |

*Source:* Gary W. Brester and Ted C. Schroeder. "The Impacts of Brand and Generic Advertising on Meat Demand." *American Journal of Agricultural Economics.* Vol. 77 No. 4 (Nov. 1995), pp. 969–979.

A decrease in demand will have the opposite results. The demand curve will shift to the left, causing a decrease in both the equilibrium price and quantity traded of the good. A decrease in the relative price of chicken causes consumers to substitute out of other meats and into chicken. This results in a decrease in the demand for beef, as shown in Figure 10.4.

Photo 10.3 Beef demand

*Source:* Marc Dietrich/Shutterstock

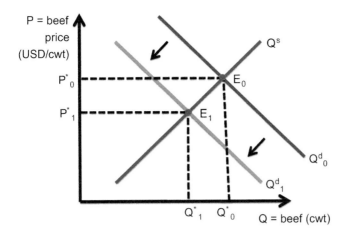

Figure 10.4 A decrease in the demand for beef

Again, the shift in the demand curve represents a change in demand and a change in quantity supplied (movement along the supply curve). The equilibrium price and quantity of beef decrease in this situation.

## 10.3.2 Supply changes

Petroleum products are a major input in the production of agricultural products such as corn. An increase in the price of petroleum stemming from increases in demand from growing economies such as China and India will be accompanied by higher costs of production faced by domestic US producers. The corn producers' marginal cost curves will shift upward due to this increase in the price of petroleum products. The market supply curve shown in Figure 10.5 is the horizontal sum of all individual firms' marginal cost curves.

This leftward shift in the supply curve is a change in supply (not a change in quantity supplied) since the source of the change is a nonprice variable (an increase in the price of an input, rather than a change in the price of corn). The equilibrium point changes from $E_0$ to $E_1$ because of the change in supply. As the supply curve shifts upward and to the left, it moves across the demand curve from the original equilibrium point to a new equilibrium point. This increases the price of corn from $P^*_0$ to $P^*_1$ and as a result causes a change in quantity demanded, or a movement along the demand curve, as shown in Figure 10.5.

**A shift in supply results in**

1   A CHANGE IN SUPPLY, and
2   A CHANGE IN QUANTITY DEMANDED.

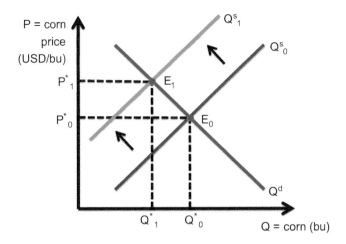

Figure 10.5  A decrease in the supply of corn

Photo 10.4  Corn supply

*Source:* Fotokostic/Shutterstock

The shift in supply in Figure 10.5 is a decrease in supply since at every price the quantity of corn supplied decreases. This can lead to confusion since the upward shift in the supply curve represents a decrease in supply. The quantity axis measures the "increase" or "decrease" in supply. The corn supply curve shifted to the

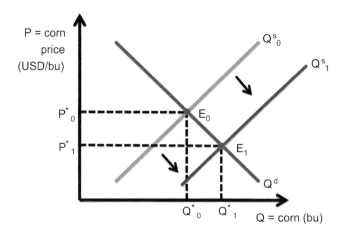

Figure 10.6 An increase in the supply of corn

left, reflecting a decrease in supply. This decrease in supply results in an increase in the equilibrium price and a decrease in the equilibrium quantity of corn. Any economic variable that decreases the supply of a good will result in a higher price and lower quantity of the good bought and sold. This type of shift could be due to a number of things, including an increase in the cost of an input, a tax on corn production, or bad weather that has a negative impact on growing conditions.

An increase in supply will have the opposite effects: the supply curve will shift downward and to the right, causing a decrease in the equilibrium price and an increase in the equilibrium quantity of the good. If plant geneticists develop a new variety of corn that yields more bushels per acre than older corn varieties, this technological change results in an increase in supply, or a rightward shift in the supply curve, shown in Figure 10.6.

Again, the shift in the supply curve represents a change in supply and a change in quantity demanded (movement along the demand curve). The equilibrium price decreases and the equilibrium quantity of corn increases in this situation. Changes in the production of a good affect the market price and quantity of a good. Examples include climate change, war, and pandemics.

## BOX 10.2

### African agriculture and food aid

In the 1960s, most sub-Saharan African nations were food exporters; today, most of these nations import millions of tons of food each year. Much of the world's hunger and poverty are concentrated in sub-Saharan Africa. Cereal yields have declined since the 1970s and are now approximately one-third of those in South Asia.

Agriculture in sub-Saharan Africa is subject to conflict, drought, a lack of government commitment to agriculture, and decreasing international aid. This tragic situation provides the opportunity for one of the greatest future increases in the welfare of humanity.

Environmental challenges include poor soil quality in many regions and drought. In Asia, irrigation provided the foundation for the introduction of high-yielding cereal varieties. In Africa, 96 percent of available arable land lacks irrigation. International aid to Africa has dropped since the 1980s, when a shift occurred in aid away from agriculture toward health, education, and governance. The World Bank has contributed to African agriculture, but the strategy has been criticized for its lack of political support in recipient nations.

Some critics have emphasized that African governments have become too dependent on international food aid. Between 1981 and 2000, national government funding for agricultural science fell by 27 percent in Africa, and many governments in sub-Saharan Africa allocate less than 1 percent of their national budgets to the sector. This could be due to a reliance on international aid. A successful strategy for increasing Africa's food production is likely to include the development of high-yielding crops, enhanced training in agricultural science, increased government commitment to agriculture, and enhanced efficiency of agricultural markets and infrastructure.

Food aid plays a unique role in reducing hunger and poverty. When famine or persistent hunger occurs, international food aid can be used to provide food to those in need. The provision of calories to hungry individuals provides a lifesaving benefit that is difficult to fault. However, food aid has costs as well as benefits. The supply of large amounts of food to a given location shifts the supply curve of food to the right, decreasing the price of food. While this is a benefit to food consumers, it lowers the food price, and thus the incentive for local producers to produce more food. Food aid can save lives in the short run, but it can decrease food availability and result in continuing dependence on food aid in the long run. Many experts promote income assistance or food vouchers, which would allow food to be purchased within Africa, instead of shipped from the US or the EU. This would increase the demand for food, based on an increase in purchasing power, resulting in upward price pressure, and increasing the incentive for local food production.

Recent analysis shows that African agriculture has not operating at full capacity, and private-sector companies could invest to enter and grow in Africa's agricultural market. The study showed that Africa could produce two to three times more cereals and grains, which would add 20 percent more cereals and grains to the current worldwide 2.6 billion tons of output. Similar increases could be seen in the production of horticulture crops and livestock (Goedde et al. 2019).

*Sources:* Hanson, S. Backgrounder: African Agriculture. Council of Foreign Relations. May 28, 2008. stephaniehanson.com/2008/05/28/african-agriculture. Retrieved January 12, 2023.

Goedde, L., A. Ooko-Ombaka, and G. Pais. "Winning in Africa's agricultural market." McKinsey and Company. February 2019. www.mckinsey.com/industries/agriculture/our-insights/winning-in-africas-agricultural-market. Retrieved January 12, 2023.

Paarlberg, Robert. *Starved for Science: How Biotechnology Is Being Kept Out of Africa*. Cambridge, Massachusetts: Harvard University Press, 2008.

BOX 10.3

## Climate Change

Climate change is a long-term change in average weather patterns. Climate change is currently reducing crop yields, decreasing the quality of major cereal grains, and negatively affecting livestock production. Farmers and ranchers throughout the world will need to invest in adaptation strategies to meet the increasing demand for food as population growth occurs.

Interestingly, moderate levels of global warming and increased carbon dioxide in the atmosphere are likely to help many crops grow faster. However, more severe warming and the increase in major weather events such as hurricanes, drought, and floods are likely to reduce food production. Livestock many have increased heat stress from higher temperatures, and fisheries will be affected by increased water temperatures that lead to increases in invasive species and affect the lifecycle of many fish and marine species. Drought also reduces pasture and feed supplies and enhances parasites. Aquaculture and fisheries are highly dependent on climate.

Although increase warning and CO2 can stimulate crop growth, it also causes greater growth in weeds and pests such as insects and fungi. Carbon dioxide can also reduce the nutritional quality of food by reductions of protein and minerals in most plant species, including wheat, soybeans, and rice.

Climate change can disrupt food availability and reduce access to food. In low-income nations, disruptions to food supply from extreme weather have a great impact on food supply and distribution, making the impact more severe in areas with lower investments in agriculture and food distribution infrastructure.

*Source:* City of Chicago.US.EPA. Climate Change Impacts. climatechange. chicago.gov. Accessed January 12, 2023.

---

## BOX 10.4

### Effect of the Russian invasion of Ukraine on agriculture

Russia's invasion of Ukraine in February 2022 had a large impact on global agriculture. Ukraine is a major grain-producing region. Ukraine was attacked and unable to harvest and export crops: wheat, sunflowers, barley, canola, and corn. In a world connected by international trade, the Ukraine war has had a major impact on global food markets. Russia is also a major exporter of energy and fertilizers. The conflict occurred immediately after the Covid-19 pandemic, when supply chains were disrupted by the disease. This timing resulted in the continued volatility of food and agricultural markets during the conflict.

Russia and Ukraine are among the most important producers of grain and produced about 13 percent of the world's wheat and accounted for 30 percent of the world's wheat exports before the war. Russia was the world leader in wheat exports. Many of the world's poorest nations relied on wheat imported from Russia and Ukraine, resulting in increased food insecurity.

The war also led to reduced access to ports in the Sea of Azov, bordered by Russia on the east, Ukraine on the northwest, and Crimea on the southwest. The conflict mainly affected Ukraine's ability to export since prior to the war over 90 percent of Ukraine's agricultural exports moved through these ports. Global trade has been restricted for products such as cereals and sugar and nitrogen fertilizer. Reduced trade in energy and fertilizer has caused increases in the price of petroleum products, fertilizer, and agricultural commodities. Transportation has switched to rail and roads. Food security is less stable given the large increase in prices. Food and agriculture are highly energy intensive, causing large increases in production costs, smaller harvests, and smaller food supplies. Large numbers of Ukrainians have been displaced, estimated at 8 million.

BOX 10.5

# Coronavirus impact on food and agriculture

Covid-19 has had a significant effect on agriculture and the food supply chain. Overall, food supply remained remarkably stable and resilient. The pandemic presented several challenges to the food production and distribution systems. The food and agricultural sectors were designated essential in most countries, making the businesses exempt from business closures and restrictions of movement. Food is a necessity, so demand remained strong throughout the Covid-19 pandemic. However, the closure of restaurants, hotels, and catering resulted in a major shift in the structure of food demand toward supermarkets.

With the onset of the pandemic, many food and agribusiness firms shifted production lines away from food consumed away from home toward grocery store food and increased capacity of inventories, switching to online platforms and direct delivery to households and hiring temporary staff.

Perhaps the largest impact of Covid-19 was on agricultural labor markets. Restrictions placed on labor mobility across borders, lockdowns, and quarantines have contributed to labor shortages in the food and agricultural sectors of many nations, particularly those with seasonal labor demands and labor-intensive production practices. As a result, fruit and vegetable production have had higher costs and a reduced workforce in high-income nations such as the US and EU. Some nations experienced short run supply issues with agricultural inputs, such as pesticides in China.

The collapse of food eaten away from home in restaurants, together with food service providers in schools, hotels, and catering businesses has devastated markets for some commodities such as potatoes for french fries, seafood, and dairy products. There has also been a shift from bulk items to smaller packaged items.

The food processing sector was greatly impacted, particularly in perishable foods, where work is in close conditions placed workers at risk to contracting the disease, and social distancing requirements were put in place, raising costs and slowing production. For example, in packing and grading fruit and vegetables and in processing livestock, worker absenteeism has increased, and the workforce has decreased due to lockdowns and limitations on worker mobility across borders. Border and port closures have also led to congestion and delays in transportation and higher food costs. Overall, the food supply system responded to the challenges of the pandemic without major problems. However, increased costs and inflation were significant.

*Source:* OECD Policy Responses to Coronavirus (Covid-19), April 29 2020.

### 10.3.3 Simultaneous supply and demand changes

Examples in the previous two sections focused on one change at a time. In the real world, supply and demand curves are constantly changing, being pushed and pulled by changes in a large number of economic forces occurring simultaneously throughout the economy and the world. In agricultural markets, supply and demand shift due to weather, input and product prices, exports, imports, expectations regarding the future, and numerous other factors. This section considers the situation when supply and demand change simultaneously. In some ways, this is more realistic than the response to changes in a single variable.

The production of agricultural products has grown over time, due to the introduction of many new foods, changes in tastes, and technological change. Consumption of food and fiber has also grown because of increases in population and increased family income. These changes are shown in the same graph, in Figure 10.7.

If the supply and demand curves shift by equal quantities over time, the equilibrium changes from $E_0$ to $E_1$, as shown in Figure 10.7. In this situation, the equilibrium price remains constant at $P^*$, while the equilibrium quantity increases from $Q^*_0$ to $Q^*_1$.

Figure 10.8 shows the case appropriate to most agricultural markets in the United States, where increases in production have outpaced increases in consumption. When supply growth outpaces demand growth, the equilibrium price of food decreases, and the equilibrium quantity of food increases. In US agriculture since the mid-1940s, the price of agricultural products has decreased in relation to most other goods. During the same period, the output of agricultural commodities has increased tremendously due to the huge productivity gains associated with mechanization, chemical and fertilizer use, and plant and animal breeding. These long-term forces taken together have made consumers better off since more food and fiber is available at a lower price. If demand increases at a faster rate than supply, then the equilibrium price will increase, reflecting the increase in scarcity of the good.

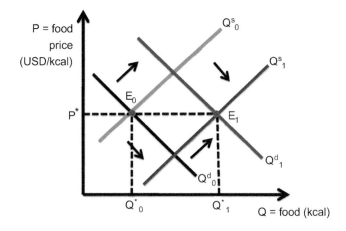

Figure 10.7 Increases in the supply and demand of food

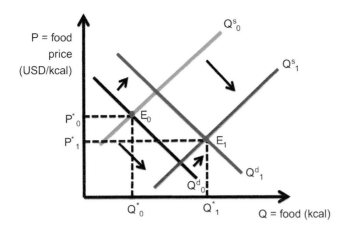

P = food price (USD/kcal)

Figure 10.8 **Supply increase outpaces demand increase**

QUICK QUIZ 10.4

QUICK QUIZ 10.4

Graph a situation where the demand of a good increases faster than the supply for the good. What happens to the equilibrium price and quantity of the good?

## 10.4 Mathematical models (optional)

Economics includes three ways to describe market phenomena: (1) graphs, (2) "stories" or verbal explanations, and (3) mathematical models. The previous sections used graphs and stories to describe the market for wheat. Simple algebra is another way to describe this market. The mathematical model presented next uses the same information to describe and analyze situations related to supply and demand.

The following equation represents the supply of wheat:

10.2 $P = 1 + 0.1Q^s$,

where P is the price of wheat in dollars per bushel, and $Q^s$ is the quantity supplied of wheat in millions of bushels. This equation is called an **inverse supply function** since price (the independent variable) is a function of quantity supplied (the dependent variable). Mathematically, a supply function could be described as $Q^s$ = f(P) since price is given and producers determine how much to produce given the independent variable, price. As before, price is measured along the vertical axis and quantity supplied is on the horizontal axis. Using the inverse supply function, P = f($Q^s$), makes the relationship easier to graph.

- *Inverse Supply Function* = a supply function that is represented with price (the independent variable) as a function of quantity supplied (the dependent variable): P = f($Q^s$).

Similarly, define an **inverse demand function** as a demand function with the dependent variable ($Q^d$) and the independent variable (P) reversed:

- *Inverse Demand Function* = a demand function that is represented with price (the independent variable) as a function of quantity demanded (the dependent variable): $P = f(Q^d)$.

Suppose that is the inverse demand function for wheat:

10.3   $P = 5 - 0.1Q^d$.

To find equilibrium, set the two equations equal to each other since P = P:

10.4   $1 + 0.1Q^s = 5 - 0.1Q^d$.

Next, recall that in equilibrium, $Q^* = Q^s = Q^d$, so replace the quantities supplied and demanded with the equilibrium quantity:

10.5   $1 + 0.1Q^* = 5 - 0.1Q^*$.

Now subtract one from each side of the equation and add $0.1Q^*$ to each side of the equation to get:

10.6   $0.2Q^* = 4$, or $Q^* = 20$ million bushels of wheat.

Substituting this equilibrium quantity ($Q^*$) into the inverse supply function yields the equilibrium price:

10.7   $P = 1 + 0.1Q^s = 1 + 0.1(20) = 1 + 2 = $ USD 3/bu of wheat.

Check this result by plugging the equilibrium quantity into the inverse demand equation:

10.8   $P = 5 - 0.1Q^d = 5 - 0.1(20) = 5 - 2 = $ USD 3/bu of wheat.

The equilibrium in the wheat market is ($P^* = $ USD 3/bu of wheat, $Q^* = 20$ million bushels of wheat). This same result found graphically requires graphing the supply and demand functions and locating the equilibrium at the intersection of supply and demand (Figure 10.9).

Economists use this type of mathematical model to study agricultural markets. Price and quantity data from markets such as the Chicago Board of Trade or the Chicago Mercantile Exchange enable the study of how changes in policies, weather, or any other economic variable will influence the prices and quantities of agricultural goods.

A model such as this helps an analyst determine the implications of how a change in the price of wheat will affect the wheat market. For example, suppose that the price of wheat increases to a level above the equilibrium level to USD 4/bu. Both the graph in Figure 10.9 and the mathematical model provide information telling that a price above the equilibrium level will increase production, decrease

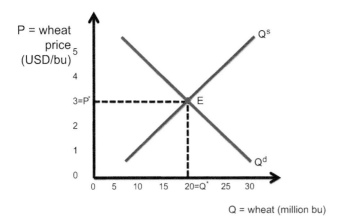

P = wheat price (USD/bu)

5

4

3=P*  ------------- E

2

1

0

0 5 10 15 20=Q* 25 30

Q = wheat (million bu)

Qˢ

Qᵈ

Figure 10.9 Quantitative wheat market equilibrium

consumption, and result in a surplus. To calculate the levels of quantity supplied and demanded, simply plug in the price of USD 4/bu into the inverse supply and inverse demand equations:

10.9a  $4 = 1 + 0.1Q^s$,
10.9b  $3 = 0.1\ Q^s$,
10.9c  $Q^s = 30$ million bushels of wheat,
10.9d  $4 = 5 - 0.1Q^d$,
10.9e  $1 = 0.1\ Q^d$,
10.9f  $Q^d = 10$ million bushels of wheat.

The surplus quantity $(Q^s - Q^d)$ can also be calculated:

10.10  Surplus $= (Q^s - Q^d) = 30 - 10 = 20$ million bushels of wheat.

This procedure also helps calculate a below-equilibrium price that leads to a shortage. Suppose that the price of wheat drops to USD 2/bu. The inverse supply and inverse demand equations yield the following estimates of quantities:

10.11a  $2 = 1 + 0.1Q^s$,
10.11b  $1 = 0.1Q^s$,
10.11c  $Q^s = 10$ million bushels of wheat,
10.11d  $2 = 5 - 0.1Q^d$,
10.11e  $3 = 0.1Q^d$,
10.11f  $Q^d = 30$ million bushels of wheat.

The shortage quantity $(Q^d - Q^s)$ can also be calculated:

10.12  Shortage $= (Q^d - Q^s) = 30 - 10 = 20$ million bushels of wheat.

This procedure also helps calculate changes in supply or demand brought about by economic variables. The next three chapters will provide additional information related to markets. They will show how outcomes depend on government policies and the number of firms in a market or market structure.

## 10.5   Chapter 10 Summary

1   A market is an institution where buyers and sellers interact. A marketplace is a physical location where buyers and sellers meet to exchange goods.
2   The interaction between buyers and sellers determines the price of a good and the quantity of the good purchased and sold.
3   Market equilibrium is the point where the quantity supplied at a given price is equal to the quantity demanded. The equilibrium price is the price at which quantity supplied equals quantity demanded. The equilibrium quantity is the point where quantity supplied equals quantity demanded.
4   Disequilibrium is a market situation in which the market price does not equate supply and demand.
5   Economic forces will result in the price always gravitating toward the equilibrium price.
6   A surplus is a market situation where quantity supplied is greater than quantity demanded.
7   A shortage is a market situation where quantity demanded is greater than quantity supplied.
8   The inverse supply function is represented by a price as a function of quantity supplied. The inverse demand function is represented by a price as a function of quantity demanded.
9   Comparative statics is a comparison of market equilibrium points before and after a change in an economic variable.

## 10.6   Chapter 10 Glossary

**Comparative Statics**—A comparison of market equilibrium points before and after a change in an economic variable.

**Disequilibrium**—A market situation in which the market price does not equalize supply and demand.

**Equilibrium**—A point from which there is no tendency to change.

**Equilibrium Price**—The price at which the quantity supplied equals the quantity demanded.

**Equilibrium Quantity**—The point where quantity supplied is equal to quantity demanded.

**Inverse Demand Function**—A demand function that is represented with price (the independent variable) as a function of quantity demanded (the dependent variable): $P = f(Q^d)$.

**Inverse Supply Function**—A supply function that is represented with price (the independent variable) as a function of quantity supplied (the dependent variable): $P = f(Q^s)$.

Market—The interaction between buyers and sellers.
Market Equilibrium—The point where the quantity supplied by producers at a given price is equal to the quantity demanded by consumers at that same price.
Market Price—The price where quantity demanded is equal to quantity supplied.
Marketplace—A physical location where buyers and sellers meet to trade goods.
Shortage—A market situation in which consumers are willing and able to purchase more of a good than producers are willing to supply at a given price $(Q^s < Q^d)$.
Surplus—A market situation in which producers are willing to supply more of a good than consumers are willing to purchase at a given price $(Q^s > Q^d)$.

## 10.7 Chapter 10 Review questions

1 If the quantity supplied is greater than quantity demanded, there is a(n)

  a  trade deficit
  b  equilibrium
  c  shortage
  d  surplus

2 If the price is higher than the equilibrium price, then

  a  quantity demanded is greater than quantity supplied
  b  quantity supplied is greater than quantity demanded
  c  the price will increase over time
  d  cannot answer with information given

3 An inverse demand function

  a  is incorrect
  b  has price as a function of quantity demanded
  c  has quantity demanded as a function of price
  d  must be inverted to graph the function

4 An increase in income results in

  a  no change in demand
  b  a change in quantity demanded
  c  a shift in demand
  d  a movement along the demand curve

5 An increase in the price of fertilizer will alter the market for wheat by a

  a  leftward shift in demand
  b  rightward shift in demand
  c  leftward shift in supply
  d  rightward shift in supply

6 Technological change results in a(n)

  a  increase in supply
  b  increase in quantity supplied
  c  decrease in supply
  d  decrease in quantity supplied

7 Technological change causes

  a  a shortage
  b  a surplus
  c  neither
  d  not enough information to know

8 Technological change results in a(n)

  a  increase in price and an increase in quantity
  b  increase in price and a decrease in quantity
  c  decrease in price and an increase in quantity
  d  decrease in price and a decrease in quantity

9 A drought will result in a shift in the

a   demand for crops to the left
b   demand for crops to the right
c   supply for crops to the left
d   supply for crops to the right

10  A drought will result in a(n)

a   increase in price and an increase in quantity of crops

b   increase in price and a decrease in quantity of crops
c   decrease in price and an increase in quantity of crops
d   decrease in price and a decrease in quantity or crops

**Answers:** 1. d, 2. b, 3. b, 4. c, 5. c, 6. a, 7. c, 8. c, 9. c, 10. b

For more study questions, flash cards, and study guides, see the online materials at the companion website: www.routledge.com/cw/barkley.

# Government policies

Photo 11.1  Government policies

*Source:* M DOGAN/Shutterstock

DOI: 10.4324/9781003367994-11

## Abstract

Price policies, including price supports and price ceilings, are analyzed, with real-world examples highlighting the consequences of agricultural price policies in low-income and high-income nations. Welfare economics is used to understand how producer and consumer well-being changes in response to changes in policies, markets, and current events. Labor immigration is analyzed to find who gains and who loses from a nation accepting new workers into the workforce. Macroeconomics, the study of economy-wide features such as inflation and unemployment, is introduced. Monetary and fiscal policy are described, and their impacts on the agricultural sector detailed. Food security, hunger, global poverty, and economic development are outlined, and public goods are comprehensively explained.

**Chapter 11 Questions**

1  What is the purpose of price supports, and what are their impacts on producers and consumers?
2  What is the purpose of price ceilings, and what are their impacts on producers and consumers?
3  What are welfare economics, and how do they help us understand economic policies and current events?
4  What are the impacts of labor immigration on the agricultural economy?
5  What is macroeconomics, and how can it help firms make better decisions?
6  What is the impact of inflation on economic decision-making?
7  How does unemployment affect business firms?
8  What is monetary policy, and how does it affect the economy?
9  What is fiscal policy, and how does it affect the economy?
10  What impact do food security, hunger, and global poverty have on the food and agriculture sectors?
11  What are public goods, and how do they impact decision-making in food and agriculture?

## 11.0   Introduction

Market economies have many advantages, including efficiency and a high standard of living. However, all real-world economies are mixed economies, with large and important roles for government programs and policies. Governments provide numerous important functions, even in the most free market economy: the provision of law and order, public safety, national defense, education, research and development, health initiatives, and environmental protection, just to name a few.

Economic programs include investments in infrastructure, research, and protection of some industries from foreign completion or market-based challenges. The government also conducts macroeconomic policies, which include fiscal and monetary policies intended to promote the functioning of the overall economy.

Agriculture in the United States, and most nations, is characterized by heavy government intervention. Governments provide many programs and policies to ensure the provision of a sufficient, safe, and nutritious food supply. So far, this book has emphasized the benefits and advantages of markets: whatever goods that consumers desire are supplied by producers at the lowest possible cost. Competitive markets ensure that consumers have access to the goods and services that provide the greatest level of utility. Market-based economies, however, require government intervention due to "market failures," or situations where markets provide undesirable outcomes.

Market failures include (1) market power (also called monopoly power, Chapter 13); (2) externalities (Chapter 15); and (3) public goods, discussed in this chapter. Market power occurs when a firm is large enough relative to the market to exert control over the price of a good. Examples include electricity providers or large agribusiness firms that can affect the price. Externalities occur when one individual's activities unintentionally affect someone else. Externalities can be either positive or negative. A positive externality occurs when a beekeeper's bees pollinate fruit crops such as apples. A negative externality occurs when a factory discharges wastewater into a river that citizens of a downstream city use for drinking water. Public goods are goods that are "nonrival," meaning that one individual's consumption of the good does not affect another individual's ability to consume the good: streetlights, sunsets, and national defense are examples.

In the three cases of market failure, government intervention can provide superior outcomes than markets alone. There is massive, continuing debate among politicians, economists, and commentators about the most beneficial type and magnitude of government interventions. In some cases, the "cure is worse than the disease," in the sense that well-intentioned policies can have unintended outcomes that are worse than the problem that they were intended to solve.

Most nations are characterized by widespread and continuing intervention in agricultural and food markets: price policies, subsidies, food safety, trade policies, nutritional programs, and environmental protection of natural resources are examples. Perhaps the most common motivation for these interventions is food security, based on the importance and urgency of food for human existence. As economic growth occurs and national incomes increase, consumers demand higher levels of food safety, better nutrition, and environmental protection. These trends are likely to continue as nations seek more effective ways of enhancing life for healthy citizens.

## 11.1   Price policies

In many nations, including the US, the government intervenes in agricultural markets in response to political pressure from either agricultural producers or consumers of food and fiber. The government has the authority to legislate the retail prices of food and agricultural commodities. If the government believes that the market price of an agricultural product is too low, it can pass a law that mandates a **price support** for the good. Since this policy increases the price, it will be promoted by producers. On the other hand, if the government believes that the market price of a good is too high, it can put a **price ceiling**, likely sponsored by consumers. This form of government intervention has been common in agricultural markets for many years.

## 11.1.1 Price supports

When the prices of agricultural goods are low, producers often place pressure on politicians to "do something about low commodity prices." A common reaction of governments is to pass a law that sets a **price support**, or a minimum price, below which the market price cannot go. In recent years, price support policies have been used to increase the prices of milk, grains, cotton, and other agricultural products both in the US and nations throughout the world.

- *Price Support* = a minimum price set by the government for a specified good or service.

When a price is higher than the market price, a surplus results, as shown in Figure 11.1. The government must enforce this market price intervention; otherwise, the surplus would quickly set in motion market forces that would return the market to the equilibrium point, where the quantity supplied equals the quantity demanded.

> QUICK QUIZ 11.1
>
> What causes this surplus?

Figure 11.1 shows a hypothetical price support for wheat, which in this example is higher than the equilibrium market price $(P_s > P^*)$.

A federal law stating that all wheat must be sold at a price at or above the price support level would force an increase in the price of wheat, as shown in Figure 11.1. This increase in price results in an increase in quantity supplied, as producers respond to the price incentive to produce more wheat, and a move upward along the supply curve. This is a change in quantity supplied, rather than a change in supply, since the price is the cause of the change. Similarly, the price rise causes

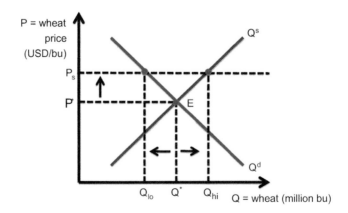

Figure 11.1 A price support for wheat

a decrease in quantity demanded, due to consumers' response to the increase in price. The consumers' action causes movement along the demand curve.

If free markets were allowed to operate, the surplus ($Q^s > Q^d$) would result in downward pressure on the price of wheat until the original equilibrium is reached. Therefore, the government must enforce this price support by removing the surplus if it expects to maintain the price at $P_s$. The government must stand ready to purchase any quantity of wheat at the price support level to keep producers from lowering the price. The government purchases the entire surplus ($Q_{hi} - Q_{lo}$) and removes this wheat from the market. The government has several options regarding the use or disposal of the surplus wheat. These include the following:

1 Give it away to US consumers through domestic food programs.
2 Give it away to foreign consumers through food aid programs
3 Export the wheat to consumers in other nations (perhaps at a below-market price).
4 Destroy the wheat (for example, dump it in the ocean).

At various times, the US government has practiced each of the four strategies. Domestic food programs include school breakfasts and school lunches.

Note that if the price support were lower than the equilibrium market price ($P_s < P^*$), the government would take no action. This is because the law requires the purchase of wheat at or above the price support level, and since the market price is above the price support level, the law is not in effect, or not "binding."

The price support is good for wheat producers since they receive a higher-than-market-equilibrium price for a larger-than-market-equilibrium number of bushels produced. The price support hurts consumers since they must pay a price higher than the equilibrium market price. Moreover, the consumers as taxpayers are made worse off since they must provide the money used to purchase the surplus and then find some way to deal with what they have purchased.

Between 1933 and 1996, the US had a complicated system of price supports. Price supports became damaging for US agriculture in the mid-1990s because the price supports raised the price of agricultural goods above the free market, world price level. Since a large percentage of all wheat and feed grains produced in the US is exported, the price supports made US food products expensive relative to exported commodities from other nations. The US was losing export opportunities to other nations due to its artificially high prices for food and feed grains. Modifications in the commodity price laws in 1996 brought US agriculture closer to a free market. Price supports remain, but they are minimum prices put in place to protect producers in times of low commodity prices, to act as a "safety net" that saves producers from low prices.

## BOX 11.1

## Government programs for risk management

Agricultural production is risky business, with uncertain prices, yields depending on weather, changes in government policies, and risky foreign markets. Risk management is therefore an important component of agricultural business decision-making. Farm operators use many strategies to manage risk, including enterprise diversification, financial leverage, vertical integration, contracting, hedging on futures markets, and insurance on crop yield and/or revenue. In addition, many farm families have access to off-farm income to help stabilize household income.

Many government programs have been developed to assist farmers and ranchers with risk management. These programs have an increasing place in food and fiber production in the US: in 2013, 295 million acres were enrolled in federal crop insurance programs, and government subsidies to agricultural producers were over USD 7 billion. The major risk management programs are described here.

Federal crop insurance (also called multiple peril crop insurance, or MPCI) was established in the 1930s to cover yield losses from most natural causes. This insurance was of limited use until the 1980s, when availability and premium subsidies were expanded to replace the earlier disaster payment program. Revenue insurance was added in the 1990s and has been the most popular form of federally sponsored agricultural insurance since that time, now providing coverage for more than 80 percent of all acres planted to major field crops in the US.

Disaster payments come in response to emergencies (storms, forest fires, floods, etc.) that prevent crops from maturing or from harvest. The payments are authorized by Congress and made on an ad hoc basis. They have diminished in use and importance since the beginning of revenue insurance.

The Agricultural Adjustment Act of 2014 (also called the 2014 Farm Act) introduced major changes to US commodity policy. The new program offers a variety of payment structures, commodity coverage, and level of yield risk and/or revenue risk. The major thrust of the 2014 Farm Act is a continuation toward consistency and linkage between the commodity programs and federal crop insurance. Many of the programs tie closely to production or anticipated production and can affect crop production levels, prices, trade, and environmental issues.

*Source:* USDA/ERS. Risk Management. www.ers.usda.gov/topics/farm-practices-management/risk-management.aspx. Retrieved January 13, 2023.

## 11.1.2  Price ceilings

At times, food prices increase, and in times of economic recession or depression, governments may intervene in the attempt to keep food affordable. In such a circumstance, a "ceiling" on food prices can protect consumers from excessively high food prices. **Price ceilings** are a government-mandated maximum price.

- *Price Ceiling* = a maximum price set by the government for a specified good or service.

When prices rise rapidly, consumers often pressure their legislators to "do something about the high prices." In the 1970s, food prices rose rapidly, creating pressure for the government to help the consumer through market price interventions. President Richard Nixon placed price ceilings on beef and many other food products. Figure 11.2 shows the impacts of such a price ceiling on meat producers and consumers.

With the imposition of the price ceiling on meat, producers and consumers cannot buy or sell meat at any price above the maximum price ($P_{max}$). If the price ceiling were set at a price greater than the equilibrium price, nothing would happen. When the price ceiling is set below the market price ($P_{max} < P^*$), however, it has consequences. The price decrease causes movements along both the supply and demand curves.

At a lower price, consumers purchase more meat due to the law of demand, resulting in an increase in quantity demanded from $Q^*$ to $Q_{hi}$. Producers reduce the quantity of meat supplied at the lower price. The result is a reduction in meat supplied from $Q^*$ to $Q_{lo}$. This creates a shortage ($Q^s < Q^d$).

This form of government intervention is interesting because the policy may or may not make consumers better off than they were prior to the mandated price ceiling. The reason is that there is less meat available to consumers at the low

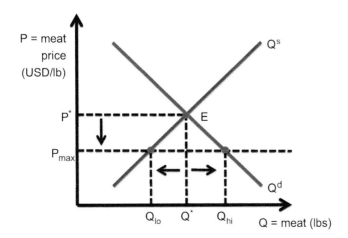

Figure 11.2  A price ceiling for meat

price of $P_{max}$. Profit-maximizing producers will decrease the supply of meat at the lower price, creating a shortage. If the law does not allow price increases, then the shortage will not self-correct through a process of consumers bidding up the price back to the equilibrium level, where the quantity supplied equals the quantity demanded.

When the price ceiling is in place, the consumers who are able to purchase meat are better off because they pay a lower price for meat. However, there is a group of consumers who are unable to locate and purchase meat due to the shortfall in production. This group of consumers is worse off because the policy restricts their access to meat.

Markets are enormously useful and adaptable institutions. Government intervention into markets typically has unanticipated consequences which distort the market mechanism. In the case of the price support, put in place to assist producers, the taxpayers and consumers must pay a large sum of money to the recipients of the price support. A price ceiling results in a shortage of the good and some unsatisfied consumers. Government intervention takes away the "self-correcting" nature of markets, which will always result in the attainment of equilibrium, or a situation where the quantity supplied is equal to the quantity demanded.

## 11.2   Welfare economics

The term **"welfare economics"** refers to the study of how well-off individual and groups are. Of particular interest is how the welfare, or well-being, of individuals or groups such as producers and consumers change due to a change in policy, market, or current event.

- *Welfare Economics* = a branch of economics that seeks to measure and understand how the well-being (welfare) of individuals changes in response to changes in policies, markets, or current events.

Note that the word "welfare" in this case does not refer to social programs or public aid intended to provide financial assistance to needy individuals. When used in economics, welfare simply refers to "well-being," or how well-off a group is, measured in dollars.

Most importantly, welfare economics provides a method for measuring how well-off different groups are in an economy by placing a dollar value on each group's welfare. In this way, welfare economic is used to quantify and evaluate proposed and actual changes in policies and markets: a simple way to describe welfare economics is "who is helped, who is hurt, and by how much."

Typically, the study of welfare economics measures how producers and consumers are affected by changes in the economy, using the concepts of **producer surplus** and **consumer surplus**.

- *Consumer Surplus (CS)* = a measure of the well-being of consumers, equal to the consumer willingness and ability to pay minus the actual price paid.
- *Producer Surplus (PS)* = a measure of the well-being of producers, equal to the price received minus the cost of production.

Consider the market for bread, and suppose that an individual is on her way to the bakery to purchase a loaf of bread. As the consumer nears the bakery, she realizes that she is willing to pay USD 5 for one loaf. This represents her reservation price. For any price higher than USD 5, she will return home empty-handed. However, when this consumer reaches the store, she is pleasantly surprised to find that the market price of bread is currently USD 4 per loaf.

We can easily calculate the consumer surplus (CS) for this individual: USD 5/loaf (willingness to pay) minus USD 4/loaf (price actually paid) results in CS = USD 1. Similarly, if the baker paid USD 2/loaf to produce the bread, then PS = USD 2: producer surplus equals price received (USD 4/loaf) minus the cost of production (USD 2/loaf).

Consumer and producer surplus are best understood using a market graph of supply and demand, as shown in Figure 11.3. Recall from Chapter 8 the derivation of a supply curve: the market supply curve is the horizontal summation of all firm's MC curves. Restated, the market supply curve represents the cost of production. Identifying producer surplus in the market graph is simply the market price (price received) minus the supply curve: this is the area of the triangle defined by the price line, the supply curve, and the vertical axis (Figure 11.3).

Calculation of producer surplus is the area of the triangle labeled PS in Figure 11.3, (0.5bh, where b = base and h = height).

11.1   $PS = 0.5bh = 0.5(10 - 0)(4 - 2) = 0.5(10)(2) = USD 10$ million.

An important and useful characteristics of PS is that it is measured in units of dollars. This is because the units of loaves cancel each other: any area in a market supply graph is price multiplied by quantity, or (USD/loaf)(million loaves) = million USD.

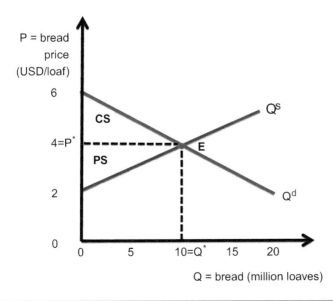

Figure 11.3 **Producer and consumer surplus**

To calculate consumer surplus, recall from Chapter 9 that the demand curve is derived from the horizontal summation of all individual consumer demand curves, which represent each individual's willingness to pay. Thus, the market demand curve represents all consumers' willingness to pay. Consumer surplus is the triangle defined by the demand curve, the price line, and the vertical axis in Figure 11.3.

### QUICK QUIZ 11.2

What is the level of consumer surplus?

Consumer surplus can also be quickly calculated, as shown in Figure 11.3.

11.2    $CS = 0.5bh = 0.5(10 - 0)(6 - 4) = 0.5(10)(2) = USD\ 10$ million.

Note that in this example PS and CS are equal due to the symmetry of the supply and demand curves.

The usefulness of welfare economics is measuring the impact of policies on producer and consumer well-being. Welfare economics provides a useful economic evaluation of a price support as it can deliver policy makers with estimates of the effects of the price support on the affected groups: producers, consumers, and taxpayers. As we have seen in Section 11.1, the purpose of the price support is to increase the well-being of producers.

## 11.2.1   Welfare economics of a price support

To demonstrate the usefulness of welfare economics, consider Figure 11.4, where a price support ($P_s$) has been legislated by the government with a law that does not

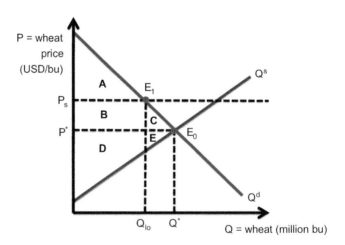

Figure 11.4 Welfare economics of a price support for wheat

allow the purchase of sale of wheat at a price below $P_s$, the level of the price support. At a high prices of $P_s$, the law of demand suggests that consumers decrease quantity demanded, *ceteris paribus*, from $Q^*$ to $Q_{lo}$ (Figure 11.4). If it is assumed that a surplus does not exist (producers only produce enough wheat to meet consumer demand at $P_s$), then $Q = \min(Q^s, Q^d)$.

---

### QUICK QUIZ 11.3

a What is the level of consumer surplus before the price support?
b What is the level of producer surplus before the price support?

---

At the initial equilibrium, consumer surplus is equal to area ABC (the area below the demand cure and above the price line). Producer surplus is equal to area DE, or the area below the price line and above the supply curve. If we denote initial values with a subscript "0," then $CS_0$ = ABC, and $PS_0$ = DE.

Wheat consumers are made worse off by the price support since they must pay a higher price for wheat. The final, or ending, value of consumer surplus (denoted with a subscript "1") is area A alone since consumers must now pay $P_s$ dollars for each bushel of wheat: $CS_1$ = A. Likewise, producer surplus is increased by area B since the support price $P_s$ is greater than the equilibrium market price $P^*$. However, producers lose area E since the quantity sold is reduced from $Q^*$ to $Q_{lo}$. Therefore, $PS_1$ = BD. The price support causes changes in the well-being of producers and consumers: $\Delta CS = CS_1 - CS_0 = -BC$ and $\Delta PS = PS_1 - PS_0 = +B - E$ (Figure 11.4). We can further understand the policy effects on the wheat market by noticing that area B is transferred from consumers to producers: in general, consumers lose and producers win. Note that society as a whole is made worse off by the price support. If we define the term "social welfare" (SW) to be the sum of all surplus in the market, it can be seen that $\Delta SW = \Delta CS + \Delta PS = -CE$. This triangle, known as a "welfare triangle," appears with any policy or program that diverges from the market equilibrium.

One of the most desirable properties of markets, and market-based economies, is that they maximize social welfare, or the total dollar value of the economy. If efficiency and market value were the only socially desirable goals, markets would dominate any government intervention in the market. The area of SW is maximized when the equilibrium price and quantity are at the market equilibrium, with no government intervention.

---

### BOX 11.2

## US farm bills

Since 1933, "agricultural acts" (frequently referred to as "farm bills") spell out the types of aid that the federal government will provide for the agricultural industry and other activities managed by the United States Department of Agriculture (USDA). Farm bills usually cover four to six years, depending on the economic condition of the industry and the composition of the Congress. The first such comprehensive law was the "Agricultural Adjustment Act of 1933." This legislation was part of the "New Deal" emergency measures during the Great Depression to address depressed farm prices and Dust Bowl droughts in the Great Plains region of the US.

Six more agricultural acts came before the Congress between 1938 and 1971, and ten such "farm bills" have become law since 1970, with the most recent in 2018. Recent legislation has broadened to include more than just food and farms. The 1990 law was called "The Food, Agriculture, Conservation, and Trade Act," and the 2008 act was the "Food, Conservation, and Energy Act of 2008." Farm bills are usually controversial because they are expensive, and they deal with subsidies, mandated payments, and regulations on what farmers can and cannot do.

The 1996 Farm Bill, officially named "The Federal Agriculture Improvement and Reform Act of 1996," drastically changed agricultural policy and the relationship between the federal government and individual farms. Beginning in 1933, agricultural producers received large subsidies (government payments) each year. The 1996 Farm Bill removed these subsidies in a movement toward free markets and free trade. The 2002 farm legislation, "The Farm Security and Rural Investment Act of 2002," reversed this course by increasing the role of the federal government in agricultural production decisions and payments. This policy shift angered some of the nation's trading partners, who had grown accustomed to lower prices for several commodities traded in world markets.

In a general sense, the 2014 Farm Bill reduced spending on agricultural activities and resulted in considerable reorganization aimed at achieving efficiency in administration of the programs. It also required individual farm operators to absorb additional risks in their farming activities. In most respects the proposed legislation makes relatively minor changes and government will remain a major presence in agricultural activities over the life of the Agriculture Act of 2014.

The 2018 Farm Bill is complicated, costly, and highly political (Evich and Boudreau).

*Sources:* 2018 Farm Bill, United States House of Representatives Committee on Agriculture.

2018 Farm Bill, United States Senate Committee on Agriculture, Nutrition and Forestry.

Evich, H.B. and C. Boudreau (December 12, 2018), "Farm bill headed to Trump after landslide House approval," Politico. www.politico.com/story/2018/12/12/house-passes-farm-bill-1060916. Retrieved January 13, 2023.

## Current agricultural policy

The Agricultural Improvement Act of 2018, also known as the 2018 Farm Bill, is an enormous bill authorizing commodity programs, crop insurance, conservation programs, agricultural trade, food aid to other nations, farm credit, rural economic development, agricultural research, forestry rules, bioenergy programs, and horticultural and organic agriculture, and nutrition policy (Supplemental Nutrition Assistance Program, or SNAP). About 76 percent of the government outlays pay for nutrition, totaling about 325 billion USD. Other expenditures include crop insurance (USD 38 billion, 9 percent), conservation programs (USD 30 billion, 7 percent), and commodity programs (USD 30 billion, 7 percent). The remaining 1 percent of outlays pay for trade, credit, rural development, and other programs.

During the Covid-19 pandemic in 2019–2021, public support for agriculture increased as never before. Most of this support was to subsidize food producers and consumers, but little of the support addressed climate change. Support for innovation, biosecurity, and infrastructure have declined in recent years. The direction of legislation is determined by the composition of the leadership of the House agricultural committee, which writes the five-year farm bills. The party in control is likely to impact the baseline spending on the farm bills, including USD 18–19 million earmarked for conservation programs. The overall size of the farm bill is likely to be affected by the composition of the agricultural committee and the budget committee.

*Source:* USDA/ERS. Farm and Commodity Policy. www.ers.usda.gov. Retrieved January 13, 2023.

Society does have goals other than efficiency such as fairness, equity, and a fair distribution of income. Governments often use market interventions to achieve these nonmarket goals. In this case, a price support was put in place to enhance producer well-being. The objective of the policy was met, but at the expense of consumers and society as a whole, who suffer a "welfare loss," also called a "deadweight loss" (DWL). In this case, DWL = $-\Delta$SW = +CE (Figure 11.4).

QUICK QUIZ 11.4

a   Graphically demonstrate the welfare economics impacts of a price support on corn.
b   What are the units for CS, PS, and SW?

The results of the welfare economic analysis demonstrate both the benefits and costs of government interventions: the redistribution of wealth from consumers to producers achieves the policy objective, but only at a cost. These results are frequently encountered during policy debates: individuals and groups who benefit from government policies emphasize the merits of redistribution, whereas the potential losers emphasize the cost and inefficiency of the proposed policy.

---

### BOX 11.4

## Multifunctionality

Multifunctionality (also called multifunctionality in agriculture) refers to the numerous benefits that agriculture provides to a region or nation. These benefits include not only market benefits but also contributions to the environment, landscape protection, food security, and positive impacts on the rural economy, including employment and economic viability.

When these positive impacts of agriculture are included in policy analyses, governments and policy makers may choose to subsidize and promote agriculture at a higher level than if the benefits were not considered. Multifunctionality has been included in agricultural trade policy discussions as a way of emphasizing the numerous positive benefits that agriculture provides to an economy. In many cases, agriculture can provide greater benefits to society when trade barriers are removed.

*Sources:* OECD (2019), Agricultural Policy Monitoring and Evaluation 2019, OECD Publishing, Paris, https://doi.org/10.1787/39bfe6f3-en. Accessed January 13, 2023.

World Trade Organization (WTO) Glossary. www.wto.org/english/thewto_e/glossary_e/glossary_e.htm. Accessed January 13, 2023.

---

### BOX 11.5

## Rent seeking

In economics, the term "rent seeking" describes the attempt to increase wealth without creating new wealth. Rent-seeking activities include lobbying regulatory agencies for favorable changes in policies using monopoly power to capture profits above the competitive level, or lobbying politicians for new programs that legislate wealth transfers to certain groups.

These activities reduce economic efficiency and social welfare, which are maximized under free markets and free trade. In many market-based economies, rent seeking takes the form of lobbying politicians through campaign donations and is legal. However, the use of bribery or corruption is in most cases against the law. Rent seeking differs from profit seeking, which is the attempt to create wealth through mutually voluntary trades. Profit seeking creates wealth and is the foundation of a market-based society, whereas rent seeking reduces wealth and is often referred to as special-interest legislation. The founders of the US were concerned about this aspect of democracy, and called the special interests "factions."

Agricultural subsidies are a form of rent-seeking behavior by farmers. Many economists argue that farmers and ranchers could thrive under free markets and free trade, rather than through government subsidies. Some economists have argued that rent-seeking actions and activities enhance income inequality since legislation is often passed that favors the wealthy lobbyists.

*Sources:* Henderson, D.R. "Rent Seeking." www.econlib.org/library/Enc/RentSeeking.html. Accessed January 13, 2023.

Investopedia. Rent Seeking. www.investopedia.com/terms/r/rentseeking.asp. Accessed January 13, 2023.

## 11.2.2   Welfare economics of a price ceiling

As we have seen earlier, price ceilings are put in place to help consumers. Welfare economic provides a way to evaluate the economic impact of a price ceiling by quantifying changes in well-being due to the policy. Consider a price ceiling on wheat (Figure 11.5). This type of policy is common in low-income nations, where politicians seek to keep food costs low in urban areas.

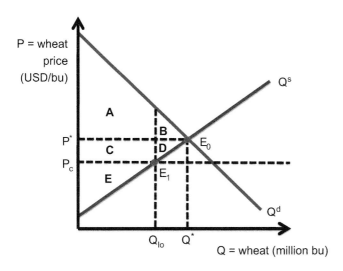

Figure 11.5 Welfare economics of a price ceiling on wheat

QUICK QUIZ 11.5

What are the initial levels of CS, PS, and SW in Figure 11.5?

Initially, $CS_0$ = AB and $PS_0$ = CDE, as shown in Figure 11.5. The price ceiling $(P_c)$ is imposed by passage of a law that does not allow wheat to be purchased or sold at a price higher than $P_c$. We will assume no surplus or shortage of wheat: $Q = min(Q^s, Q^d)$. In this case, the quantity of wheat produced will be $Q_{lo}$ since producers will decrease the quantity supplied do what to $Q_{lo}$, due to the law of supply.

QUICK QUIZ 11.6

a    Is this a change in demand or a change in quantity demanded? Why?
b    Is this a movement along, or a shift in, the demand curve? Why?

The price ceiling results in a low price, causing CS to change from area $CS_0$ = AB to $CS_1$ = AC. Consumers gain area C, but lose B: $\Delta CS$ = +C –B. The final producer surplus is $PS_1$ = E, and $\Delta PS$ = –CD. Social welfare change is $\Delta SW$ = –BD, the welfare triangle or deadweight loss (DWL). As in the case of the price ceiling, the policy objective is met, consumers are helped, but at a cost to producers and society as a whole.

QUICK QUIZ 11.7

Is it possible for the price ceiling to be put in place and the policy objective of increasing consumer well-being not be met? What conditions would cause the price ceiling to make consumers worse off?

Note that some consumers are made worse off by the price ceiling: those consumers who no longer purchase the wheat, located between $Q_{lo}$ and $Q^*$. Interestingly, if area B is larger than area C, consumers as a group are made worse off by the price ceiling, which was intended to help them. This is possible when the demand is highly price inelastic and supply is relatively price elastic. The success of the policy depends crucially on the own-price elasticities of supply and demand.

Welfare economics is a powerful and useful tool to quantify, analyze, and evaluate government policy proposals and market changes. Calculation of changes in the dollar value of well-being for all affected groups provides a solid contribution to policy analysis and decision-making. One important feature of welfare analysis is the identification and quantification of policy consequences, both intended and unintended.

BOX 11.6

## Consumer food subsidies

One major objective of all nations is to provide enough food to feed all people and to reduce or eliminate hunger, good insecurity, and malnutrition. The major policy that addresses this goal in the US is the Supplemental Nutrition Assistance Program (SNAP, also called "food stamps"). Even with food assistance programs, Feeding America reports that 34 million people in the US are food insecure, including 8 million children. A major part of the USDA's budget is for nonagricultural programs, primarily food assistance programs. More than 66 percent (about USD 283 billion in 2022) of the total USDA budget is for these subsidies to low-income consumers.

Consumer food subsidies originated in the Great Depression, when food stamps were issued to reduce agricultural surpluses by providing paper vouchers ("food stamps") that could be traded for food. After World War II, the surpluses has been depleted, and the food stamp program was discontinued. The Food Stamp Program was legislated by Congress in 1964 after a pilot program had been in place since 1961. Initially, program participants purchased food stamps at a discounted rate, but beginning in 1977, food stamps became free for qualified participants. During the 1990s, paper food stamps were replaced with electronic cards. The program name was changed from Food Stamps to SNAP in 2008. To be eligible, a household must have gross income below 130 percent of the federal poverty level (USD 27,750 per year for a family of four in 2022). Participation in SNAP increases during periods of poor economic conditions, such as during the Great Recession of 2008. At that time, about 10 percent of all food expenditures in the US were SNAP purchases. Benefits were increased during the Covid-19 pandemic, through both temporary increases in benefit levels and supplemental emergency allotments.

Additional assistance is provided by the Women, Infants, and Children (WIC) program, which provides nutrition services and food stamps to low-income pregnant and postpartum women, infants up to one year of age and children up to five years of age.

In addition to SNAP, private charities contribute to ending hunger through food banks, food pantries, soup kitchens, and emergency shelters. Several aspects of the SNAP program are controversial. Many critics believe that there should be a stronger work requirement for SNAP program eligibility. There is currently a work requirement, but this rule is often waived. Others believe that benefits to needy individuals and families should be provided in money, rather than food. The agricultural industry benefits from increased food sales and lobbies for continuation of the food assistance programs.

*Sources:* Coleman-Jensen, A., M.P. Rabbitt, C.A. Gregory, and A. Singh. September 2022. Household Food Security in the United States in 2021, ERR-309, U.S. Department of Agriculture, Economic Research Service.

Feeding America. www.feedingamerica.org/. Accessed January 13, 2023.

Wilde, Parke. *Food policy in the United States: An introduction.* Routledge, 2018.

## 11.3   Immigration

In high-income nations immigrant workers are hired in labor-intensive agriculture, such as fruit and vegetable production. These workers offer an enormous contribution to the agricultural economy through hard work in the production of food and fiber. Yet the wages for immigrant workers are low. Additionally, it is possible that immigration can be costly to rural areas due to the high cost of the provision of public services such as medical facilities, schools, and housing for low-wage workers.

Most farm workers in the US are immigrants, in spite of the massive labor-saving technological change over many decades. Technological change has occurred in the production of many crops through mechanization and the use of agricultural chemicals: over time, machines and chemicals have replaced farm workers in the US and other high-income nations such as the EU, Australia, and Japan. The number of persons employed on US farms has been stable for several decades, due to two offsetting forces: (1) a large increase in the production of hand-harvested fruits and vegetables and (2) rapid labor-saving technological change. In the US, most of these farm workers live in "farm work communities," defined as cities with a population under 20,000 that are typically poor and growing rapidly.

In theory, the economic impact of immigration on rural communities could be either positive or negative. New immigrants can stimulate job and wage growth through economic activity resulting from increased demand for housing, food, clothing, and services. However, it is possible that immigration and growth in the local labor supply could result in lower wages and displaced employment opportunities for existing workers. The actual economic outcome is highly complex, dynamic, and difficult to measure. Immigration has resulted in the description of the US as a "melting pot" of people and groups all nationalities, ethnicities, races, and religions. Immigration is often controversial, as existing groups may clash with more recent immigrants. Those in favor of immigration and open borders emphasize the positive benefits of a nation of immigrants, whereas opponents of immigration emphasize the need for new workers to follow the law to maintain law and order.

## 11.3.1  Welfare analysis of immigration: short run

Welfare analysis can be utilized to understand the economic impact of immigration. Adjustments take time, so initial impacts in the short run can differ markedly from long-run impacts. The economic impacts depend crucially on both the number of migrants and the skill level of new migrant workers. Economic theory suggests that the destination, or receiving nation, has large economic benefits from immigration, but there are winners and losers. Who wins and who loses depends on the wage structure and availability and mobility of capital, as explained later. For example, if a nation has a shortage of workers in computer skills, then immigration of workers with technical skills could be a net gain for the receiving nation. However, even in this case, workers in the receiving nation will face lower wages due to an increase in the labor supply from immigration.

It is important to emphasize that if capital is mobile and can adjust quickly, and technology can adapt to changing labor composition, then the economy with migrants is a larger version of the original economy that existed before immigration. In this case, the native-born workers are neither winners nor losers. Economic adjustments to new immigrants require time, and it is during the transition to the new workers that gains and losses occur. When immigration occurs, goods that are produced using migrant labor have an increase in production. In Figure 11.6, the wage rate is the price of labor, the initial demand for labor is given by $Q^d_0$, and the labor supplied by native workers (original workers in the receiving nation) is $Q^s_0$, which is assumed to be perfectly inelastic at $L_0$ million workers. The real-world labor supply is not fixed, as is shown in Figure 11.6, as higher wages can result in more work supplied to the market. However, the inelastic labor supply model illustrated in Figure 11.6 is good approximation of labor markets: the qualitative results of the model accurately depict the real world.

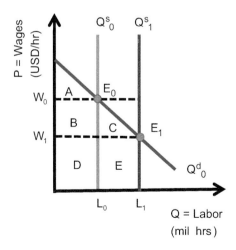

Figure 11.6  Welfare analysis of immigration impact on labor market: short run

The initial, pre-immigration labor market equilibrium occurs at $E_0$, characterized by wage rate $W_0$ and labor supply $L_0$. The total social welfare in this market is the sum of producer surplus and consumer surplus (SW = PS + CS). This is the area under the demand curve at $L_0$ (= ABD). Recall that the workers are the suppliers of labor; thus, producer surplus is the economic value of worker well-being. The consumer in this case is the firms since the employers purchase (hire) labor. The consumer surplus in the labor market shown here is the economic value to the business firms, or employers.

Before immigration occurs, producer surplus received by the workers is the entire rectangle (BD). The supply curve is vertical in this case, causing the area under the supply curve to be nonexistent. The workers receive this amount of income since area BD is equal to the wage rate times the quantity of labor employed in the economy ($W_0 * L_0$). Firms, or employers of workers, receive the consumer surplus, which before immigration occurs is equal to area A in Figure 11.6.

After immigration occurs, the labor force is increased by the number of migrants (M): $L_1 = L_0 + M$ (restated, $M = L_1 - L_0$). In the short run, no adjustments in the labor and capital market take place, and the result of an increase in the quantity of labor is a decrease in the price of labor: the wage rate falls from $W_0$ to $W_1$. Native workers lose area B in producer surplus, with a new level of economic surplus equal to D (= $W_1 * L_0$). Migrants receive wage rate $W_1$, and migrant earnings are equal to area E (= $W_1 * M$). Presumably, the wage rate earned in the receiving nation is larger than the wage rate that was available to the immigrants in their nation of origin. The wage rate is also likely to be large enough to induce workers to change locations, which can be a costly transition. Employers in the receiving nation are the winners, as consumer surplus (economic value for the firms who hire either native workers or migrants) increases from area A before immigration to area ABC after immigration.

The welfare analysis of immigration (an increase in the workforce of M workers) can be summarized in the usual way:

$\Delta$CS = employer gains = + B + C,
$\Delta PS_L$ = native worker gains = – B,
$\Delta PS_M$ = migrant worker gains = + E,
$\Delta$SW = net gain to entire economy = + C + E.

Notice that there is a net gain in total economic activity due to immigration: the magnitude of economic activity in the receiving nation is larger after immigration occurs. This is due to the influx of new resources bringing economic value and spending. This differs from government interventions in the free market economy, which are characterized by deadweight losses, or losses in societal welfare. This is because government programs and policies all result in a loss of voluntary exchange between buyers and sellers and deadweight loss. In the case of labor immigration into a nation, more voluntary exchange takes place, with large overall economic benefits to the receiving nation. The controversy surrounding immigration is the distributional effects: in the short run, native workers lose due to declining wages. As the economy adjusts to the new workers, the benefits become larger and the negative impacts are diminished, as will be explained in the next section.

## 11.3.2   Welfare analysis of immigration: long run

Workers and firms can make many adjustments once the new migrants join the workforce. In an economy with many types of skilled and unskilled workers, native workers can take jobs in areas of their comparative advantage and invest in human capital (education and training) to allow them to increase wages by moving out of low-paying jobs and into high-paying jobs. Given sufficient time, migrants can do this, too, and will move into higher-paying jobs as new waves of immigration occur.

Migrants who bring capital or work skills with them can enter growing sectors, such as technology, medicine, and services. The demand for labor in these areas is large and growing, so wages continue to increase as new workers enter the economy.

In the long run, these types of adjustment in capital and labor markets, together with technological change, will result in economic growth and broad-based wage and income growth in the receiving economy. The US has had high levels of immigration simultaneous with high and growing levels of income for most of its history: immigration has catalyzed economic growth in the high-income nations of the world. This desirable outcome requires change, adjustment, and in many cases labor migration, both occupational and locational. Growth mandates change, and change is often difficult. This is one of the major features of free markets and free trade. When economic agents are free to make decisions in their own interest, great things can happen. But improvement requires change. When workers and their families are free to locate where they desire to live and work, economic growth is likely to occur, but the transition can be challenging, and when cultures and values differ, controversy can occur.

The long-run effects of immigration can be seen in Figure 11.7. New workers joining the economy (M) cause an increase in the aggregate demand for goods in the economy, and this economic growth entices firms to produce more goods. More production requires more workers, and the demand for labor increases from $Q^d_0$ to $Q^d_1$. Equilibrium in the labor market shifts from the short-run equilibrium ($E_0$) to long-run equilibrium ($E_1$). The increase in labor demand offsets the downward pressure on wage rates, resulting in wages returning to their original level, $W_0$. The economy grows, so consumer surplus (economic value of employers, or business firms) increases to include the area under the demand curve and above the new price line: AFG. Native worker earnings are restored to their initial level (BD), and migrant worker surplus is increased to CHE.

The overall economy gains significantly once these adjustments have occurred. Adding more resources to an economy in the long run, given sufficient time for the transition to occur, will yield large economic growth as the economy is growing by the size of the new migrant labor force, and these immigrants bring new resources and larger demand for consumer goods and services.

$\Delta CS$ = employer gains = + F + G,
$\Delta PS_L$ = native worker gains = 0,
$\Delta PS_M$ = migrant worker gains = + C + H + E,
$\Delta SW$ = net gain to entire economy = + C + E + F + G + H.

The potential gains from immigration can be thwarted during periods of economic recession, when the overall demand for goods increases at a decreasing rate. This

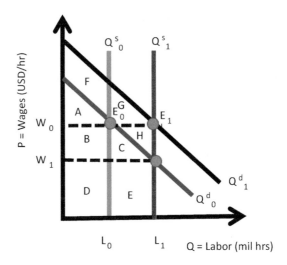

Figure 11.7 **Welfare analysis of immigration impact on labor market: long run**

economic stagnation can lead to a decrease in the demand for labor. When native workers face poor economic conditions, they are less likely to favor new migrants.

In agriculture, recent immigrants perform many tasks that native workers would not do at the low wages offered to migrants. These tasks can include meatpacking, chemical application, and harvesting fruit and vegetables. The US currently allows millions of workers to enter the country and work in farm jobs. If this supply of workers were to be eliminated, the cost of labor would rise enormously causing the cost of food to increase.

## 11.4 Macroeconomics

As we learned in Chapter 1, macroeconomics is the application of economic principles to "economy-wide aggregates," meaning issues, policies, and events at the national or international level. Macroeconomics is broad, general, and affects the entire economy. As a result, macroeconomics affects all individual production and consumption decisions, often unnoticed, in the background in ways that may not be obvious. Knowledge of macroeconomics provides a useful and powerful tool for economic decision-making in food and agriculture. In this section, a broad overview and description of basic macroeconomic principles is provided as a brief introduction to the fascinating and impactful study of the overall economy.

Macroeconomists use the same approaches as microeconomists, including cost-benefit analysis, marginal analysis, and measurement of value and well-being in currencies such as dollars and euros. However, macroeconomics is often used to better understand the overall function of the economy and provide forecasts of future business climates, economic growth, and the value of currencies.

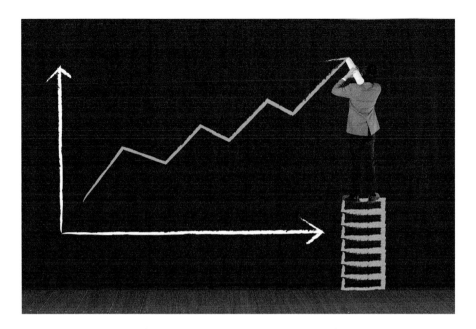

> **Photo 11.2** Macroeconomics
>
> *Source:* Singkham/Shutterstock

## 11.4.1    Macroeconomic basics

Macroeconomics seeks to measure, understand, and forecast the overall value of a national economy. The most common measurement of the overall size of the economy is gross domestic product (GDP).

● *Gross Domestic Product (GDP)* = a measure of the value of total expenditures of all goods and services in an economy in a given time period, usually one year or one quarter.

The intuition of GDP is simply the sum total value of all goods and services produced in an economy. The official GDP is measured by economists in the US Department of Commerce and reported on a quarterly basis. In 2022, the GDP equaled approximately USD 23 trillion (Table 11.1).

Although the calculation and measurement of GDP may appear straightforward, it is an enormously complicated procedure due to price volatility, the definition of goods, how to aggregate and average goods into a single measure, and how to account for goods not paid for such as child rearing and housekeeping. A second measure of the overall value of an economy is the **national income (NI)**.

● *National Income* (NI) = a measure of the total value of all factor payments (capital, labor, and land) during a period of time, usually one year or one quarter.

Recalling the circular flow diagram of an economy from Chapter 1, the measures of GDP and NI capture the value of an economy in two different places: GDP

> ### Table 11.1  United States gross domestic product (GDP)

| Year | GDP (USD trillion) | Price index (percent) | GDP (2012 USD trillion) | Farm income (2012 USD billion) | Ag GDP share (percent) |
|------|------|------|------|------|------|
| 2018 | 20.5 | 0.907 | 18.6 | 133.1 | 0.01 |
| 2019 | 21.4 | 0.888 | 19.0 | 125.0 | 0.01 |
| 2020 | 20.9 | 0.880 | 18.4 | 142.5 | 0.01 |
| 2021 | 23.0 | 0.843 | 19.4 | – | – |

*Source:* Department of Commerce. Bureau of Economic Analysis. Economic Report to the President, Table B—3 (2022). Economic Report to the President, Table B—9 (2022, Farm Income).

measures the value of goods and services, and NI quantifies the input, or factor, markets. If the measurements are done with care and the data are solid, the two measures should be equal, at least conceptually. The real work is complicated, however, and as a result, the two measures differ. Numerous macroeconomists and government employees devote their careers to improving the definition, measurement, and use of NI accounts, given their importance and usefulness in providing information to the financial sector and businesses.

One of the major issues in macroeconomics is that of business cycles, or volatility in NI. The rate of change in GDP over time is used to define several important macroeconomic terms.

- *Recession* = a time period when the rate of growth of GDP is negative.
- *Boom* = a time period when the rate of growth of GDP is positive.
- *Depression* = a time period when the rate of change in GDP is negative.

The goal of macroeconomic policy is to provide an economy with the desirable attributes of full employment, stable prices and currency values, and economic growth. These conditions provide the decision-makers in an economy (producers and consumers) with a solid foundation upon which to make forward-looking choices. Since all decisions, including business, career, and personal decisions, are intended to make the future better than the past, a steady, predictable economy is desirable and provides for economic growth.

## 11.4.2  Money

Throughout the study of economics, we have used **money**, usually measured in dollars, to quantify the value of goods and services.

- *Money* = anything generally accepted and commonly used as a measure of payment.

Money provides three major functions in a society:

- Medium of exchange
- Store of value, or purchasing power
- Unit of account

In ancient societies without money, goods and services had to be traded through barter, or direct exchange. Barter requires a simultaneous coincidence of wants: I would like to give you two chickens for one coconut, but the transaction will not take place unless you are willing to trade at the same rate of exchange. Money makes life simpler and vastly more efficient: I can separate the sales of chickens from coconut purchases.

Money is also a store of wealth, allowing trades to be separated across time: if I sell two chickens today for money, I can keep the money (store of wealth) and use the purchasing power to buy coconuts in the future. For money to be most useful, it must retain a constant value over time. If the value of money changes over time, the function of a store of wealth is weakened since money holders do not know the value of goods that could be purchased with the money in the future. The third function of money is a unit of account, or a measurement of the value of a good or service.

In each of these three functions, money that retains the same value is most useful: if currency lost value over time, consumers and producers would not use it as a store of value. The value of money can be defined by the term "**purchasing power**."

- *Purchasing Power* = the value of money in terms of units of goods that money can purchase or command.

In a real-world economy, the value of money, or purchasing power, can rise and fall based on market conditions: the supply and demand of money. Inflation refers to price increases of goods.

- *Inflation* = a sustained, rapid increase in prices, as measured by a price index over months or years, resulting in a decrease in purchasing power of the currency.
- *Deflation* = a general decrease in prices, as measured by a price index, resulting in an increase in purchasing power of the currency.

If purchasing power remains stable, economic decision-makers will continue to hold and use money. If inflation erodes the purchasing power of money, it becomes less attractive as a medium of exchange, store of value, and unit of account. Therefore, one of the major goals of macroeconomic policy is to provide steady, stable prices by keeping the value of money (currency) constant over time.

A large branch of macroeconomic studies "money and banking," includes the money supply, the commercial banking system, financial markets, savings, and investment. The importance of these topics is paramount, given the need for businesses and individuals to borrow funds to pay for inputs into the production of goods and services in a modern economy. Credit is particularly important in many aspects of agriculture since food production takes time: production costs often occur a long time before final production and sales. Also, weather and other biological uncertainties cause agricultural and food markets to be volatile relative to other markets. Risk management and financial management are necessary to keep food and agricultural sectors operating efficiently.

### 11.4.3   Real and nominal GDP

The purchasing power of all currencies changes over time due to changes in the supply and demand for each currency. As a result, all prices and measures of national income are subject to errors in measurement unless corrected for the rate of inflation, or the rate of change in purchasing power. Macroeconomists at the US Department of Commerce measure changes in purchasing power with the use of price indexes. A price index captures the "average" value of money by averaging, or indexing, a "market basket" of goods and services most commonly purchased by consumers. This is a weighted average of goods most frequently purchased in an economy. To account for inflation, actual prices must be corrected, or "deflated," into prices measured with a common value, or constant purchasing power. For example, if the price of eggs rose from one USD per dozen eggs in 2023 to USD 1.2 per dozen eggs in 2024, the rate of inflation would be 20 percent.

Economists refer to actual market prices as **nominal prices**, and corrected prices as **real prices**.

- **Nominal Prices** = prices observed at any point in time, measured in dollars of that time.
- **Real Prices** = prices of goods or services adjusted for inflation.

The calculation of real prices is straightforward, as shown in the example of egg prices.

11.3   Real $P_{egg(2020)}$ = (Nominal $P_{egg(2019)}$ ÷ Price Index) * 100.

In our case, the price index would equal 100 in 2023 and 120 in 2024. Therefore, the real price of eggs in 2024 is equal to USD 1 per dozen eggs. This simple calculation is also used to correct, or deflate, nominal GDP into a more accurate measure of real GDP:

11.3   Real GDP = (Nominal GDP ÷ Price Index) * 100.

This procedure is shown in Table 11.1. Real GDP per capita is commonly used as a measure of welfare, or well-being, of individuals in an economy. Per capita GDP for several selected nations appears in Table 11.2. The figures range from US 2,257 per capita in India to USD 70,249 per capita in the United States. A limitation of the measure of per capita GDP is that there is no distinction between nations with very different income distributions. The average can mask highly divergent levels of inequality. A second limitation is that nonmarket goods are not included. Therefore, in many low-income nations, a larger share of goods are not transacted in markets, so the measured per capita GDP is lower in those cases.

### 11.4.4   Monetary policy

Recall that the overall objectives of macroeconomic policy include (1) full employment; (2) to provide stable prices, or low inflation; and (3) the promotion of economic growth. Macroeconomic policies that are used to achieve these objectives are broken down into two broad categories: (1) monetary policy and (2) fiscal

Table 11.2 Per capita GDP, selected nations, 2021

|  | Agricultural employment (% of total male employment) | Fertilizer consumption (kg/ha) | GDP per capita (current USD) | Cereal yield (kg/ha) | Trade to GDP ratio (present) |
|---|---|---|---|---|---|
| India | 43 | 209 | 2,256.6 | 3,161 | 45 |
| Thailand | 31 | 143 | 7,066.2 | 3,016 | 117 |
| Ghana | 30 | 107 | 2,363.3 | 1,925 | 58 |
| China | 25 | 383 | 12,556.3 | 6,296 | 37 |
| Romania | 21 | 83 | 14,858.2 | 3,453 | 87 |
| Brazil | 9 | 365 | 7,507.2 | 5,256 | 39 |
| Japan | 3 | 238 | 39,312.7 | 6,050 | 37 |
| USA | 1 | 126 | 70,248.6 | 8,175 | 25 |

*Source:* World Bank

policy. International trade is highly interconnected to these policies, and as a result, trade policy is a third area of macroeconomic policy.

● *Monetary Policy* = changes in the rate of growth of the quantity of money in the economy to achieve macroeconomic objectives.

In the US, monetary policies are conducted by the Federal Reserve Bank, an independent agency of the federal government. In Europe, the EU is in charge of the euro and conducts monetary policy on behalf of the member nations. Since money is a "good" that provides the useful functions of medium of exchange, store of value, and unit of account, money can be understood using market analysis, using the concepts of the supply and demand for money. The monetary authority produces and supplies money to the market, and firms and households demand money to make their business transactions less time-consuming and more efficient. The value of money is determined by the interaction of the supply and demand for money, just as with other goods and services.

This is accomplished by providing more currency to the economy, making the currency less scarce, and thus less valuable. In the US, this process is conducted by the Federal Reserve Bank through the purchase of government securities (bonds). The dollars used to buy these bonds are introduced into the economy through "open market operations." The monetary authority can also alter the "discount rate," a key interest rate charged by the Federal Reserve Bank for loans to commercial banks. The interest rates charged to all borrowers are affected by the discount rate since it influences the quantity of credit available in the economy.

If the supply of money is increased by the monetary authority, the value of money decreases, and inflation occurs, *ceteris paribus*. This is called an expansionary monetary policy. By introducing more money (dollars or euros, for example) into the economic system, the monetary authority desires to make more credit available to business firms and consumers, who will in turn purchase more goods and services. Expansionary monetary policy therefore is used to stimulate the economy by making more money and credit available.

At times, inflation can be considered an issue, where purchasing power decreases over time. During periods of high inflation, households with fixed incomes lose some of their ability to purchase goods since the overall price level is increasing. One of the major functions of money is a unit of account, and inflation erodes the usefulness of this function. For example, if the price of corn increases from one year to the next, it is not immediately known if this price increase indicates an increase in the relative price of corn or an increase in all prices due to inflation. Business decisions for the corn producer are quite different in each case. If the relative price of corn increases, the farm will increase production of corn by planting more acres of land to corn and increasing the purchase of inputs such as chemicals and fertilizers (Chapter 4). On the other hand, if the price increase is due to inflation, then relative prices have not changed, and the profit-maximizing firm will not increase acreage planted to corn or input use.

Given these issues caused by inflation, a monetary authority may use restrictive monetary policy to reduce the supply of money and credit in the economy to reduce inflation rates. The desired outcome of this policy is to restrain economic growth to reduce inflation and thereby increase purchasing power. Monetary policy is extremely important to an economy, as it determines purchasing power and the rate of inflation. However, monetary policy is an inexact policy instrument: changes in the money supply cause predictable changes in unemployment levels, economic growth, and inflation, *ceteris paribus*. Given the huge range of other economic activities occurring in an economy, including international trade, technological change, and income growth, monetary policy is a crude instrument. Particularly vexing to the monetary authority is the time lag between when monetary policies are conducted and the corresponding changes in economy-wide activities. Given the huge size of the economy, it takes time for monetary policy to work.

## 11.4.5   Fiscal policy

Fiscal policy is the second type of macroeconomic policy.

- *Fiscal Policy* = attempts by a government to influence macroeconomic variables through taxes and government spending.

There is a great deal of disagreement and debate among economists about the most appropriate form of fiscal policy. Expansionary fiscal policy is employed during times of recession: the government will increase government spending and/or lower tax rates with the goal of spurring economic growth. Restrictive fiscal policy involves reducing government spending and/or increasing taxes to reduce economic activity.

The legislative branch of government typically appropriates money for government expenditures and sets tax rates. In the US, Congress has authority to enact fiscal policies. The goals of fiscal policy are identical to those of monetary policy: to reduce or eliminate fluctuations in business cycles, keep inflation low and steady, and promote economic growth. However, the policy instruments differ substantially: fiscal policy uses tax rates on individuals and corporations to expand or contract economic activity. The main idea is that if household and firms are able to keep more of their earnings, they will spend the retained earnings and have an incentive to earn more. Thus, the economy can be stimulated through lower tax rates. Similarly, government expenditures can be used to induce higher levels of economic activity.

## 11.4.6 Macroeconomic policy and agricultural-sector linkages

Agricultural firms are land and capital intensive relative to nonfarm businesses. This means that food production is more heavily reliant on land and machinery than other industries. Agricultural goods are also widely traded between nations. These characteristics cause the food and agricultural sectors to be strongly influenced by macroeconomic conditions and the two forms of government intervention in the macroeconomy: monetary and fiscal policy.

Figure 11.8 shows the linkages between macroeconomic policies and the agricultural sector. While the linkages are strong and direct, it is important to emphasize that it is difficult to quantify or predict the exact impact of each policy on agricultural prices, incomes, and productivity. The difficulty in measurement and understanding is due to the complexity and magnitude of the overall economy, combined with the simultaneous occurrence of millions of market events, price changes, and other economic events that affect the overall economy. Given this complexity, to isolate the impact of macroeconomic policies, *ceteris paribus*, is difficult and most often crude. This makes it easy for politicians and economists to attribute macroeconomic changes to the policy of their choosing.

Economists can say with certainty, however, that monetary and fiscal policy have important and widespread impacts on the food and agricultural economy, as shown in Figure 11.8. Both fiscal policy and monetary policy have a strong influence on interest rates and inflation. These both have a truly crucial influence on the agricultural sector. Interest rates reflect the cost of borrowing funds, which allow agricultural producers to purchase inputs such as land, machinery, seed,

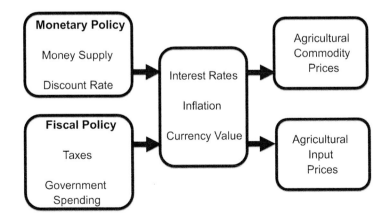

Figure 11.8 Macroeconomic policy linkages to agriculture

fertilizer, and chemicals ahead of production and sales. Food storage is an important component of food and agricultural markets, and the interest rate is one of the major costs of storage. Inflation affects agriculture due to the time lags associated with food and fiber production, processing, storage, and transportation. For example, if wheat producers make planting decisions in the fall but do not harvest the wheat until the summer of the following year, inflation (or deflation) could alter the expected value of the crop.

Expansionary monetary policy can have a large influence on the food and agricultural sector by increasing the money supply. To summarize, through these policy mechanisms, the monetary authority has a strong influence on interest rates (the cost of credit and cost of storage) and inflation, the value of a currency. Chapter 14 demonstrates the importance of the large influence that the value of nation's currency has on the exchange rate. Since exchange rates determine the quantity of goods and services traded, monetary policy has a huge impact on international trade of food and agricultural products. Fiscal policy also has important impacts on the macroeconomy and therefore on the agricultural economy (Figure 11.8).

## 11.5 Food security, hunger, and global poverty

Almost every day, we hear messages about society's desire to "feed the world," or ensure that enough food is produced to feed "10 billion people by 2050." Many government programs and policies exist to alleviate hunger and poverty. Unfortunately, a huge proportion of the world's population lives without enough food to eat. It has been shown that global hunger is a result of poverty, rather than food scarcity. There is enough food produced in the world to feed the world's population. Unfortunately, hunger continues to exist due to lack of purchasing power: world hunger is a direct result of world poverty. Producing more food is unlikely to eliminate poverty and hence unlikely to resolve hunger.

### BOX 11.7

**Science policy**

Science policy concerns the allocation of resources to scientific endeavors to best serve the public. Science policy in agriculture is enormously important since huge gains in food supplies have resulted from investments in science applied to agricultural production practices. Science funding has led to truly dramatic increases in the standard of living though technological change in food and agriculture.

Agricultural science funding is important, complex, and changing rapidly. Traditionally, agricultural science was funded by the public sector through agricultural programs in the USDA and global institutions. Over time, funding in agriculture has switched to private sources. Debate and controversy continue about the optimal role of government in research and development of agricultural technology.

Historically, investments in agriculture have led to large rates of return. However, the returns to investments in science often require a long period of time to materialize. The US has supported science through federal and state governments for a very long time. Most science policy is determined by congressional budget appropriations, which are then administered through federal agencies such as the USDA, the National Science Foundation (NSF), and the National Institutes of Health (NIH).

The US has decreased its commitment to agricultural research and development, while China, India, and Brazil have enhanced the funding of agricultural innovation. Important trade-offs exist between research in basic science, applied science, and commercial product development. Scientific policy focuses on knowledge production, which occurs across private firms, public institutions, and individual scientists. The Foundation for Food and Agriculture Research (FFAR) originated in the Agricultural Act of 2014. The FFAR allocated USD 200 million of startup funds to invest in public agricultural research and development, requiring a one-to-one match of nonfederal dollars. This type of funding is likely to enhance food production over a long period of time.

*Sources:* Pardey, P. and V.H. Smith. "Waste Not, Want Not Transactional Politics, Research and Development Funding, and the US Farm Bill." Chapter 4 in: Smith,

V.H., J.W. Glauber, and B.K. Goodwin, eds. *Agricultural Policy in Disarray.* Vol. 2. Rowman & Littlefield, 2018.

The attempt to assist in the reduction or elimination of hunger, particularly since the end of World War II, has led to the concept of **food security.**

● *Food Security* = a situation where all people at all times have access to sufficient, safe, and nutritious food to maintain a healthy and active life.

The concept of food security most often includes not only physical access to food but also economic access to meet all dietary, nutrition, and safety needs. There continues to be a great deal of debate about the appropriateness of national food security. Should each nation produce sufficient food to adequately feed the entire population? Or should nations grow the crops most suited to their specific growing conditions and environment and use international trade to meet their citizens' food requirements? This is a much-debated issue. Some argue that national food security is paramount, while others suggest that it is less costly to purchase imported food, and therefore a superior choice.

Photo 11.3 Food aid

*Source:* Adrian Lindley/Shutterstock

Both strategies have benefits and costs. It can be difficult to assess the overall strengths and weaknesses of these crucial food, hunger, and poverty strategies, given the complexity and persistence of the issues. **Food aid** is a policy intended to help hungry people.

● *Food Aid* = international provision of food or cash to purchase food to address hunger or undernutrition.

Food aid comprised over 20 percent of global assistance in the 1960s, but is now less than 5 percent. Food aid remains important, however, due to the prevalence of world hunger and food emergencies. Problems associated with food aid include the following: (1) food aid is often a result of a surplus of food produced in the donor nation, (2) food aid is used as a foreign policy tool, (3) economic development may not be the objective of food aid, and (4) cash could provide superior outcomes to food in many circumstances. Changes in relative prices demonstrate two major issues associated with food aid. First, food aid often removes surpluses of grain from the donor nation, resulting in higher grain prices. These higher prices are often one of the major motivations for food aid. Second, food aid makes food more plentiful in the recipient nation, decreasing food prices. Lower prices in agriculture diminish producer incentives to produce more food. Economists emphasize the "self-correcting" nature of markets: high prices result in an increase in supply. To the extent that food aid lowers prices, it decreases the ability of the recipient-nation farmers to compete in food and agriculture. This can exacerbate poverty, food insecurity, and lead to dependence on food aid.

Many argue for the use of food aid in emergencies for relief. As a short-run policy, relief aid is not intended to resolve the underlying causes of poverty and hunger. Instead, it is intended to help in times of emergency.

---

**BOX 11.8**

## Global hunger

Hunger is defined as physical discomfort in the short run resulting from chronic food shortage or a life-threatening lack of food. Global hunger, also called world hunger, refers to hunger aggregated to the global level. The term "food insecurity" refers to limited or unreliable access to safe and nutritionally adequate food, whereas "malnutrition" results from insufficient intake of biologically necessary nutrients. There are two types of malnutrition: (1) protein-energy malnutrition, defined as a lack of calories and protein, and (2) micronutrient deficiency, or a shortage of vitamins and minerals.

The United Nations Food and Agriculture Organization (FAO) estimates that about 828 million people of the 7.1 billion people in the world (11.7 percent) suffered from chronic undernourishment in 2021. The vast majority of hungry persons live in lower-middle-income regions, which saw a 42 percent decrease in undernourished people between 1990–1992 and 2012–2014. Unfortunately, global hunger has been rising since 2016. The highest prevalence of hunger occurs in sub-Saharan Africa, where about 22 percent of people remain undernourished in 2020.

The world produces enough food to feed everyone. Growth in food availability and improved access to food helped reduce the percentage of chronically undernourished people. The main cause of global hunger is the inability to purchase food due to low incomes: poverty is the cause of hunger. Sadly, hunger is also a cause of poverty; there is a cyclical relationship between hunger and poverty.

*Sources:* National Research Council. 2006. Food Insecurity and Hunger in the United States: An Assessment of the Measure. Washington, DC: The National Academies Press. https://doi.org/10.17226/11578. Retrieved January 13, 2023.

United Nations Food and Agricultural Organization (FAO). "The State of Food Security and Nutrition in the World." 2019. data.unicef.org/resources/sofi-2022. Retrieved January 13, 2023.

## 11.6  Economic development

Market-based economies have achieved high levels of wealth and income over the
past few centuries, and particularly since 1950. Unfortunately, however, a majority of the world's population does not have high incomes. Examples are seen in
Table 11.2. The term "**economic development**" is used by economists and politicians to denote actions and policies that promote the standard of living and economic health of a nation, region, or area. Economic development is typically used
in a broader context than economic growth, which refers solely to an increase in
GDP. Economic development encompasses improvements in economic, political,
and social well-being of people.

● *Economic Development* = actions and policies that promote the standard of
   living and economic health of a nation, region, or area, encompassing improvements in economic, political, and social well-being of people.

The history of economic development provides a fascinating look at the challenges
of helping others. After World War II, US president Harry S. Truman identified the
development of low-income nations as a priority for the US and Western European
nations. For several decades, the focus was on the promotion of industrialization
in low-income nations. These policies included import substitution and self-sufficiency. In the 1970s, the focus changed to investments in education, training, and
human capital, as well as the redistribution of wealth. In the 1980s, globalization,
free markets, and free trade were highlighted.

Optimal economic development strategies are highly controversial, heavily
debated, and remain uncertain. Some economists focus on property rights and rule
of law as prerequisites for economic growth and development. Without enforcement of property rights, businesses and households have little incentive to partici-
pate and invest in the mainstream economy.

### BOX 11.9

### Global poverty

Seven percent of the world's people lived in extreme poverty in 2020
(World Bank 2022). This percentage has decreased over time: from
1990 to 2015, more than 1 billion people have lifted themselves out
of poverty: the extreme poverty rate dropped from 36 to 10 percent.
Since then, poverty reduction has slowed. Although large gains
have been made in the reduction of global poverty, poverty remains
difficult to eliminate, particularly in low-income nations and
countries characterized by conflict and political upheaval.

One in ten people in low-income nations live below the
international poverty line, defined as less than USD 2.15 per day.
The decrease in poverty has slowed since 2013, especially in sub-
Saharan Africa, where up to 35 percent of the population continues

to live below the poverty line. This comprises 60 percent of the global poor.

The causes of poverty include lack of resources, unequal income distribution, conflict, and hunger. More than half of the hungry people in the world live in nations afflicted by conflict, and about 75 percent of the children across the globe who are stunted live in conflict areas (FAO 2022).

*Sources:* United Nations Food and Agricultural Organization (FAO). "The State of Food Security and Nutrition in the World." 2022. Data/unicef.org/ resources/sofi-2022. Retrieved January 13, 2023.

World Bank. 2022. Poverty and Shared Prosperity 2022: Correcting Course. Washington, DC: World Bank. License: Creative Commons Attribution CC BY 3.0 IGO.

Free market economists emphasize the importance of specialization and gains from trade that occurs in market-based economies. Others suggest that infrastructure-based economic development is most appropriate, characterized by investments in transportation, housing, education, and health care. Most economists agree that economic growth is an important precursor to economic development: higher income levels allow governments, private individuals, and business firms to enhance social services, health care, and the level of social well-being of a nation. Although there is debate and disagreement about appropriate policies for economic development, the world has experienced a massive increase in per capita GDP since 1950. The objective of economic development remains to promote and encourage this level of wealth and high standard of living with all people in all nations.

## BOX 11.10

### Farm consolidation

Farms in the United States have been consolidating and becoming larger for several decades due to technological changes that allow one farmer to work more land. As a result, the average size of farm in the US has increased over time. It is important to note that the size distribution of family farm is highly skewed (asymmetric): there are a large number of small farms, but most food is produced by a small number of very large farms.

Consolidation of crop farms has occurred for a long time across all crops. This consolidation has been accompanied with enhanced specialization (MacDonald et al., 2018). Even with consolidation, most food and fiber production is from family farms, which accounted for approximately 90 percent of farms with at least USD 1 million in sales during 2015. The exceptions are hog and poultry production, which are characterized by corporate farming, typically through contracts.

Larger-sized farms capture economies of scale, allowing for lower per-unit costs of production. Technological change in agriculture, particularly advances in mechanization, chemical use, and fertilizer application practices continue to provide a strong economic incentive for further consolidation in US agriculture.

In 2017, 105,453 farms (5 percent) produced 75 percent of all farm sales (USDA/NASS). The largest farms, defined as farms with sales of 5 million USD or higher, accounted for less than 1 percent of all farms, but 35 percent of all farm sales. Small farms (less than $50,000 in sales) accounted for 76 percent of farms, but only 3 percent of sales. These statistics demonstrate a long trend in concentration of farms into larger farms producing more of the agricultural products in the US, a trend that is mirrored in the global economy.

*Sources:* J.M. MacDonald, R.A. Hoppe, and D. Newton. Three Decades of Consolidation in U.S. Agriculture, EIB-189, U.S. Department of Agriculture, Economic Research Service, March 2018.

United States Department of Agriculture, National Agricultural Statistics Service. 2017 Census of Agriculture. Cen V1 (5–14). United States, Summary and State Data. Volume 1. Geographic Area Series. Part 51, AC-17–A-51. Issued April 2019.

## 11.7   Public goods

Most goods and services are bought and sold in markets, where the price is determined by the interaction of supply and demand. Interestingly and importantly, there are many goods and services for which there is no market. Police protection is an example: there is supply and demand for a police force, but no market where price and quantity are determined in equilibrium. No markets exist for goods such as police, fire protection, radio and television broadcasts, and Wi-Fi connections. These are examples of public goods, and price and quantity decisions are most often made by political and administrative bodies.

Public goods are defined as goods that are (1) nonrival and (2) nonexcludable.

- *Public Good* = a good that is both (1) nonrival and (2) nonexcludable.
- *Rival Good* = a good in which the consumption of the good by one person precludes the consumption of the good by a second person.

- *Nonexcludable Good* = a good in which everyone can consume the good whether they pay for it or not.

The purchase and consumption of most goods is rivalrous, meaning that if one person consumes the good, no one else can: if I eat an apple, you cannot, so apples are rival goods. For nonrival goods, one individual's consumption of the good does not diminish another person's ability to consume the good: watching a sunset, listening to an Internet radio broadcast, and national security are examples.

Nonexcludable goods in agriculture include food security and rural landscapes. An excludable good is one that nonpaying customers can be stopped from consuming, such as a hamburger or a cell phone. A nonexcludable good occurs when it is not possible to prevent nonpaying consumers from gaining access to the good. Fresh air, public parks, and beautiful vistas are nonexcludable goods. Since farmers cannot exclude consumers form a fresh, healthy secure food supply or beautiful agriculture landscapes, these goods are nonexcludable. It can be argued that farmers are "undercompensated" for these aspects of farming.

Agriculture has two other attributes that are public goods: agricultural research and development and food safety are also characterized by nonrivalry and nonexcludability. It could be argued that pubic goods are "underproduced" since producers are not fully compensated for the production of public goods. Subsidies are provided to agriculture in most high-income nations, including the US, EU, and Japan. These large subsidies are controversial since farmers who receive the subsidies have higher levels of wealth and income than the taxpayers who pay for the subsidies. The subsidies are often justified by the public good characteristics of agriculture: to the extent that agriculture is underproduced, the subsidies provide compensation to farmers. Public goods are related to externalities, a topic that is explored in Chapter 15.

---

### BOX 11.11

## Food safety

Food safety is a crucial policy goal for all nations. In low-income nations, food safety issues result in sickness and death. High-income nations are not immune: in the US, millions get sick each year and thousands die from food safety problems.

Food safety issues are divided into two broad categories: (1) foodborne illnesses (for example, *Escherichia coli* and *Salmonella*) and (2) toxic chemicals and new technologies (Wilde 2018). Food safety is often preventable, but costly. As a result, policy makers are challenged to supply the "optimal" level of food safety, using risk assessment and risk management tools.

The Food and Drug Administration (FDA) is charged with oversight activities of food safety. The Centers for Disease Control (CDC) monitors and investigates foodborne diseases. Many agricultural chemicals have been found to be carcinogenic or otherwise potentially harmful to human health. The Environmental Protection Agency (EPA) assesses consumer exposure to pesticides, sets maximum allowable tolerances for pesticides residues, and regulates pesticides use in agricultural production. The Animal and Plant Health Inspection Services (APHIS) is in charge of preventing animal and plant diseases, including foreign diseases and pests.

The FDA Food Safety Modernization Act (FSMA) was passed by Congress in 2010. This act granted more authority to the FDA for food oversight and safety. Food safety issues are important, complicated, and ever-changing. As the food production practices continue to evolve and adopt large-scale technologies, food safety regulation must continue to adapt and will continue to play an important part of government regulatory activities.

*Sources:* US General Accounting Office. FOOD SAFETY: A National Strategy Is Needed to Address Fragmentation in Federal Oversight. GAO-17–74: Published: Jan 13, 2017. Publicly Released: Feb 13, 2017.

Wilde, Parke. Food policy in the United States: An introduction. Routledge, 2018.

## 11.8  Mathematical welfare economics of price policies (optional)

Recall from Chapter 10 the equations for the inverse supply and demand of wheat:

11.5   $P = 1 + 0.1Q^s$,
11.6   $P = 5 - 0.1Q^d$,

where P is the price of wheat in dollars per bushel and $Q^s$ is the quantity supplied of wheat in millions of bushels.

### QUICK QUIZ 11.8

Find the equilibrium price and quantity of wheat.

To find equilibrium, set the two equations equal to each other since P = P and $Q^* = Q^s = Q^d$ to get P* = USD 3/bu of wheat and Q* = 20 million bushels of wheat (Figure 11.9).

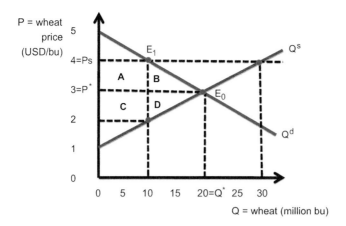

**Figure 11.9** Mathematical welfare economics of a price support for wheat

## 11.8.1 Mathematical welfare economics of a price support

Suppose that a price support is put in place by the government at $P_s$ = USD 4/bu. To calculate the levels of quantity supplied and demanded, simply plug in the price of USD 4/bu into the inverse supply and inverse demand equations to get

11.7  $Q^s$ = 30 million bushels of wheat, and
11.8  $Q^d$ = 10 million bushels of wheat.

Assuming that there is no surplus, or that wheat producers do not overproduce, the equilibrium quantity will be $Q = min(Q^s, Q^d)$, in this case $Q$ = 10 million bushels of wheat (Figure 11.9). Since consumers face a higher price and a lower quantity, the change in consumer surplus is as follows:

11.9  $\Delta CS = -AB = -(10 - 0)(4 - 3) - 0.5(20 - 10)(4 - 3)$
$\qquad = -10 - 5 = $ USD $-15$ million.

Wheat producers gain area A due to the higher price but lose area D due to lower quantity produced and sold.

11.10  $\Delta PS = +A - D = +(10 - 0)(4 - 3) - 0.5(20 - 10)(3 - 2) = +10 - 5 = $ USD $+5$ million.

The change in social welfare is the sum of the changes in producer and consumer welfare.

11.11  $\Delta SW = \Delta CS + \Delta PS = -BD = $ USD $-10$ million.

Define and explain deadweight loss (DWL) for the price support policy. Calculate the level of DWL.

Recall that the deadweight loss of a policy is the loss in social welfare, or the dollar value of the loss to all groups, in this case DWL = $-\Delta$SW = USD 10 million.

## 11.8.2 Mathematical welfare economics of a price ceiling

This procedure also helps calculate a below-equilibrium price that leads to a shortage. Suppose that the government legislates a price ceiling on wheat equal to USD 2/bu (Figure 11.10). The inverse supply and inverse demand equations can be used to calculate the quantities:

11.12 $Q^s$ = 10 million bushels of wheat,
11.13 $Q^d$ = 30 million bushels of wheat.

As before, no shortage or surplus is assumed, so Q = min($Q^s$, $Q^d$). In the case of the price ceiling, the equilibrium quantity of wheat will be Q = 10 million bu of wheat (Figure 11.10).

Since consumers face a lower price and a smaller quantity, the change in consumer surplus is as follows:

11.14 $\Delta$CS = +C $-$B = +(10 $-$ 0)(3 $-$ 2) $-$ 0.5(20 $-$ 10)(4 $-$ 3) = +10 $-$ 5 = USD +5 million.

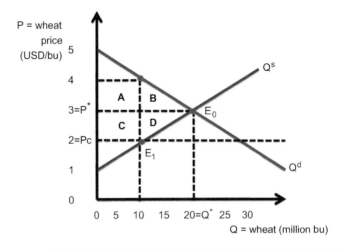

Figure 11.10 Mathematical welfare economics of a price ceiling on wheat

The policy has met the objective of increasing consumer well-being. Note, however, that not all consumers are made better off since consumers with a lower willingness to pay are excluded from the market. Wheat producers lose areas C and D due to the lower price and lower quantity produced and sold.

11.15 $\Delta PS = -CD = -(10 - 0)(3 - 2) - 0.5(20 - 10)(3 - 2) = -10 - 5$
$= USD\ -15$ million.

The change in social welfare is the sum of the changes in producer and consumer welfare.

11.16 $\Delta SW = \Delta CS + \Delta PS = -BD = USD\ -10$ million.

Recall that the deadweight loss of a policy is the loss in social welfare, or the dollar value of the loss to all groups, in this case $DWL = -\Delta SW = USD\ 10$ million.

## QUICK QUIZ 11.10

What conditions would cause this policy to make consumers worse off?

## 11.9 Chapter 11 Summary

1   A price support is a minimum price set by the government for a specified good or service, typically used by high-income nations to support agricultural producers.
2   A price ceiling is a maximum price set by the government for a specified good or service, typically used by low-income nations to support urban consumers.
3   Welfare economics is a tool used by economists to measure and understand how the well-being of individuals and groups changes in response to changes in policies, markets, and current events.
4   Consumer surplus (CS) is a measure of the well-being of consumers, equal to the consumer willingness to pay minus the price actually paid.
5   Producer surplus (PS) is a measure of the well-being of producers, equal to the price received minus the cost of production.
6   Immigration results in lower wages in the receiving nation in the short run, resulting in losses to native workers, gains to employers, and gains to new migrants.
7   In the long run, immigration is a net gain to the economy, new workers, employers, and native workers.
8   Macroeconomics is the application of economic principles to economy-wide aggregates, meaning issues, policies, and events at the national or international level.
9   The overall size of the economy is measured by the concepts gross domestic product (GDP) and national income (NI).
10  The overall economic situation is described by the terms recession, boom, and depression.

11 Money is anything generally accepted and commonly used as a means of payment.

12 Money provides three services to an economy: (1) a medium of exchange, (2) a store of value, and (3) a unit of account.

13 Inflation and deflation are terms used to describe changes in the purchasing power of money.

14 Nominal prices are prices as they exist at a point in time, and real prices are adjusted for inflation.

15 Monetary policy changes the rate of growth in the quantity of money to achieve macroeconomics objectives. Expansionary monetary policy is used to stimulate the economy, and restrictive monetary policy is used to control inflation.

16 Fiscal policy uses tax rates and government spending to achieve macroeconomic objectives. Tax cuts and increased government spending are used to stimulate the economy, and higher tax rates and reductions in government spending are used to slow the economy.

17 Strong linkages exist between macroeconomic policies and the agricultural sector since agriculture is greatly influenced by interest rates, prices, and exchange rates.

18 Food security is a situation where all people at all times have access to sufficient, safe, nutritious food for maintaining a healthy and active life.

19 Food aid is the international provision of food or cash to purchase food to address hunger or undernutrition.

20 Economic development refers to actions and policies that promote the standard of living and economic health of a nation, region, or area, encompassing improvements in economic, political, and social well-being of people.

21 A public good is a good that is both (1) nonrival and (2) nonexcludable. A rival good is a good in which the consumption of the good by one person precludes the consumption of the good by a second person. A nonexcludable good is a good in which everyone can consume the good whether they pay for it or not.

## 11.10   Chapter 11 Glossary

**Boom**—A time period when the rate of growth of GDP is positive.

**Consumer Surplus (CS)**—A measure of the well-being of consumers, equal to the consumer willingness and ability to pay minus the actual price paid.

**Deflation**—A general decrease in prices, as measured by a price index, resulting in an increase in purchasing power of the currency.

**Depression**—A time period when the rate of change in GDP is negative.

**Economic Development**—Actions and policies that promote the standard of living and economic health of a nation, region, or area, encompassing improvements in economic, political, and social well-being of people.

**Fiscal Policy**—Attempts by a government to influence macroeconomic variables through taxes and government spending.

**Food Aid**—International provision of food or cash to purchase food to address hunger or undernutrition.

**Food Security**—A situation where all people at all times have access to sufficient, safe, nutritious food to maintain a healthy and active life.

**Gross Domestic Product (GDP)**—A measure of the value of total expenditures of all goods and services in an economy in a given time period, usually one year or one quarter.

**Inflation**—A sustained, rapid increase in prices, as measured by a price index over months or years, resulting in a decrease in purchasing power of the currency.

**Monetary Policy**—Changes in the rate of growth of the quantity of money in the economy to achieve macroeconomic objectives.

**Money**—Anything generally accepted and commonly used as a measure of payment.

**National Income (NI)**—A measure of the total value of all factor payments (capital, labor, and land) during a period of time, usually one year or one quarter.

**Nominal Prices**—Prices observed at any point in time, measured in dollars of that time.

**Nonexcludable Good**—A good in which everyone can consume the good whether they pay for it or not.

**Price Ceiling**—A maximum price set by the government for a specified good or service.

**Price Support**—A minimum price set by the government for a specified good or service.

**Producer Surplus (PS)**—A measure of the well-being of producers, equal to the price received minus the cost of production.

**Public Good**—A good that is both (1) nonrival and (2) nonexcludable.

**Purchasing Power**—The value of money in terms of units of goods that money can purchase, or command.

**Real Prices**—Prices of goods or services adjusted for inflation.

**Recession**—A time period when the rate of growth of GDP is negative.

**Rival Good**—A good in which the consumption of the good by one person precludes the consumption of the good by a second person.

**Welfare Economics**—A branch of economics that seeks to measure and understand how the well-being (welfare) of individuals changes in response to changes in policies, markets, or current events.

## 11.11   Chapter 11 Review questions

1  A price support results in

    a   off-farm migration
    b   shortages
    c   surpluses
    d   lower prices

2  A price ceiling will result in

    a   higher returns to producers
    b   higher prices
    c   surpluses
    d   shortages

3  The role of government

    a   should be minimized
    b   should be maximized
    c   is necessary in the case of market failures
    d   is to provide food to citizens

4  Market failures include all except

    a   externalities
    b   monopoly power
    c   market competition
    d   public goods

5 Welfare economics

a is about people who receive government handouts
b is not useful in a market based economy
c shows how well-off consumers and producers are from policy changes
d is too difficult to understand

6 Producer surplus is

a willingness to pay for a good minus the price actually paid
b price received for a good minus the cost of production
c quantity supplied minus quantity
d quantity demanded minus quantity supplied

7 Consumer surplus is

a willingness to pay for a good minus the price actually paid

b price received for a good minus the cost of production
c quantity supplied minus quantity
d quantity demanded minus quantity supplied

8 A price support

a increases PS and increases CS
b increases PS and decreases CS
c decreases PS and increases CS
d decreases PS and decreases CS

9 A price ceiling

a increases PS and increases CS
b increases PS and decreases CS
c decreases PS and increases CS
d decreases PS and decreases CS

10 Money is all except:

a a medium of exchange
b used in a barter economy
c a store of value
d a unit of account

**Answers:** 1. c, 2. d, 3. c, 4. c, 5. c, 6. b, 7. a, 8. b, 9. c, 10. b

For more study questions, flash cards, and study guides, see the online materials at the companion website: www.routledge.com/cw/barkley.

# The competitive firm

Photo 12.1 The competitive firm

*Source:* Dmitriy Shironosov/Shutterstock

DOI: 10.4324/9781003367994-12

## Abstract

This chapter examines market structure. Emphasis is placed on the four character-istics of perfect competition: (1) numerous buyers and sellers, (2) a homogeneous product, (3) freedom of entry and exit, and (4) perfect information. Special atten-tion is given to the desirable property of firms in perfectly competitive industries: efficiency. The chapter uses timely and relevant examples from agriculture and agribusiness to describe strategies for perfectly competitive firms. Since competi-tive firms cannot influence the prices of the commodities they sell, their best strat-egy is to continuously attempt to lower production costs by being early adopters of new technologies.

### Chapter 12 Questions

1 How is market structure defined, and what does it mean?
2 What are the four characteristics of a perfectly competitive market?
3 Why are perfectly competitive industries considered to be ideal, and why are they efficient?
4 What are strategies for perfectly competitive farmers, ranchers, and agribusiness firms?
5 Why is early adoption of new technology a good strategy for perfectly competitive firms?

## 12.1 Market structure

The previous chapter described how the interaction of buyers and sellers deter-mines the market price and quantity of a good or service in a market economy. Here, attention turns to **market structure**, or how an industry is organized.

- *Market Structure* = the organization of an industry, typically defined by the number of firms in an industry.

Market structure, sometimes referred to as "industrial organization," has a major influence on the prices and quantities of goods and services sold in a market. In general, the number of sellers in an industry is an important indicator of market structure. If there are only a few firms, their behavior and business strategies will be quite different from the behavior and strategies of firms in an industry with numerous competitors.

The number of firms in an industry varies considerably in a free market econ-omy, especially an economy as large and complex as that of the US. In the US, resi-dents in a given town or city often purchase electricity from a single firm with no option to purchase power from an alternative source. Similarly, software for the nation's computers is provided primarily by Microsoft, with a few other options such as Linux. Fast food is available from numerous sources, including McDon-ald's, Burger King, KFC, Taco Bell, Wendy's, and many others. Clothing purchases come from huge chain stores (Macy's), small locally owned stores, catalogs, used clothing stores (often operated by churches and charities), and the Internet.

The US automobile industry is dominated by three large firms (General Motors, Ford, and Chrysler), originally called the "Big Three," but now often referred to as the "Detroit Three." This name change stems from the growth in dominance of non-US automobile producers such as Toyota, Volkswagen, Hyundai, and others. When the agricultural giant Archer Daniels Midland (ADM) buys soybeans to crush into oil, it purchases beans from thousands of independent soybean growers found mainly in the Midwest and Great Plains. Together with Bunge and Cargill, ADM has crushed approximately three-quarters of all US-grown soybeans in recent years. When grocery stores and restaurants purchase meat for their customers, over 80 percent of their meat purchases are from four large meatpackers: Tyson, Cargill, JBS-USA, and National Beef Producers. Smithfield Foods dominates hog production with over 1.2 million sows in 2020, perhaps more in the years since then. The next-largest US hog producer is Triumph Foods, with 443,000 sows in 2020.

The diversity of market structures, and the frequent changes in ownership and management of processing and handling firms, has attracted the attention of economists interested in the economic effects of the number of firms that comprise an industry. These analysts have organized the types of market structures, or industrial organizations, into several categories listed in Table 12.1.

In this chapter, discussion of market structures begins with **monopoly**, the extreme case of a single firm that, by itself, is also the industry.

- *Monopoly* = a market structure characterized by a single seller.

In many locations, the local utility company is the sole source of natural gas and electricity. Consumers cannot purchase these types of energy from any other firm. Most towns and cities also use locally operated monopolies to provide such things as water, natural gas, electricity, sewage disposal, and landline phone service. These products are essential to everyone in the community. However, the firms that produce these products or services require huge investments in infrastructure and often lend themselves to some degree of government control or oversight. As a result, they are "public utilities," and they exist in a peculiar web of regulations, typically one firm per location.

---

Table 12.1 Market structure (industrial organization)

| Structure | Number of firms | Examples |
|---|---|---|
| Monopoly | Single seller | Electricity company, water company |
| Oligopoly | Few sellers | Automobiles; beef packing |
| Monopolistic competition | Many sellers of branded goods | Gasoline stations; grocery stores |
| Perfect competition | Numerous sellers | Agricultural commodities: wheat, corn |

**Perfect competition** lies at the other end of the market structure spectrum. In a perfectly competitive market structure, the industry has numerous firms producing an identical product.

- *Perfect Competition* = a market or industry that has four characteristics: (1) numerous buyers and sellers, (2) a homogeneous products, (3) freedom of entry and exit, and (4) perfect information.

**Oligopoly** and **monopolistic competition** lie between these two extremes. Oligopoly is an industry composed of a few firms, such as the automobile industry. Monopolistic competition is a market structure that combines some features of monopoly with some characteristics of competition. In a monopolistically competitive industry, many firms produce similar, but not identical, products. Toothpaste, soap, clothing, and many kinds of retailing are examples.

The next two chapters explain how the behavior and performance of an industry depend on its market structure. Competitive firms strive to maximize profits, taking prices as fixed and given. Monopolists maximize profits by selecting and manipulating the price and accessibility of the product. Firms located between the two extremes of monopoly and competition have some ability to influence price, usually within a narrow range. "**Market power**" is the term used to designate the firm's ability to affect to price of its product.

- *Market Power* = the ability to affect the price of output. A firm with market power faces a downward-sloping demand curve.

Whereas individual competitive firms have no market power, monopolists have complete market power. Business firms in production agriculture and agribusiness most often have no control over the prices they receive. They are in competitive industries.

## 12.2  Characteristics of perfect competition

The behavior and outcomes of competitive firms depend on four characteristics discussed in Chapter 4. These are (1) numerous buyers and sellers, (2) a homogeneous product, (3) freedom of entry and exit, and (4) perfect information. Real-world firms seldom meet all four of these characteristics, making the concept of a perfectly competitive firm an idealized case. However, small farms and the shore-bound commercial fishery are industries that come close. Firms in industries that closely match the model are studied to provide analysts with a greater understanding of firm behavior in order to make useful predictions about how prices change and how competitive firms respond to price changes. The implications of each of the four characteristics of a competitive firm requires special examination. Assumptions used to simplify the complex real world reduce the four issues or characteristics to their most important elements and make their study tractable.

The four characteristics of a perfectly competitive industry form the basis for models of competitive firms and industries. This modeling helps analysts understand how firms behave, how they use specialized resources, and how managers of firms in competitive settings can increase their profitability.

## 12.3    The perfectly competitive firm

Each firm in a perfectly competitive market is a **price taker** that can exert no influence over output prices, as discussed in Chapter 4. For example, the wheat seller
takes whatever price the buyer offers. A price taker is a firm that has no market
power. It must take input and output prices as given and fixed. Even though competitive firms exert no influence on product prices, the prices themselves fluctuate
in response to forces outside the firms' control.

Firms that have market power are price makers. These firms have at least some
ability to influence the price of outputs because of the large size of the firm relative to the market. They produce and sell enough product to affect the price of the
good. Restated, a price maker is a firm that faces a downward-sloping demand
curve. These price maker firms are the subject of Chapter 13.

### 12.3.1    The demand curve facing a competitive firm

A competitive firm is small relative to the industry, so small that it cannot influence the price of the product that it sells. Consider an individual rice producer in
Jackson County, Arkansas. Figure 12.1 shows the relationship between the rice
market on the left and the individual rice producer on the right. The interaction of
all (aggregated) rice producers and consumers appears in the supply and demand
curves on the left. Market forces establish an equilibrium price at the intersection
of supply ($Q^s$) and demand ($Q^d$). In equilibrium, a quantity of $Q^*$ billion cwt of
rice are produced and sold at a price of $P^*$ dollars per hundredweight (cwt). The
demand curve slopes downward due to the law of demand, and the supply curve
slopes upward due to the law of supply (Chapter 8).

> ### QUICK QUIZ 12.1
>
> What does the market demand curve show? How is the market demand for rice
> derived?

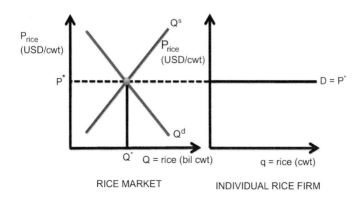

**Figure 12.1  Rice market and individual rice producer**

QUICK QUIZ 12.2

How is the market supply of rice derived?

The units shown on the graph are crucial. Farmers produce rice over most of the world, so the rice market is global in scope and is very large. The units for quantity of rice in the rice market graph are in billions of hundredweight (Q).

The graph on the right side of Figure 12.1 represents the individual firm. The individual rice producer is so small that the quantity produced on the one farm is measured by numbers of hundredweight (q). The demand curve facing the individual firm is perfectly elastic (horizontal). This means that the price elasticity of demand for one and every producer is infinite. The first hundredweight of rice sold by a producer will receive the same price as the last ($|E^d| = \infty$). The demand curves in Figure 12.2 show why this is true.

The demand curve in the left-hand panel (a) is perfectly inelastic: the consumer purchases the same quantity, regardless of price. No substitutes exist for this good. This demand is perfectly inelastic ($|E^d| = 0$). In the next panel (b), the demand curve is inelastic ($|E^d| < 1$) since consumers do not make large changes in the quantity demanded in response to price changes. Panel (c) shows an elastic demand ($|E^d| > 1$), where consumers are responsive to price. If the price increases by even a small amount, the quantity demanded decreases significantly. Finally, panel (d) depicts a perfectly elastic demand curve ($|E^d| = \infty$).

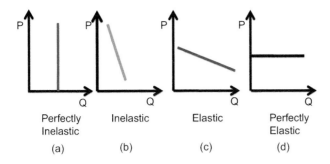

P | P | P | P

Q | Q | Q | Q

Perfectly Inelastic | Inelastic | Elastic | Perfectly Elastic

(a) | (b) | (c) | (d)

**Figure 12.2 Elasticity of demand over time**

When demand is perfectly elastic, the price is the same regardless of the quantity purchased. This is the defining characteristic of the perfectly competitive industry. The good is homogeneous, so consumers do not care which firm supplies the good. If the individual rice farmer in Figure 12.1 tried to raise the price of rice by one cent above the market price, P\*, no buyer would purchase the farmer's rice at this higher price since there is a large quantity of rice available at the market price, P\*. At any price higher than P\*, the demand facing this firm would fall to zero.

If one individual firm were to charge a price slightly lower than the equilibrium price, all of the consumers in the market would flock to the producer charging the lower price. The demand facing a competitive firm is perfectly elastic since consumers are extraordinarily responsive to price. Any rational producer would not charge less than the market price since the firm can always receive P\* dollars per hundredweight. The elastic, or horizontal, demand curve facing the individual producer reflects the ability to sell as much or as little produce as desired at the prevailing market price. The firm is so small relative to the market that the quantity it supplies does not affect the market price.

To see this, consider how large the quantity of rice is for the individual farmer relative to the world rice market. The quantity of rice in the right-hand panel of Figure 12.1 is trivial compared to the billions of hundredweight of rice traded in the world market at the equilibrium price shown in the left panel of Figure 12.1.

The demand curve (D) facing the competitive rice farmer in Figure 12.3 is identical to the price line (P\*). The revenue of a competitive firm is calculated using the fixed and given market price. Total revenue (TR) is the market price (P) multiplied by the quantity produced (q) and sold by the firm.

12.1    $TR = P * q$

Total revenue for the rice producer is the rectangle defined by the price (0P\*) multiplied by the quantity sold (0Q\*), shown by the rectangle TR in Figure 12.3. Average revenue (AR) is the per-unit level of revenue earned by the firm:

12.2    $AR = TR / q = P^* q / q = P.$

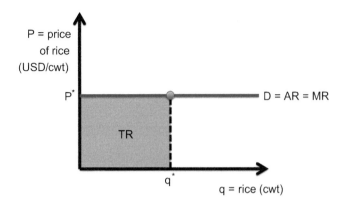

P = price
of rice
(USD/cwt)

P*

TR

D = AR = MR

q*

q = rice (cwt)

**Figure 12.3** Revenues for a perfectly competitive firm

The AR for the rice producer is equal to the price (P = AR). Lastly, the marginal revenue (MR) for the competitive firm is the change in TR (ΔTR) brought about by a small change in quantity sold (Δq). Price does not change, and ΔTR = Δ(Pq) = PΔq, so the only source of change in revenue must come from changes in the quantity sold (q):

12.3    MR = ΔTR / Δq = Δ(Pq) / Δq = PΔq / Δq = P.

The additional (marginal) revenue that the firm receives from the sale of one unit of output is always equal to the constant price (P*). The demand curve for the firm is a horizontal line at the same level as average revenue, marginal revenue, and the equilibrium market price, so D = AR = MR = P*.

## 12.3.2   Profit maximization for a competitive firm

A competitive firm will maximize profits by setting marginal revenue equal to marginal cost (MR = MC). This profit-maximizing condition holds true for the competitive firm, shown in Figure 12.4.

Figure 12.4 shows the typical U-shaped cost curves, together with the market price derived from the intersection of market supply and market demand for a rice-producing firm. The rice producer in Arkansas maximizes profits by meeting the two conditions of profit maximization: (1) MR = MC, and (2) MC must cut MR from below. The profit-maximizing level of output is q*, which satisfies the two conditions. The large rectangle represents total revenue accruing to the rice producer. Total revenue is found by multiplying the equilibrium price by the equilibrium quantity (TR = P*q*). Profits are found by subtracting all costs of production from the total revenue (π = TR – TC). Total costs are found by substituting the output level (q*) into the ATC curve. This is because ATC = TC / q, so TC = ATC * q. The level of profits for the rice producer is the rectangle denoted by π in Figure 12.4. The firm in the diagram is earning positive economic profits.

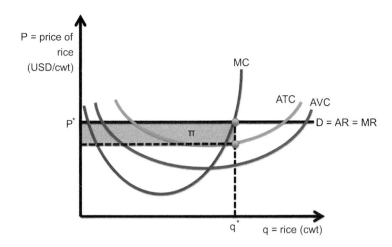

Figure 12.4 **Profits for a perfectly competitive firm**

QUICK QUIZ 12.3

What is the difference between accounting profits and economic profits? Hint: see Chapter 3.

## 12.4   The efficiency of competitive industries

Perfectly competitive industries have many desirable features. The most important of these concerns efficiency. Competition among firms results in **efficiency** of resource use in the economy.

● *Efficiency* = a characteristic of competitive markets, indicating that goods and services are produced at the lowest possible cost and consumers pay the lowest possible prices.

Efficiency is a desirable result of competition. The industry uses scarce resources in such a way as to produce goods and services at the lowest possible cost. Prices charged by competitive firms are no higher than the cost of production (MC). The numerous firms and homogeneous product criteria guarantee this result. If a competitive firm were to try to charge a price higher than the competitive market price, customers would quickly shift to producers charging the lower market price. Consumers will never by "gouged" by producers trying to raise the price above the competitive level.

   The second characteristic of perfectly competitive industries that leads to efficient market outcomes is the freedom of entry and exit. When an industry is earning high levels of profits, new firms will enter the industry to produce the profitable good or service. This eliminates the possibility of market power, or monopoly prices, in a competitive industry. When a competitive firm is unprofitable, it will drop out of the industry to find a more profitable way to use its resources. As more firms leave, the industry supply diminishes (the supply curve shifts upward and to the left) and prices to the consumer increase.

The agricultural sector of the United States has been subject to decreasing farm numbers since the mid-1930s, when the nation had 6.8 million farms. The number in 2021 stood at about 2.0 million. Why? Because the opportunities to earn a living outside of agriculture became greater than the opportunities inside of agriculture for many individuals and families. In recent years (2019–2021), an economic recession due to the Covid-19 pandemic in the overall economy, together with growing demand for agricultural commodities, reversed this trend. The returns to agriculture and agribusiness were high during the period, relative to positions available in other sectors of the economy.

In an economy with freely operating markets, resources flow to their highest (most profitable) use. The efficiency captured by the producer allows production at the lowest possible cost per unit. Consumers enjoy this efficiency because it allows them to purchase goods at very low prices, much lower than would be the case under monopolistic conditions.

The retail fresh flower market in New York City provides an example of how this flow of resources takes place. The New York flower market depicted in Figure 12.5 shows market situations for the entire market, as well as for a hypothetical individual florist, "Frank's Flowers."

The left-hand panel in Figure 12.5 represents the aggregate market for flowers in New York City. The supply curve reflects all of the florists in the market, and the demand curve represents all of the consumers. The intersection of supply and demand at P* determines the market price for flowers. All of the florists in the area charge the same price of P* per dozen flowers, or customers will shift their business to the firms that charge P*. This result is the perfectly elastic demand curve facing Frank and other individual flower shops in the area.

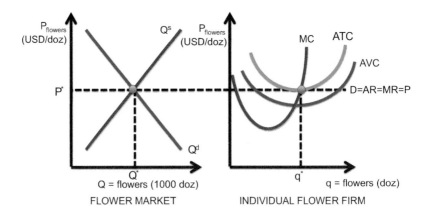

Figure 12.5 Flower market and individual flower producer

Frank sells flowers (in dozens) by setting marginal revenue (D = MR = P*) equal to marginal cost (MC) at a quantity q* dozen flowers. Economic profits are equal to zero, indicating that the resources employed by Frank (K, L, A, and M) are all earning exactly their opportunity cost.

QUICK QUIZ 12.4

List and describe the four factors of production for Frank: K, L, A, and M.

QUICK QUIZ 12.5

What are opportunity costs? Why are economic profits equal to zero an acceptable outcome for Frank?

Figure 12.5 shows a market equilibrium (left side) and a firm equilibrium (right side). The quantity supplied equals the quantity demanded in the market, the firm (which is one of many similar firms) is earning zero economic profits, and the price is equal to the marginal cost. The efficiency that results from this outcome is considered to be highly desirable because the resources employed by Frank's firm, including Frank himself, are earning at least as much as they could earn in their next best use. Consumers are paying the exact cost of production for a dozen flowers.

Suppose there is an increase in the population of New York City. Figure 12.6 demonstrates how the New York flower market responds.

The demand for flowers increases with the increase in New York City's population. The shift in demand results in a movement along the supply curve to the new equilibrium point, showing an increase in quantity supplied. The new equilibrium price is $P_1{}^*$, and the new quantity is $Q_1{}^*$.

The increase in price translates into increased economic profits for Frank's shop. The right panel of Figure 12.6 shows the positive economic profits in the rectangle denoted $\pi$, where $\pi = TR - TC$. The market price increased from $P_0{}^*$ to $P_1{}^*$, while the costs of production remained the same as they were prior to the population increase.

Frank's and every other florist in New York City will earn positive economic profits. The positive profits that result from population growth help explain economic behavior in other locations even where conditions may not be the same. The analysis in Figure 12.6 shows why businesses in a college town favor (1) increased enrollment at the college, (2) a good football team, (3) an active industrial park that hires graduates, (4) new golf courses, and (5) new housing developments that will attract new individuals and families. Population growth is a good thing for businesses!

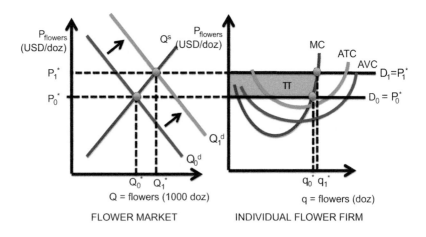

FLOWER MARKET                    INDIVIDUAL FLOWER FIRM

Figure 12.6 An increase in demand for flowers

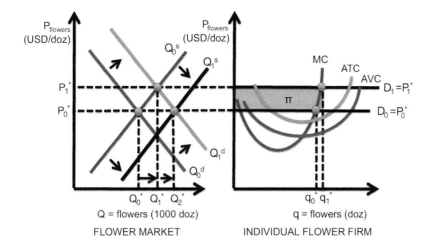

Figure 12.7 **An increase in supply following an increase in demand for flowers**

The flower story, however, is not over. The high level of earnings by Frank and the other florists will result in entry of other florists and floral-related businesses. This means that college graduates with a degree in horticulture or landscape design will locate in New York City to take advantage of the profitable conditions. The entry of new firms will shift the supply curve of flowers to the right (an increase in supply) as long as positive economic profits exist. The supply of flowers will continue to shift to the right until the original price ($P_0$*) is reached, as shown in Figure 12.7.

The increase in supply results in an increase in the equilibrium level of output from $Q_1$* to $Q_2$* and a decrease in the equilibrium price back to the original level, $P_0$*. This lowers the price facing Frank since the new florists in New York City take some of Frank's original business. Frank still maximizes profits by setting marginal revenue equal to marginal cost at the new but lower price, $P_0$*, and produces the original level of output, $q_0$*. Frank is now back at its original equilibrium point. Frank's positive economic profits attracted new firms that attracted some of Frank's customers and reduced profits back to the equilibrium level: zero economic profits.

The analysis can also show how a decrease in demand results in the exit of firms from an industry. In Frank's case, if the demand for flowers fell, the result would be a lower market price for flowers, which would lower the perfectly elastic demand curve facing the flower shop. If the price drop is small, and price remains above the shutdown point (P > min AVC), then Frank's would stay in business to minimize costs in the short run. However, if price falls below the shutdown point, Frank's would have to shut down and exit the industry. In this case, the resources originally employed by Frank's would move to other industries.

## Cut flower production

Cut flowers are big business. In the past two decades, floriculture, the cultivation of ornamental and flowering plants, has become one of the fastest growing sectors in US agriculture. In 2019, floriculture sales in the United States exceeded USD 34 billion. Slightly more than two-thirds (by dollar volume) of the fresh flowers sold in the US were produced in other countries. By value of flower sales to the US, the top three nations that export cut flowers to the US are Colombia (65 percent), Ecuador (16 percent), and the Netherlands (6 percent). Most domestic production comes from California (76 percent), followed by Washington (9 percent), Oregon (3 percent), and New Jersey (3 percent).

Floral crops are typically grown in greenhouses or covered areas and are usually sold in bunches or as bouquets. The most popular cut flowers are roses, carnations, gladioli, and pompon chrysanthemums. Flower demand is highly seasonal. Sales are highest in February through May and in the fall. Cut flower sales peak on Valentine's Day and Mother's Day; poinsettias are sold between Thanksgiving and Christmas. Since cut flowers are highly perishable, they require cool temperatures and storage conditions to prolong their quality. The increasingly automated US floral industry deals with the year-round production of high-value crops such as Easter lilies, orchids, and forest azaleas. Automation in greenhouses such as extended exposure to natural and artificial light accelerates plant production.

Flower sales are highly dependent on consumer income, and cut flowers are a luxury good (Chapter 8). Cut flower sales are higher for consumers with high incomes, and sales are highly responsive to fluctuations in consumer income. Most of the recent increase in cut flower sales in the US depends on imported stocks of flowers. About 40 percent of the imports are roses, followed by carnations (10 percent) and chrysanthemums (10 percent). Low production costs and a strong US dollar drive the import market. During the 1980s and 1990s, production of the major cut flowers shifted from US growers to Central and South America to take advantage of year-round production, lower labor costs, and lower energy costs for heating and lighting greenhouses.

The US cut flower industry faces two major trends, the major growth in mass-market sales in big discount stores and supermarkets and highly automated production (growing) operations resulting from the rising cost of labor. This is the substitution of capital for labor highlighted in Chapter 5. A related trend is the movement of farmers out of traditional agricultural commodities into contract floriculture: a movement along the production possibilities frontier (PPF) due to change in relative prices (Chapter 6). Many former tobacco farmers in the southeast US have contracted with large retailers such as Home Depot and Walmart. Many US companies have invested in flower farms in South America to supply the growing US demand for flowers.

*Source:* "Industry and Trade Summary: Cut Flowers." US International Trade Commission. February 2003. www.usitc.gov/publications/332/pub3580.pdf. Retrieved January 13, 2023.

## QUICK QUIZ 12.6

Use a two-panel graph of a competitive market and a firm to show the impact of an increase in the price of chicken on the beef market.

The exit of scarce resources from unprofitable industries is efficient from a societal point of view, although it can be devastating to the persons involved. In a free market economy, the consumers determine what to produce and what not to produce. If the demand for a good is not sufficient for the number of firms producing it, then some firms will close and resources will flow out of the unprofitable industry and into enterprises with higher-earning opportunities.

This chapter focuses on the behavior of a competitive firm. To this point it has explained how competition brings about desirable results for society. The next section investigates strategies that competitive firms use to maximize profits in the long run.

## 12.5   Strategies for perfectly competitive firms

Competitive firms are price takers, so the development of an elaborate pricing strategy would be a waste of the firm's manager's resources. Since the market determines the price through the supply and demand mechanisms in the entire market, the price is outside the control of the individual competitive firm. Similarly, the goods produced by competitive firms are homogeneous, so trying to compete through quality differences or branding does not help the competitive firm. This means that advertising and other marketing activities are not profitable for competitive firms.

These conditions and qualifications are desirable and help make life less complicated for producers and consumers. Producers do not waste money on advertising and marketing, and consumers pay only the costs of producing and distributing the

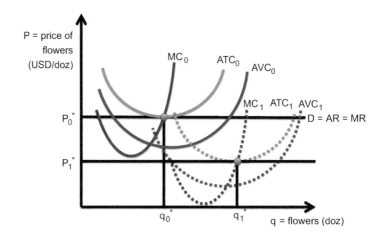

Figure 12.8 **Early adoption of technology: a perfectly competitive firm**

good. If price and product quality are outside the firm's control, what can a competitive firm do to maximize its earnings? It can concentrate on minimizing costs.

A competitive firm's best strategy is to lower its costs of production at every opportunity. This could involve adopting new technologies or purchasing inputs at the lowest possible price. In a competitive industry, firms must continue to keep up with the other firms to stay in business. If other firms reduce costs, the firm will have to match these cost reductions or face lower profits in the future. This helps explain why agricultural producers constantly search for new technologies in the form of new equipment, new farm management practices, and new farming methods. Indeed, the history of agriculture is one of continuous technological innovation and adoption.

This technological change allows for higher levels of output from the same level of inputs. Figure 12.8 traces the impact of a firm in the flower business adopting a new technology.

The technological change lowers the costs of production from $MC_0$ to $MC_1$. This allows the florist to go from a position of zero economic profits at the original equilibrium ($q_0^*$) to positive economic profits at the new equilibrium ($q_1^*$). If Frank's Flowers adopts this technology before the other florists in New York City, Frank will earn positive economic profits. These high earnings, however, will attract new entrants into the industry. The new entrants will increase the supply of flowers in the market until the market price drops to a new equilibrium price at the minimum point on the ATC curve. Therefore, profits are always temporary in a competitive industry. Positive profits encourage entry, and entry causes supply to increase until the profits are dissipated.

The conclusion or lesson of this analysis is that the early adopters of a new technology capture the benefits of the advance. Firms not adopting the technology must leave the business, as their costs remain high while the market price drops. The best strategy recommendation for a firm in a competitive industry, such as an agricultural firm, is for it to develop and adopt technology as rapidly as possible. These businesses must continuously adopt more efficient production methods in order to remain profitable in the long run.

The nation's land grant universities, such as Kansas State University, Texas A&M University, the University of Wisconsin, and dozens of others, conduct much of the agricultural research done in the United States. The research, often partially funded by producer groups such as the Oregon Livestock Association or the North Dakota Wheat Growers, help firms find the best strategy for firms in competitive industries struggling to remain on the cutting edge. The suggested strategy often includes using the most up-to-date production technology. Not only do producers who adopt technology benefit, but the consumers of agricultural products also benefit from research and development of food and fiber since technological change places downward pressure on the price of these goods.

Economists have a great deal of confidence in the ability of markets to allocate scarce resources efficiently. Resources move into industries where profits are high, and resources exit industries where profits are negative. The process of adjustment to new methods and new market conditions makes society better off. Producers earn the maximum profits possible by investing factors of production in the most profitable areas, and consumers pay the lowest possible prices for goods and services.

To be sure, the real world is more complicated than the stories, examples, and models presented here. Few, if any, industries exactly meet the four qualifications of perfect competition. Many real-world industries have fewer firms than the competitive ideal. Similarly, few industries include only firms that produce homogeneous products. Wheat, milk, and soybeans may be close to homogeneous no matter where they are produced, but a bouquet of red roses from Frank's may differ from the flowers purchased down the street. The next chapter describes the performance of markets that do not qualify as perfectly competitive. The differences are large and consequential for both buyers and sellers.

## 12.6   Chapter 12 Summary

1   The market structure of an industry refers to the number of sellers in the industry.
2   A monopoly has only a single firm in an industry.
3   A perfectly competitive industry has numerous firms that produce an identical product.
4   An oligopoly in composed of a "few" firms.
5   Monopolistic competition combines some factors of monopoly with some characteristics of competition. Monopolistic competitors produce similar, but not identical, products.
6   Market power is the ability of a firm to set price. Monopolists have complete market power; competitive firms have no market power.
7   A perfectly competitive firm has four characteristics: (1) numerous buyers and sellers, a homogeneous product, (3) freedom of entry and exit, and (4) perfect information.

8  A price taker is a firm so small relative to the industry that it has no influence over price. A price maker has the ability to influence price.
9  The demand curve facing an individual competitive firm is perfectly elastic.
10  Profit maximization conditions for a competitive firm are MR = MC, and the MC cuts MR from below.
11  Efficiency is a condition indicating that production of goods and services occurs at the lowest cost and consumers pay the lowest possible prices. Efficiency is consistent with all resources earning their opportunity costs.
12  A competitive firm's best strategy for maximizing profits is to minimize costs.

## 12.7  Chapter 12 Glossary

**Efficiency**—A characteristic of competitive markets, indicating that goods and services are produced at the lowest possible cost and consumers pay the lowest possible prices.
**Market Power**—The ability to affect the price of output. A firm with market power faces a downward-sloping demand curve.
**Market Structure**—The organization of an industry, typically defined by the number of firms in an industry.
**Monopolistic Competition**—A market structure defined by (1) many sellers; (2) a product with close, but differentiated, substitutes; (3) some freedom of entry and exit; and (4) some availability of knowledge and information.
**Monopoly**—A market structure characterized by a single seller.
**Oligopoly**—A market structure characterized by a few large firms.
**Perfect Competition**—A market or industry that has four characteristics: (1) numerous buyers and sellers, (2) homogeneous products, (3) freedom of entry and exit, and (4) perfect information.

## 12.8  Chapter 12 Review questions

1  Which type of firm has complete market power?

   a   monopoly
   b   competitive firm
   c   oligopoly
   d   monopolistic competition

2  Which good may be a homogeneous product?

   a   furniture
   b   automobile
   c   wheat
   d   toothpaste

3  A competitive firm is a(n)

   a   oligopolist
   b   price maker
   c   price taker
   d   monopolist

4  The demand curve facing an individual firm in a competitive industry is

   a   perfectly elastic
   b   perfectly inelastic
   c   the aggregate demand curve
   d   equal to the supply curve

5  Competition results in

   a   monopoly prices
   b   prices higher than the cost of production

c    cutthroat price wars that leave consumers worse off

d    efficient prices

6   A competitive firm's best strategy for maximizing profits is to:

a    set a monopoly price for the product

b    differentiate the product

c    reduce output to increase price

d    minimize costs

7   If a competitive firm has positive economic profits

a    entry occurs

b    exit occurs

c    neither entry nor exit occurs

d    a firm must earn positive economic profits to stay in business

8   The most profitable firms in competitive industries

a    advertise

b    market their product most effectively

c    adopt new technology early

d    wait to see if the new technology works out

9   A competitive firm is

a    efficient due to entry and exit

b    efficient due to high costs

c    inefficient due to entry and exit

d    inefficient due to high costs

10  A competitive firm is characterized by all except:

a    perfect information

b    free entry and exit

c    barriers to entry

d    a homogeneous product

**Answers:** 1. a, 2. c, 3. c, 4. a, 5. d, 6. d, 7. a, 8. c, 9. a, 10. c

For more study questions, flash cards, and study guides, see the online materials at the companion website: www.routledge.com/cw/barkley.

# Chapter 13

## Market power

Photo 13.1 Market power

*Source:* Tan Kian Khoon/Shutterstock

DOI: 10.4324/9781003367994-13

## Abstract

This chapter explores the causes and consequences of market power—the ability to charge prices higher than the competitive equilibrium price. Monopoly, monopolistic competition, oligopoly, and cartels are market structures characterized by market power. Examples from agriculture include the international wheat trade, major beef packers, and fruit and vegetable marketing orders. This chapter also explains how buyers (consumers) interact with firms characterized by different market structures. Game theory is used to demonstrate how economic models can be made more useful by incorporating the actions and reactions of other firms into the model.

### Chapter 13 Questions

1  What is market power, and how does it affect consumers and producers?
2  What is a monopoly, and how does it help us understand the economy?
3  What is monopolistic competition, and why is it an important concept?
4  What is an oligopoly, and what characteristics does an oligopoly have?
5  What is a cartel, and how does it operate?
6  How do buyers interact with firms in each market structure category?
7  What is game theory, and how is it applied to the study of market structures?

## 13.1   Market power

Competitive markets depend on free, voluntary trade between numerous buyers and numerous sellers to assure efficiency in resource use. This chapter discusses noncompetitive **market structures** in which individual firms can influence the price charged for their products. This occurs when there are so few firms in the industry that each one can affect product prices by altering the quantity of goods they place on the market. When there are only a few firms, the rivalry among them does not necessarily result in competitive outcomes similar to those discussed in Chapter 12. Discussion here turns to situations where free markets may not, and most likely will not, yield efficient outcomes. When efficiency is absent, consumers pay more for products than manufacturers spend to make them. Using terms studied in earlier chapters, buyers pay more than a product's cost of production in order to obtain a good. In addition, potential entrants may find it difficult or impossible to enter an industry. The discussion begins with an explanation of **market power**.

Market power is the ability of a firm to set the price of a good higher than the cost of production. A firm with market power can influence the price of its product, or the competitive market price.

● *Market Power* = the ability to affect the price of output. A firm with market power faces a downward-sloping demand curve for its product.

When there are numerous firms in an industry, price competition forces each firm to charge the competitive market price, P = MC. If a competitive firm raises the price of the good it produces, it will sell nothing because its customers shift their purchases to other firms that are selling the same product at the lower competitive price.

When there are only a few firms in an industry, individual firms may be able to charge a price higher than the competitive price, forcing consumers to pay more than the product's cost of production. Since this outcome is inefficient, the US government has legislated against the blatant use of market power. In 1890, the United States passed the Sherman Antitrust Act (1890) to protect consumers from firms that used excessive amounts of market power to influence the prices charged for their products. Giant firms like Standard Oil and the American Tobacco Company were among the first to be regulated by the antitrust laws. Why? Because they used their immense market power to set prices of their products at a level above the cost of production. They, and others, made huge profits from their price-setting activities. Since these practices placed a heavy burden on individual consumers and other sectors of the economy, the government took steps to limit the price-setting abilities of monopolistic firms.

## 13.2   Monopoly

A monopoly is easy to define and understand because the entire industry is a single firm. No other firm produces the same or similar goods.

- *Monopoly* = a market structure characterized by a single seller. The firm is the industry.

> ### QUICK QUIZ 13.1
>
> Is McDonald's a monopoly since it is the only firm that produces and sells a Big Mac?

While it is true that McDonald's is the only firm that sells the Big Mac, McDonald's is not a monopolist since many firms produce hamburgers, many of which are close substitutes for Big Macs. A monopoly is the only producer of a good that has no close substitutes. In a monopoly, the firm is the industry. Since the monopolist is not subject to competition, the monopolist is a **price maker**, instead of a **price taker**. These terms were discussed in Chapter 4. A monopoly has characteristics that differ from those of a competitive firm. These two types of market structure are on opposite ends of a spectrum (recall Table 12.1). Table 13.1 compares the characteristics of the two types of industrial structure.

Table 13.1 shows the reasons why the monopoly's situation is different from that of a firm in a competitive industry. The monopoly firm produces a good for which there are no close substitutes, whereas a competitive firm produces a good that is identical in every way to the product of the numerous other firms. Competitive firms are characterized by freedom to enter and exit the industry, whereas potential entrants into the monopoly industry face a legal or financial barrier that does not allow a firm to produce and sell the same product as the existing

---

### Table 13.1 Monopoly and competition

| Monopoly | Competitive firm |
| --- | --- |
| One seller | Numerous sellers |
| No close substitutes | Homogeneous product |
| Barriers to entry and exit | Freedom of entry and exit |
| Unavailability of information | Perfect information |

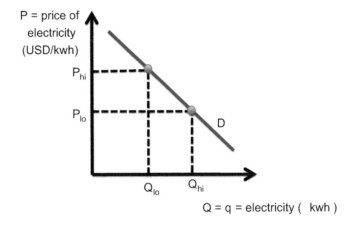

Figure 13.1 The demand curve facing an electricity company

monopolist. Lastly, the monopoly can withhold market information from others, the opposite of the perfect information situation of competitive firms. Recall that the perfectly competitive case assumes that all firms know everything about technology and prices.

The profit-maximizing behavior of a monopolist is quite different from the behavior exhibited by a competitive firm. The demand curve facing the local electricity company (or perhaps the local natural gas company) provides a useful starting place. Businesses and firms in most locales must purchase electricity from the same company since that firm has a legal monopoly on the sale of electricity. The status of the legal monopoly is not hard to understand. Electricity reaches residential and commercial areas through extensive and complex distribution networks of overhead wires and underground cables. If two companies delivered electric power to the same area, a second set of wires and cables would be needed. A second delivery system would be expensive—more expensive than local consumers would like to pay or could afford to pay. The problem is avoided by the formation of a delivery area in which only one company is given the authority to deliver electric power. The firm, called a "public utility," is the industry in this area, so its market demand curve (Figure 13.1) is the same as the demand curve facing the firm. For every practical purpose, this locally sanctioned power delivery firm is a monopoly that exhibits all of the characteristics shown in Table 13.1. Electricity is sold in units of kilowatt-hours (kwh). A kwh is a measure of the working power supplied by a specified amount of electricity. Household utility bills usually specify the number of kwhs the household has used during a billing period and calculates the charges for that use.

## QUICK QUIZ 13.2

How is the market demand curve for electricity derived?

## QUICK QUIZ 13.3

What does the demand curve facing a competitive firm look like?

The notation for the monopolist's demand curve is unique. Both Q (the market quantity) and q (a firm's quantity) identify the quantity of electricity demanded. The reason is that the delivery company is both the firm and the industry. The monopolist's goal, like the goal of every competitive firm, is to maximize profits. A monopolist is sometimes perceived by society as a firm that behaves differently from other firms. It may behave differently, but the underlying objective, maximizing profit, is the same.

Although the monopolist is called a "price maker," the public utility monopoly does not have complete control over the price of the firm's product. The monopoly's price-making behavior is subject to the willingness and ability of consumers to purchase the product. These characteristics are represented by the demand curve. If the price of electricity is set higher than consumers are willing to pay, the monopolist will not sell any electricity.

Figure 13.1 shows the demand curve facing a monopolist. The monopolist can either (1) set a price and let consumers determine how much to purchase at that price or (2) set a quantity and let consumers determine the price. Restated, since the consumers' purchases control the slope and location of the demand curve, the monopolist can manipulate either price or quantity, but not both.

Figure 13.1 shows this. If the local power company sets a high price ($P_{hi}$), it will sell only a small quantity of electricity ($Q_{lo}$). If the monopolist sets a low price ($P_{lo}$), it will sell a larger quantity of electricity ($Q_{hi}$). Contrast this with the competitive case, where any firm in the industry can sell as much or as little as it desires at a constant price. The monopolist is not a price taker so must determine a price at which to sell the product while keeping in mind the constraints imposed by consumer demand. Note that real-world electricity firms are highly regulated and make price and quantity decisions under government supervision. For simplicity, the example presented here is for an unregulated monopolist. Examples of unregulated monopolies are difficult to find.

**Photo 13.2** Electricity distribution

*Source:* Wallenrock/Shutterstock

BOX 13.1

## Electricity

Electricity is used 24 hours a day, seven days a week, and is an important input into most economic and social activities in advanced countries. The availability of electricity is constant and reliable, so people do not usually consider how dependent they are on electrical power. In the 1820s and early 1830s, Michael Faraday, a British scientist, discovered the fundamental principles of electricity generation and management. Faraday's basic method of generating the power was based on moving a loop of wire, or a disc of copper between the positive and negative poles of a magnet. This method is still used today, using a turbine. When the blades on the shaft of a turbine are rotated, the generator produces electricity through a process called magnetic induction. Commercial electricity is all produced using turbines, with the main differences being the size of the generator and the source of power used to turn the blades.

Electricity has been generated at central generating stations since 1881. The first power plants were run using water power or coal. Today (early twenty-first century), fossil fuels, including coal, natural gas, and petroleum, are the major sources of energy used in electricity production. These fuels are used to convert water into steam, and a steam turbine is used to produce electricity. In 2021, coal produced approximately 23 percent of all electricity produced in the US, and natural gas around 37 percent.

Coal is abundant in the US and provides the lowest cost of producing electrical power. However, coal-fired electricity plants produce by-products: carbon dioxide, nitrous oxides, particulates, and mercury. Modern technology and "scrubbers" have reduced these emissions, but coal-generating plants still account for 20 percent of the nation's carbon dioxide emissions. As population and incomes rise, the demand for electricity is likely to increase significantly. Coal will most likely help meet this increased demand.

Natural gas is the cleanest burning fossil fuel but is more expensive than coal. A new technology, "hydraulic fracturing," or "fracking," has increased access to natural gas by injecting fluid into rock formations to allow the natural gas underneath to escape. Electricity is also produced using nuclear energy. The US now (2021) has 93 operating nuclear power plants that produce 8 percent of the nation's electrical power. Nuclear plants have low operating costs but produce dangerous amounts of radioactive wastes. Hydropower provides about 3 percent of the nation's energy. Renewable forms of electricity production include geothermal, solar, and wind.

Electric utilities provide the delivery of electricity to consumers. The electric power industry is learning more about transmission, distribution, power storage, and recovery using pumped storage methods, although pumped storage methods are still not a significant part of the industry.

*Source:* US Department of Energy. US Energy Information Administration. www.eia.gov/. Retrieved January 13, 2023.

A monopoly firm's cost structure is the same as for any other type firm. The cost curves are the typical "U-shaped" curves first mentioned in Chapter 3. The revenue received by a monopoly, however, differs greatly from the revenue of a competitive firm. To show this, first review the revenue of a competitive firm. Recall that the demand curve facing a competitive firm such as a firm producing wheat is perfectly elastic, or horizontal, as shown by $D = AR = MR = P^*$ in Figure 13.2.

Since total revenue is the quantity sold multiplied by the price of the product ($TR = P * q$), the total revenue line is upward sloping and of constant slope (Figure 13.2). The competitive wheat firm can sell any quantity of the wheat it produces, but it must be sold at the given market price, $P^*$. Figure 13.3 shows the

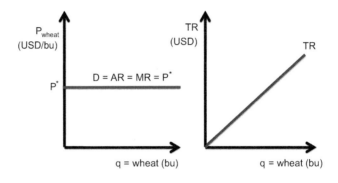

Figure 13.2 Revenues for a competitive wheat firm

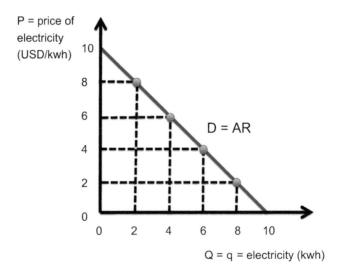

Figure 13.3 The quantitative demand curve facing an electricity company

demand curve faced by a monopolistic firm. Suppose that the inverse demand function for electricity is given by

13.1   $P = 10 - q,$

where q is the quantity of electricity sold measured in kilowatt-hours (kwh), and P is the price of electricity (USD /kwh).

A graph of this demand curve shows why the monopolist is unable to set the price of electricity without regard for the consumers' willingness to pay. The monopolist is constrained by the demand curve. If the electric company charged USD 10/kwh, it could not sell any electricity. By lowering the price of electricity to USD 8/kwh, the firm will sell 2 kilowatt-hours of electricity for total revenue (TR) equal to USD 16. The law of demand reveals that as the price of electricity drops, consumers will purchase more. At a price of USD 0/kwh (electricity is given away free), the company delivers 10 kilowatt-hours of electricity, but the total revenue is zero since no price is charged. Table 13.2 shows some of the possible combinations of prices, quantities, and total revenues faced by the firm selling electricity.

The revenue curves for the company are drawn in Figure 13.4. For the monopolist, average revenue can be read directly from the demand curve (D = AR), as shown in the left-hand graph of Figure 13.4. This result is derived from the definition of total revenue (TR = Pq). Average revenue is the revenue per unit of output, or total revenue divided by the quantity produced and sold:

13.2   $AR = TR / q = Pq / q = P.$

Since average revenue is equal to the price of the good, the demand curve is identical to the average revenue curve. Recall the relationship between average and marginal. The average always "chases" the marginal. Putting this idea to use, if the average revenue curve is decreasing, then the marginal revenue curve must be located below

Table 13.2 Revenues for the electricity company

| Price (USD/kwh) | Quantity (kwh) | Total revenues (USD) | Average revenues (USD/kwh) | Marginal revenues (USD/kwh) |
|---|---|---|---|---|
| 10 | 0 | 0 | — | — |
| 9 | 1 | 9 | 9 | 9 |
| 8 | 2 | 16 | 8 | 7 |
| 7 | 3 | 21 | 7 | 5 |
| 6 | 4 | 24 | 6 | 3 |
| 5 | 5 | 25 | 5 | 1 |
| 4 | 6 | 24 | 4 | −1 |
| 3 | 7 | 21 | 3 | −3 |
| 2 | 8 | 16 | 2 | −5 |
| 1 | 9 | 9 | 1 | −7 |
| 0 | 10 | 0 | 0 | −9 |

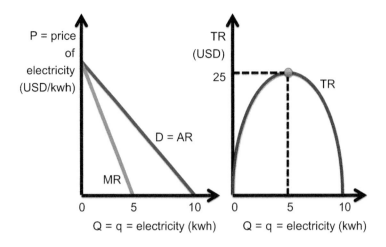

Figure 13.4 Revenues for the monopolist: an electricity company

the average revenue curve (Figure 13.4). The slope of the marginal revenue curve represents the rate of change of the total revenue curve (MR = ΔTR / ΔQ).

Since marginal revenue is declining, the slope of the total revenue curve declines throughout. The marginal revenue curve crosses the x-axis at $q_0$ (= 5) units of output. This is the same quantity of output at which the slope of the total revenue curve becomes negative. To maximize revenue, the monopolist would sell five units of output since that is the highest level of revenue (TR = 25) that the firm can earn.

The firm, however, must also consider the costs of production in deciding what level of output will maximize its profit. Depending on the firm's cost structure, it may be too costly for the firm to produce five units of output. Figure 13.5 shows

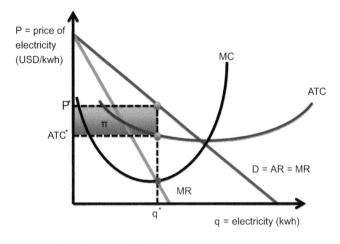

Figure 13.5 Profit maximization by an electricity company

the typical U-shaped cost curves together with the average revenue and marginal revenue curves. The profit-maximizing strategy for the monopolist is to set MR = MC, with MC cutting MR from below.

This profit-maximizing solution is an example of incremental decision-making. The firm sets MR = MC at q* kilowatt-hours of electricity. The profit-maximizing price of electricity is found by taking the quantity (q*), where MR = MC, and using the demand curve to find the price (P*).

At this quantity, the firm earns positive economic profits by selling q* kilowatt-hours of electricity at P* dollars per kilowatt-hour. Profits are equal to the rectangle denoted by $\pi$ below P* and above ATC*, to the left of q*.

---

### QUICK QUIZ 13.4

What would happen if the electricity company in Figure 13.5 charged a price higher than P*? A price lower than P*?

---

Profits are maximized at q* kilowatt-hours. If one additional unit of electricity were produced and sold, the size of the profit rectangle would decrease since the MC curve is higher than the MR curve at all quantities greater than q*. If electricity sales dropped by one unit, profits would be lower since MR > MC at all quantities to the left of q*.

Monopolists search for maximum profits by offering different prices and discovering the levels of demand and total revenue at each price. The monopolist's solution is to restrict output to a level lower than the competitive market output level to receive a price above that which would be charged by a competitive firm. By restricting output, the monopolist is making its good less available and thus more valuable. Notice in Figure 13.5 that the price charged by the monopolist is significantly higher than the cost of production (ATC) at quantity q*. This is one major reason why economists and society favor competitive markets over monopoly. The monopoly solution is inefficient since price is greater than the cost of production.

Monopolies exist for several reasons, including (1) large fixed costs (public utilities), (2) locational monopolies (electricity distributors), (3) limited markets for highly specialized goods (fine jewelry, art), and (4) patents or licenses. Certain kinds of firms must incur large fixed costs prior to the sale of any product at all. These firms are **natural monopolies**.

- *Natural Monopoly* = a situation where a single firm has large fixed costs, making it most efficient (lowest cost) for production to be concentrated in a single firm.

Think of the firm that sells and distributes electricity. Prior to selling electricity, the firm must build and operate a power generator (a huge dam, or a nuclear generator, or a sizeable coal-burning plant), together with an expensive distribution network that includes poles, huge amounts of wire, switches, and transformers. These items are large and costly to install and maintain. The marginal cost of producing one additional kilowatt-hour is small relative to these large fixed costs, but it does no good to produce even one kilowatt-hour of electricity if the firm cannot deliver it to a purchaser. The firms that incur these huge fixed costs are poorly suited to provide electricity to only a few customers, but their vast distribution grid allows them to serve many, perhaps thousands, of customers with one generating plant. In a situation like this, only one firm is needed. A second firm producing the same product would increase the distribution costs and, hence, the price of electricity for consumers. In more technical terms, price competition between two or more firms would drive price down to the competitive level, where neither firm could remain in business, since at this level of output, costs are greater than revenue.

This is why many public utilities such as electricity, natural gas, local telephone service, mail delivery, and municipal water are either regulated monopolies or goods provided by some level of government. In these cases, huge fixed costs require firms to charge prices greater than marginal costs to recover their production costs and the large fixed costs associated with maintaining the distribution system.

Firms that own a unique location can act like a monopoly and charge a high price for the uniqueness of the good. The golf course at Pebble Beach, California, for example, has fairways bordering the Pacific Ocean. It is a one-of-a-kind facility, and it can act like a monopoly. In other areas, prime real estate locations can charge high prices to willing customers who desire to locate homes and businesses in the areas of highest demand.

Most national governments issue patents to the inventors and originators of new machines, powerful medicines, and even new varieties of plants. The same governments issue copyrights (a kind of patent) on works of literature, music, and art. Patents and copyrights are government licenses issued to the developers of new products and techniques. Any inventor can apply for a patent that grants exclusive use of a product or technique to the inventor for a period of 17 years. This is a legal barrier to entry that gives the firm a monopoly for 17 years if no close substitutes for the product exist. In 1996, Monsanto, a huge agricultural biotechnology firm, invented, perfected, and was licensed to sell a cotton seed called Bollgard. The seed had built-in biological (genetic) protection against several weevils (insects) that had been problematic for cotton producers. Monsanto's special seed protected cotton producers from the insects. The same year, Monsanto perfected the herbicide (weed killer) Roundup. Both Bollgard and Roundup were extraordinarily good at doing their jobs of killing undesirable pests in agricultural fields. The patent on Roundup gave Monsanto the exclusive right to produce and sell the product in the United States for 17 years, until the patent expired in 2003.

Patents protect firms and give them the opportunity to recover the high research and development (R&D) costs required before the product is available on the market. Patents make goods more expensive to consumers, but many argue that research and development would not occur, or would slow drastically, in a world with no patent protection.

In the real world, few industries fit the strict definitions of monopoly or competition. Instead, real-world industries usually fall somewhere between these two extreme forms of market structure. The next section explores a market structure that combines aspects of both monopoly and competition.

## 13.3   Monopolistic competition

Many real-world industries include many firms that produce similar, but not identical, goods. The structure of firms in a similar-but-not-identical industry is referred to as **monopolistic competition**.

- *Monopolistic Competition* = a market structure defined by (1) many sellers; (2) a product with close, but differentiated, substitutes; (3) some freedom of entry and exit; and (4) some availability of knowledge and information.

The key ingredient of monopolistic competition is product differentiation, or competition to attract customers by making a good that is different from the other goods but produced by firms in the (same) industry. Almost all consumer products fall into this form of market structure: gasoline stations, cake mixes, toothpaste, milk, soap, soft drinks, and hundreds of other items. Many, if not most, items available in big-box stores such as Walmart or Target are manufactured in a monopolistic competitive industry. Since the products are very much alike, advertising and marketing activities become key characteristics of monopolistic competition. Firms attempt to show consumers how their product differs from that of their rivals.

Since the products in a monopolistic competition industry are not homogeneous, the individual firm faces a downward-sloping demand curve. The slope, or elasticity, of demand depends upon the degree of uniqueness of the good and the consumers' loyalty to the product. Consumers who prefer Colgate toothpaste are willing to pay more for this brand than switch to Crest. If this is true, then the demand for Colgate is relatively inelastic when compared to Crest. Alternatively, if consumers perceive Crest to be a close substitute for Colgate, then the demand curve for Colgate would be relatively elastic.

---

### BOX 13.2

#### Monopolistic competition in the soft drink industry: Coke and Pepsi

On May 8, 1886, a pharmacist named Dr. John Pemberton carried a jug of Coca-Cola syrup to Jacobs' Pharmacy in downtown Atlanta, Georgia, where after being mixed with carbonated water, it sold for five cents a glass. In the decades since that time, Coca-Cola has evolved from one product, Coca-Cola, to the more than 500 brands of soft drinks available in 2014. The Coca-Cola Company currently sells 1.9 billion soft drinks a day, in more than 200 nations. It is the largest beverage company in the world, with over 200 brands worldwide. Products include sparkling drinks and still beverages such as bottled water, juice, juice drinks, teas, coffees, sports drinks, and energy drinks. The company is headquartered in Atlanta,

Georgia, and employs roughly 700,000 workers worldwide. It manufactures concentrates, beverage bases, and syrups that are sold to bottlers, who bottle and sell the finished products. The company reports a 46 percent market share in the US, earns USD 38 billion in annual revenue, and had an advertising budget of USD 4.1 billion in 2021.

In the summer of 1898 a pharmacist named Caleb Bradham invented Pepsi-Cola in Bern, North Carolina. Pepsi-Cola and the company behind it, PepsiCo, has grown into a large marketer of beverages, juices, and snack foods. Pepsi-Cola and Frito-Lay merged in 1965. In 2001, the larger PepsiCo merged with The Quaker Oats Company. Today, PepsiCo is a USD 79 billion company, employing more than 291,000 people. PepsiCo sells products in nearly 200 countries, and offers more than 500 beverages, with a 25 percent market share in the United States, and advertising expenditures over USD 1.96 billion in 2021.

Coke and Pepsi have been engaged in a "marketing war" for decades, as the combined market share for the two companies is over 71 percent of the carbonated soft drink market.

*Sources:* Coca-Cola. www.coca-colacompany.com/. Retrieved January 13, 2023.

Pepsi-Cola. www.pepsi.com/. Retrieved January 13, 2023.

While the characteristics of goods across firms differ in monopolistic competition, the prices among similar products do not vary by much. If price differences become large, consumers will switch to the close substitutes offered by competing firms. In other words, firms do not have a great deal of control over price in monopolistic competition. Figure 13.6 shows a graph of such a firm. The demand curve is downward sloping, showing the market power of the monopolistic competitor, in this case, the soft drink producer Coca-Cola. The cost structure of the firm includes the typical "U-shaped" curves.

Figure 13.6 shows that the monopolistic competitor is in a situation similar to that of a monopolist: it sets MR = MC, produces q* units of output, and sells them at a price P*. Positive profits are shown by the rectangle between the price (P*) and average total cost (ATC*) lines, and to the left of q*. A major difference between a monopolist and a monopolistic competitor is that the monopolistic competitor has less influence over price and must use other strategies to compete with rival firms that produce similar products.

The monopolistic competitor has two major strategies to increase profits. First, the firm could reduce costs. This is the same as in the case of a competitive firm or a monopoly: do anything possible to lower production costs, including adopting new technology, adding a new product line, or purchasing inputs at lower prices. Second, the monopolistic competitor can attempt to influence demand through

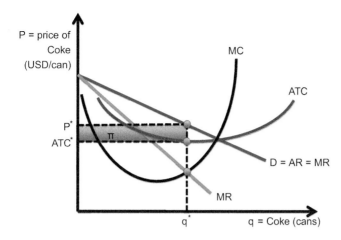

**Figure 13.6** **Profits for a monopolistically competitive firm: Coke**

advertising and marketing efforts that strive to show how his product is "better" than others in this closely fought marketing battle. If consumers believe that a certain brand of toothpaste will make their teeth whiter and control cavities, then the demand for that brand of toothpaste will shift to the right (increase). This strategy is called "**nonprice competition.**"

● *Nonprice Competition* = a market situation where firms compete over good characteristics other than price, such as quality, quantity, services, color, taste, branding, packaging, etc.

Competition to win customers over to a certain brand is often intense. The automobile manufacturers in Detroit, Michigan, for example, often hold much information privately (or secretly) for fear the other car companies will steal their new products and ideas. Coke and Pepsi do battle on prime-time television and on college campuses in their efforts to convince consumers that their product is better than the rival's cola. Coke and Pepsi also attempt to acquire exclusive contracts with colleges and universities, requiring the rival products to not be sold in exchange for money or profit sharing.

Software companies and technology firms, also operating as monopolistic competitors, compete for the best workers and to advertise as the first and best firm to sell new and powerful software applications, or "apps."

Monopolistic competition has been used as a criticism of free market capitalism. Under this type of market structure, many resources are "wasted" on advertising and marketing. Millions of dollars are paid to celebrities from the entertainment and sports industries to endorse a large number of products. Command economies, such as China in the 1950s, produced just one type of clothing and used the resources that market economies use for advertising and marketing to produce other goods. Many individuals believe that the variety of goods offered in a free market economy is not wasteful, but rather provides consumers with information and choices regarding what they might wish to purchase. If consumers were not willing to pay for and pay attention to advertising, the advertising industry would not survive in a market system. Is advertising wasteful? This depends on your viewpoint. Since economists try to purge value judgments from their analyses, the point must rest on individual cases.

Monopolistic competition is a form of market structure that lies between the two extremes of monopoly and competition. It lies close to competition because there are many firms. It is also similar to monopoly since the products of the different firms have special qualities that make them distinct and result in a downward-sloping demand curve. The next section considers a form of market structure that is closer to monopoly since there are only a few firms in the industry.

## 13.4 Oligopoly

An **oligopoly** is a market structure where only a few firms engage in production activities.

● *Oligopoly* = a market structure characterized by a few large firms.

The key characteristics of firms in an oligopoly are that the firms are rivals even though they form an interdependent group. The behavior of one firm has an impact on the behavior of other firms in the industry. Oligopolists must take into consideration the actions of other firms. Firms in an oligopoly are considered to have market power, and their ability to set price is determined by their own actions and the actions (and reactions) of other firms in the industry.

Taken together, agricultural implement manufacturers operate as an oligopoly. There is much interdependence within the group. Both price and nonprice competition are prevalent. The John Deere farm implement manufacturer must pay close attention to its rival, Case-IH, if it wants to maximize profits, or even if it wants to stay in business. If one of these giant firms lowers the price of certain lines of implements, the other firm, also a giant, will most likely match the new low price in order to retain its customers. If the price is lowered by both firms, then both firms earn lower levels of profits. Both firms would be better off maintaining a higher price. Similarly, if one firm raises its price, it will lose some customers to the other firm, unless the price hike is matched. Profit levels and market shares are determined by all firms in an oligopoly, rather than just the one firm acting alone.

The central strategy of an oligopolist is to form an alliance with the other firms in the industry to maintain prices at a level higher than the competitive market price. Firms **collude** when they agree to make decisions as a group.

● *Collusion* = when firms in an industry jointly determine the price of the good.

Collusion is a form of monopoly. If all of the firms in an oligopoly agree to act as a single firm, they would be a de facto monopoly, and the monopoly pattern for profit maximization would be appropriate. The collusive price and quantity solution would be the monopoly solution. This form of business strategy has been illegal in the United States since passage of the Sherman Antitrust Act in 1890.

## 13.4.1 Cartels

**Cartels** are groups of independent firms that join together for the express intent of regulating and controlling their price and production decisions. Cartels arise when several firms in an industry attempt to band together and act like a monopoly.

- *Cartel* = a group of independent firms that join together to regulate price and production decisions.

While this form of market structure is illegal within the United States (due to the Sherman Anti-Trust Act), it is legal in some other nations. The Organization of Petroleum Exporting Countries (OPEC) is a famous international cartel that limits oil production in its 12 member nations in an attempt to drive up the world price of oil.

---

**BOX 13.3**

### The Organization of Petroleum Exporting Countries (OPEC)

OPEC is a permanent intergovernmental organization created in 1960 to coordinate petroleum supply and price policies among member countries. OPEC includes 13 oil-producing countries as members: Algeria, Angola, Congo, Equatorial Guinea, Gabon, Iran, Iraq, Kuwait, Libya, Nigeria, Saudi Arabia, the United Arab Emirates, and Venezuela. The OPEC headquarters are in Vienna, Austria.

OPEC is a cartel: a group of producers that restricts output in an attempt to raise prices above the competitive level. The group meets twice each year to decide overall oil output and assign output quotas for each member nation. As a cartel, OPEC is faced with enforcement problems: overproduction and price cheating by its members. Each individual member could make itself better off by producing more than its quota and charging a lower price for oil since the cartel price is higher than the cost of production. In reality, cheating takes the form of credit discounts or extensions, selling higher grades of oil for a lower-grade price, transportation discounts, side payments, and rebates.

Economists are suspicious of the ability of OPEC to increase oil prices, as the real price of oil fell from 1974 to 2003. Since then, oil prices have climbed, but much of this increase in oil prices has been due to the increased demand stemming from economic growth in Asia. OPEC's ability to control the price of oil has diminished due to discovery and development of large oil reserves in Alaska, the North Sea, Canada, the Gulf of Mexico, the opening of Russia to trade, and market modernization. As of 2023, OPEC members collectively controlled 80 percent of world crude oil reserves and 40 percent of the world's crude oil production, affording them considerable strength in the global market.

*Source:* OPEC. www.opec.org/. Retrieved January 13, 2023.

In a fashion similar to OPEC's intense interest in world crude oil production and distribution, US cattle producers and the US government pay a great deal of attention to the market structure of the beef packing industry since there is a large concentration of market power in four firms: Tyson, Cargill, JBS USA, and National Beef. The fear is that these firms may form a cartel and attempt to exert detrimental levels of control over livestock producers, processors, and consumers. Figure 13.7 is a hypothetical demonstration of the supply and demand for the meat industry (on the left) and for an individual packing plant (on the right). Assume that the packers were able to form a cartel, with the objective of reducing output in order to increase the price of beef.

The competitive solution in Figure 13.7 occurs at the intersection of beef supply and beef demand in the market graph on the left ($P^*$, $Q^{comp}$). If a successful

**Photo 13.3** Oil production

*Source:* TebNad/Shutterstock

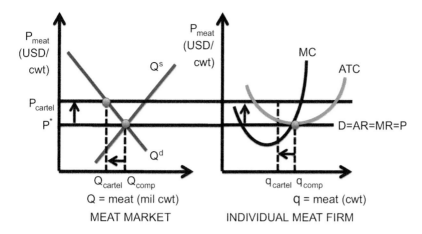

Figure 13.7 Hypothetical cartel in the meat industry

cartel makes an agreement to restrict the output of meat from $Q^{comp}$ to $Q^{cartel}$, the agreement reduces the quantity of beef and drives the price up to $P^{cartel}$. Assume that this restricted level of output is 80 percent of the original market. If the four packers collude perfectly, they charge the monopoly price and act as if they were a single firm.

## BOX 13.4

### Meatpacking

The meatpacking industry operates the slaughtering, processing, packaging, and distribution of meat from animals such as cattle, pigs, sheep, poultry, and other livestock. The industry is primarily focused on producing meat for human consumption, but it also yields a variety of by-products, including hides, feathers, dried blood, and through the process of rendering, fat such as tallow and protein meals such as meat and bone meal for use in the animal feed industry. The meat industry is the largest agricultural sector in the United States. Meat and poultry sales are greater than USD 218 billion annually, and the meat processing industry employed a total of over 500,000 people in 2021.

The meatpacking industry has changed greatly in the past 30 years due to the movement of packing plants to the small cities of the Great Plains, where large numbers of feedlots are now located. New meatpacking companies such as Iowa Beef Processors (IBP, now owned by Tyson) brought new technology and captured economies to scale in large plants located in areas where labor unions did not have a strong history. This, coupled with increasing worker speed and productivity, cutting labor costs, and consolidation provided new sources of profits to large firms that operated large plants on small margins.

Over the past three decades, the number of immigrant laborers in meatpacking plants, and in the Midwestern areas where they are located, has increased dramatically. The industry has been criticized for hazardous working conditions and low pay.

*Source:* "Meatpacking." Dictionary of American History. http://Encyclopedia.com. www.encyclopedia.com. Retrieved August 24, 2019.

## BOX 13.5

### Monopoly power in agribusiness industries

The US meatpacking industry is highly concentrated among the "Big Four" largest firms: Cargill, Tyson, JBS-USA, and National Beef. These four firms represent approximately 85 percent of all beef packing. The size of these companies brings both benefits and costs to the beef producers and consumers.

The potential problem with market concentration is monopoly pricing: large firms might control enough of the market to offer lower price to cattle, pork, and poultry producers relative to competitive firms. The Big Four might also be able to charge higher prices than price charged by numerous competing firms. Livestock producers have often cited monopoly power as a source of financial hardship and loss of cattle ranches over time.

The potential benefit to the meat industry is economies of scale: larger production plants and companies result in lower per unit costs. Modern meatpacking plants are enormous, requiring complex coordination of inputs that include labor, cattle, water, electricity, safety, and waste management. Meat is perishable, requiring additional complex decision-making and coordination to get the product to consumers in a timely, safe fashion. Larger firms provide meat to grocery stores, restaurants, and institutions at a lower cost than could smaller meat packers such as local butcher shops.

Economists suggest approaching issues by comparing benefits and costs. Packer concentration allows for operation at higher volumes and lower costs relative to smaller plants. Agricultural economists who study this issue tend to conclude that the benefits of large, concentrated production might outweigh the costs. Restated, the lower consumer meat prices provided by economies of scale provide benefits larger than the potential costs of monopoly power.

*Source:* Azzam, A. and J. Schroeter. 1995. "Tradeoffs between Oligopsony Power and Cost Efficiency from Horizontal Consolidation: An Example from Beef Packing."

*American Journal of Agricultural Economics 77:835–836.*

If the four firms were able to agree to cut back on beef production by 20 percent each, they would earn positive economic profits, as shown in the right side of Figure 13.7. The problem with collusive agreements is the constant temptation of each firm to "cheat" once the agreement has been made. At the collusive price, a single meatpacking plant could increase its production slightly, then take advantage of the cartel price. It would sell the added output at the agreed-to price. If a single firm could do this at the cartel price, it would set MR = MC at the intersection of those two curves in the right-hand section of Figure 13.7.

There are only a few firms (in the case of beef packers, only four dominant firms) in an oligopoly. Therefore, one firm's cheating behavior puts downward pressure on the price of beef. This, in turn, erodes the cartel agreement and leads to a breakup, and the price falls back toward the competitive level, limiting the effectiveness of the cartel. The issue is that the cheating firm assumes that all other firms stick to the agreement—an assumption that is inconsistent with the firm's own behavior. If all of the firms cheat on the agreement, then the competitive output and price would result. This being the case, any cartel must spend money on monitoring other firms to make sure that they don't violate the original conditions of the agreement.

Strategic behavior among oligopolists can be complicated. The rivalry between firms can lead to aggressive price competition, or effective collusion, or anything in between these extremes. Volatility is a major feature of oligopoly. Rivalry among firms may maintain a price agreement for a short period, but it is often followed by a price war that keeps the price at a competitive level. The next section discusses the benefits and costs of highly concentrated market structures.

## 13.5   Is big necessarily bad?

There have been a large number of mergers and acquisitions in the agribusiness industry in the past several years. These have occurred on both the factor side and the output side of agricultural and food markets. Many small firms have merged to form larger firms, which farmers and other market participants often think of as having too much power. While it is true that if the large firms in concentrated industries have the ability to use market power to charge higher than competitive prices to consumers, the consolidation of firms into larger entities would be an inefficient outcome for society. It would result in a transfer of resources from consumers to the large firms.

There are major economic advantages to the production of goods and services by very large firms, however. The primary benefit stemming from growth in firm size is **economies of scale**, which refers to lower production costs at larger levels of output:

- *Economies of Scale* = when the per-unit costs of production decrease as output increases.

There is a trade-off between large-scale firms in agricultural production and agribusiness. If these large firms exploit their market power by charging prices above the competitive level, then consolidation could be considered a negative aspect of the agricultural economy. However, to the extent that large firms capture economies of scale, they are contributing to the efficiency of the economy by producing goods at lower per unit costs relative to smaller firms.

Mergers and large firms are controversial. Some people are likely to emphasize the market power abuses (real or imagined) of a large firm, and others are likely to emphasize efficiency gains. Individual cases of consolidation should be considered on an individual case bases. Even then, it is likely to be very difficult to determine the exact impact on prices and output that will follow after consolidation of small into large entities. Most evidence suggests that large firms do not have a great influence on price due to the potential competition from other firms. Also, there are huge cost savings associated with large production facilities that allow production at a low cost per unit of output. Thus, in most cases, it is likely that the benefits of bigness outweigh the costs. Just as there are gains stemming from the size of large firms, there are also gains from the large firms trading with other nations, a theme developed in the next chapter.

## 13.6  Game theory

Although game theory has a playful name, it concerns a useful and important topic: strategic interactions between interdependent economic decision-makers. Strategic interactions are actions taken by one individual or group that affect others and, importantly, consider the possible reactions or retaliations of the affected parties. In this way, forward-looking decisions help anticipate others' responses. Game theory can be summarized as a series of strategic interactions: actions and responses.

Many economic decisions made by either competitive firms or monopolies do not need to consider the possible reactions of other stakeholders. Competitive industries are characterized by numerous firms, each producing a homogeneous product (Chapter 12). A competitive firm is a price taker and cannot affect the price of the good or service. In this sense, competitive firms are not rivals. They do not need to be concerned about the actions of other competitive firms, because the actions of one firm have no impact on any other firm in the industry. Likewise, a monopoly does not need to consider how other firms in the industry will react to an action it takes: there are no other firms in the industry. Strategic interactions occur in between the market structure extremes of competition and monopoly. Oligopolies are considered "players" in this economic "game."

- *Game* = A decision-making situation in which the participants (players) make strategic decisions.
- *Player* = A stakeholder who makes decisions in games.
- *Game Theory* = The study of strategic decision-making.

In many situations, a firm's profits depend on the decisions of others who are outside of the firm's control. Game theory provides a useful and informative way for a firm to improve its decisions by including the anticipated actions and reactions of others in its own decision-making process. For example, a fast-food company that integrates rival fast-food company reactions to a new product may make more effective decisions than those restaurants that do not. One of the major conclusions of game theory is that cooperating with rivals may result in superior outcomes than retaliating or doing nothing. Decision-makers, or players, in a game theory situation will consider the impact of their decisions on other affected parties and the possible responses of those parties. By thinking two or more steps ahead, game theory can save firms from unnecessarily losing profits and consumers from losing money. Game theory provides insight into the optimal course of actions by incorporating the possible reactions of others. As such, game theory provides a method of using forward-looking and realistic decision-making processes.

Strategic decisions result in payoffs, which are the outcomes that generate benefits or costs to the players (stakeholders). These payoffs can be summarized in a "payoff matrix," which shows the benefits or costs accruing to each player given her decision and the decision of her competitor. Figure 13.8 illustrates a simple game regarding what price to choose using the payoff matrix.

- *Payoffs* = the outcomes that generate benefits or costs to the players (stakeholders) in a game.

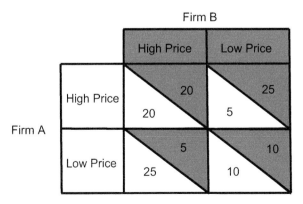

Payoffs in USD (millions)

Figure 13.8 **Pricing game**

## 13.6.1  Price game

This game formalizes a hypothetical situation similar to issues that arise in the food and agriculture industry when two firms are deciding what price to charge for a new product. Their decisions will determine which firm will end up with up to USD 40 million, the total amount of consumer willingness to pay for the good in this market. Both firms earn USD 10 million selling at the low price. Suppose a higher price doubles the size of the market to USD 20 million for each firm. Game theory can summarize this situation, where there is an obvious large monetary incentive to charge a higher price in this market.

If both firms charge the low price for the product, they split the market evenly at USD 10 million each. The payoffs in Figure 13.8 show the payoffs to Firm A in the lower-left triangle of each quadrant, and the payoffs to Firm B are in the shaded upper-right triangle. If both Firm A and Firm B continue to sell at the low price, they are in the lower-right quadrant, where each firm earns USD 10 million. If either A or B charges a high price, the outcome is shown in the lower-left (Firm A) or upper-right (Firm B) quadrants, indicating the competitive nature of this strategic pricing game. If both firms charge the high price, the outcome appears in the upper-left quadrant, where the firms split the market evenly, and each firm earns USD 20 million.

The earnings in this situation depend not only on the firm's (either A or B) own decisions but also on the actions and reactions of other firms. How do firms decide what to do? There are two ways of thinking about a solution. The first is called a "**dominant strategy**." A dominant strategy is one that is optimal no matter what the opponent does.

● *Dominant Strategy* = a strategy in game theory that is optimal no matter what the opponent does.

To find Firm A's dominant strategy, consider Firm A's decision in light of the decision made by Firm B. If Firm B chooses to charge a high price (left column of the payoff matrix), then Firm A can choose between a high price, which would yield USD 20 million, or a low price, which would result in profits equal to USD 25 million. Therefore, Firm A will select "low price" if B chooses "high price." Similarly, if Firm B selects "low price" (right column), Firm A will again select "low price," since 10 > 5. Firm A has a dominant strategy in "low price" because it is better off choosing "low" no matter what Firm B does.

What is Firm B's dominant strategy? Using the same logic, if Firm A selects low, then B selects low: 10 > 5. If A chooses high, B is still better off with low: 25 > 20. The dominant strategy outcome of the product pricing game is "low, low" shown in the lower-right quadrant where each firm chooses to charge the low price, no matter what the other firm does. This outcome describes the real-world incentive to maintain a competitive price to maintain market share. The game is a simplistic game showing a straightforward dominant strategy for both players.

> ### QUICK QUIZ 13.5
>
> Is the dominant strategy outcome the optimal outcome for the two players? Why or why not?

In many games, one or more player may not have a dominant strategy. In such cases there is a second method of searching for an optimal strategic decision. Named for the mathematician John Nash, the "Nash equilibrium" allows each player to do the best that she can, given what the other player is doing. The result is stable because no player is left with an incentive to change.

- *Nash Equilibrium* = an equilibrium in game theory where each player does the best that she can, given what the other player is doing. The result is stable because no player is left with an incentive to change.

### QUICK QUIZ 13.6

Is the Nash equilibrium the same as a dominant strategy outcome? Why or why not?

Nash strategies are often the same as the dominant strategies, but need not be. In the product pricing game depicted in Figure 13.8, the Nash strategies are identified in the following way: focus on each quadrant and determine if each firm would like to stay or change strategies. If Firm B chooses "low" and Firm A chooses "low," then Firm A does not have an incentive to change since it would lose money (10 > 5). Similarly, B desires to stay with "low" if A selects "low," (10 > 5). So the "low, low" solution is a Nash equilibrium with neither firm desiring to change. The solution "low, low" qualifies as both a dominant strategy (each firm is doing the best that it can, no matter what the other firm chooses) and a Nash equilibrium (each firm is doing the best that it can, given what the other firm is doing).

In each of the other three quadrants, at least one of the firms desires to change strategies. In the "high, low" quadrant, A would like to move (10 > 5), given B's choice of "low." However, B would not like to change from low to high (25 > 20), given A's selection of "high." Likewise, Firm B would not stay in quadrant "low, high." Both firms desire to leave the upper left quadrant, "high, high." In this game, there is no good reason for either firm to charge a high price. Interestingly, when the firms both charge a high price, there is an incentive for each firm to charge a lower price to earn more profits. However, this positive outcome depends on the reaction of the other firm: if the other firm meets the price decrease, both firms lose 10 million USD. The game's outcome has both firms charging a low price since the incentive is the same for both firms, given the choices of the rival firm.

The outcome of this pricing game demonstrates a dilemma: both the dominant strategy and the Nash equilibrium lead to an inferior outcome (low, low). Both firms would be better off at "high, high". However, the concern over a rival's reaction and potential for retaliation create incentives that cause the game to end in a less desirable outcome. This result is common in agribusiness and food oligopolies. A similar outcome results from marketing and advertising expenditures. Oligopolists may get into an "advertising war" in which firms all spend money on advertising but do not increase their market share. Game theory incorporates realism into economic models of oligopoly by including the actions and reactions of firms.

## 13.6.2 Firm location decision: a game that brings firms together

The Nash equilibrium concept is used extensively in economics, social sciences, biology, and military science. The crucial thing to remember is that a firm will only stick with a decision if it is the best that the firm can do, given the reactions of other firms. Nash's insights provide a useful solution to a problem that is pervasive in market economies and politics: firms that are apparent competitors locate near each other, and politicians, regardless of party, select policies that represent the "average voter." In most towns or cities, the fast-food restaurants, the car dealerships, and the gasoline stations are located in close proximity to each other. This is often due to zoning regulations, but it is also a result of optimal strategic decision-making by the business owners: game theory. Consider Firm A's choice of where to locate a business in Figure 13.9.

---

**QUICK QUIZ 13.7**

What is the optimal location for a firm in Figure 13.9? Why?

---

Firms A and B both sell coffee, and coffee drinkers (potential customers) are spread evenly across the 100 blocks of a city. Coffee drinkers purchase from the nearest coffee vendor. In this case, the Nash equilibrium says both firms should locate as close to the middle of the city as possible. Why? Suppose that Firm B locates at block 75 (b' in Figure 13.9). In this case, Firm A could move to block 74 and receive nearly three-quarters of the coffee market since all customers to the left of Firm A's location will purchase from it. Firm B would lose customers and would desire to move closer to the middle to recover lost sales. Thus, in equilibrium, Firms A and B will both locate in the middle, at block 50, which is a stable location: a Nash equilibrium. Obviously, but importantly, the real world is more complicated than this simple model. For example, product differentiation causes one firm to move away from the other firm. However, the simple example provides a prediction that holds in many real-world cases.

This simple game explains a great deal about market and political behavior. Firms will locate near each other, not only in physical space, but also with respect to other strategic attributes. Similarly, if the sugar content of packaged cereals is important to consumers, firms producing these products will move their products toward the sugar content desired by the average consumer. Politicians will align themselves as closely as possible to the median voter. This outcome explains why

0       50      75      100

**Figure 13.9 Firm location game**

many partisan voters are frustrated at election time when candidates may appear to be advocating the same things, rather than reflecting the preferences of strong right- or strong left-leaning voters.

The outcome of this game has important implications for polarized issues in food and agriculture since it suggests that firms starting in different places have economic (or political) incentives to move toward the same location. Economic incentives provide the catalyst to bring divergent groups together in many situations and issues. Extreme groups can provide a starting point, and can bring an important issue into the spotlight, but the policy process typically brings opposing groups together through compromise and negotiated solutions. Similarly, highly specialized niche markets can often serve a portion of a larger market, but firms often face irresistible economic incentives to provide goods and services that are acceptable to a majority of consumers.

## 13.7   Chapter 13 Summary

1   Market power is the ability to affect the price of output. A firm with market power faces a downward-sloping demand curve.
2   Monopoly is a market structure characterized by a single seller.
3   The profit-maximizing condition for a monopolist is when MR = MC, with MC cutting MR from below.
4   A natural monopoly has large fixed costs.
5   Monopolistic competition is a market structure defined by (1) many firms; (2) a product of close, but differentiated, substitutes; (3) some freedom of entry and exit; and (4) some availability of knowledge and information.
6   Nonprice competition is when firms compete over good characteristics other than price, such as quality, quantity of services, etc.
7   An oligopoly is a market structure characterized by a few large firms.
8   Collusion occurs when the firms in an industry jointly determine the price of a good.
9   A cartel is a group of independent firms that join together to regulate price and production decisions.
10   Economies to scale exist when per-unit costs of production decrease as output increases.
11   Game theory is the study of strategic decision-making and can be summarized as looking at the world as a series of strategic interactions: actions and responses.
12   Game theory provides insight into the optimal course of action by incorporating the possible reactions of others.
13   By thinking two or more steps ahead, game theory can save firms from unnecessarily losing profits and consumers from losing money.
14   A dominant strategy is a strategy in game theory that is optimal no matter what the opponent does.
15   A Nash equilibrium is an equilibrium in game theory where each player does the best that she can, given what the other player is doing. The result is stable because no player is left with an incentive to change.
16   Game theory explains why firms often locate near each other and produce similar products.

## 13.8   Chapter 13 Glossary

**Cartel**—A group of independent firms that join together to regulate price and production decisions.

**Collusion**—When the firms in an industry jointly determine the price of the good.

**Dominant Strategy**—A strategy in game theory that is optimal no matter what the opponent does.

**Economies of Scale**—When the per-unit costs of production decrease as output increases.

**Game**—A decision-making situation in which the participant (players) make strategic decisions.

**Game Theory**—The study of strategic decision-making.

**Market Power**—The ability to affect the price of output. A firm with market power faces a downward-sloping demand curve for its product.

**Market Structure**—The organization of an industry, typically defined by the number of firms in an industry.

**Monopolistic Competition**—A market structure defined by (1) many sellers; (2) a product of close, but differentiated, substitutes; (3) some freedom of entry and exit; and (4) some availability of knowledge and information.

**Monopoly**—A market structure characterized by a single seller. The firm is the industry.

**Nash Equilibrium**—An equilibrium in game theory where each player does the best that she can, given what the other player is doing. The result is stable because no player is left with an incentive to change.

**Natural Monopoly**—A situation where a single firm has large fixed costs, making it most efficient (lowest cost) for production to be concentrated in a single firm.

**Nonprice Competition**—A market situation where firms compete over good characteristics other than price, such as quality, quantity, services, color, taste, branding, packaging, etc.

**Oligopoly**—A market structure characterized by a few large firms.

**Payoffs**—The outcomes that generate benefits or costs to the players (stakeholders) in a game.

**Player**—Stakeholder who makes decisions in games.

## 13.9   Chapter 13 Review questions

1  Profit maximization is the goal of which type of firm:

a   competitive firm
b   monopolist
c   oligopolist
d   all of the above

2  A monopolist produces a good that

a   is a public utility, such as electricity
b   has no close substitutes
c   has numerous substitutes
d   is inferior

3  A natural monopoly has

a   numerous competitors
b   large fixed costs
c   large variable costs
d   zero fixed costs

4  The key characteristics of a monopolistic competitor is

a    freedom of entry and exit
b    homogeneous product
c    product differentiation
d    monopolistic prices

a    monopoly
b    oligopoly
c    monopolistic competition
d    perfect competition

5  A group of firms that join together to regulate price and production decisions is

a    the teamsters
b    an oligopoly
c    collusion
d    a cartel

6  Large firms can take advantage of

a    natural monopoly
b    monopoly pricing strategies
c    economies of scale
d    collusion

7  Game theory involves

a    fairness and following the rules of the game
b    monopoly
c    the actions and reactions of other players
d    competition

8  Game theory is most useful in studying which market structure?

9  A dominant strategy is

a    the best strategy for a dominant firm
b    the best strategy for all firms
c    a strategy that is optimal no matter what the other players do
d    a strategy that is optimal given what the other players are doing

10  A Nash equilibrium is

a    the best strategy for a dominant firm
b    the best strategy for all firms
c    a strategy that is optimal no matter what the other players do
d    a strategy that is optimal given what the other players are doing

**Answers:** 1. d, 2. b, 3. b, 4. c, 5. d, 6. c, 7. c, 8. b, 9. c, 10. d

For more study questions, flash cards, and study guides, see the online materials at the companion website: www.routledge.com/cw/barkley.

# Agriculture and the global economy

Photo 14.1 Agriculture and the global economy

*Source:* TFoxFoto/Shutterstock

DOI: 10.4324/9781003367994-14

## Abstract

This chapter explains why international trade and globalization occur. It also tells why most economists are enthusiastic supporters of free trade among nations. The chapter uses examples from food and agriculture to explain the motivation behind international trade. The chapter also explains the principle of comparative advantage as it applies to the globalization of trade in food and agriculture. The chapter includes an explanation of the advantages of diversity in national resources. A three-panel diagram of trade is presented to demonstrate who wins and who loses from trade. The benefits and losses from labor immigration are analyzed in detail. The impact of exchange rates and transportation costs on trade are examined.

**Chapter 14 Questions**

1   Why does international trade and globalization occur?
2   Why do most economists favor free trade?
3   What is the motivation behind international trade?
4   What is the principle of comparative advantage, and how does it explain why trade occurs?
5   How does international trade relate to diversity in natural resources?
6   Who wins and who loses from trade?
7   What are the benefits and costs of labor migration?
8   How do exchange rates and transportation costs affect international trade?

## 14.1   Globalization and agriculture

Watching television news, listening to the radio, or surfing the Internet repeatedly brings a person into contact with terms such as "internationalization," "globalization," "immigration," and "the global economy." This relatively recent focus on international issues stems from the rapid reduction in economic, political, and cultural barriers between nations. High-profile examples of globalization include free trade agreements such as the NAFTA, the 2011 free trade agreement between the US and South Korea, and the adoption of the euro as the official currency of 17 European nations. Most adults in the US are familiar with current events that have international implications. However, the underlying causes and consequences of globalization are often less clearly understood.

   With few notable exceptions, politicians favor free trade between nations. Similarly, elected officials frequently join together to support free trade, even while disagreeing on many other issues. Economists have even stronger feelings. They are unyielding proponents, obsessed with the idea of goods flowing freely between nations without obstructions due to **trade barriers**, such as **tariffs, import quotas,** embargoes, or unnecessary searches by government officials. Free markets and free trade are the lifeblood of economists, who typically oppose government interventions in the voluntary exchange of goods and services in both domestic and international markets.

- *Trade barriers* = laws and regulations to restrict the flow of goods and services across international borders, including tariffs, duties, quotas, and import and export subsidies.
- *Tariff* = a tax on imports of a good.
- *Import Quota* = a trade restriction that sets a physical limit on the quantity of a good that can be imported during a given time period.

## BOX 14.1

### European agriculture

The EU is an economic and political confederation of 27 member nations. The EU was first developed as the European Economic Community (EEC) beginning with six members in 1958. In 1993, the EEC became the EU, which is a single market with standardized laws and institutions to ensure the free movement of people, goods, services, and capital. The EU also maintains common policies on international trade, agriculture, fisheries, and regional development. The EU is the largest food importer in the world and among the largest food exporters.

Agriculture within the EU is highly diverse and productive. Europe is approximately the same size as the US: 4 million square miles. European agriculture includes colder climates such as Sweden and Finland, where wheat, barley, oats, and timber are grown. In the south, Mediterranean nations such as Spain and Italy produce wine, olives, cork, almonds, and tomatoes. France is the largest agricultural producer in the EU, with 35 percent of the total land area devoted to agriculture. France produces dairy, wine, beef, wheat, and corn, among many other food products. The Eastern European nations of the EU have agricultural sectors that employ large numbers of workers. Over one-third of Bulgaria's workforce, for example, finds employment in agriculture. In Turkey, the figure approaches 50 percent.

After the devastation of World War II, the farm policies of the several European countries focused on providing enough food for a war-torn population. At the beginning of the European Community, its Common Agricultural Policy (CAP) had objectives of increasing agricultural production, stabilizing markets, providing certainty in food markets, and ensuring adequate incomes for farmers. The policy's high price supports and market interventions met these objectives but also resulted in large and unintended overproduction and surpluses. To dispose of these food surpluses, the EEC often sold the excess on the world market at prices considerably below the world price. This system was criticized as unfair competition for farmers outside of the EU, especially those in low-income nations.

Since the 1990s, EU agricultural policy has evolved, and the community has implemented policy reforms. The CAP now concentrates on food quality, environmental quality, rural economic development, animal welfare, and food safety. Policy reforms have made the policies less harmful to competing nations.

*Sources:* Europa Agriculture. https://europa.eu/european-union/topics/agriculture_en. Retrieved January 16, 2023.

Stead, David; (02 January 2010). "Common Agricultural Policy." http://EH.Net Encyclopedia. Retrieved January 16, 2023.

## BOX 14.2

## Trade disputes

Free trade brings large benefits. However, trade results in winners and losers: not everyone gains because of trade. Thus, trade policies and actual trade flows may affect the economic welfare of nations, groups, and individuals. It is not surprising, then, that disputes arise over trade, trade policies, and trade barriers. Trade disputes have been a major feature of US history since the nation was founded. England's King George helped to cause the American Revolution by imposing difficult tax and trade laws and regulations on residents in the New World.

Now, two and a half centuries after King George's edicts, the US has two major types of trade policies: import barriers on goods such as sugar and cotton, and export subsidies on grains such as wheat. The US sugar import quota restricts the quantity of sugar imported into the US, resulting in higher sugar prices in the US and reduced sugar prices abroad. Foreign sugar producers and sugar-exporting nations lose revenue from the lack of the ability to trade sugar with the US. This example of a loss of export markets can lead to trade disputes between nations. Grain export subsidies also result in higher internal (US) grain prices and lower external (foreign) grain prices. Policies such as these can also lead to economic loss and the potential for trade disputes.

In the modern era of globalization, trade disputes are common and important both economically and politically. For example, Brazil brought a case against US cotton subsidies and export credits. These subsidies resulted in lower world cotton prices, causing economic losses for cotton producers in Asia, Africa, and South America. The policies violated US trade agreements, and the US now makes cash payments to Brazilian farmers to compensate for their losses. The World Trade Organization (WTO) is a trade agreement with more than 140 member nations. Its objective is to reduce trade barriers between nations. The WTO has formal procedures for rationalizing disputes about trade agreements. The WTO can provide recommendations but does not have legal authority to cause nations to alter their trade policies.

Given the enormous and growing importance of trade between nations, trade disputes and their resolution will continue to have an important place in the modern international economy. Resolution of trade disputes provides for a movement toward the elimination of trade barriers, which will increase the net economic welfare of all trading nations. However, recall that free trade does not benefit all individuals and groups. Thus, such disputes will continue as nations progress toward improved methods of producing, processing, trading, and consuming food and fiber products.

*Source:* Wilde, Parke. 2018. *Food Policy in the United States: An Introduction, Second Edition.* Chapter 4. New York: Routledge/Earthscan.

## BOX 14.3

## International trade policies

Governments of trading nations use a large variety of trade policies. The major trade policies include import tariffs and quotas, export taxes and subsides, export restrictions, and dumping. Import tariffs are taxes on imported goods. Tariffs are frequently imposed to help domestic producers and raise revenue for government. The major impact is an increase in the domestic price of a good, by reducing foreign competition. An import quota restricts the quantity of a good that can be imported. The impact of an import quota is the same as that of an import tariff: higher domestic prices.

An export tax is a tax on an exported good. An export tax results in lower domestic prices and higher foreign prices. This type of tax helps domestic consumers and/or raises government revenue. An export subsidy pays exporters a given amount per unit of exported good. The outcome is an increase in the domestic price of a good and a decrease in prices abroad. Thus, export subsidies benefit domestic producers.

Export restrictions are a limit on the quantity of an exported good to lower prices at home. At times, exports can be prohibited to maintain lower prices for domestic consumers. For example, during the food price crisis in the late 2000s, some nations banned exports in an effort to maintain low domestic food prices.

Dumping is a trade practice used to sell a product overseas at a price lower than the production cost. Dumping often results from domestic agricultural subsidy policies that increase the price and quantity of a good. If there is a surplus, dumping provides a method of removing the domestic surplus while maintaining a high domestic price. Producers in nations where goods sell at low prices often criticize dumping.

High-income nations such as the US, EU, Australia, and Japan, typically subsidize agricultural producers though import tariffs, quotas, and export subsidies. Low-income nations typically tax agriculture. In many low-income nations, agriculture is a large portion of the total economy, resulting in a major source of government revenue. In high-income nations, agriculture comprises a small percentage of the total economy, causing subsidies to be affordable.

Non-tariff barriers (NTBs), also called technical trade barriers, include food safety and food labeling policies. Many nations impose technical trade barriers or requirements related to the quality of a traded good. One major difficulty of this form of regulation is that NTBs can protect domestic producers from foreign competition, without violating trade agreements.

*Source:* Wilde, Parke. 2018. *Food Policy in the United States: An Introduction, Second Edition*. Chapter 4. New York: Routledge/Earthscan.

## BOX 14.4

### Recent changes in international trade policies

The US agricultural sector depends on exports to maintain profitability: about one-half of all agricultural products produced in the US are exported. Although there has been a movement by most nations toward free trade for many decades, in 2017 the US President imposed a 25 percent tariff on steel imports and a 10 percent tariff on aluminum imports on most nations. Six nations

(Canada, China, EU, India, Mexico, and Turkey) imposed retaliatory tariffs on US agricultural exports to those nations. China applied additional retaliatory tariffs of 5–25 percent on thousands of agricultural products, including 25 percent tariffs on soybeans and pork, the main products that the US exports to China. The USDA estimates that these retaliatory tariffs reduced agricultural trade by 27 billion USD from mid-2018 to the end of 2019.

These losses were regained through negotiation and tariff reduction in 2020. Prices and profits in US agricultural crucially depend on exports to China, so future relations between the two nations will play a major role in the future well-being of US agriculture.

*Source:* Morgan, Stephen, Shawn Arita, Jayson Beckman, Saquib Ahsan, Dylan Russell, Philip Jarrell, and Bart Kenner. January 2022. The Economic Impacts of Retaliatory Tariffs on U.S. Agriculture, ERR-304, U.S. Department of Agriculture, Economic Research Service.

## 14.2   Interdependence and gains from trade

It does not take long to notice the advantages of buying and selling goods from other parts of the world. A typical breakfast in a typical US household, for example, most likely includes coffee produced from beans grown in Brazil and orange juice squeezed from oranges grown in either Florida or Mexico. Similarly, China uses cotton grown in Arizona or Mississippi to make clothes worn in the US. The Ford 350 pickup trucks in the university parking lot required imported component parts manufactured in several different nations. The paper used to make the printed versions of this book likely came from trees grown either in the southern US or Canada.

People living in North America rely on goods produced in many nations in all parts of the world. This is unquestionably good because it expands the number and variety of goods available for consumption. Similarly, domestic producers acknowledge that international trade allows the US population to be more productive and efficient since specializing in the production of a limited number of goods brings advantages in the production process.

Adam Smith (1723–1790), an early Scottish economist, stated this in his 1776 book, *An Inquiry into the Nature and Causes of the Wealth of Nations*. Smith's key argument advocating economic interdependence among nations focused on the advantage that comes by working full-time in a specialized area, then using the earnings from this work to purchase goods and services from other specialized workers possibly working in other nations. Smith's simple insight that an individual should "do what he or she can do best" is the basis for international trade. A modern example of this concept stems from the question, "Should a professional tennis player mow her own lawn?" The tennis player may be an exceptional athlete who has earned millions of dollars playing in lucrative matches. Given her youth and athleticism, it is likely that she would also be good at mowing lawns. She may be faster and more efficient at mowing than anyone else in town. In fact, she may even enjoy mowing grass as a way of unwinding from the stress of fame and fortune that she receives from the United States Tennis Association Tour.

Given her ability as a professional tennis player, she is most likely better off spending her time practicing her tennis game while someone else mows the lawn. She could make herself better off by "trading" a portion of her winnings to another person for lawn care services. And the individual who cuts her lawn is better off by accepting payment for mowing the grass.

Suppose that the football coach at a major football-famous university is an excellent typist and can type more words per minute than his administrative assistant. Should the coach type his own letters? No. Economic reasoning suggests that the coach should maintain focus on how to win football games, rather than type letters, even though letters are an important part of the coach's position.

The concept "do what you can do best, and trade for the rest" appears straightforward. However, it can be difficult to apply. Should farm managers cut (harvest) their own wheat or hire custom cutters? Should ranchers hire workers to work cattle, or do the work themselves? Should agribusinesses do their own recordkeeping or hire it done by an accountant? These common questions require answers and explanation.

## 14.3    Gains from trade example: Oklahoma beef and wheat

The best way to understand the source of the gains from trade is to work through a numerical example. Suppose that the year is 1889, and two rugged individuals have made the decision to homestead in the panhandle region of Oklahoma, perhaps near the present town of Goodwell. To make things simple, also assume that (1) there are only two persons living in the county: a farmer (wheat) and a rancher (beef), (2) there are only two goods available: beef and wheat, and (3) both individuals like to eat meat and bread. If the farmer insisted on being self-sufficient, he would only be able to eat bread; if the rancher were self-reliant, she could eat all of the beef that she desired but would be unable to enjoy bread of any type.

If all people were very good at producing one of the two goods, then it would be easy to show that they could make each other better off by specializing in the production of what they do best and trading with the other person. This is simply Adam Smith's idea of doing what you do well (you have an advantage) and trading for other goods. The concept is appealing since humans are born with different abilities and interests. Specialization allows for efficient production, and trade allows for a more diverse and interesting consumption package. Both individuals increase their level of satisfaction through specialization and trade: they produce what they are good at and trade for the other good.

This simple exchange becomes more interesting and more realistic when one of the individuals is better at producing both goods, a situation that is probably

quite common in real life. Suppose the rancher acquires a homestead (usually 160 acres) of productive, high-quality land. This allows her to be more productive at producing both beef and wheat, while the farmer, whose homestead is located on poor-quality land, must continue to produce only a fair, or even poor, wheat crop. Specialization and trade can benefit both parties. Table 14.1 shows the productivity levels of both the farmer and the rancher, assuming that each can work 40 hours a week and can raise beef, wheat, or a combination of both.

Figure 14.1 shows all possible combinations of beef and wheat that the farmer can produce, given the production possibilities shown on the left side of Table 14.1. If the farmer devotes all his effort to beef production, he ends up with two pounds

Table 14.1 **Production possibilities of the farmer and the rancher**

| | Hours needed to make 1 pound of: | | Amount produced in 40 hours (in lb): | |
|---|---|---|---|---|
| | *Beef* | *Wheat* | *Beef* | *Wheat* |
| Farmer | 20 | 10 | 2 | 4 |
| Rancher | 1 | 8 | 40 | 5 |

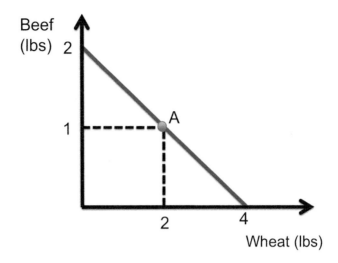

Figure 14.1 Farmer's production possibilities

of beef and no wheat. If the farmer spent all available hours on wheat production, he would produce four pounds of wheat but no beef. If the farmer allocates half his time to the production of each product, 20 hours are spent producing beef, and 20 hours are devoted to wheat production. Point A in Figure 14.1 shows that in this case, the output of beef equals one pound and the output of wheat equals two pounds.

Figure 14.2 is a graph of the rancher's production possibilities. The rancher can produce more of each product since she has resources that are more productive. If

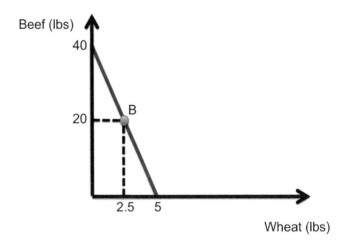

Figure 14.2 Rancher's production possibilities

the rancher divided her time evenly between the two products, she could produce at point B: 20 pounds of meat and 2.5 pounds of wheat. These differences in productivity provide the necessary conditions for both the farmer and the rancher to become better off through specialization and trade.

Eventually, the rancher finds a way to increase the level of consumption of both individuals through trade and without either person having to work any more hours. Her suggestion goes like this:

> The farmer spends 40 hours each week growing wheat (this is what he does best). Specializing in this way the farmer produces four pounds of wheat in a week. The farmer could trade one pound of wheat to the rancher for three pounds of beef in return. This would result in a higher level of consumption for both the farmer and the rancher.

Figure 14.3 shows that with no trade, the farmer is at point A, consuming one pound of beef and two pounds of wheat. If the farmer follows the advice of the rancher, he produces four pounds of wheat, trades one pound of the wheat for three pounds of meat (a trade that both parties favor), and ends at point A*, consuming three pounds of both beef and wheat. The farmer is now in a position to consume more of both goods (Figure 14.3, Table 14.2).

The rancher is also made better off through this trade. The rancher started with no trade and consumed 20 pounds of beef and 2.5 pounds of wheat (point B in Figure 14.4). After trade, she moves her productive activities toward beef (her specialty) by allocating 24 hours a week to cattle and 16 hours per week to wheat. This allocation of her time results in 24 pounds of beef and 2 pounds of wheat. The rancher then trades 3 pounds of beef for 1 pound of wheat (recall the rancher's proposal earlier). Because of the trade, the rancher consumes 21 pounds of beef

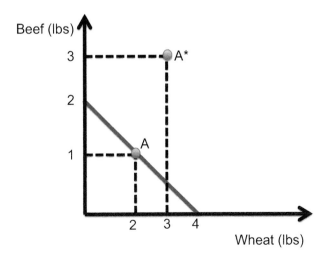

Figure 14.3 Farmer's consumption with trade

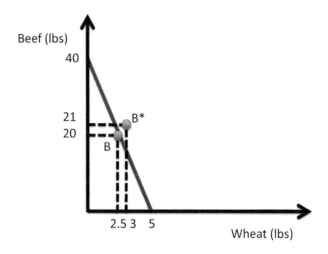

Figure 14.4 Rancher's consumption with trade

Table 14.2 Outcome of specialization and trade for the farmer and the rancher

|  | Before trade | | After trade | | Net gain | |
|---|---|---|---|---|---|---|
|  | Beef | Wheat | Beef | Wheat | Beef | Wheat |
| Farmer | 1 | 2 | 3 | 3 | +2 | +1 |
| Rancher | 20 | 2.5 | 21 | 3 | +1 | +0.5 |

and 3 pounds of wheat (shown at point B* in Figure 14.4 and Table 14.2). The rancher is able to consume more of both products.

What is happening here? By each specializing in what he or she does best, the total production of goods available to the entire Oklahoma Panhandle economy grows and thrives. Although both the farmer and the rancher are better off with trade than without it, trading seems odd because the rancher is actually more productive in the production of both goods. This outcome, making all individuals better off through specialization and trade, holds true in a wide variety of situations and examples. The idea is formalized in the principle of comparative advantage.

## 14.4 The principle of comparative advantage

The key to understanding how interdependence between individuals in an economy, and international trade between nations, can make all trading partners better off is to understand the distinction between **absolute advantage** and **comparative** advantage. These ideas are explained by asking the question from the example in a slightly different way: "Who is better at producing wheat, the farmer or the rancher?" One possible answer is that the rancher is more efficient at producing wheat since it takes her only eight hours of effort to produce one pound of wheat, whereas it takes the farmer ten hours to produce the same amount. Economists use the term "absolute advantage" to compare the productivity of two persons, firms, or nations. Whoever is the more productive (or has the lowest cost of production) has an absolute advantage in the production of a good.

- *Absolute Advantage* = lower costs of production for a specific good or service.

In the farmer/rancher example, the rancher has an absolute advantage in the production of both beef and wheat. Absolute advantage was one of Adam Smith's great insights.

---

### QUICK QUIZ 14.1

Define absolute advantage. Does trade require that each trading partner have a different absolute advantage? Why or why not?

---

### BOX 14.5

## Adam Smith and absolute advantage

Adam Smith (1723–1790), a Scottish philosopher/economist, is considered by many to be the most important economist of all time. In his major work, *An Inquiry into the Nature and Causes of the Wealth of Nations*, Smith explained how rational self-interest in a free market economy could lead to economic well-being. The book, considered the first modern work of economics, promoted free markets, free trade, and a capitalistic form of economic organization. Smith explained, "It is not from the benevolence of the butcher, the brewer, or the baker, that we expect our dinner, but from their regard to their own self-interest. We address ourselves, not to their humanity but to their self-love, and never talk to them of our own necessities but of their advantages."

Absolute advantage is one of the many contributions made in *The Wealth of Nations*. Smith argued that all nations would gain simultaneously if they specialized in accordance to their absolute advantage and then traded with other nations. This was controversial at the time since many nations were exporting goods in order to stockpile gold, a form of commercial economic policy called mercantilism. Even though there are possible economic gains stemming from absolute advantage, the gains are not always beneficial for all parties. David Ricardo (1772–1823) extended Smith's idea of absolute advantage to comparative advantage, the foundation for mutually beneficial exchanges.

The centerpiece of Smith's economic thought is the division of labor. *The Wealth of Nations* describes a pin (nail) factory where ten workers each specialize in different tasks and produce a great number of pins, whereas if each worker performed all of the tasks associated with making a pin, he would produce only a small number of pins. Smith suggested that self-interest was the major motivating force that allocated resources to their highest return. This profit-seeking behavior leads to the equality of returns since all uses of a resource will eventually yield the same rate of return; otherwise, more reallocations of resources will occur.

Smith's work is encyclopedic, but the themes related to self-interest, the division of labor, specialization and trade, and free markets continue to be seminal aspects in modern twenty-first-century economics.

*Source:* The Concise Encyclopedia of Economics. Library of Economics and Liberty. Adam Smith. www.econlib.org/library/Enc/bios/Smith.html. Retrieved January 13, 2023.

The second way to answer the question about who is better at producing wheat is to look at what must be given up to produce one pound of wheat. Using language learned in Chapter 3, what is the **opportunity cost** of a pound of wheat? In the example, each person has 40 hours per week to allocate to the production of beef and wheat. There is a trade-off between producing these two goods since an hour spent producing beef is unavailable for the production of wheat, and vice versa. The opportunity cost to the rancher producing wheat shows the sacrifice of beef required to produce a pound of wheat. Since it takes the rancher one hour to produce one pound of wheat and one hour to produce eight pounds of beef, every hour that the rancher spends producing wheat takes away the possibility of using that hour to produce eight pounds of beef. Put another way, the "cost" to the rancher of producing one pound of wheat is the lost opportunity (or opportunity cost) associated with giving up eight pounds of beef. Figure 14.4 shows this: the slope of the production possibilities line (rise over run) is equal to eight.

For the farmer, the opportunity cost of producing one pound of wheat is equal to how much beef must be given up to produce one pound of wheat. The farmer requires ten hours to produce one pound of wheat. If those 10 hours were spent producing beef, he could produce 0.5 pounds of beef since it requires the farmer 20 hours of time to produce one pound of beef (Table 14.1). The slope of the farmer's production possibilities line in Figure 14.3 shows that the farmer can use some of his resources to produce either one pound of wheat or one-half pound of beef. The slope is equal to 0.5.

The term **comparative advantage** indicates that one firm has different comparative advantages from another. The firm with the smaller opportunity costs has the comparative advantage. The concept of comparative advantage works not only for individuals but also for firms, nations, or blocs of nations such as the EU.

- *Comparative Advantage* = the superior productive capacity of one individual, or nation, or region, or industry, relative to all others, based on opportunity cost.

QUICK QUIZ 14.2

Define comparative advantage. Which is needed for trade: absolute advantage or comparative advantage?

The producer who has the smallest opportunity cost of producing a good has a comparative advantage in the production of a good. In the rancher/farmer example, even though the rancher has an absolute advantage in the production of wheat, the farmer has the comparative advantage. It is not possible for a single person to have a comparative advantage in both goods. Since the farmer has a comparative advantage in producing wheat, the rancher has the comparative advantage in producing beef.

BOX 14.6

## David Ricardo and comparative advantage

David Ricardo was born in London in 1772, the third of 17 children. Ricardo's father was a successful stockbroker of Portuguese origin who had recently moved to England. When Ricardo was 21, he eloped to marry Priscilla Anne Wilkinson. This elopement led to David Ricardo's rejection by his father, and his mother never spoke to him again. David, like his father, became a successful stockbroker.

Interestingly, Ricardo was exposed to economics when, at the age of 27, he read Adam Smith's *Wealth of Nations*. Ricardo maintained his interest in economics and went on to make important contributions to the emerging discipline. He was friends with contemporary economists James Mill, Jeremy Bentham, and Thomas Malthus. Like Smith, Ricardo was a proponent of the free trade of goods between nations, without government intervention. Ricardo opposed England's tariffs on agricultural products (called the Corn Laws). Parliament repealed these tariffs in 1846.

Ricardo's major contribution to economics was the refinement of the theory of comparative advantage, which stated simply that there is a mutual benefit from trade, even if one trading partner is more productive at every activity than the trading partner. The theory was introduced in his book, *Principles of Political Economy*, published in 1817. The basic idea of the theory is that a nation that trades for low cost products is better off than if the nation produced the goods at home. When each nation specializes in the goods that it can produce at lower costs than other nations, all nations can gain from trade. This simple, elegant, and powerful economic model has been used to justify and promote free trade between nations ever since.

*Source:* The Concise Encyclopedia of Economics. Library of Economics and Liberty. David Ricardo. www.econlib.org/library/Enc/bios/Ricardo.html. Retrieved January 13, 2023.

## 14.5  Comparative advantage and trade

Differences in comparative advantage or differences in the opportunity costs between trading partners (individuals, firms, and nations) allow for specialization and eventually lead to gains for all traders. Anytime that one person has opportunity costs that are different from another person's, the total production of the two persons will increase if they each specialize in the production of the product in which they have the comparative advantage. Benefits arise because each person is doing what he does best, followed by trade. As a result, the total production of both products increases, making all trading parties better off.

The benefits of increasing production for two individuals also hold for groups of individuals, and nations. Nations trade in order to take advantage of other nations doing what they do best. They trade to buy goods and services from a less expensive source. A nation produces and exports the goods and services in which it has a comparative advantage. The US exports huge tonnages of agricultural products. The Midwest, for example, sells a majority of its wheat and feed grain production overseas and its exports of beef products expands each year.

### BOX 14.7

### Agricultural productivity growth in Brazil

Brazil is a vast nation, with huge agricultural resources and increasing productivity. Brazilian agriculture is highly diverse, and the nation is self-sufficient in food. Brazil is one of the BRIC (Brazil, Russia, India, and China) nations, characterized by high economic growth that stems partially from rapid growth in agricultural productivity. The agricultural growth has come about by bringing new land into production and improving the productivity of crops and livestock through scientific knowledge.

In the 1970s, Brazil was concerned about future food supplies. The nation made the decision to expand agricultural production though scientific research and free trade. Since then, Brazil has become the first tropical agricultural giant. The other large agricultural exporters are all in temperate climates: the US, Canada, Australia, the EU, and Argentina. In less than 30 years, Brazil transformed itself from a net food importer to one of the world's biggest food exporters. Between 1996 and 2006, the total value of Brazil's crops increased 365 percent, and beef exports in 2006 were ten times higher than they had been a decade earlier. Brazil has a comparative advantage in many agricultural products and is the world's leading exporter of poultry, coffee, orange juice, sugarcane, and ethanol. It is the second largest exporter of soybeans, behind the US.

Brazil has accomplished all of this without the help of large government subsidies. State support accounted for 5.7 percent of total farm income in Brazil during 2005–2007, compared to 12 percent in the US and 29 percent in the EU. The massive growth in agriculture was based on investments in agricultural research. Contemporary research has led to improvements of the soil, which was originally too acidic and of low quality, together with advances in crop and livestock genetics. Genetically modified (GM) soybeans have led increases in soybean production of 10.5 percent each year since 1990. Brazil produced 51 million metric tons of soybeans on 23 million hectares in 2005.

Brazilian farms are many times the size of those found in the US. Critics of the Brazilian agricultural growth have accused Brazil of destroying the Amazonian tropical rainforest to grow food. While some rainforest has been destroyed, most of the new farms are located in the cerrado, or savannah, which are grasslands located some distance from the Amazon. One limitation of Brazilian agriculture is transportation. The fields of Mata Grasso, in the Center-West part of the country, are located a long distance from outdated port facilities. Improvements in both rail transport and ports will allow Brazil to become more competitive with US soybean exports and provides an excellent example of comparative advantage.

*Sources:* "Brazil's Agricultural Miracle: How to Feed the World." *The Economist.* August 26, 2010.

Cremaq, Piaui. "Brazilian Agriculture: The Miracle of the Cerrado." *The Economist.* August 26, 2010.

Table 14.3 Exports and imports of selected nations, 2021

| | Exports (USD bil) | | | | | Imports (USD bil) | | | | |
|---|---|---|---|---|---|---|---|---|---|---|
| | Brazil | China | Niger | Switz | USA | Brazil | China | Niger | Switz | USA |
| Food | 97 | 77 | 0.12 | 10 | 170 | 12 | 206 | 0.89 | 14 | 194 |
| Manufactures | 70 | 3,145 | 0.13 | 268 | 1,079 | 178 | 1,562 | 1.57 | 193 | 2,256 |
| Chemicals | 13 | 264 | 0.004 | 144 | 270 | 64 | 262 | 0.36 | 62 | 329 |
| Machinery | 26 | 1,622 | 0.12 | 44 | 538 | 80 | 1,008 | 0.69 | 58 | 1,167 |
| Textiles | 0.85 | 146 | 0.06 | 1 | 13 | 4 | 16 | 0.05 | 2 | 40 |
| Clothing | 0.17 | 176 | 0 | 3 | 6 | 2 | 12 | 0.01 | 9 | 106 |

Source: WTO Statistics Database. www.stat.wto.org/StatisticalProgram.

Table 14.3 shows the trade activities among five exporting and importing nations. The diversity of trade among them is apparent. The US exports and imports a large amount of food and imports a great deal of clothing. China has truly large exports of manufactured goods and clothing, whereas Brazil is a major net exporter of food. Switzerland imports clothing and other goods and has a large net export of chemicals. Niger has lower trade volumes, with imports greatly exceeding exports in all categories.

Table 14.4 shows the composition of agricultural trade for the same five nations. The US is a net exporter of grains, including wheat and rice, and meat. The US is a net importer of bananas, coffee, and sugar. Brazil has large net exports of coffee and meat but imports a large amount of wheat. China imports more cereals and

Table 14.4 Food exports and imports of selected nations, 2021

| | Exports (USD mil) | | | | | Imports (USD mil) | | | | |
|---|---|---|---|---|---|---|---|---|---|---|
| | Brazil | China | Niger | Switz. | USA | Brazil | China | Niger | Switz. | USA |
| Bananas | 37 | 18 | 0 | 0 | 442 | 0 | 1,040 | 0 | 110 | 2,557 |
| Cereals | 4,546 | 104 | 0 | 1 | 27,002 | 2,843 | 14,719 | 3 | 247 | 1,251 |
| Coffee | 5,805 | 160 | 0 | 3,796 | 1,026 | 4 | 833 | 4 | 1,035 | 7,425 |
| Dairy and Eggs | 101 | 162 | 0 | 904 | 6,485 | 515 | 9,205 | 17 | 716 | 2,741 |
| Meat | 17,448 | 852 | 0 | 7134 | 20,582 | 321 | 28,562 | 7 | 587 | 11,117 |
| Rice | 73 | 95 | 0 | 0 | 511 | 32 | 5 | 0 | 1 | 0 |
| Sugar and Honey | 342 | 1,697 | 0 | 144 | 735 | 33 | 877 | 16 | 263 | 3,235 |
| Wheat | 284 | 2 | 0 | 0 | 7,286 | 1,851 | 3,039 | 0 | 0 | 402 |

Source: FAOSTAT.

dairy products than it exports. Niger has low trade volumes for all food categories. Switzerland is a net meat importer and net tobacco exporter.

These trade volumes in all goods (Table 14.3) and in agricultural goods (Table 14.4) demonstrate that specialization and gains from trade can lead to large volumes of food and goods being produced in one place and consumed in another location. Adam Smith argued, and now most economists agree, that this is perhaps the single most important ingredient to a high standard of living: specialization and gains from trade.

## 14.6   The motivation for and consequences of free trade

Globalization, also called free trade between nations, provides enormous economic benefits to many producers and consumers of trading nations. A great deal of the increase in national incomes that has occurred since 1950 can be attributed to free trade between nations. Interestingly, although free trade provides net benefits to trading nations, not every individual or group will be made better off from trade. There are benefits and costs to trade, as with all decisions, policies, and choices. In this section, the motivation behind trade is identified, as well as the economic consequences of free trade between nations.

One of the major benefits of trade is expanding a nation's consumption possibilities. For example, consumers in the US, China, EU, and Japan can purchase fresh fruit and vegetables in the winter months by importing produce from nations in the Southern Hemisphere, where it is summer. Likewise, nations in temperate climactic zones can purchase tropical products from nations in warmer climates: coffee, cocoa, sugar, orange juice, and pineapple, for example. This expansion of available consumer goods provides one major impetus for trade. A second motivation behind free trade is the principle of comparative advantage. Comparative advantage allows individuals, regions, and nations to specialize in what they do best and trade for other products, expanding the consumption possibilities. Expanded consumption occurs due to the efficient use of resources brought about by specialization and trade. For example, if Canada specializes in wheat production and Costa Rica specializes in banana production, both nations benefit from specialization and trade.

In order to understand the concepts of open and closed economies are defined and explained.

- *Closed Economy* = a nation that does not trade. All goods and services consumed must be produced within the nation.
- *Open Economy* = a nation that allows trade. Imports and exports exist.

In a closed economy with no trade, quantity demanded must equal quantity supplied since the nation must produce everything that is consumed: $Q^s = Q^d$. Trade allows this equality to be broken, allowing for imports ($Q^d > Q^s$) and exports ($Q^s > Q^d$). The concepts of **excess supply** and **excess demand** can be used to further understanding of the motivation and consequences of free trade.

What follows is based on the international trade in cocoa as an example of why and how free trade occurs. Consider a nation such as Brazil that exports cocoa.

The left panel of Figure 14.5 depicts Brazil's cocoa market. At the price $P_e$, domestic consumption equals domestic production in Brazil ($Q^s = Q^d$). **Excess supply (ES)** is equal to zero at $P_e$ since there is no ES (also known as exportable surplus). As cocoa prices increase above $P_e$, there is an increase in quantity supplied, or movement along the supply curve. Producers respond to higher prices by producing more cocoa, following the law of supply.

> ### QUICK QUIZ 14.3
>
> Why is this an increase in quantity supplied and not an increase in supply?

As cocoa prices increase, there is also a decrease in quantity demanded of cocoa, caused by cocoa consumers shifting purchases out of the now relatively higher priced cocoa. This is the law of demand in action: higher relative prices result in smaller purchases, holding all else constant.

At a given, arbitrarily selected, world price ($P_w$), where $P_w > P_e$, quantity supplied ($Q^s$) is larger than quantity demanded ($Q^d$). At prices greater than $P^e$, a surplus, or ES, of cocoa exists in Brazil. In a closed economy, this surplus would bring market forces into play moving the price back to the equilibrium level $P^e$. In an open economy, however, the excess supply of cocoa at the world price $P^w$ (Figure 14.5) could be exported to enhance revenues. Free trade allows Brazil to use its vast resources of land and tropical weather to produce enough cocoa to meet the consumption requirements of its own people and provide an exportable surplus of cocoa to other nations. The ES curve shown in the right panel of Figure 14.5 can now be defined.

- *Excess Supply (ES)* = quantity supplied minus quantity demanded at a given price. $Q^s - Q^d$.

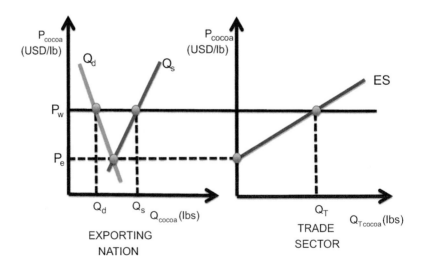

**Figure 14.5** Exporting nation: excess supply

Similarly, an importing nation is characterized by a domestic demand that is larger than domestic supply: $Q^d > Q^s$ (left panel, Figure 14.6). Consider the United Kingdom (UK), a high-income nation in a northern climate. Citizens of the UK enjoy chocolate products, yet cocoa production is relatively expensive in the northern maritime climate. If the UK were a closed economy, the equilibrium price of cocoa would be $P^i$, shown in the left panel of Figure 14.6. Cocoa could be grown in the UK, but at great expense, with high production costs from glasshouse production. At price P, the domestic cocoa market is in equilibrium: $Q^s = Q^d$. At $P^i$, there is no surplus or shortage of cocoa. As the price decreases from $P^i$, the quantity demanded of cocoa increases due to the law of demand, and the quantity supplied of cocoa decreases due to the law of supply.

## QUICK QUIZ 14.4

Are the changes forthcoming from a price change in quantity supplied or changes in supply? Why?

The concept of excess demand (ED) now forms the basis for summarizing a nation's imports.

● **Excess Demand (ED)** = Quantity demanded minus quantity supplied at a given price. $Q^d - Q^s$.

Thus, the ED equals zero at price $P_i$. At price $P_i$ in the right panel of Figure 14.6, the quantity traded ($Q_T$) is equal to the excess demand in the left panel ($Q^d - Q^s$). Note that any change in the domestic supply or domestic demand of cocoa causes

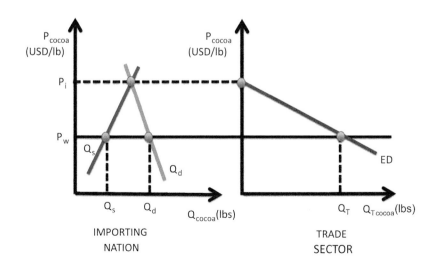

Figure 14.6 Importing nation: excess demand

a shift in the excess demand curve: domestic behaviors and market shifts have global consequences. In what follows, the high-price importing nation (UK) will be linked with the low-price exporting nation (Brazil) to show how trade occurs and the consequences of trade.

## 14.7 Three-panel diagram of international trade

Next, consider the two cocoa trading partners in the same diagram, as shown in Figure 14.7. Here, the nations are linked by international trade, depicted in the middle panel of the figure. The ES curve in the center panel is upward sloping since higher cocoa prices cause increased quantity supplied and decreased quantity demanded in the exporting nation, Brazil. Similarly, ED is downward sloping since lower cocoa prices induce increased quantity demanded and decreased quantity supplied in the importing nation UK. Equilibrium in the global cocoa market is found in the center trade panel of Figure 14.7, where ES = ED. In a multination setting, this equilibrium would occur where the sum of all product supplied is equal to the sum of all individual-nation demands. The quantity traded, $Q_T$, is equal to the level of cocoa imports of the UK, and the total level of cocoa exports from Brazil ($Q_T$ = imports = exports).

The point where exports equals imports is the equilibrium quantity traded ($Q_T$), where ES = ED. This equilibrium in the trade sector determines the world price ($P_w$), or the price of cocoa for both of the trading partners, in this case Brazil and the UK. Figure 14.7 highlights two important points about free trade. First, the motivation for trade is simple: "buy low and sell high." If there is a price difference between two locations, arbitrage provides profit opportunities to traders. A firm that buys at the lower price in Brazil and sells at the higher UK price can earn profits through this act of arbitrage. Second, anything that affects cocoa supply or demand in either nation affects the global price and quantity traded. Thus,

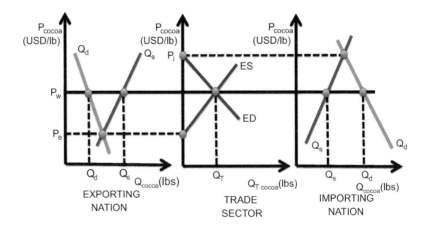

Figure 14.7 The motivation for and consequences of trade: cocoa

all producers and consumers of a good are interconnected in the sense that their welfare is affected by weather, growing conditions, demand, and all other supply and demand determinants in all trading nations. This point cannot be emphasized enough: in a global economy, the well-being of all producers and consumers depends on people, policies, and current events throughout the world. This simple model is useful in understanding the determinants of food and agricultural exports: all of the supply and demand shifters in the exporting nations and the importing nations. This is a truly huge number of things that affect the income levels of all producers in both exporting and importing nations in a global economy.

The consequences of free trade are also captured in Figure 14.7. Both nations have net economic benefits from cocoa trade. However, not all groups are made better off. This outcome demonstrates why free trade agreements continue to be timely, important, and interesting. Nations can gain from trade, but only at the expense of some citizens. In Brazil, the exporting nation, cocoa producers are made much better off by international trade: the cocoa price increases from $P_e$ to $P_w$, and the quantity sold increases. Brazilian consumers are made worse off; however, since they face a higher cocoa price and smaller quantity demanded. Producers in exporting nations will support free trade, whereas consumers in exporting nations lose. Effective policy could use the overall net benefits to compensate the losers, in this case the Brazilian cocoa consumers.

In the importing nation (UK), domestic consumers are able to consume larger quantities of cocoa at lower prices. These benefits are often large for buyers of products that are expensive to produce in the importing nation. In high-income nations, low-cost imports often include clothing, tropical fruit, coffee, electronic products, and many manufactured goods. Opposition to free trade is likely to be concentrated in producer groups in importing nations. These groups will face lower prices due to competition from lower-cost imports. Domestic producers of an imported good will face real economic losses due to free trade. However, the net economic benefits accruing to the importing nation are positive. If the losing producers could be compensated, then free trade could bring positive benefits to all groups in trading nations.

Trade barriers and trade wars such as the tariffs imposed by the US and China during 2018/2019 will reduce or eliminate the gains from trade. In the case of a tariff, the free trade price of cocoa ($P_w$) will no longer hold in both nations. A trade barrier drives a wedge between the cocoa prices ($P_i > P_e$). The difference between the prices will be the magnitude of the tariff: $P_i = P_e +$ tariff.

## BOX 14.8

### Rise of China impact on US food and agriculture

Economic reforms in China have led to unprecedented economic growth, rapid urbanization, and industrialization. Increased income level have led to slower population growth and increased migration to cities. Higher income levels have led to a large increase in food consumption and a dietary shift out of grains such as wheat and rice and into meat, including beef and pork. Increased meat consumption requires large increases in purchases of feed grains such as corn and soybeans, which have been increasing imported.

Policy makers in China seek to reduce imports, to enhance self-sufficiency. In December 2012, General Secretary Xi emphasized food security: "the food of the Chinese people must be made by and remain in the hands of the Chinese. Everyone need to take responsibility for food security." In 2021, China purchased over 50 percent of US soybean exports, and 27 percent of US corn exports. China purchased 20 percent of all agricultural exports from the US. Trade wars reduce US agricultural exports to China and result in lower prices and profits for US grain farms. Since China has become a major customer of US agriculture in recent years, the US will continue to closely monitor China's continued desire to buy food from the US.

China has invested in US farmland and US meatpacking as a strategy to control more of the food supply for Chinese customers. China's rise in global power has created new challenges for relations between the US and China.

*Source:* Zhang, Phoebe. "China's Xi Jinping puts focus back on food security." *South China Morning Post.* December 26, 2021.

## 14.8  Labor immigration into the US from Mexico

To demonstrate the effects of the movement of labor from one nation to another, the three-panel diagram of Section 14.7 can be usefully employed. The graph of agricultural labor migration from Mexico to the US provides a summary of the economic winners and losers. The analysis demonstrates that both Mexico and the US have net gains from labor migration. As in all economic changes, there are winners and losers. Figure 14.8 shows labor movements for the receiving nation (US) in the right panel and the source nation (Mexico) in the left panel. The trade sector is represented in the middle panel.

If the two nations have isolated labor markets, wages in the US ($W_{USA}$) would be higher than wages in Mexico ($W_{MEX}$). This wage differential ($W_{USA} > W_{MEX}$) is the source of arbitrage since workers are motivated to leave Mexican jobs and migrate to the US for higher wages. When the movement of labor is legal and affordable, the number of migrants is shown in the middle panel, equal to $Q_T$ million hours of work. If $Q_T$ hours of work were transferred from Mexico to the US through labor immigration, the wage rates would be equalized at $W^*$ in both nations. Note that this model ignores exchange rates and transportation costs of migration.

The graphical model demonstrated in Figure 14.8 also assumes freedom of movement between the two nations. In agriculture, there is considerable freedom for farm workers to enter the US from Mexico to supply labor to farms. The H-2A Temporary Agricultural Program allows foreign-born workers to legally enter the United States

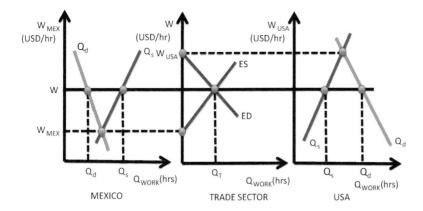

Figure 14.8 Labor migration into the US from Mexico

to perform seasonal farm labor on a temporary basis for up to ten months. The seasonal needs of crop farmers (fruit, vegetables, and grains) can be met with this program, but most livestock producers (ranches, dairies, and hog and poultry operations) are not able to use the program. An exception is made for livestock producers on the range (sheep and goat producers), who can use H-2A workers year-round.

The analysis in Figure 14.8 shows the same results for labor as were obtained for commodities such as wheat in Section 14.7. Winners include consumers (employers) in the importing (receiving) nation and producers (workers) in the exporting (source) nation. In this case, US farmers who employ migrant workers are made better off, but native workers (US workers employed prior to immigration) are made worse off. The gains and losses are due to the decrease in wages from $W_{USA}$ to $W^*$. The movement of workers out of Mexico results in gains for Mexican workers but losses for employers of workers in Mexico. This is due to the wage increase in Mexico from $W_{MEX}$ to $W^*$.

Both origin and receiving nations have net benefits. This result explains why immigration has been a large, significant feature in US history (the US is often referred to as a "nation of immigrants"). The gains and losses in each nation demonstrate why immigration continue to be controversial issue: large economic gains and losses in each nation.

In the long run, the gains to immigration are large for the recipient nation. This is for two reasons: (1) migrant workers are most often complementary to native workers: low-skill immigrants combine with high-skill native workers to enhance productivity for all workers in the receiving nation and (2) increased population generates increased demand for all goods and services in the US, resulting in enhanced economic conditions for all workers in the receiving nation.

## 14.9   Exchange rates and transportation costs

So far, the analysis has ignored transportation costs and international currencies. To incorporate these important features of international trade, consider US grain exports. A large percentage of all grain produced in the US is exported to other nations. Japan is a major importer of US wheat. When a Japanese firm purchases wheat, it must convert Japanese currency (yen) into US dollars (USD) and pay for the cost of transporting the grain from a US port such as Galveston, Texas, or Kalama, Washington, to Japan. These features of international grain purchases are summarized in equation 14.1. Grain is often sold in units of bushels (bu).

14.1   $P_J = a(P_{US} + T)$.

In this equation, a is the exchange rate and equals the number of yen that can be purchased with one US dollar, $P_{US}$ is the price of US wheat (USD/bu), $P_J$ is the price of wheat in Japan, and T is the per-unit transportation costs (USD/bu). The equation can be best understood with an example. Suppose that the price of wheat in the US is equal to 6 USD/bu, and transportation costs (T) are equal to 2 USD/bu. Further assume that 1 USD is equivalent to 100 yen: it requires 100 yen to purchase 1 USD. In this case, a = 100 yen/USD, so that the price of wheat in Japan ($P_J$) is 800 yen. Equation 14.1 is an "arbitrage condition," meaning that if prices differed from 800 yen/bu in Japan or 6 USD/bu in the US, arbitrage would take place until the equilibrium prices were restored.

   Now consider how changes in the exchange rate and transportation costs affect the international wheat market. Transportation costs represent a cost of production and affect the price paid by consumers in a location different from the location of origin. The major determinant of transportation costs is distance between the point of production and the point of sale. In our example of grain trade between the US and Japan, suppose that T increases due to an oil price increase. This fuel cost increase will increase the relative price of US wheat in Japan. This would result in substitution out of US wheat and into wheat produced in other nations. If T increases from 2 USD/bu to 3 USD/bu. Holding all else constant, the increase in transportation costs will raise the price of US wheat in Japan ($P_J$) from 800 yen/bu to 900 yen/bu. Japan will shift some wheat purchases to Australia, if possible, since transportation costs for Australian wheat to Japan are much lower given the much shorter distance between ports.

   Gains in modern technology in transportation and communication have lowered transportation costs dramatically over time, particularly since World War II. This has been one of the major causes behind increased globalization, particularly in food and agriculture.

   Another major determinant of international trade is the exchange rate. An exchange rate is simply the rate of exchange between two different currencies. The value of a currency is determined by the supply and demand of the currency. For example, if foreign consumers desired to make more purchases in the US, they would demand more US dollars to make the purchases possible. This increase in demand for US dollars would drive the value of the US dollar higher. Changes in exchange rates have large consequences for international trade.

   Suppose that the exchange rate between yen and USD increases from 100 yen/USD to 120 yen/USD, assuming that the price of US wheat is 6 USD/bu and transportation costs equal 2 USD/bu. In this case, the price of wheat in Japan would increase from 800 yen/bu to 960 yen/bu. Interestingly, even if the demand for wheat in Japan and the supply of wheat in the US remained stable, international trade in wheat is greatly affected by a change in the value of the currency of either trading partner. It is therefore crucial to understand the causes and consequences of exchange rate fluctuations in a global economy. Exports and imports are sensitive to the value of national currencies.

The arbitrage equation (equation 14.1) suggests that exports will increase when the exchange rate (a) is low. A low exchange rate occurs when the value of the US dollar is "weak," or the purchasing power of the dollar is low. For example, if the exchange rate decreases from 100 yen/USD to 80 yen/USD, then consumers in the US could only receive 80 yen for 1 USD, down from 100 yen per US dollar. The lower value represents a loss in purchasing power of the US dollar.

One major cause of a weak currency is monetary policy. Specifically, when the money supply increases at a rate greater than the rate of growth in money demand, the value of currency is diminished, and purchasing power declines. Therefore, monetary and fiscal policies, described in Chapter 11, have large and significant impacts on agricultural exports and imports. If the money supply (M) is increased, holding all else constant, this results in a decrease in a nation's exchange rate (a). A lower exchange rate causes the prices of the nation's goods to decrease since the value of the trading partner's currency is now higher: in our example, more USD can be obtained for the same level of yen. This makes imported goods more affordable in Japan, and US exports will increase. Likewise, US imports of Japanese goods will decline since the higher exchange rate (lower value of USD) results in higher prices of Japanese goods in the US.

China sets the exchange rate of the Chinese currency, the yuan. By keeping the yuan undervalued (lower than the market rate), China encourages exports and discourages imports. This policy has been a source of controversy in the US and was the major source of the **trade war**. A trade war is situation where one nation retaliates against another by imposing import tariffs or placing other restrictions on the opposing country's imports. These policies can result in retaliation and escalation of trade barriers between the two nations.

In summary, exporters desire weak currencies and expansionary monetary and fiscal policies. Any decrease in the value of the exporting nation's currency will result in higher levels of exports. On the other hand, importers desire strong currencies due to the greater purchasing power associated with higher exchanges rates. Therefore, importers prefer contractionary monetary and fiscal policies, which result in more purchasing power for foreign goods.

## 14.10 Chapter 14 Summary

1 Absolute advantage is a situation where one nation has lower costs of production for a specific good or service.
2 Comparative advantage is the superior productive capacity of one nation or region or industry relative to others, based on opportunity cost.

3  Differences in comparative advantage or differences in the opportunity costs between individuals, firms, and nations allow for specialization and gains from trade.

4  Diversity in resources leads to large gains in trade. Differences between regions and nations lead to economic benefits through specialization and trade.

5  Globalization has led to large increases in national incomes since 1950.

6  There are benefits and costs to trade. The overall benefits are greater than the overall costs: the net benefits are positive.

7  The benefits to trade include expanding a nation's consumption possibilities.

8  A closed economy is a nation that does not trade. An open economy is a nation that allows imports and exports.

9  Trade of one good between two nations can be summarized and understood using a three-panel diagram of trade.

10  Opposition to free trade is concentrated in producer groups in importing nations, who face lower prices due to trade.

11  Changes in the exchange rate and transportation costs have major effects on international trade.

## 14.11   Chapter 14 Glossary

**Absolute Advantage**—Lower costs of production for a specific good or service.

**Closed Economy**—A nation that does not trade. All goods and services consumed must be produced within the nation.

**Comparative Advantage**—The superior productive capacity of one individual, or nation, or region, or industry, relative to all others, based on opportunity cost.

**Excess Demand (ED)**—Quantity demanded minus quantity supplied at a given price. $Q^d - Q^s$.

**Excess Supply (ES)**—Quantity supplied minus quantity demanded at a given price. $Q^s - Q^d$.

**Import Quota**—A trade restriction that sets a physical limit on the quantity of a good that can be imported during a given time period.

**Open Economy**—A nation that allows trade. Imports and exports exist.

**Opportunity Cost**—The value of a resource in its next-best use. What an individual or firm must give up to do something.

**Tariff**—A tax on imports of a good.

**Trade Barriers**—Laws and regulations to restrict the flow of goods and services across international borders, including tariffs, duties, quotas, and import and export subsidies.

**Trade War**—A situation where one nation retaliates against another by imposing import tariffs or placing other restrictions on the opposing country's imports. These policies can result in retaliation and escalation of trade barriers between the two nations.

## 14.12   Chapter 14 Review questions

1  The nation with the lowest cost of production has a(n)

   a   comparative advantage
   b   absolute advantage
   c   unfair advantage
   d   competitive advantage

2  The nation with the lowest opportunity costs of producing a good has a(n)

   a   comparative advantage
   b   absolute advantage
   c   unfair advantage
   d   competitive advantage
   e   a shortage of Swiss Army knives

3  Trade will most likely take place between two nations that are

   a   very different
   b   much the same
   c   in close proximity to each other
   d   have similar access to resources

4  Globalization results in

   a   increases in overall income
   b   decreases in overall income
   c   damage to international relations between nations
   d   higher prices for all goods in trading nations

5  The benefits of trade include

   a   lower prices for producers in importing nations
   b   expanding production of all goods in all nations
   c   expanding the consumption possibilities of trading nations
   d   higher prices for consumers in nations

6  A closed economy is

   a   better off due to specialization
   b   better off since it is self-sufficient
   c   a goal that all nations aspire to
   d   worse off than an open economy

7  Excess supply is

   a   demand minus supply
   b   supply minus demand
   c   supply plus demand
   d   a surplus of goods that must be consumed

8  Excess demand is

   a   demand minus supply
   b   supply minus demand
   c   supply plus demand
   d   a surplus of goods that must be consumed

9  An increase in the exchange rate is

   a   good for exporting producers
   b   bad for exporting producers
   c   bad for importing producers
   d   good for importing consumers

10  An increase in transportation costs between nations is:

   a   good for exporting producers
   b   bad for exporting producers
   c   bad for importing producers
   d   good for importing consumers

**Answers:** 1. b, 2. a, 3. a, 4. a, 5. c, 6. d, 7. b, 8. a, 9. b, 10. b

For more study questions, flash cards, and study guides, see the online materials at the companion website: www.routledge.com/cw/barkley.

# Economics, agriculture, and the environment

**Photo 15.1** Economics, agriculture, and the environment

*Source:* B Brown/Shutterstock

DOI: 10.4324/9781003367994-15

## Abstract

Natural resources and environmental quality are increasingly important aspects of the US economy. This is particularly true in the agricultural industry, which is heavily dependent on land, agrochemicals, and water. This chapter explores how rational actors can overuse, or exploit, resources such as cropland, water from an underground aquifer, or grazing land. Externalities such as air and water pollution from agricultural production and processing can result in suboptimal or harmful outcomes for society. Possible solutions to externality problems include bans, taxes, quantitative standards, and subsidies. Under certain circumstances, private bargaining can also lead to efficient environmental outcomes.

### Chapter 15 Questions

1   Why are natural resources and the environment increasingly important in food and agriculture?
2   Why do rational people exploit resources such as land and water through too much use?
3   What are externalities, and how are they used to help understand air and water pollution in agriculture?
4   What are solutions to pollution, and what is the optimal role of the government in solving pollution?
5   How can bans, taxes, quantitative standards, and subsidies be used to help solve pollution issues in agriculture?

## 15.0   Introduction

The impact of agricultural production and processing on the natural environment has become increasingly important over the past several decades. Modern agriculture is characterized by the increased use of inputs such as agrochemicals and fertilizer, which can influence both the environment and human health. The rapid industrialization of economic activity in the eighteenth and nineteenth centuries led to greater levels of air and water pollution, which, in turn, led to increased concern for the environment. The desire for improved environmental quality is partially the outcome of the large increase in national incomes since about 1950. At that time, the populations of North America, Western Europe, Japan, Australia, and some other areas became wealthy enough to meet the basic needs for food, clothing, and housing. As these needs were met, some resources and income shifted to uses related to providing clean air, clean water, and safe food. Given the current high, and generally increasing, levels of economic growth, the environmental issues have taken on increasing importance, and a growing fraction of societal income has been devoted to goals related to the environment. As low-income nations grow and prosper, they, too, have become more interested in environmental goals. A clean environment, food safety, human health, and animal welfare are luxury goods, with Engel curves that appear to increase at an increasing rate.

## QUICK QUIZ 15.1

Define and explain the terms "luxury good" and "Engel curve" (Chapter 9). Explain why environmental goals are considered a "luxury good."

The modern environmental movement began in 1962 with the publication of Rachel Carson's book, *Silent Spring*. Carson highlighted the potential problems associated with the use of chemical pesticides in agricultural production. The book received a large amount of attention and was championed, as well as heavily criticized. Carson notified the public of the potential dangers of DDT (dichloro-diphenyl-trichloroethane) and other chemicals used in agriculture, leading to a growing concern for the environment. This widely read book led to political action and legislation.

In 1968, Garrett Hardin, a professor of human ecology at the University of California–Santa Barbara, wrote "The Tragedy of the Commons," an article published in *Science* magazine. Hardin illuminated the failure of market economies to solve a common situation of shared, or commonly owned, resources. Hardin's classic publication resulted in a greater understanding of and concern for environmental resources.

Earth Day gave impetus to the growing number of individuals and groups who supported and promoted environmental goals. Prompted by environmentalists, Senator Gaylord Nelson (D-WI) led the effort to pass legislation for the creation of Earth Day, held on April 22, 1970. The initial efforts of Carson, Hardin, and Nelson led to the formation of the United States Environmental Protection Agency (USEPA), proposed by President Richard M. Nixon in 1970. Since that time, the concern for the environment has grown, and the "green movement" seems likely to have an increasing impact on the agriculture and food industries.

Two major possibilities, the **tragedy of the commons** and **externalities**, lead to important and controversial issues in the area of agriculture and the environment. The "tragedy of the commons" occurs when a publicly owned resource is overused or exploited because no one person or institution has exclusive private rights to use the resource. An "externality" is a situation where the production or consumption of a good results in positive or negative impacts to individuals or groups external to the market. Air pollution is a common example. The local coal-fired power generating plant emits large clouds of sulfur dioxide (sulfuric acid). Its nearby neighbors must inhale the pollution, but they have no voice in the production of the pollution, or the manufacture of electricity, or the mining of the coal. The air pollution is "external" to the economic processes that create it. Other common examples include noise, odors, congestion, and creating reservoirs that flood productive land.

## Climate change

Climate change and global warming are related to the level of greenhouse gases (GHG) there are in the atmosphere. Greenhouse gases occur naturally and are essential to the survival of humans and millions of other living things. The concentration of GHGs has been rising steadily, and mean global temperatures along with it, since the time of the Industrial Revolution. The most abundant GHG, accounting for about two-thirds of GHGs, carbon dioxide ($CO_2$), is largely the product of burning fossil fuels (United Nations 2017).

Natural disasters have become more prevalent in the past 30 years (FAO 2017). Global warming and an increase in the volatility of rainfall and temperatures have resulted in less stable weather conditions, leading to drought in some locations and flooding in others. El Niño caused conditions of severe food insecurity in 2016 for 20 million people (FAO et al. 2018). More powerful hurricanes and cyclones have resulted in greater damage to food production and other economic activity, particularly in nations of the Caribbean and Asia. Drought in Africa has also led to crises in food production, economic activity, and hunger.

Climate change can also have an impact on disease, particularly those carried by mosquitos and fleas. These insects thrive in warm, humid environments (FAO 2017). Disease caused by these insects can prolong the cycle of malnutrition. It is easy to see why climate change is considered to be the defining issue of our time.

*Sources:* United Nations Food and Agricultural Organization (FAO). "The Future of Food and Agriculture: Trends and Challenge." Rome, 2017. www.fao.org/publications/fofa. Retrieved January 16, 2023.

United Nations Food and Agricultural Organization (FAO), World Food Programme, and European Union. "Global Report of Food Crises 2018." www.wfp.org/publications/global-report-food-crises-2018. Retrieved January 16, 2023.

United Nations. Climate Change. www.un.org/en/climatechange. Retrieved January 16, 2023.

## 15.1 The tragedy of the commons

Huge tracts of open land in the American West are owned by the federal government. Much of this land is dry grassland, best used for grazing sheep or cattle. Other parts of the land area throughout the West are privately owned. A Nevada rancher who owns her own grazing land will behave as a profit-maximizing firm that finds the optimal level of input, in this case grassland, as discussed in Chapter 4. The rancher will continue to add cattle to the land until the additional benefit (marginal revenue product, MRP) is equal to the additional cost (marginal factor cost, MFC).

### QUICK QUIZ 15.2

Define the terms "marginal revenue product" and "marginal factor cost." What are these two terms used for? (Hint: recall Chapter 4.)

On the publicly owned land, however, a cattle rancher typically pays fees for a permit to graze cattle on a well-defined part of the range. To acquire a greater understanding of the tragedy of the commons, consider the case when a cattle rancher does not bear any costs for grazing the cattle. Assume that grazing on public land (the "commons") is free and can be used simultaneously by many ranchers.

If all ranchers desire to use the public land for grazing, they will continue to add animals to the land until the additional benefit (MRP) is equal to the additional cost, in this case zero (MFC = 0), as seen in Figure 15.1. This can lead to the tragedy of the commons, or in this case, overgrazing, where the resource is depleted beyond beneficial use by ranching. In Figure 15.1, $Q_0$ acres of land would be used if there were no costs associated with land use, and $Q^*$ is the profit-maximizing, efficient rate of use. In the long run, $Q_0$ acres will result in depleted resource stocks since the land would be overgrazed. Resource depletion would shift the MRP curve down and to the left over time as overgrazed grass is not sustainable.

● *Tragedy of the Commons* = a situation where a group of rational individuals, acting in their own self-interest, depletes a shared limited resource, resulting in destruction of the resource and a negative outcome for all parties.

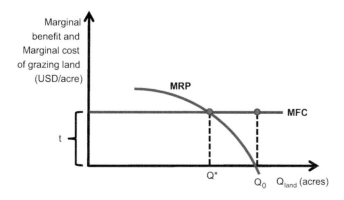

Figure 15.1 The tragedy of the commons: cattle grazing on public land

The tragedy of the commons is often described in terms of grazing and overgrazing publicly owned ranch land. However, the effect applies to all commonly owned or shared resources, including such things as public parks of all sizes, swimming pools, and fishing streams. The outcome of the tragedy of the commons seems irrational. After all, the story of the tragedy of the commons asserts that rational, profit-maximizing individuals will use a resource beyond its optimal, sustainable use. The reason is that there are no costs (or very low costs) associated with using the land, so ranchers continue to use the land past the point of sustainability, to exploitation, or overuse. This outcome is typical of public land use for grazing animals, hunting, fishing, and camping. Use of water from an underground aquifer and deforestation can also result in a similar kind of tragedy.

There are several possible solutions to tragedy of this kind. The land can be privatized (sold or gifted) to individuals for private use. Use can be regulated and held at lower levels, or the government can charge the users (for example, cattle owners) a fee for the use of the resource (in this case, grazing land). If a permit is sold for the right to use the resource, the rate of use can be brought back in line with a sustainable rate of resource use (Q*), as in Figure 15.1. The user fee (t) could be set equal to MFC, which would result in the optimal, sustainable level of resource use, Q*. This analysis explains why the federal government uses permits and user fees for cattle grazing on public lands in the American West. Without these fees, the land would be overgrazed. Figure 15.1 shows this and is similar to the tax placed on atrazine in the example from Chapter 4.

---

### BOX 15.2

## Carbon sequestration

Carbon sequestration is the process of capturing carbon dioxide from the atmosphere and storing it in the soil. Carbon dioxide is naturally captured from the air through biological, chemical, and physical processes. Carbon sequestration is importantly related to global warming since it reduces the amount of carbon dioxide in the atmosphere, which can mitigate or deter global warming. It has been proposed as a strategy to slow the accumulation of greenhouse gases, which are released when fossil fuels are burned.

Agriculture is an important source of carbon sequestration since soils hold a large amount of carbon. Carbon emissions from agriculture can be reduced by increasing yields and efficiency and applying fertilizer more accurately. Reduced-till and no-till practices use less fuel per acre. However, reduced tillage is often accompanied by greater use of weed-control chemicals, which could increase the release of carbon to the atmosphere.

Carbon removal in agriculture can be enhanced by selecting farming methods that return biomass to the soil, by using cover crops, concentrating livestock grazing in small pens, and restoring degraded land. Although there are environmental benefits to agricultural sequestration of carbon, farmers may be reluctant to adopt more expensive agricultural practices without a financial benefit or incentive. The governments of Australia and New Zealand are considering a program that would allow farmers to sell carbon credits in the attempt to lower carbon emissions.

*Sources:* "FACTBOX: Carbon farming on rise in Australia." Reuters. June 16, 2009. www.reuters.com/article/us-australia-soilcarbon-factbox-sb/factbox-carbon-farming-on-rise-in-australia-idUSTRE55G01B20090617. Retrieved January 16, 2023.

Poeplau, C., and A. Don. "Carbon sequestration in agricultural soils via cultivation of cover crops—A meta-analysis." *Agriculture, Ecosystems & Environment* 200 (2015): 33–41.

## 15.2   Externality

Both the buyer and the seller benefit in a market transaction. Otherwise, the exchange would not take place. The buyer considers the good to have value greater than the price, and the seller believes that the price is greater than the value of the good, resulting in a mutually beneficial exchange. Sometimes, the production and sale of a good affects a third party. A farm that uses fertilizer and chemicals to maximize crop yields may create multiple effects on many people. If the fertilizer and chemicals seep into the water supply, the chemicals could affect the health and happiness of someone living downstream. Similarly, a feedlot of cattle could result in offensive odors and a polluted water supply. When this happens, a downstream third party is said to be subject to an **externality,** or an economic loss suffered by someone who had no voice in the market transaction. Externalities can also be positive, such as the smell of chocolate from a candy store, or a beautiful view of a verdant farming area.

● *Externality* = a consequence of an economic activity that affects unrelated third parties. The externality can be either positive or negative. Thus, an externality is a transaction spillover that creates a cost or a benefit not transmitted through market prices.

The economic analysis of an externality is similar to that of the tragedy of the commons. The key to both situations is the costs that are not included in the market decisions or transactions. Figure 15.2 shows that producers consider their private costs of producing a good ($MC_{private}$), but not the additional, public costs of an externality like water pollution ($MC^* = MC_{private} +$ external costs). If the negative externality is not included in the production and consumption decisions, the privately produced quantity ($Q_{private}$) will result in price $P_{private}$.

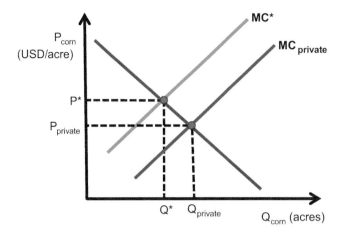

Figure 15.2 Externality: chemical runoff in corn production

Photo 15.2 Corn

*Source:* Fotokostic/Shutterstock

This level ($Q_{private}$) is considered to be "too high" relative to society's best interests, which include both the private and external (public) costs of producing corn. When the external costs are considered, or "internalized," the equilibrium quantity decreases to $Q^*$, and the price of corn increases to $P^*$. The equilibrium that incorporates the externality is considered to be "optimal" for society since it includes the costs of the negative externality (in this case, water pollution). In agriculture, negative externalities occur in chemical runoff from fields, animal waste, odor, noise, soil conservation, climate change, endangered species, deforestation, and water use for irrigating crops.

- **Negative Externality** = a situation where the market price does not include the full cost of producing or consuming a good or service.

A negative externality occurs when a firm emits pollutants into the air or water and creates a cost that is not included in the firm's costs of production. Positive externalities also occur in agriculture when tourists or travelers receive pleasure, or benefits, from viewing agricultural fields and activities. Since the travelers pay no cost for the view, private costs are larger than the societal costs and no monetary benefits include the value of the externality. The societal MC curve is to the right of the private MC curve, and the optimal equilibrium quantity would be larger than $Q_{private}$, indicating a larger level of corn production than would occur if no positive externality were present. Another example of a positive externality is the increased productivity of a fruit orchard that arises from a colony of bees that pollinate the fruit. The bees cost nothing but bring significant increases in production.

- **Positive Externality** = a situation where the market price does not include the full benefit of producing or consuming a good or service.

Honeybees provide an example of a positive externality. Although many insects and birds help in the pollination of tree fruits (apples, peaches, almonds, etc.), common honeybees are likely the most efficient at performing this task. A beekeeper (Farmer A) makes her living by maintaining many, sometimes hundreds, of hives, or colonies, of bees. Her annual income comes from selling honey and beeswax. More importantly, she earns income by renting the hives to orchardists (Farmers B), who need the bees to pollinate their fruit trees but who do not typically own their own bee colonies. During the pollination season the hives are transported from Farmer A's farm to Farmer B's farm to do their work.

The bees move from flower to flower and from tree to tree carrying the pollen needed for the fruit to form and mature. However, the bees don't recognize property lines and will stray to Farmer C's orchard, which adjoins Farmer B's property. The bees carry pollen between the two orchards pollinizing all the trees regardless of ownership. In many, perhaps most cases, Farmer C does not share in paying the rent for the bees even though his trees receive the essential benefit that the bees provide. The bees are performing an act that is external to the (monetary) transaction between A and B. Farmer C is getting the service for nothing. This service is called a "positive externality." Such externalities occur in many situations in agriculture.

A similar positive externality occurs in urban areas where home maintenance affects the property value of neighboring homes. Similarly, a nation that desires high levels of food security could value higher levels of domestic food production than would occur from market forces alone. In such cases, consumers and taxpayers might be willing to subsidize food production in order to provide stronger probabilities of having an adequate food supply during an emergency or war. The positive externality argument often justifies continued levels of government subsidies to agricultural producers in the US and Europe.

QUICK QUIZ 15.3

Is living on a farm in a remote rural area a positive externality? How about living in New York City? Explain carefully.

An externality can be "internalized," or included in the market equilibrium, via three mechanisms: (1) a tax, (2) government regulation such as quantitative restrictions, or (3) private bargaining between affected parties. First, consider the tax. A tax used to internalize an externality is called a **Pigouvian tax**, named for British economist Alfred C. Pigou (1877–1959), who studied the possibility of using such taxes as early as 1932. If a tax equal to the cost of a negative externality is levied on the person or firm that creates the externality, the socially optimal equilibrium will result. This solution justifies taxes on goods that may be considered "overconsumed" compared to goods produced (sold) at their socially optimal levels: agrochemicals such as pesticides and herbicides, grazing cattle, fertilizer, or water use from an aquifer. A Pigouvian tax can reduce use of such goods by making them more expensive.

- *Pigouvian Tax* = a tax levied on firms that pollute the environment or create other negative externalities during the production of goods and services.

The imposition of a tax has limitations. It may be difficult to measure the level of externality, or to know the appropriate tax level to charge to achieve a desired outcome. Perhaps the biggest drawback to Pigouvian taxes is the measurement issue associated with externalities, including (1) identification of the externality's source; (2) physical measurement of the externality source, such as the presence of a pollutant, which differs across time and space; (3) economic damage caused by the externality, which can be highly variable; and (4) societal preferences for nonmarket goods such as clean air, clean water, or human health. The measurement problem makes policy decisions related to resources and the environment challenging. To complicate the decision further, many environmental policies are interconnected and have unanticipated consequences that fall on other environmental goals and resources. However, externalities call for policies even if inexact, because of the potentially large negative external consequences associated with agricultural production: soil erosion, water quality, future water availability, human health problems, and others.

Regulation is a second option for dealing with externality problems. If the government or other authority could set a quantitative limit equal to $Q^*$ in Figure 15.2, the socially desirable level of output could be reached, and the externality effectively internalized. This strategy also faces difficulties in measurement, and can be more difficult to enforce due to measurement and enforcement issues.

## BOX 15.3

### Water in agriculture

Agriculture is the largest consumer of water. Over the past 50 years, agricultural water use has tripled, and by 2050 global water demand for agriculture is estimated to increase by 19 percent for additional irrigation. Approximately 40 percent of the world's food supply is produced under irrigation (Aquastat 2019), and 69 percent of freshwater withdrawals are for agriculture (Schlosser et al. 2014).

Food production was enhanced greatly during the period 1960–1990 through huge irrigation projects, particularly in South Asia. In many dry areas of the world, agriculture competes with human uses of water. Climate change is predicted to bring about increased volatility in precipitation and thus more unpredictable water availability. The combination of population expansion, economic growth, and climate change are expected to result in about half of the world's population under water pressure (WHO 2018). According to the OECD, global demand is projected to increase by 55 percent due to increase in water demand from manufacturing, thermal power plants, and domestic use (OECD 2012). These competing demands will make water more expansive for many of the world's farmers.

Agriculture faces two major water challenges: reducing the negative impact on freshwater resources and increasing water risks resulting from water scarcity, water overabundance, and water quality degradation. These challenges will worsen without effective design and implementation of water and agriculture policies.

Policy solutions need to address water prices, which are below prices charged to other sectors in many nations. Policies also need to address water pollution resulting from agriculture nutrient and pesticide runoffs in many OECD countries (Gruere et al. 2018).

*Sources:* Aquastat 2019. www.fao.org/aquastat/en/. Retrieved January 16, 2023.

Gruère, G., C. Ashley and J. Cadilhon (2018), "Reforming water policies in agriculture: Lessons from past reforms," OECD Food, Agriculture and Fisheries Papers, No. 113, OECD Publishing, Paris, https://doi.org/10.1787/1826beee-en. Retrieved January 16, 2023

Organization for Economic Co-Operation and Development (OECD). The OECD Environmental Outlook to 2050 (OECD, 2012) www.oecd.org/environment/indicators-modelling-outlooks/49846090.pdf. Retrieved January 16, 2023.

Schlosser, C.A., K.M. Strzepek, X. Gao, A. Gueneau, C. Fant, S. Paltsev, B. Rasheed, T. Smith-Greico, É. Blanc, H.D. Jacoby and J.M. Reilly, (2014). The Future of Global Water Stress: An Integrated Assessment. Joint Program Report Series Report 254, 30 p. (http://globalchange.mit.edu/publication/16014) Retrieved January 16, 2023

World Health Organization (WHO). Drinking Water. Key Facts. February 2018. www.who.int/news-room/fact-sheets/detail/drinking-water. Retrieved January 16, 2023.

## 15.3  Private bargaining: Coase

A third solution was suggested by Nobel Prize–winning economist Ronald Coase (1910–2013) in 1960. Coase suggested that there may be no need for a tax or regulation to internalize an externality. Instead, Coase suggested that the affected parties could voluntarily negotiate a solution. The party that is negatively affected has an incentive to bargain with the party creating the externality. If a business firm or household downstream from a cornfield is harmed by chemical runoff, the affected party could offer a payment to the corn farmer to reduce chemical use. The affected party is willing to pay up to the total cost of the externality, and the externality producer will accept a payment as long as it is greater than the economic benefit gained from chemical use.

● *Coasian Bargaining* = when an externality affects a third party, the affected parties have an incentive to bargain with each other to reach an efficient outcome.

**Coasian bargaining** between affected parties is a popular solution among economists since each party is allowed to bargain voluntarily until the optimal solution is reached. Suppose that a cotton producer (denoted by i) uses chemicals to control pests. The producer uses a herbicide to control weeds. These chemicals provide increased productivity to the cotton producer in the form of increased cotton yields per acre, but their use imposes costs on a nearby horticultural nursery (j), which grows plants, shrubs, and trees for sale to suburban homeowners. The benefits to the cotton producer are the marginal revenue product ($MRP_i$), introduced in Chapter 4 and shown in Figure 15.3. Agrochemical use in cotton production is subject to diminishing returns: the first gallon of chemical applied is the most productive (most effective at killing weeds), and each successive gallon of chemical applied is less effective and provides lower additional revenue. At $Q_0$ gallons, all of the productivity gains (and therefore monetary gains) are exhausted. So far, the story is identical to the profit-maximizing solutions explored in Chapter 4.

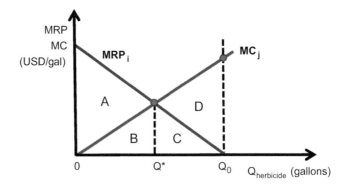

**Figure 15.3  Coase solution: herbicide drift in cotton production**

Now consider the addition of the second party (j). The horticultural producer adjacent to the cotton fields makes this story an interesting and real-world resource issue. Chemical "drift" occurs when the herbicides are applied. In this case, the unintentional herbicide drift damages the flowers, shrubs, and trees that are the source of revenue for the nursery. As chemical use is increased, the damage to the horticultural crops is assumed to increase at an increasing rate: higher levels of herbicide result in proportionally larger plant damage to the nursery plants. The $MC_j$ curve in Figure 15.3 captures the damage done to the horticultural producer j.

The externality occurs because the cotton producer desires to use $Q_0$ gallons of herbicide to maximize profits, whereas the nursery owner desires zero gallons of chemical use in order to escape the damage caused by drift. The outcome will depend on who has the legal rights to use the chemical. If the cotton producer owns the right to apply chemicals, $Q_0$ will result; whereas if the nursery has the legal right to limit pesticides, zero chemical use will result. Coase suggested that if the costs of negotiation are low, then the optimal use of chemicals will result, regardless of which party owns the property rights. This claim is often difficult to believe, but the analysis presented in the following paragraphs shows how private bargaining results in the optimal outcome ($Q^*$) in either case. The optimal outcome is "best" since it considers all benefits and costs to all affected parties. The Coasian solution internalizes the externality, without the use of government intervention in the form of a tax, subsidy, or quantitative restriction.

Photo 15.3 Agricultural chemical application

*Source:* Federico Rostangno/Shutterstock

Suppose that the cotton producer owns the right to use chemicals and applies $Q_0$ gallons of herbicide. This will cost the nursery BCD dollars since the total costs of damage are equal to the additional costs ($MC_j$) times the quantity used (Q), or the area under the MC curve. To reduce the quantity of chemical used to $Q^*$, the nursery would be willing to pay any amount up to CD dollars (the total value of economic damage from using $Q_0 - Q^*$ gallons of chemical), and the cotton producer would be willing to accept any payment above C dollars (the economic gains from using $Q_0 - Q^*$ gallons of chemical). At $Q^*$, the nursery owner's willingness to pay ($MC_j$) is equal to the cotton producer's willingness to accept the payment to reduce chemical use ($MRP_j$). Thus, the equilibrium quantity of chemical applied to the cotton is $Q^*$.

If the nursery owns the right to chemical use and can legally halt all chemical use by the cotton producer, the initial value of chemical use is zero. However, if the cotton producer can negotiate with the nursery owner, she will be willing to pay up to AB dollars (the economic benefit of chemical use for $Q^*$ gallons), and the nursery owner will accept any dollar amount above B dollars (the amount of economic damage caused by $Q^*$ gallons of chemical use). In this case, the equilibrium quantity of chemical use is also $Q^*$ gallons. This is truly an unexpected result: private bargaining will result in the optimal use of chemical ($Q^*$), regardless of who owns the right to use or prevent the use of the chemical.

Coase's contribution suggests that in many externality cases, there is no need for government regulation or market intervention. In particular, if the costs of negotiating are low, the best solution to many externality problems may be to let the affected parties negotiate a solution. According to the analysis described here, this will result in the socially optimal level of resource use.

It is important to note that the optimal level of chemical use is greater than zero, a result that many dedicated environmentalists will not accept. Some individuals and groups call for zero use of agrochemicals, fertilizer, and other agricultural inputs that frequently have environmental consequences. This extreme and often-rigid position ignores the societal benefits from more efficient food production and often lower food and fiber costs.

Negotiation is often expensive enough to eliminate the possibility of a Coasian bargaining solution. In agricultural resource issues, the costs of negotiation are often high due to the large number of affected parties and measures of benefits and costs that are difficult to obtain. If many individuals are negatively affected by use of agricultural chemicals and fertilizer, they may not be able to negotiate effectively with a group of agricultural producers. Getting all of the affected parties to work together could increase the costs associated with this type of negotiation. In such cases, there may be a role for government regulation of resources used in agriculture or a government-assigned negotiator to assist in the process. In reality, agriculture is heavily regulated by the government: input bans, quantitative restrictions, taxes, and subsidies are pervasive in agriculture. This type of regulation reflects the high costs of developing and enforcing agreements between affecting and affected parties. Similarly, government regulation is not costless, and policy analysis often overlooks these costs.

The agricultural sector relies more heavily on land, pesticides, and water than other sectors of the economy. As such, the application of economic principles to resource use in agriculture is timely, important, and interesting. As society meets the basic needs for food, clothing, and housing, the general population will increasingly demand higher environmental quality, higher levels of human health, and greater food safety. Although this chapter has merely introduced the economic problems associated with resources and the environment, society can expect to see an increasing fraction of its wealth devoted to higher quality food, resources, and environmental goals.

## 15.4   Chapter 15 Summary

1   As nations grow wealthier, more income is spent on achieving higher goals, including clear air, clean water, and food safety.
2   A tragedy of the commons can result when groups of individuals, acting rationally and in their own self-interest, deplete a limited resource, resulting in a negative outcome for all parties.
3   The production and sale of a good can result in an externality that positively or negatively affects third parties. Externalities reflect a spillover of a transaction not incorporated into the market price.
4   If agricultural production results in external or public costs, such as air or water pollution, deforestation, or global warming, then the market-based level of agricultural output may exceed the socially optimal level.
5   One solution to an externality is a Pigouvian tax, equal to the public costs of the activity. The socially optimal level of output results if the tax is set equal to the public costs.
6   Coasian bargaining provides a potential solution to an externality, when the affected party and the individual or firm creating the externality bargain until a solution is reached. This form of voluntary bargaining can result in the socially optimal level of resource use if negotiation costs are low.
7   Successful bargaining requires accurate knowledge of the costs and benefits associated with the externality and its resolution. The negotiating can be quite expensive.

## 15.5   Chapter 15 Glossary

**Coasian Bargaining**—When an externality affects a third party, the affected parties have an incentive to bargain with each other to reach an efficient outcome.
**Externality**—A consequence of an activity that affects unrelated third parties. The externality can be either positive or negative. Thus, an externality is a transaction spillover that creates a cost or a benefit not transmitted through market prices.
**Negative Externality**—A situation where the market price does not include the full cost of producing or consuming a good or service.
**Pigouvian Tax**—A tax levied on firms that pollute the environment or create other negative effects during the production of goods and services.
**Positive Externality**—A situation where the market price does not include the full benefit of producing or consuming a good or service.
**Tragedy of the Commons**—A situation where a group of rational individuals, acting in their own self-interest, depletes a shared limited resource, resulting in a negative outcome for all parties.

## 15.6   Chapter 15 Review questions

1   As societal incomes grow, we expect that the largest increase in spending will be on

a   food
b   housing
c   health and environment
d   clothing

2   A tragedy of the commons results when

a   individuals are irrational
b   the costs of using a resource are not charged to the user
c   transactions costs are high
d   property rights are well specified and assigned

3   A Pigouvian tax resolves an externality if it is set equal to

a   the cost of enforcing a quantitative restriction
b   marginal private costs of the activity
c   marginal social costs of the activity
d   transactions costs

4   Coasian bargaining does not work well when there are

a   high transactions costs
b   low transactions costs
c   property rights assigned to the affected party
d   property rights assigned to the creator of the externality

5   Agriculture in high-income nations such as the US and EU is

a   mostly subject to Coasian bargaining

b   subject to the law of nature, but not the law of government regulation
c   heavily regulated
d   not a generator of externalities

6   In a tragedy of the commons situation, an input will be used until

a   MRP = 0
b   MRP = MFC
c   MFC = 0
d   Not enough information to answer

7   A tragedy of the commons could occur in all except

a   public parks
b   fishing streams
c   highways
d   private homes

8   Negative externalities in agriculture include all except

a   agricultural chemical runoff
b   feedlot odor
c   deforestation
d   bees

9   A positive externality in agriculture is

a   chemicals
b   machinery
c   nice views of farmland
d   taxes

10   A Pigouvian tax is used to

a   enhance government efficiency
b   resolve a negative externality
c   resolve a positive externality
d   resolve a tragedy of the commons

**Answers:** 1. c, 2. b, 3. c, 4. a, 5. c, 6. a, 7. d, 8. d, 9. c, 10. b

For more study questions, flash cards, and study guides, see the online materials at the companion website: www.routledge.com/cw/barkley.

# Farm and agribusiness management

Photo 16.1 Agribusiness management

*Source:* cosma/Shutterstock

DOI: 10.4324/9781003367994-16

## Abstract

Farm and agribusiness management is described as making good economic decisions in an industry characterized by large and ever-present changes. Strategic planning and human resource management are crucial components of farm and agribusiness management. The terms risk and uncertainty are defined and explained. Futures markets are a common form of risk management by agribusiness firms. This chapter provides examples of hedging and commodity options. Agricultural finance is introduced by investigating the opportunity cost of time, the time value of money, compounding, and discounting money flows. Net present value, a useful tool used to value projects, investments, and firms, is presented.

### Chapter 16 Questions

1  Why are the food and agricultural sectors subject to constant change?
2  How can strategic planning and human resource management help managers make better decisions?
3  How are risk and uncertainty defined, and how do they differ?
4  What can managers do to reduce risk in farm and agribusiness firms?
5  What are hedging and options, and how are they used to reduce risk?
6  What are the basic principles of agricultural finance?
7  What is the opportunity cost of time, and how is it used to make financial decisions?
8  What is the net present value, and how can it enhance decision-making for farm and agribusiness managers?

## 16.1   The food supply chain

The food industry can be divided into four major sectors: farm services, producers, processors, and marketers. Interestingly, for every dollar spent at the grocery store, the farm value was approximately 15 cents in 2019. The remaining 85 cents went to farm services, producers, processors, and marketers.

### 16.1.1   The farm service sector

The farm service sector includes firms that produce or sell inputs used in the production of agricultural products. This sector includes such things as feed, seed, insurance, fertilizer, chemicals, fuel, and equipment.

Many of the large agribusinesses that serve the agribusiness sector are in the farm service sector, including DuPont chemicals and seeds, Monsanto, John Deere, International Harvester, and many other large input suppliers. Increasingly important are economic and financial consultants, who provide services to farmers and ranchers. Banking, insurance, accounting, law services, and agronomic consulting have increased greatly in recent years as producers have become larger and more business and economic minded. In addition to these private firms, many federal and state agencies provide financial information, credit, and general advising to individuals operating in the agribusiness sector.

## BOX 16.1

### Banking

The banking sector provides a valuable service to agricultural producers by lending money for inputs such as land, machinery, seeds, fertilizer, and chemicals. In many cases, farmers and ranchers would be unable to use modern agricultural production practices without the ability to borrow money from banks and the financial sector.

Modern banking practices emerged in Europe in the seventeenth and eighteenth centuries. Merchants stored gold with goldsmiths, who began to lend money out on behalf of the depositor, leading to the creation of promissory notes and bank notes. Banks borrow money by accepting funds deposited and issuing debt instruments such as bank notes or bonds. Banks lend money by making advances to customers and generate revenue by charging interest and transaction fees. A bank profits from the difference between the level of interest it pays for deposits and the interest rate paid to it on lending activities, or the "spread" between the cost of funds and the local interest rate.

Commercial banks are highly regulated by the central bank, which in the US is the Federal Reserve System. Many banks in the US are also insured by the Federal Deposit Insurance Corporation (FDIC).

## 16.1.2 The producer sector

The producer sector includes all firms that purchase inputs to produce food and fiber outputs. In most cases, these are biological processes. The substitution of capital for labor and consolidation of small firms into larger enterprises have resulted in massive changes in the number and size of farms in most nations. These trends are likely to continue. A major concern in the processing sector is the concentration of markets in the hands of a small number of large firms. To the extent that firms have market power, they could have negative economic consequences for both producers and consumers, as was discussed in Chapter 13.

## 16.1.3 The processor sector

Large agribusinesses that purchase raw materials such as agricultural crops and commodities and then transforms them into food products comprise the food processor sector. As explored in Chapter 13, many of the processes in this sector are characterized by enormous economies to scale, leading to large firms and plants in meat processing and food manufacturing. Large businesses capture cost saving as fixed costs are spread over greater levels of output, providing for enormous financial gains from large firm and plant size.

### 16.1.4 The marketing sector

Advertising and marketing efforts are commonly used to enhance sales of food products. This is particularly true for new food products in order to inform and persuade consumers to purchase innovative foods in grocery stores and restaurants. Agricultural commodity markets for grains and meat are competitive industries composed of numerous firms selling a homogeneous product: hamburger, wheat, cocoa, or rice. These markets do little or no advertising or marketing since the firms face a perfectly elastic demand curve (Chapter 12). Firms with differentiated products, however, often spend large sums on marketing efforts designed to distinguish one product (McDonald's Big Mac, for example) from another (Burger King's Whopper).

The following paragraphs provide information regarding agribusiness management, marketing, and finance, including a description of how futures markets work and how money is valued across time.

## 16.2 Farm and agribusiness management

It has been emphasized throughout this book that good decisions are based on a simple decision-making tool frequently used by economists: the comparison of benefits and costs. Farm and agribusiness managers who employ this tool are likely to make superior decisions and be more successful than managers who do not. In a market-based economy, good management decisions are the single most important ingredient for firm survival and success. This is true for family farms and ranches, large agribusiness firms, and everything in between. One of the defining characteristics of market-based economies is change, caused by continuous changes in the determinants of supply and demand: technological advances, input costs, and income growth are examples.

The history of agriculture is one of continuous, enormous technological change. Farm and ranch managers must stay informed of new production techniques and market conditions. Producers must make decisions about which technologies to adopt: if the technology is not as efficient as anticipated, economic losses can occur. Similarly, if a farm or agribusiness manager does not adopt a successful technology, the firm will be at a competitive disadvantage.

Technological advance is not the only characteristic of food and fiber production that is subject to change. Earlier chapters have shown that public policies for agriculture are under constant revision, market prices fluctuate, and environmental regulations are frequently modified to protect natural resources. Consumer tastes and preferences for food products change rapidly with income increases and the discovery and introduction of new foods. And international trade has an ever-increasing impact on food and agriculture as greater levels of globalization lead to more imports and exports.

Good decision-making is crucial, given these constant changes and, as indicated earlier, the economic approach provides a useful tool for making changes in a dynamic setting. In today's global economy, farm and agribusiness managers are required to continually observe, reflect, and act on ubiquitous and enormous change.

## 16.2.1   The functions of management

Management of a firm can be summarized by four major functions of management: planning, implementation, control, and adjustment. Planning is simply choosing a course of action, a policy, or a process. Solid plans make use of economic decision-making: identification of alternatives and analysis of the benefits and costs of each. Implementation may require acquiring new and different inputs and producing new and different outputs, frequently by combining labor, capital, and land in unfamiliar ways.

The control function includes monitoring, recording, and analyzing results. These records are used in the adjustment function, which allows managers to modify continuously, update, and upgrade their decisions.

## 16.2.2   Strategic planning and management

Strategic farm and agribusiness management is an ongoing process, which includes analysis and assessment of the firm's internal and external situation through the following:

1   Strategy formulation of the best course of action for the firm.
2   Strategy execution of the course of action.
3   Continuing evaluation, assessment, and improvement of firm performance, culture, communications, data reporting, and other strategic management issues.

### BOX 16.2

## Human resource management in food and agriculture

Increasingly over time, agribusinesses rely on hired workers and employees to produce food and fiber. Agribusiness firms have become larger due to economies to scale, and as a result, the importance of good working relationships and labor practices has grown. Working with other people and managing others have become important skills for agribusiness managers. Those managers who are successful at hiring, motivating, communicating, evaluating, and training personnel will enhance the value of the firm.

Since agricultural labor markets compete with nonfarm labor markets, agribusiness managers must offer wages, salaries, benefits, and working conditions at a level at least as high as competing firms to attract and retain a quality workforce. Regulations and laws have become more complex over time, requiring a greater investment in worker training, management, evaluation, and compensation.

Many aspects of agricultural production decisions are outsourced to experts, including advisors, and consultants. Specialization of work has led to more individuals involved in almost all farm and food operations. These trends are likely to continue, requiring effective and efficient agribusiness managers to become capable and competent managers of their most valuable asset: human resources. In Chapter 13, continuous interactions between workers were describes as a "game," with cooperative solutions often much more profitable than conflict or poor relations.

The strategic farm and agribusiness management procedures are closely related to the decision principles described earlier in the book: weighing benefits and costs of every alternative. For example, firms choose production or output levels by setting marginal revenue equal to marginal cost (Chapter 4). Optimal input levels are selected by setting marginal revenue product equal to marginal factor cost (Chapter 4). These profit-maximizing procedures are given special importance in economics since continual adjustment of inputs and outputs most often provides the highest level of profits. Optimal input combinations (Chapter 5) and optimal output combinations (Chapter 6) were also analyzed. These are all examples of how the economic principles presented can be used to evaluate profit-maximization decisions.

## 16.3   Agricultural and food marketing

Marketing agricultural and food products is subject to a great deal of risk and uncertainty, two terms that will be defined and explored in what follows.

### 16.3.1   Risk and uncertainty

Food and agriculture are characterized by a great deal of risk: production risk due to weather, price risk due to volatile market conditions, and market risks due to international trade and globalization, to name just a few. Managers in the food and agricultural sector use risk management as a method of reducing risk and providing a more stable financial environment. To better understand market volatility, it is worthwhile to define risk and uncertainty.

- *Risk* = a situation where the outcome is unknown, but the probability of different outcomes is known.

- *Uncertainty* = a situation where the probability of different outcomes is unknown.

A coin toss represents risk, for example, since the outcome (heads or tails) is unknown, and the probability of outcomes is known (0.5 for each outcome). Price changes in agricultural markets represent uncertainty since farm managers have no way of assigning a probability to the future occurrences of any commodity price.

Agricultural producers have many sources of uncertainty, the primary source being weather, comprising temperature, moisture, and wind. Biological production is subject to diseases, pests, predators, and insect damage. In addition to production risk, agriculture is known to have high market risks: agricultural prices are volatile.

Insurance can be used to reduce risk but not uncertainty. In agriculture, insurance types include crop production insurance, property insurance, liability insurance, and life/health/accident insurance. However, insurance is not available for all risks in food and agriculture. Examples include egg breakage, grain spills, and food safety issues. Risks such as these are too costly for private insurance contracts to be available. Uncertainty describes situations where probabilities of possible outcomes are unknown. In many situations, uncertainty is a negative feature of running a business, or a cost. However, uncertainty is also a major favorable characteristic of a market-based economic system. If nothing changed, there would be no progress. New innovations, technologies, and markets provide the foundation for a well-functioning, prosperous economy. Strategies used by producers to reduce uncertainty include flexibility, diversification, production contracts, futures contracts (described in the next section) and government programs (described in Chapter 11).

---

## BOX 16.3

### The Great Recession: the financial crisis of 2008

No nation, regardless of its form of economic organization, is immune to economic fluctuations. Capitalism, the form of organization embraced by the US, has suffered many periods of economic unrest. Among the more severe of these have occurred in 1873, 1893, 1929–1937, and recently 2008–2009. The two most talked about are the Great Depression of the 1930s, and the Great Recession of the 2000s. The recession of the 2000s was the most recent, so it deserves special attention.

The global economic decline of 2008–2009 has been considered the worst global recession since World War II (1939–1945). The years leading up to the crisis were characterized by strong global economic growth, increasing capital flows, and prolonged economic stability. In the US, investment banks had grown rapidly and were not subject to the same regular oversight as the depository banking system. This increased the risk facing the economic system and enhanced the vulnerability to recession.

Prior to the crisis, US mortgage-backed securities were marketed around the globe and provided higher yields than US government bonds. Many of these securities were backed by subprime mortgages, which collapsed in value in 2006 when many homeowners began to default on their mortgage payments. This led to a loss of confidence in the banking and investment industries and resulted in many large investment banks and commercial banks in the US and Europe suffering large losses. Governments tried to come to the industry's rescue using massive "bailouts."

In a global economy, the financial sectors of all nations are interdependent and synchronized, and markets are integrated across all trading nations. This interdependence made it difficult for any single nation to pull out of the recession. The global recession resulted in a decline in international trade and increased unemployment. Governments and central banks responded with fiscal and monetary policies to stimulate national economies. One characteristic of the economic recovery since the Great Recession is an increasing concentration in wealth: the distribution of income has become an important policy issue in the time period since the recession.

Photo 16.2 Futures market

*Source:* lassedesignen/Shutterstock

## 16.3.2   Futures markets

Farmers today are not only managers of the production process but also managers of the market and crop risks associated with agriculture.

- *Cash Markets* = markets in which delivery of the good occurs simultaneously with payment.
- *Futures Markets* = markets in which price is determined now, and delivery of the good is specified for a future point in time.

To reduce the severity of price risk, producers use a method of shifting the risk to someone else while retaining the role as producer. Grain buyers developed forward prices for agricultural products to help absorb the price and market risk.

- *Forward Price* = an agreement today for a price that will be paid for the delivery of a commodity at a specified future date.

Forward prices have been used by producers in both commodity (output) markets and in input markets such as seed, fertilizer, fuel, and chemicals. In a typical example of forward pricing, a farmer negotiates a price with the buyer of a crop at planting time, even though the crop will not be delivered until harvest time. If cash prices are lower than the negotiated price at harvest, the farmer is pleased; if the cash price is higher at harvest, the buyer is better off. Thus, the forward price shifts the risk of price movement and price volatility from the producer to the buyer.

Agricultural producers are thus able to reduce or eliminate price risk, but continue to face significant risk and uncertainty from weather, pests, diseases, and weeds. Many of these physical risks are managed by the purchase of insurance covering the possible loss of a crop. These insurance contracts are similar to family insurance on houses, cars, and other physical assets. By pooling physical risk, business manages and households shift the risk to insurance companies, which are able to make a competitive rate of return by absorbing and managing risk for a large number of customers. Producers use of insurance has increased in recent years.

- *Contract Farming* = a production contract between a producer and a buyer, which specifies both physical production attributes and prices.

Many producers take advantage of forward prices offered by commodity buyers, and many of the buyers shift their price risk on to futures markets, as discussed in what follows.

- *Futures Contract* = a written document calling for the future delivery of a commodity of a specific grade at a particular time and place.
- *Futures Market* = a marketplace where futures contracts are bought and sold. Also called futures exchanges.
- *Speculator* = a trader who strives to earn profit by buying at a low price and selling at a high price without taking physical possession of the commodity.
- *Hedger* = a trader who buys and sells futures contracts to reduce price risk.

- ***Pit*** = the physical location of futures contract trades on the floor of a futures market.

A futures contract is a standardized contract traded in a market, where it was created. Two types of traders buy and sell futures contracts. A **speculator** seeks profit by accepting risk on futures contracts without actually owning the physical commodity. A **hedger**, on the other hand, seeks to reduce or eliminate price risk. The movement of risk from hedgers to speculators is what allows futures markets to work.

The major futures markets for agricultural commodities in the US are the Chicago Board of Trade (CBOT) for grains and the Chicago Mercantile Exchange (CME) for livestock. These exchanges earn money by providing a physical location for trading futures contracts and charge a commission (fee) for each trade. Most large brokerage houses such as Merrill Lynch have representatives who trade on the exchanges. Traditional commodity markets took place in the "pit," where buyers and sellers interacted. Each commodity has a pit, and traders use hand signals to buy and sell contracts. The futures contracts represent a legal contract to deliver or take delivery of a commodity in the future. The commodities themselves are not traded in these futures markets.

Hedging is a risk management practice that reduces risk through the sale of a commodity futures contract instead of the actual commodity. Grain producers can hedge before the crop is planted, during the growing season, or while the grain is stored. Livestock can be hedged at the time of purchase or at any time during the feeding period. Buyers of the contracts often are a food processing firms desiring to lock in the price of a commodity for future use or a speculator striving to sell the contract later for a higher price.

Futures contracts often allow for delivery upon expiration of the contract; however, the contract is typically repurchased, and the commodity is sold on the cash market. Cash and futures prices usually move up or down together. Any gain or loss that occurs when the cash market goes up or down is offset by a corresponding loss or gain on the futures contract. To hedge successfully, a manager should have a good understanding of "**basis**."

- ***Basis*** = the difference between the futures contract price and the local cash market price.

The basis will become larger and smaller while the futures contract is held, resulting in differences between the gains and losses in the cash market and futures market. This variation is called **basis risk**.

- ***Basis Risk*** = the risk that offsetting investments in a hedging strategy will not experience price changes in entirely opposite directions from each other. This imperfect correlation between the two investments creates the potential for excess gains or losses in a hedging strategy, thus adding risk to the position.

Although futures contracts carry some risks of their own, the price of a contract usually does not fluctuate as much as cash prices. Hedging is used to lock in prices for both commodities and inputs such as feed for livestock.

## Hedging example: selling corn in Iowa

A corn producer in Iowa has just planted 1,000 hectares of corn (maize), with expected production costs of USD 5/bu. This represents the farm's break-even price from Chapter 4. At planting time, the cash corn price is USD 7/bu, and corn futures contracts for delivery at harvest sell for USD 8/bu. The corn producer can hedge by selling a futures contract for delivery at harvest.

### Case one

Suppose that at harvest time, the cash price has decreased to USD 5/bu. The producer sells the harvested corn for USD 5/bu and buys back the futures contract for USD 6/bu. The farm's net price per bushel is as follows:

| | |
|---|---|
| Sold futures contract | USD +8/bu |
| Bought back futures contract | USD –6/bu |
| Sold corn for cash price | USD +5/bu |
| Net gain | USD +7/bu |

Although the cash market declined from USD 7 to 5/bu, the farmer still had a net gain equal to USD 2/bu, gained from the futures contract.

### Case two

Suppose that the cash market price had increased to USD 10/bu at harvest time, and the cash price was USD 8.75/bu. In this case, the net price per bushel of corn would be as follows:

| | |
|---|---|
| Sold futures contract | USD +8/bu |
| Bought back futures contract | USD –10/bu |
| Sold corn for cash price | USD +8.75/bu |
| Net gain | USD +6.75/bu |

The net selling price is nearly the same in both Case One and Case Two, regardless of whether the cash corn market increases or decreases. The only determinant of the net price received by the farm is the basis, or the difference between the futures price and cash price at the time the corn is sold: USD 1/bu in Case One and USD 1.25/bu in Case Two. The futures market allows the producer to hedge or reduce risk resulting from market volatility.

**Commodity options** allow traders to bet on the price of a futures contract to go higher or lower.

- *Commodity Option* = an option is the right, not the obligation, to buy or sell a futures contract at a designated **strike price**.
- *Strike Price* = the price at which the buyer of a commodity option could buy or sell the underlying futures contract.

An example is the best way to explain how a commodity option works. Suppose that a September USD 5.50/bu corn call allows you to buy a September futures contract at USD 5.50/ bu any time before the option expires. As in futures contracts, most traders do not convert options, they just close the option position and take the profits. There are two main types of options: **calls** and **puts**.

- *Calls* = a call option is purchased when the underlying futures price is expected to increase.

If a trader believes that corn futures are going to move higher, she would want to buy a corn call option.

- *Puts* = a put option is purchased when the underlying futures price is expected to decrease.

For example, if a trader expects soybean futures to move lower, he might want to buy a soybean put option. Options are valuable tools that assist agricultural producers mitigate risk.

## 16.4   Agricultural finance

Agribusiness managers, including farmers and ranchers, rely heavily on obtaining financial assets from the farm credit system, including banks and credit institutions. The following paragraphs describe and explain some principles of finance to enhance knowledge of how agribusiness managers make financial decisions and how financial institutions evaluate proposed projects and potential investment opportunities in the food and agribusiness sector.

### 16.4.1   The opportunity cost of time

Many economic decisions involve time, with benefits and costs occurring in different time periods. When this is the case, it is important to understand that one dollar today is worth a different amount than the same dollar in the future or the past. This is due to the time value of money. One dollar received today is worth more than one dollar received next year. Why? Because of the opportunity cost of money: one dollar today could be invested in a financial institution or used to purchase an asset. If the rate of return, called the interest rate, is equal to i, then one dollar today is worth USD 1(1 + i) next year. This amount can be broken down into two components: (1) the principal (USD 1) and (2) the interest earned (USD i).

For decisions involving revenues and costs over time, economic decisions are made using **present value** analysis.

- *Present Value (PV)* = the present value of money or an economic good that will be received in the future.

The best way to understand the concept of present value is with an example. Suppose that you could receive USD 1.10 exactly one year from today (t + 1). What is the present value (PV) of this amount today (t)? If you invested the dollar today at an interest rate equal to 10 percent (i = 10), then one year from today the dollar would be worth USD 1.10 [1.10 = 1(1 + i)]. The dollar investment would earn 10 percent interest, or USD 0.10. Therefore, the present value of receiving USD 1.10 one year from today equals USD 1.

## 16.4.2 Compounding and discounting

The principle of opportunity cost, or the time value of money, provides the ability to value dollars (or any currency) at any point in time—past, present, or future. For example, one dollar today will be worth $1(1 + i)^n$ n years into the future. This procedure is called "compounding," or valuing current dollars in future values. The same dollar today was worth $1/(1 + i)^n$ n years in the past. This calculation is called "discounting" dollars to their value at a previous point in time.

> ### QUICK QUIZ 16.1
>
> a   What is the PV of 2.10 USD received next year if the interest rate is equal to 5 percent?
> b   What is the PV of 12 USD received next year if the interest rate is equal to 20 percent?

The mathematical formula for present value is given in equation 16.1, where PV is present value, FV is future value, the interest rate is i, and n is the number of years in the future.

16.1   $PV = FV / (1 + i)^n$

For example, the present value of USD 1,000 in ten years with a 6 percent interest rate is equal to USD 558.39, as shown in equation 16.2.

16.2   $PV = FV / (1 + i)^n = 1000 / (1.06)^{10} = 1,000 / 1.7908 = 558.39$ USD

Intuitively, this means that if a sum of USD 558.39 were invested today at 6 percent interest, it would be worth USD 1,000 in ten years.

Interest rates play a crucial role in present value analysis. Since the interest rate appears in the denominator of PV, the larger the interest rate, the smaller the PV of future dollars. Likewise, the smaller the interest rate, the larger the PV of future dollars. If the interest rate were equal to zero, then PV = FV, and there would be no opportunity cost of money.

Present value analysis can also calculate the value of a sequence of future payments by extending equation 16.1 to include money received in multiple years in the future.

16.3 $PV = FV_1 / (1 + i) + FV_2 / (1 + i)^2 + FV_3 / (1 + i)^3 + \ldots + FV_n / (1 + i)^n.$

This can be rewritten as a sum:

16.4 $PV = \Sigma\, FV_t / (1 + i)^t.$

## 16.4.3  Net present value

If asked to calculate the value of an income stream arising from a project or investment, we could calculate the **net present value** (NPV) of the project.

- *Net Present Value (NPV)* = the present value (PV) of the income stream generated by a project minus the current cost ($C_0$) of the project. [NPV = PV – $C_0$].

The NPV is a widely used measure of the economic viability of a project or investment. If a project's NPV is positive, then the project is profitable because the present value of the future stream of earnings for the project is greater than the current cost of the project. A project with a negative NPV would not be profitable, and funds could be better invested in other projects or investments. The NPV of a project can be written as in the equation 16.4.

16.5 $NPV = FV_1 / (1 + i) + FV_2 / (1 + i)^2 + FV_3 / (1 + i)^3 + \ldots + FV_n /$
$(1 + i)^n - C_0,$

16.6 $NPV = \Sigma\, FV^t / (1 + i)^t - C_0.$

---

### QUICK QUIZ 16.2

The manager of an agribusiness firm is considering the purchase of a new machine that will cost USD 250,000 and last four years. The machine will provide earnings in the form of cost savings equal to USD 50,000 in year one, USD 75,000 in year two, and USD 80,000 in years three and four. (a) What is the PV of cost savings if the interest rate is 7 percent? (b) Should the manager purchase the machine?

---

Some projects and investments provide positive revenues that continue forever. Consider a project or asset that provides equal future value indefinitely into the future, as in equation 16.7.

16.7 $PV_{asset} = FV_1 / (1 + i) + FV_2 / (1 + i)^2 + FV_3 / (1 + i)^3 + \ldots$

In the special case where FVs are equal forever ($FV_1 = FV_2 = FV_3 = ...$) and the interest rate (i) is constant, the asset is called a perpetuity, and the present value of the asset can be calculated in a simple manner

16.8  $PV_{perpetuity} = FV / i.$

Perpetual bonds and preferred stocks are examples of this type of perpetuity. The owners of these assets are paid a fixed amount at the end of each period, forever.

> QUICK QUIZ 16.3
>
> Calculate the PV of a perpetuity that pays the owner USD 1,000 at the end of each year, when the interest rate is fixed at 5 percent.

The present value method is also useful in determining the value of a firm. The present value of any business enterprise (firm) is equal to the present value of the future stream of profits ($\pi$), or revenues minus costs.

16.9  $\pi_{firm} = \pi_0 + \pi_1 / (1 + i) + \pi_2 / (1 + i)^2 + \pi_3 / (1 + i)^3 + ...$

This equation simply states that the value of a firm today is the present value of its current and future profits. Good decision-making, including agribusiness management decisions, involves thinking like an economist, by comparing the benefits and costs of every activity. This approach to problem solving and decision-making yields enormous advantages, particularly in a dynamic agricultural economy.

## 16.5  Chapter 16 Summary

1  Agriculture is only a small component of a very complex food industry.
2  Food and agriculture are characterized by large and small agribusinesses throughout the food supply chain, including farm services, agricultural producers, processors, and marketing firms.
3  Agribusiness management is described as making good economic decisions in an industry characterized by large and ever-present changes.
4  The economic approach to decision-making provides a useful tool for making decisions in a dynamic economy.
5  Strategic planning is a crucial component of agribusiness management and includes analysis, assessment, strategy formulation, execution, and continuing evaluation and improvement of the firm's performance.
6  Human resource (labor) management is an increasingly important feature of agribusiness management.
7  Food and agriculture are subject to a great deal of risk and uncertainty, and these terms are defined and explained.
8  Futures markets are a common form of risk management by agribusiness firms, and examples of hedging and commodity options are described and analyzed.

9 Agricultural finance is introduced by investigating the opportunity cost of time, the time value of money, compounding, and discounting money flows.
10 Net present value is defined and used to value projects, investments, and firms.

## 16.6 Chapter 16 Glossary

**Basis**—The difference between the futures contract price and the local cash market price.

**Basis Risk**—The risk that offsetting investments in a hedging strategy will not experience price changes in opposite directions from each other. This imperfect correlation between the two investments creates the potential for excess gains or losses in a hedging strategy, thus adding risk to the position.

**Calls**—A call option is purchased when the underlying futures price is expected to increase.

**Cash Markets**—Markets in which delivery of the good occurs simultaneously with payment.

**Commodity Option**—An option is the right, not the obligation, to buy or sell a futures contract at a designated strike price.

**Contract Farming**—A production contract between a producer and a buyer, which specifies both physical production attributes and prices.

**Forward Price**—An agreement today for a price that will be paid for the delivery of a commodity at a specified future date.

**Futures Contract**—A written document calling for the future delivery of a commodity of a specific grade at a particular time and place.

**Futures Market**—A marketplace where futures contracts are bought and sold. Also called futures exchanges.

**Futures Markets**—Markets in which price is determined today, and delivery of the good is specified for a future point in time.

**Hedger**—A trader who buys and sells futures contracts to reduce price risk.

**Net Present Value (NPV)**—The present value (PV) of the income stream generated by a project minus the current cost ($C_0$) of the project. [NPV = PV – $C_0$].

**Pit**—The physical location of futures contract trades on the floor of a futures market.

**Present Value (PV)**—The present value of money or an economic good that will be received in the future.

**Puts**—A put option is purchased when the underlying futures price is expected to decrease.

**Risk**—A situation where the outcome is unknown, but the probability of different outcomes is known.

**Speculator**—A trader who strives to earn profit by buying at a low price and selling at a high price without taking physical possession of the commodity.

**Strike Price**—The price at which the buyer of a commodity option could buy or sell the underlying futures contract.

**Uncertainty**—A situation where the probability of different outcomes is unknown.

# 16.7   Chapter 16 Review questions

1  The farm value of one US dollar spent on food is equal to

   a   15 cents
   b   35 cents
   c   65 cents
   d   85 cents

2  The farm service sector includes all except

   a   bankers
   b   insurance
   c   chemicals
   d   processors

3  Banks generate revenue by

   a   charging interest and fees on loans
   b   charging interest and fees on savings
   c   renting space out to business
   d   home and business ownership

4  Risk is

   a   unknown outcomes and unknown probabilities of outcomes
   b   unknown outcomes and known probabilities of outcomes
   c   known outcomes and unknown probabilities of outcomes
   d   known outcomes and known probabilities of outcomes

5  Uncertainty is

   a   unknown outcomes and unknown probabilities of outcomes
   b   unknown outcomes and known probabilities of outcomes
   c   known outcomes and unknown probabilities of outcomes
   d   known outcomes and known probabilities of outcomes

6  A futures market

   a   takes place in the future
   b   is a market where price is determined today for future delivery of a good
   c   is a market where good delivery is today and price is determined in future
   d   Increases price risk

7  If the NPV of a proposed project is positive

   a   the project is expected to be profitable
   b   the project is expected to be unprofitable
   c   the project is expected to have zero economic profits
   d   not enough information to know

8  If the NPV of a proposed project is positive

   a   investors should invest in the project
   b   investors should not invest in the project
   c   the project should be undertaken
   d   not enough information to know

9  A perpetuity is

   a   always worth more than an asset of fixed life
   b   never worth more than an asset of fixed life
   c   a good investment
   d   not enough information to know

10  Good agribusiness management decisions

    a    compare the benefits and costs of all activities

    b    are made by thinking like an economist

    c    discount future revenues and costs into today's dollars

    d    all of the above

**Answers:** 1. a, 2. d, 3. a, 4. b, 5. a, 6. b, 7. a, 8. c, 9. a, 10. d

For more study questions, flash cards, and study guides, see the online materials at the companion website: www.routledge.com/cw/barkley.

# Glossary

**Absolute Advantage**—Lower costs of production for a specific good or service.

**Absolute Price**—A price in isolation, without reference to other prices. Example: the price of wheat is $3/bushel (see **Relative Prices**).

**Accounting Costs**—Explicit costs of production; costs for which payments are required.

**Accounting Profits** $[\pi_A]$—Total revenue minus explicit costs. $\pi_A = TR - TC_A$ (see **Economic Profits**).

**Agricultural Economics**—Economics applied to agriculture and rural areas.

**Agriculture**—The science, art, and business of cultivating the soil, producing crops, and raising livestock useful to humans. Farming.

**Arc Elasticity**—A formula that measures responsiveness along a specific section (arc) of a supply or demand curve and measures the "average" price elasticity between two points on the curve.

**Average Costs (AC)**—Total costs per unit of output. AC = TC/Y. Note that **average costs** (AC) are identical to **average total costs** (ATC).

**Average Fixed Costs (AFC)**—The average cost of the fixed costs per unit of output. AFC = TFC/Y.

**Average Physical Product (APP)**—The average productivity of each unit of variable input used [=Y/X].

**Average Revenue (AR)**—The average dollar amount received per unit of output sold. AR = TR/Y.

**Average Total Costs (ATC)**—The average total cost per unit of output. ATC = TC/Y. Note that **average costs** (AC) are identical to **average total costs** (ATC).

**Average Variable Costs (AVC)**—The average cost of the variable costs per unit of output. AVC = TVC/Y.

**Barriers to Entry and Exit**—Legal or economic barriers that hinder or prevent a new firm from entering or exiting an industry.

**Basis**—The difference between the futures contract price and the local cash market price.

**Basis Risk**—The risk that offsetting investments in a hedging strategy will not experience price changes in opposite directions from each other. This imperfect correlation between the two investments creates the potential for excess gains or losses in a hedging strategy, thus adding risk to the position.

**Boom**—A time period when the rate of growth of GDP is positive.

**Break-Even Point**—The point on a graph that shows that total revenue (TR) is equal to total cost (TC).

**Budget Constraint**—A limit on consumption determined by the size of the budget and the prices of goods.

**Budget Line**—A line indicating all possible combinations of two goods that can be purchased using the consumer's entire budget.

**Calls**—A call option is purchased when the underlying futures price is expected to increase.

**Capital**—Physical capital: machinery, buildings, tools, and equipment.

**Cardinal Utility**—Assigns specific, but hypothetical, numerical values to the level of satisfaction gained from the consumption of a good. The unit of measurement is the hypothetical util (see **Ordinal Utility**).

**Cartel**—A group of independent firms that join together to regulate price and production decisions.

**Cash Markets**—Markets in which delivery of the good occurs simultaneously with payment.

**Ceteris Paribus**—Latin for "holding all else constant." This assumption is used to simplify the real world.

**Change in Demand**—When a change in the quantity of a good purchased is a result of a change in an economic variable other than the price of the good. A shift in the demand curve.

**Change in Quantity Demanded**—When a change in the quantity of a good purchased is a result of a change in the price of the good. A movement along the demand curve.

**Change in Quantity Supplied**—A change in the quantity of a good placed on the market due to a change in the price of the good. A movement along the supply curve.

**Change in Supply**—A change in the quantity of a good produced due to a change in one or more economic variables other than the price of the good. A shift in the supply curve.

**Closed Economy**—A nation that does not trade. All goods and services consumed must be produced within the nation.

**Coasian Bargaining**—When an externality affects a third party, the affected parties have an incentive to bargain with each other to reach an efficient outcome.

**Collusion**—When the firms in an industry jointly determine the price of the good.

**Command Economy**—A form of economic organization where resources are allocated by whoever is in charge, such as a dictator or an elected group of officials (see **Market Economy** and **Mixed Economy**).

**Commodity Option**—An option is the right, not the obligation, to buy or sell a futures contract at a designated **strike price**.

**Comparative Advantage**—The superior productive capacity of one individual, or nation, or region, or industry, relative to all others, based on opportunity cost.

**Comparative Statics**—A comparison of market equilibrium points before and after a change in an economic variable.

**Complements in Consumption**—Goods that are consumed together (e.g., peanut butter and jelly; see **Substitutes in Consumption**).

**Complements in Production**—Goods that are produced together (e.g., beef and leather; see **Substitutes in Production**).

**Constant Returns**—When each additional unit of input added to the production process yields a constant level of output relative to the previous unit of input. Output increases at a constant rate.

**Consumer**—An individual or household that purchases a good or a service.

**Consumer Surplus (CS)**—A measure of the well-being of consumers equal to consumer willingness and ability to pay minus the actual price paid.

**Contract Farming**—A production contract between a producer and a buyer, which specifies both physical production attributes and prices.

**Costs of Production**—The payments that a firm must make to purchase inputs (resources, factors).

**Cross-Price Elasticity of Demand**—A measure of the responsiveness of the quantity demanded of a good to changes in the price of a related good.

**Cross-Price Elasticity of Supply**—A measures of the responsiveness of the quantity supplied of a good to changes in the price of a related good.

**Decreasing Returns**—When each additional unit of input added to the production process yields less additional output relative to the previous unit of input. Output increases at a decreasing rate.

**Deflation**—A general decrease in prices, as measured by a price index, resulting in an increase in purchasing power of the currency.

**Demand**—Consumer willingness and ability to pay for a good.

**Demand Curve**—A function connecting all combinations of prices and quantities consumed for a good, *ceteris paribus*.

**Demand Schedule**—Information on prices and quantities purchased.

**Depression**—A time period when the rate of change in GDP is negative.

**Disequilibrium**—A market situation in which the market price does not equalize supply and demand.

**Dominant Strategy**—A strategy in game theory that is optimal no matter what the opponent does.

**Economic Development**—Actions and policies that promote the standard of living and economic health of a nation, region, or area, encompassing improvements in economic, political and social well-being of people.

**Economic Good**—A good that is scarce (see **Noneconomic Good**).

**Economic Profits [$\pi_E$]**—Total revenue minus both explicit and opportunity costs. $\pi_E = TR - TC_A -$ opportunity costs (see **Accounting Profits**).

**Economics**—The study of the allocation of scarce resources among competing ends.

**Economies of Scale**—When the per-unit costs of production decrease as output increases.

**Efficiency**—A characteristic of competitive markets indicating that goods and services are produced at the lowest possible cost and consumers pay the lowest possible prices.

**Elastic Demand**—A change in price that brings about a relatively larger change in quantity demanded.

**Elastic Supply**—A change in price brings about a relatively larger change in quantity supplied.

**Elasticity**—The percentage change in one economic variable resulting from a percentage change in another economic variable.

**Elasticity of Demand**—The percentage change in the quantity demanded in response to a percentage change in price.

**Elasticity of Supply**—The percentage change in the quantity supplied in response to a percentage increase in price.

**Engel Curve**—The relationship between income and quantity demanded, *ceteris paribus*.

**Engel's Law**—As income increases, the proportion of income spent on food declines, *ceteris paribus*.

**Equilibrium**—A point from which there is no tendency to change.

**Equilibrium Price**—The price at which the quantity supplied equals the quantity demanded.

**Equilibrium Quantity**—The point where quantity supplied is equal to quantity demanded.

**Excess Demand (ED)**—Quantity demanded minus quantity supplied at a given price: $Q^d - Q^s$.

**Excess Supply (ES)**—Quantity supplied minus quantity demanded at a given price: $Q^s - Q^d$.

**Externality**—A consequence of an economic activity that affects unrelated third parties. The externality can be either positive or negative. Thus, an externality is a transaction spillover that creates a cost or a benefit not transmitted through market prices.

**Factors**—Inputs provided by nature and modified by humans who use technology to produce goods and services that satisfy human wants and desires. Also called **inputs, factors of production**, or **factors**. Resources include **capital** (K), **labor** (L), **land** (A), and **management** (M).

**Factors of Production**—Inputs provided by nature and modified by humans who use technology to produce goods and services that satisfy human wants and desires. Also called **inputs, factors of production**, or **factors**. Resources include **capital** (K), **labor** (L), **land** (A), and **management** (M).

**Fiscal Policy**—Attempts by a government to influence macroeconomic variables through taxes and government spending.

**Fixed Costs**—Those costs that do not vary with the level of output; the costs associated with the fixed factors of production.

**Fixed Input**—An input whose quantity does not vary with the level of output.

**Food Aid**—International provision of food or cash to purchase food to address hunger or undernutrition.

**Food Security**—A situation where all people at all times have access to sufficient, safe, nutritious food to maintain a healthy and active life.

**Forward Price**—An agreement today for a price that will be paid for the delivery of a commodity at a specified future date.

**Free Trade Agreement**—Agreements between nations to reduce or eliminate trade barriers.

**Futures Contract**—A written document calling for the future delivery of a commodity of a specific grade at a particular time and place.

**Futures Market**—A marketplace where futures contracts are bought and sold. Also called futures exchanges.

**Futures Markets**—Markets in which price is determined today, and delivery of the good is specified for a future point in time.

**Game**—A decision-making situation in which the participant (players) make strategic decisions.

**Game Theory**—The study of strategic decision-making.

**Good**—An **economic good**.

**Gross Domestic Product (GDP)**—A measure of the value of total expenditures of all goods and services in an economy in a given time period, usually one year or one quarter.

**Hedger**—A trader who buys and sells futures contracts to reduce price risk.

**Homogeneous Product**—A product that is the same no matter which producer produces it. The consumer cannot identify the producer of a good.

**Immediate Run (IR)**—A period of time in which all inputs are fixed.

**Imperfect Substitutes**—Inputs that are incomplete substitutes for each other in the production process.

**Import Quota**—A trade restriction that sets a physical limit on the quantity of a good that can be imported during a given time period.

**Income Elasticity of Demand**—The percentage change in the demand for a good in response to a 1 percent change in income.

**Increasing Returns**—When each additional unit of input added to the production process yields an increasing level of output relative to the previous unit of input. Output increases at an increasing rate.

**Indifference Curve**—A line showing all possible combinations of two goods that provide the same level of utility (satisfaction).

**Industry**—A group of firms that all produce and sell the same product.

**Inelastic Demand**—A change in price brings about a relatively smaller change in quantity demanded.

**Inelastic Supply**—A change in price brings about a relatively smaller change in quantity supplied.

**Inferior Good**—A good whose consumption declines in response to an increase in income.

**Inflation**—A sustained, rapid increase in prices, as measured by a price index over months or years, resulting in a decrease in purchasing power of the currency.

**Inputs**—Inputs provided by nature and modified by humans who use technology to produce goods and services that satisfy human wants and desires. Also called **inputs, factors of production,** or **factors.** Resources include **capital** (K), **labor** (L), **land** (A), and **management** (M).

**Inverse Demand Function**—A demand function that is represented with price (the independent variable) as a function of quantity demanded (the dependent variable): $P = f(Q_d)$.

**Inverse Supply Function**—A supply function that is represented with price (the independent variable) as a function of quantity supplied (the dependent variable): $P = f(Q_s)$.

**Isocost Line**—A line indicating all combinations of two variable inputs that can be purchased for a given, or same, level of expenditure.

**Isoquant**—A line indicating all combinations of two variable inputs that will produce a given level of output.

**Isorevenue Line**—A line depicting all combinations of two outputs that will generate a constant level of total revenue.

**Law of Demand**—The quantity of a good demanded varies inversely with the price of the good, *ceteris paribus*.

**Law of Diminishing Marginal Returns**—As additional units of one input are combined with a fixed amount of other inputs, a point is always reached at which the additional output produced from the last unit of added input will decline.

**Law of Diminishing Marginal Utility**—Marginal utility declines as more of a good or service is consumed during a given time period.

**Law of Supply**—The quantity of goods offered to a market varies directly with the price of the good, *ceteris paribus*.

**Long Run (LR)**—A time span during which no inputs are fixed; all inputs are variable.

**Luxury Good**—A good whose consumption increases at an increasing rate in response to an increase in income.

**Macroeconomics**—The study of economy-wide activities such as economic growth, business fluctuations, inflation, unemployment, recession, depression, and booms (see **Microeconomics**).

**Marginal Analysis**—Comparing the benefits and costs of a decision incrementally, one unit at a time.

**Marginal Costs (MC)**—The increase in total costs due to the production of one more unit of output: $MC = \Delta TC / \Delta Y$.

**Marginal Factor Cost (MFC)**—The cost of an additional (marginal) unit of input; the amount added to total cost of using one more unit of input: $MFC = \Delta TC / \Delta X$.

**Marginal Physical Product (MPP)**—The additional amount of total physical product obtained from using an additional, or marginal, unit of variable input $[=\Delta Y / \Delta X]$.

**Marginal Rate of Product Substitution (MRPS)**—The rate at which one output must decrease as production of another output is increased. The slope of the production possibilities frontier (PPF) defines the MRPS. $MRPS = \Delta Y_2 / \Delta Y_1$.

**Marginal Rate of Substitution (MRS)**—The rate of exchange of one good for another that leaves utility unchanged. The slope of an indifference curve. $MRS = \Delta Y_2 / \Delta Y_1$.

**Marginal Rate of Technical Substitution (MRTS)**—The rate at which one input can be decreased as the use of another input increases to take its place. The slope of the isoquant. $MRTS = \Delta X_2 / \Delta X_1$.

**Marginal Revenue (MR)**—The addition to total revenue from selling one more unit of output. $MR = \Delta TR / \Delta Y$.

**Marginal Revenue Product (MRP)**—The additional (marginal) value of output obtained from each additional unit of the variable input. $MRP = MPP * PY$.

**Marginal Utility (MU)**—The change in the level of utility as consumption of a good is increased by one unit. $MU = \Delta TU / \Delta Y$.

**Market**—The interaction between buyers and sellers.

**Market Demand Curve**—The relationship between the price and quantity demanded of a good, *ceteris paribus*, derived by the horizontal summation of all individual consumer demand curves for all individuals in the market.

**Market Economy**—A form of economic organization where resources are allocated by prices. Resources flow to the highest returns in a free market system (see **Command Economy** and **Mixed Economy**).

**Market Equilibrium**—The point where the quantity supplied by producers at a given price is equal to the quantity demanded by consumers at that same price.

**Market Power**—The ability to affect the price of output. A firm with market power faces a downward-sloping demand curve.

**Market Price**—The price where quantity demanded is equal to quantity supplied.

**Market Structure**—The organization of an industry, typically defined by the number of firms in an industry.

**Market Supply Curve**—The relationship between the price and quantity supplied of a good, *ceteris paribus*, derived by the horizontal summation of all individual supply curves for all individual producers in the market.

Marketplace—A physical location where buyers and sellers meet to trade goods.

Microeconomics—The study of the behavior of individual decision-making units such as individuals, households, and firms (see **Macroeconomics**).

Mixed Economy—A form or economic organization that has elements of both a **market economy** and a **command economy**.

Monetary Policy—Changes in the rate of growth of the quantity of money in the economy to achieve macroeconomic objectives.

Money—Anything generally accepted and commonly used as a measure of payment.

Monopolistic Competition—A market structure defined by (1) many sellers; (2) a product with close, but differentiated, substitutes; (3) some freedom of entry and exit; and (4) some availability of knowledge and information.

Monopoly—A market structure characterized by a single seller.

Nash Equilibrium—An equilibrium in game theory where each player does the best that she can, given what the other player is doing. The result is stable because no player is left with an incentive to change.

National Income (NI)—A measure of the total value of all factor payments (capital, labor, and land) during a period of time, usually one year or one quarter.

Natural Monopoly—A situation where a single firm has large fixed costs, making it most efficient (lowest cost) for production to be concentrated in a single firm.

Necessity Good—A good whose consumption increases at a decreasing rate in response to an increase in income.

Negative Externality—A situation where the market price does not include the full cost of producing or consuming a good or service.

Negative Returns—When each additional unit of input added to the production process results in lower total output relative to the previous unit of input. Output decreases.

Net Present Value (NPV)—The present value (PV) of the income stream generated by a project minus the current cost ($C_0$) of the project. [$NPV = PV - C_0$].

Nominal Prices—Prices observed at any point in time, measured in dollars of that time.

Noneconomic Good—A good that is not scarce; there is as much of this good to meet any demand for it. A free good (see **Economic Good**).

Nonexcludable Good—A good in which everyone can consume the good whether she pays for it or not.

Nonprice Competition—A market situation where firms compete over good characteristics other than price, such as quality, quantity, services, color, taste, etc.

Normal Good—A good whose consumption increases in response to an increase in income.

Normative Economics—Based on statements that contain opinions and/or value judgments. A normative statement contains a judgment about "what ought to be" or "what should be" (see **Positive Economics**).

Oligopoly—A market structure characterized by a few large firms.

Open Economy—A nation that allows trade. Imports and exports exist.

Opportunity Costs—The value of a resource in its next-best use. What an individual or firm must give up to do something.

Opportunity Set—The collection of all combinations of goods within the budget constraint of the consumer.

**Ordinal Utility**—A way of considering consumer satisfaction in which goods are ranked in order of preference: first, second, third, etc. (see **Cardinal Utility**).

**Own-Price Elasticity of Demand**—The percentage change in the quantity demanded in response to a percentage change in price.

**Own-Price Elasticity of Supply**—Measures the responsiveness of the quantity supplied of a good to changes in the price of that good.

**Payoffs**—The outcomes that generate benefits or costs to the players (stakeholders) in a game.

**Perfect Competition**—A market or industry with four characteristics: (1) a large number of buyers and sellers, (2) a homogeneous product, (3) freedom of entry and exit, and (4) perfect information.

**Perfect Complements (consumption)**—Goods that must be purchased together in a fixed ratio.

**Perfect Complements (production)**—Inputs that must be used together in a fixed ratio. They operate in fixed proportions in the production process.

**Perfect Information**—A situation where all buyers and sellers in a market have complete access to technological information and all input and output prices.

**Perfect Substitutes (consumption)**—Goods that are completely substitutable, or the consumer is indifferent between the two goods.

**Perfect Substitutes (production)**—Inputs that are completely substitutable in the production process.

**Pigouvian Tax**—A tax levied on firms that pollute the environment or create other negative externalities due to production of goods and services.

**Pit**—The physical location of futures contract trades on the floor of a futures market.

**Player**—Stakeholder who makes decisions in games.

**Positive Economics**—Based on factual statements. Such statements contain no value judgments. Positive economic statements describe "what is" (see **Normative Economics**).

**Positive Externality**—A situation where the market price does not include the full benefit of producing or consuming a good or service.

**Present Value (PV)**—The present value of money or an economic good that will be received in the future.

**Price Ceiling**—A maximum price set by the government for a specified good or service.

**Price Maker**—A firm characterized by market power, or the ability to influence the price of output—a price-making firm faces a downward-sloping demand curve.

**Price Support**—A minimum price set by the government for a specified good or service.

**Price Taker**—A firm so small relative to the industry that the output price is fixed and given, no matter how large or how small the quantity of output it sells.

**Producer**—An individual or firm that produces (makes; manufactures) a good or provides a service.

**Producer Surplus (PS)**—A measure of the well-being of producers equal to the price received minus the cost of production.

**Production Function**—The physical relationship between inputs and outputs.

**Production Possibilities Frontier (PPF)**—A curve depicting all possible combinations of two outputs that can be produced using a constant level of inputs.

**Profits [$\pi$]**—Total revenues minus total costs: $\pi = TR - TC$. The value of production sold minus the cost of producing that output.

**Public Good**—A good that is both (1) nonrival and (2) nonexcludable.

**Purchasing Power**—The value of money in terms of units of goods that money can purchase, or command.

**Puts**—A put option is purchased when the underlying futures price is expected to decrease.

**Rational Behavior**—Individuals do the best that they can, given the constraints they face. Rational behavior is purposeful and consistent.

**Real Prices**—Prices of goods or services adjusted for inflation.

**Recession**—A time period when the rate of growth of GDP is negative.

**Relative Prices**—The prices of goods relative to each other. Example: the price of wheat increased relative to the price of corn (see **Absolute Price**).

**Resources**—Inputs provided by nature and modified by humans who use technology to produce goods and services that satisfy human wants and desires. Also called **inputs, factors of production,** or **factors.** Resources include **capital** (K), **labor** (L), **land** (A), and **management** (M).

**Risk**—A situation where the outcome is unknown, but the probability of different outcomes is known.

**Rival Good**—A good in which the consumption of the good by one person precludes the consumption of the good by a second person.

**Scarcity**—Because resources are limited, the goods and services produced from using those resources are also limited, which means consumers must make choices, or trade-offs, among different goods.

**Service**—A type of economic good that is not physical. For example, a haircut or a phone call is a service, whereas a car or a shirt is a good.

**Short Run (SR)**—A time span during which some factors are variable and some factors are fixed.

**Shortage**—A market situation in which consumers are willing and able to purchase more of a good than producers are willing to supply at a given price ($Q_s < Q_d$).

**Shutdown Point**—The point on a graph where marginal revenue (MR) is equal to average variable costs (AVC).

**Social Science**—The study of society and of individual relationships in and to society, generally regarded as including sociology, psychology, anthropology, economics, political science, and history.

**Speculator**—A trader who strives to earn profit by buying at a low price and selling at a high price without taking physical possession of the commodity.

**Strike Price**—The price at which the buyer of a commodity option could buy or sell the underlying futures contract.

**Substitutes in Consumption**—Goods that are consumed either/or (e.g., wheat bread and white bread; see **Complements in Consumption**).

**Substitutes in Production**—Goods that compete for the same resources in production (e.g., wheat and barley; see **Complements in Production**).

**Supply**—The relationship between the price of a good and the amount of a good available at a given location and at a given time.

**Supply Curve for an Individual Firm**—The firm's marginal cost curve above the minimum point on the average variable cost curve.

**Supply Schedule**—A schedule showing the relationship between the price of a good and the quantity of a good supplied.

**Surplus**—A market situation in which producers are willing to supply more of a good than consumers are willing to purchase at a given price ($Q_s > Q_d$).

Tariff—A tax on imports of a good.

Technological Change—Change that allows the same level of inputs to produce a greater level of output. Alternatively, technological change allows production of the same level of output with a smaller number of inputs.

Total Costs (TC)—The sum of all payments that a firm must make to purchase the factors of production. The sum of **total fixed costs** and **total variable costs**. TC = TFC + TVC.

Total Factor Cost (TFC)—The total cost of a factor, or input. TFC = $P_X$ * X.

Total Fixed Costs (TFC)—The total costs of inputs that do not vary with the level of output.

Total Physical Product (TPP)—The relationship between output and one variable input, holding all other inputs constant.

Total Revenue (TR)—The amount of money received when the producer sells the product. TR = $P_Y$ * Y.

Total Revenue Product (TRP)—The dollar value of the output produced from each level of variable input. TRP = TPP * $P_Y$.

Total Utility (TU)—The total level of satisfaction derived from consuming a given bundle of goods and services.

Total Variable Costs (TVC)—The total costs of inputs that vary with the level of output.

Trade Barriers—Laws and regulations to restrict the flow of goods and services across international borders, including tariffs, duties, quotas, and import and export subsidies.

Trade War—A situation where one nation retaliates against another by imposing import tariffs or placing other restrictions on the opposing country's imports. These policies can result in retaliation and escalation of trade barriers between the two nations.

Tragedy of the Commons—A situation in which a group of individuals, acting rationally and in their own self-interest, deplete a shared limited resource, resulting in a negative outcome for all parties.

Uncertainty—A situation where the probability of different outcomes is unknown.

Unitary Elastic Demand—The percentage change in price brings about an equal percentage change in quantity demanded.

Unitary Elastic Supply—The percentage change in price brings about an equal percentage change in quantity supplied.

Util—Hypothetical unit of satisfaction derived from consumption of goods or services.

Utility—Satisfaction derived from consuming a good.

Variable Costs—Those costs that vary with the level of output; the costs associated with the variable factors of production.

Variable Input—A variable input is one that when changed, affects the level of output.

Welfare Economics—A branch of economics that seeks to measure and understand how the well-being (welfare) of individuals changes in response to changes in policies, markets, or current events.

# Index

Note: Page numbers in *italic* indicate a figure. Page numbers in **bold** indicate a table or a box on the corresponding page.

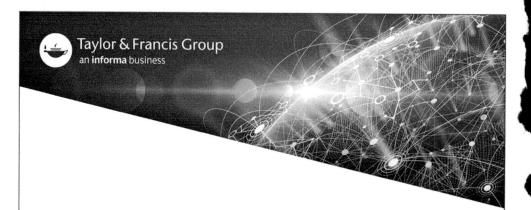